VEDIC ARY AND WESTERN IDENTITY CRISIS

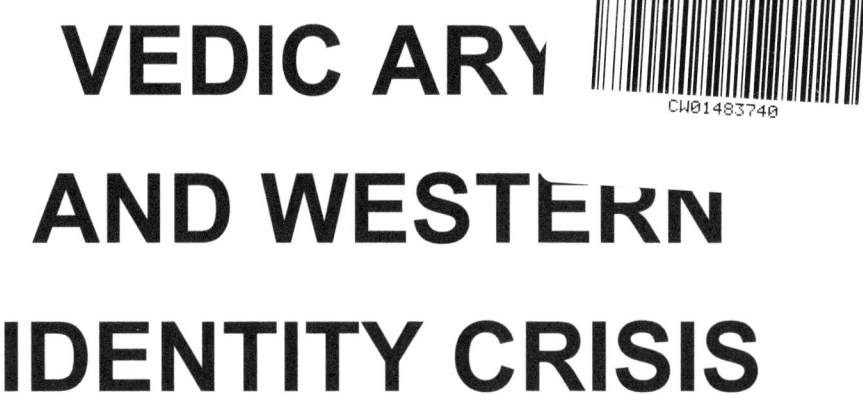

M. K. Agarwal

First they stole Our Wealth

then Our Soul

Recent Books by the Same Author

Agarwal M. K., The Vedic Core of Human History, iUniverse 2013.

Agarwal, M. K., From Bharat to India, Vol. 1 Chrysee the Golden, iUniverse, 2012.

Agarwal, M. K., From Bharat to India, Vol. 2 The Rape of Chrysee, iUniverse, 2012.

Agarwal, M.K. and Sharma, A.K., Yoga-Ayurveda Miracle, Dog Ear, 2011.

Further information on Authors' Page, Amazon.com

And author website aumco.net

TABLE OF CONTENTS

Preface

The origin of world civilization can be traced back to Indus world that came into being as a result of pristine ideation by great rishis (sages) who had discovered natural laws governing human body and its relationship to the universe. They epitomized an Aryan ideal of self-sacrifice for serving humanity, built great urban centers, conducted maritime trade around the globe, and amassed wealth as never before in human history. They were mathematicians *par excellence* and had discovered the reality underlying the temporal phenomena. The insights they gained in Numerology, Astrology (*jyotish*) and Symbolism are now followed around the globe. They were to discover writing and linguistics that reached an acme in Sanskrit which became a lingua franca to record pioneering discoveries and advances in natural and medical sciences. Meditation on causation and reality permitted path breaking discoveries that were to form the **basis of world civilization**. Her archaeologists had deciphered the secrets of *Vastu shastra* to lift human spirit to the grandest spiritual heights while her scientists had harnessed the laws of mathematics, natural, physical, chemical, and medical sciences, **thousands of years before Europeans**. Her literary genius had invented story telling that was to become the staple backbone of European folklore. Her freedom of thought was so total that the individual was to strive to become an **Arya** or as **similar to God** as possible through righteous *karma* **and** *dharma.* Life was celebrated by music, song, dance, drama, games and sports, whereas the sexual act of creation could be freely enjoyed for salvation through *Tantra Yoga,* even within the temple precincts. Although her vaults were overflowing with the world's wealth, her philosophers and thinkers had understood the inevitable reality of an afterlife so renunciation and detachment were integrated into everyday life in order to prepare the individual for the last moments of physical existence.

From 5000 BC on, Bharat of old was held in awe the world over for her wealth and wisdom. She was both a highly developed manufacturing country and an agricultural country. Right up to the 18th century, no other peoples could compete with her methods of production, distribution and commercial organization. So refined were her products that the British and others came to buy the luxury articles made in Bharat for resale at high profits in Europe. So efficient and highly organized were her methods of production that they had to be stifled by heavy import duties in Europe and export taxes in Bharat. So reliable and efficient was her banking system that the bills of exchange issued by her financial houses were honored everywhere in Asia and beyond. So elaborate was her network of agents, brokers and middlemen that the news of market reached them even before they reached the Western colonizers. Sir George Bidwood was to observe:

"The whole world has been ceaselessly pouring its bullion for 3000 years into India to buy products of her industries".

Like a loving mother, she provided religious and cultural models for her adapted siblings in most of Asia as her glory spread through the Shri Vijaya and the Majapahit Empires, Indonesia, Malaysia, Fu-nan, Khmer strongholds, Champa, Myanmar, Sri Lanka, Siam and Philippines. To the West, her influence reached Persia, Arabia, Turkey, Syria, Mesopotamia, Central Asia, the Russia Republics, Greece and the Roman Empire. To the north, she took China, Korea and Japan in her embrace while to the south her message reached the East Coast of Africa. She inspired the Celts who brought culture to Europe where many countries now vie with each other to claim Celtic heritage. Sea farers from her bosom landed in the Americas, Oceania, Africa, and Polynesia, thousands of years before the Europeans. Instead of sending armies to kill, mutilate, torture, rob and enslave, she sent ambassadors of hope, learning, and peace to peoples in alien lands who begot great Empires and monuments to honor their foster mother.

Lured by the Eastern Bounty, primitive barbarians came as conquerors to unleash a reign of physical and mental terror in the name of dogmatic faiths that had prohibited free thinking, enterprise and inquiry in their native lands. Consequently, the believers there toiled in general depravity, perpetual misery, superstition, poverty, disease, hunger, filth, and the like, all of which were written off as **God's will** that was never to be questioned. The Arabs came wielding the sword of Islam in the one hand, and Koran in the other, to usurp the riches of Bharat by sheer plunder, murder, theft, torture, rape, castration and slavery, leading to some 80 million dead. The foundation of Arabic literature and sciences was laid only between 750-850 CE where everything is foreign, except the religion. Arabs even changed Sanskrit names into Arabic to camouflage the real origin and to pass Vedic patrimony off as Arabic whose translations into European script were to spur the revival of Europe that had remained mired in superstition, cannibalism, magic, sorcery, bestiality, homosexuality, disease epidemics, poverty, prostitution, slavery, illiteracy, and the like, because the Bible had become a despotic instrument in the hands of the clergy to stifle all inquiry.

The British entered Bharat with Bible and Guns, first to expropriate its riches and then its culture. Whereas the European miasma suffered from the same privations as the Arabs before their conquests, the British nevertheless dubbed their plunder a *"noble mission of ruling a lesser people for their own good"*. Having acquired affluence through stolen riches, the British could no longer tolerate the fact that the Vedic heritage was far superior to their own barbaric past. Attention was therefore turned to Greece as the sole source of Western Civilization and to rewrite Indian history according to foreign conquests and their aftermath. To this end, a comparative genealogy was advanced where the Vedic literature would merely be repeating the events described in the Bible although Vedic patrimony forms the core upon which Greece and the Abrahamic religions are based. An effort was finally mounted to manipulate the time maps such that all scientific and literary knowledge of ancient Bharat could be derived from Alexandrian Greece and the feigned "Greek miracle". The myth of "Aryan invasion", manipulated solely by comparative linguistics, was furthermore invented to pass off Vedic culture as stemming from the patrimony of the European stock. The British now dubbed themselves to be the original Aryans, much like the Germans had done bofore, and Americans were to do later, who in some remote past had been the teachers of Vedic sages, seers, and Brahmins although they had failed to create anything worthwhile in their native habitat.

After decimating some 70 million Indians, the British engineered a local fifth column, in the form of an education system, designed to create an English educated sub caste that would ape the British to repudiate its own Vedic tradition, and look instead to the west as the fount of its civilization. Consequently, post-independence Indians acquired an inferiority complex, starting with Nehru and Gandhi, who exploited India much as the invaders had done. The present generation in the West profits from the wealth looted by its ancestors through sheer genocide, unspeakable cruelty, theft, swindling, and the like, but refuses to accept the true legacy via which such wealth was procured. The cause has thus been severed from the effect.

It is the purpose of this book to spread awareness regarding the true core of world civilization and to cudgel the Hindu out of his self-destructive slumber. Contrary to the myth propagated by the likes of Gandhi, Vedic civilization was never pacifist. All great Hindu Epics and scriptures deify just war to neutralize evil, so much so that the primeval unmoved mover (God) reincarnated nine times in different forms to annihilate demons, devils and miscreants. In fact Gita, the most venerated scripture of all, was recited during the great Epic Mahabharata to admonish against cowardice and weakness. In Shrimad Bhagvad Gita, Lord Krishna, one of the nine incarnations, actually espouses annihilation of kith and kin by the right *karma* of war to defend *dharma*. The overt militancy of Abrahamic faiths cannot be countered by the self-effacing meekness of a mewing lamb. A clashing sword only understands another clashing sword, not the philosophical greatness of spiritual surrender. Hindus must in keep in mind the great ideals intimately spun into the fabric of the eternal, all-encompassing Vedas, and assume responsibility for right dharma and karma.

Krinvanto Vishwam Aryam. Bande Mataram. Satyam Shivam Sundaram.

Acknowledgments

The research conducted for this book stems from my lifelong quest to assign correct historical perspective to the rich patrimony of ancient Bharat. Any undertaking of this size requires concerted effort of a large number of individuals and institutions. I am indebted to the staff and facilities of libraries at Bryn Mawr College, the Tri-College collections and their Inter library loan services, as also the libraries at the University of Pennsylvania, Columbia University, Sarasvati Research Center, and many others. Some of the rare books were made available to me by various sources in India where several leading experts in Sanskrit provided valuable insights into the message hidden behind the apparently specious poetry of Vedic aphorisms. For illustrations, I am thankful to the patient enterprise of many who went through the trouble of understanding technical terms for a non-specialist public. Many colleagues at the University of Paris, despite their own hectic schedule, gave me their invaluable advice, ideas, criticisms, and suggestions for improvement. Last, but not the least, I thank the hospitality and goodwill of peoples who generously welcomed me during my field work around the globe: from the vast expanses of Africa to the tip of South America, from the remote outposts of native reservations in the US to the isolated hamlets of Australia and Papua New Guinea, from the bubbling generosity of nature in the islands of the Pacific Ocean to the warm depths of a multicultural Caribbean. Needless to say that I felt most at home with peoples in the cultural orbit of Bharat of Old: China, Japan, Singapore, Malaysia, Indonesia, Vietnams, Laos, all of South East Asia and particularly Cambodia that shares a cherished cultural link with her cultural mother of a bygone era.

M. K. Agarwal   July 2015

List of Abbreviations

Archeological Survey of India (ASI)

Bharatiya Janata Party (BJP)

Central Intelligence Agency (CIA)

Christian Missionary Society (CMS)

Deoxyribonucleic acid (DNA)

East India Company (EIC)

Grand Trunk Road (GTR)

Indian Council for Historical Research (ICHR)

Indus-Sarasvati Civilization (ISC)

New York Times (NYC)

Painted Grey Ware (PGW)

Prime Minister (PM)

Prime Minister's Office (PMO)

Rashtriya Swayamsevak Sangh (RSS)

Rig Veda (RV)

South East Asia (SEA)

Times of India (TOI)

Traditional Chinese medicine (TCM)

Vishva Hindu Parishad (VHP)

World War (WW)

1.   Epistemology of Bharat

During its 10,000 years of history, modern India was known by name although Bharat was adopted officially after independence in 1947, along with India imposed by the British. Tradition speaks of three different apparitions in three distant *yugas* (ages) all of which carry the name Bharata. The Bharats were a venerable and ancient tribe mentioned in the 3rd mandala of RigVeda, whereas the 7th Mandala informs us that they were on the victorious side during the Battle of the Ten Kings. The first Bharat was born in Satyuga as the son of Rishabh deva, also known as Adinath, who was designated as the first Jain Tirthankara, and synonymous with Shiva in the Hindu tradition, as desribed by Jinasena in *Adipurana*. He sired 100 sons and the eldest Bharat carried the *chakra* (wheel) in his armory to claim the title of a *cakravartin* (emperor). The *cakravartin* was thus an ancient political concept to conquer by means of superior moral and political powers in all directions *(digvijay)*. Bharata subjugated rival kings without violence, by compassion *(daya),* divine wisdom *(Brahma-jñana)* and penance *(tapas)*. Adinath's youngest son Marich became lord Mahavira or the 24th teerthankar. *Ashtapad* records that idols of all early teerthankars are to be found in a Jain temple in the Mansarovar region. The second Bharata was born in the Tretayuga as the son of King Dasharatha of Ayodhya, and younger half brother of Lord Rama. Bharata here epitomizes dharma, idealism, family values, truth, righteousness, filial love and duty, as epitomized in Ramayana that was to transform peoples and cultures around the globe.

In the *Adi Parva* (The Book of the Beginning) of the Maha Bharat epic, the third Bharat is mentioned as the son of King Dushyanta and Shakuntala and thus a descendant of the Lunar Dynasty of the Kshatriya varna. The story goes like this: A heavenly nymph called Maneka was sent by Indra to distract the great sage Vishvamitra from his deep penance. She conceived but Vishvamitra distanced himself from the child and mother to return to his earlier vocation. Maneka left the newborn baby on the banks of the Malini River, some 10 km west of Kotdwara in the Shivalik range. The child was found by a Rishi Kanva surrounded and protected by birds (*Shakunton* in Sanskrit), and so she was named Shakuntala. King Dushyanta encountered her when she was nursing her pet deer wounded by the King and fell in love with her. Before departing for the capital, the King gave her a ring as a memory of their encounter but never came back. In due course, Shakuntala conceived and the Sage Kanwa named the boy *Sarvadamana* (the subduer of all) because, even at the age of six, he was able to seize and restrain wild animals. Shakuntala reached King's palace with her son and after much discourse the King accepted her as his wife. A celestial messenger now advised the King Dushyanta:

> abhūtir eṣā kas tyajyāj jīvañ jīvantam ātmajam
> śākuntalaṃ mahātmānaṃ dauḥṣantiṃ bhara paurava
> bhartavyo 'yaṃ tvayā yasmād asmākaṃ vacanād api
> tasmād bhavatv ayaṃ nāmnā bharato nāma te sutaḥ

(Therefore, O thou of Puru's race, cherish thy high-souled son born of (Queen) Shakuntala and because this child (Bharat) is to be cherished by thee even at our word, therefore shall this thy son be known by the name of Bharat (the cherished or the supported).

Thereafter, *Sarvadamana* came to be called *Bharat* who conquered the entire Asian heartland and reached the top of 'Meru' or 'Sumeru' mountain (the center of the world and the tallest mountain in Hindu mythology). There he planted a flag but he saw numerous such flags of world conquerors before him. This made him feel very insignificant and he took the *diksha* to attain nirvana. Bharatavarsha represented the ideal of great empires dominated by social harmony, truth, knowledge, wealth and prosperity. **Bharatvarsha**, is defined thus in *Vishnu Purana*:

> uttaraṃ yatsamudrasya himādreścaiva dakṣiṇam
> varṣaṃ tadbhārataṃ nāma bhāratī yatra santatiḥ

(The country that lies north of the ocean and south of the snowy mountains is called *Bharatam*; there dwell the descendants of Bharat).

In the shloka: *visvāmitrasya rakṣati brahmedam bhāratam janam* RV 3.053.12. Rishi Vishvamitra seems referring to a people identified as *Bharatam Janam*, or 'Bharata folk', who occupied the Indus Saraswati heartland and who could be the distant forefathers of the present day Hindu traditions (Chapter 5:I). They harnessed metal technology, carried out brisk maritime trade from Hanoi to Haifa, devised hieroglyphs for the Indus script and much more, as described in the following sections.

Vedic texts like 'Shatapatha Brahmana 'and 'Aitereya Brahmana' mention lands of the Aryans from Gandhara (Afganistan) in the west to Videha (Nepal) in the east, and south to Vidarbha (Maharashtra). Hence the Vedic people were in these regions by the Krittika equinox or before 2400 BC. According MahaBharat, as well as numerous puranas, Bharat Empire included the whole territory of the Indian subcontinent, including the present day Pakistan, Afghanistan, China, Iran, Tajikistan, Uzbekistan, Kyrgyzstan,

Russia, Turkmenistan, North-west Tibet, Nepal and Bangladesh. This corresponds to the approximate extent of the historical Maurya Empire under Chandragupta and Ashoka (4th to 3rd BC). Afghanistan actually stems from Sanskrit upa gana stan = the place inhabited by allied tribes.

Rig Veda states that the main Bharat region was located from Parushni (Ravi) in the west to Ganga in the east, from Afghanistan (Kabul or Gandhara or the Druhyus) in the west, across the Sarayu river in the east down to the Vindhyas and the Narmada river (Yadu country) in the south; Anus were centered around Chenab. Kashmir may have been named after the sage Kashyapa, whereas Afghanistan is mentioned as Balkh or Bactria inhabited by shudras or lower classes. Bharat ruled virtuously, earned great fame and was bestowed with the titles of *Chakravarti* (emperor) as well as *Sarvabhauma*. Bharat Chakravarti also figures in *Vishnu Purana* (2,1,31), *Vayu Purana* (33,52), *Linga Purana*(1,47,23), *Brahminda Purana* (14,5,62), *Agni Purana* (107,11-12), *Skanda Purana* (37,57) and *Markandaya Purana* (50,41) as also in sacred Jain texts. Foreign sources have described Bharat as well. Herodotus (440 BC) defines the land thus:

"Eastward of India lies a tract which is entirely sand. Indeed, of all the inhabitants of Asia, concerning whom anything is known, the Indians dwell nearest to the east and the rising of the Sun".

Megasthenes (300 BC) was to write in *Indika:*

"India then being four-sided in plan, the side which looks to the Orient and that to the South is the Great Sea; that towards the Arctic is divided by the mountain chain of Hemodus from Scythia, inhabited by that tribe of Scythians who are called Sakai, and on the fourth side, turned towards the West, the Indus marks the boundary, the biggest or nearly so of all rivers after the Nile".

Arrian (140 CE) defines in *Indoi,* Indou:

"The boundary of the land of India towards the north is Mount Taurus (Caucasus). The western part of India is bounded by the river Indus right down to the ocean. Towards the south this ocean bounds the land of India, and eastward the sea itself is the boundary".

Subsequent dynasties stem from the great law giver Manu who had ten children; the eldest Ikshvaku was the founder of the Suryavansha or the solar line of kings. Manu's daughter Ila married Budha (mercury), son of Chandra (Moon), thus founding the Chandravansha or the lunar line. In one tradition, Puru, Bharat, Rama, Kuru, and Pandavas, have been suggested to have come 7, 43, 65, 71 and 94 generations after Manu. Yayavati, 6th in line after Manu, had five sons who ruled five regions of Bharat: Puru (central, Yamuna Ganga), Anu (north Punjab, Bengal and Bihar), Druhyu (west or northwest Gandhara and Afghanistan), Turvasa (Bengal, Bihar and Orissa and the ancestors of Dravidians and Yavanas) and Yadu (southwest, Gujarat, Rajasthan). Yadu's descendants are known as Yadavas whose most famous elite Krishna was Yadu's 87th descendant. Sita (means furrow) belongs to the Videha dynasty and is a cousin of Rama 61 generations removed; Jains and Buddhists regard Rama and Sita as brothers and sisters. Thirty generations separate Rama from the Bharat battle; Buddha is also a descendant of Ikshvaku.

Bharatavarsha in Sanskrit literally means the continent (*'varsha'*) that is dedicated/devoted (*'rata'*) to light or wisdom (*'bha'*) = **'devoted to light/knowledge'**. Bharat could also mean 'The Cherished' where Bha = Bhava (Expression), Ra = Raga (Melody Notes) and Ta = Tala (Rythmic pattern). The Bharats were an Aryan tribe mentioned in the Rig Veda, notably participating in the Battle of Ten Kings. A version of the *Bhagavata Purana* says that the name Bharat stems from *Jata Bharatha* who appears in the fifth canto of the *Vishnu Purana* (2.3.1). Our Vedic Rishi ancestors devoted themselves to the quest for the eternal truth and ultimate reality, *kevala jnana, satchidananda.* Eventually, the three Bharats (two kings, one prince) were to unite all of land mass as divine Bharat Mata, the **very first nation** of humanity. Bharatvarsha was to give birth to the loftiest of all ideals in human ideation to form the core human history for all ages. Some of the maxims of the Aryans went like this: The Song of the Hindu (5085 BC).

"Hinduism is the law of life, not a dogma; its aim is not to create a creed but a character and its goal is to achieve perfection through spiritual knowledge which rejects nothing yet refines everything through continuous testing... No external force can crush him, except when he is divided and betrays his own... He who seeks to convert another to his own faith offends against his own soul, the will of God, and the law of humanity... the goal of the Hindu is to reach the ultimate in being awareness and bliss for all...A Hindu must enlarge the spirit of mankind and may worship an idol of his choosing to attain the ultimate in ideation".

Songs of Munidasa (5385 BC) state:

"Knowledge of itihasa (history) without feeling is an empty shell. It will not preserve the fire of the past but only its ashes. Civilizations are kept alive only if their knowledge and visions are recreated in people's minds..."

Many Xtian authors have lauded the message contained in the vedic Hindu scriptures. Christian author Godfrey Higgins :

*"The peninsula of India would be one of the first peopled countries, and its inhabitants would have all the habits of **progenitors of man** before the flooding as much as perfection of more of any nation…In short, whatever learning man possessed before his dispersion…may be expected to be found here; and of this Hindustan affords innumerable traces…notwithstanding all…the fruitless efforts of our (Christian) priests to disguise it".*

2. Sanskrit Personifies Eternal Vibrations

Man's progress from savagery to civilization is intimately bound up with abstract ideation which permits a human being to rise above the chaos of primitive sensations and to fashion an ordered cosmos. This is causally linked to the development of language that forms the building bloc of human psyche and subconscious. Sanskrit words personify objects, actions, and attributes related to the underlying reality, perceived by the ear in the same way as visual forms are perceived by the eye. **Sanskrit personifies the cosmic vibration** revealed to the rishis as sound, audible to the human ears, and stemming from the Divine word OM (AUM).

"I am the father of the Universe, the mother, the support and the grandsire. I am the object of knowledge, the purifier and the syllable OM. I am also the Rig Veda, Sama Veda and the Yajur Veda".

In *Brahminagrantha* we are told nine times that:

"Word is God, the speech is God, whatever is speech is God, God is the supreme space of speech".

According to *Shabda Brahma*, attributed to Bhartrhari 450 CE:

"The Word-Principle is Brahman, God itself…The purification of the Word is the very siddhi, attainment of God, the Supreme Self".

The Bible was to observe much later:

"In the beginning was the Word, the Word was with God, the Word was God" (John 1:1).

According to some Greek philosophers *logos* 'word', or speech', was the governing principle of the universe.

All creation arose out of the primeval sound vibration **AUM** or **OM** and will return to it at the end of time. Mundaka Upanishad stated that "*OM is the bow, the soul is the arrow, and Brahma is the target*". In Bhagvada Gita, OM is recognized as a *mantra* which existed from the beginning of creation. Krishna was to extol the universality of the syllable OM:

'Oh son of Kunti, I am the taste in waters, I am the Moon and Sun, I am the syllable OM in all Vedas, I am the sound in ether and manhood in man (VI 8)…I am the father of the Universe, the mother, the support and the grandsire. I am the object of knowledge, the purifier and the syllable OM. I am also the Rig Veda, Sama Veda and the Yajur Veda".

The original Om later expanded into the sacred **Gayatri mantra**, as explained in the *Chatuh-sloki* of *Srimad Bhagvatam* that was taught by Vishnu to Brahma at the time of creation. One Harvard team has recently shown that Gayatri mantra evoked the highest level of meditative vibrations.

In *Surat Shabda Yoga*, initiation by an Outer Living Satguru (Sat = true, Guru = teacher) is required to reconnect the soul to the Shabda by stationing the Inner Shabda Master (the Radiant Form of the Master) at the third eye chakra. A derivative view was held by tantrists who ascribed incarnate divine powers to sacred Sanskrit letters that characterized the seven chakras in Kundalini yoga. Consequently, language became the metaphor for the eternal truth like a divine spirit "*descending and embodying itself in phenomena…*" In *Shabdapurvayoga*, liberation was to be attained through the purification of one's everyday language from grammatically incorrect forms.

The **eternal sound of creation**, captured as the Sanskrit language, underwent systematization by a number of sages. Yasks's *Nirkuta* appears to be the very first attempt at an objective structural analysis of a language, followed by the tradition *vakarana,* one of the six *Vedanga* disciplines that culminated in the *Ashtadhyayi* of Panini, which consists of 3990 *sutras,* composed around 400 BC. Panini's grammar is based on 14 *Shiva sutras* (aphorisms) such that the whole *Matrika* (alphabet) is abbreviated by *Pratyahara.* Panini started out with 1700 consonants, nouns, pronouns, verbs, prefixes and suffixes to construct compound words in a mathematical manner where phonetics and grammar produced a language far more perfect than anything else available anywhere. He laid down 4000 grammatical rules and the language was now called *Samskrta,* meaning perfected or refined. Its most striking feature consisted of an objective resolution of speech and language into their component element according to their function. Sound in each group of alphabets was arranged according to the place where they are produced in the mouth (guttural, palatals, cerebrals, dentals and labials). Starting from simple roots, complex words grew by the addition of prefixes and suffixes. Rules were worked out to defining the conditions according to which consonants and vowels influence each other, undergo change, or drop out.

The Sanskrit grammar of Panini, the earliest and the most perfect of its kind in the world, gave rise to the science of **Philology**. The concept of Sandhi invented in Bharat is now adopted by Western linguists and is now being used in computer programing. A century after Panini, Katyayana composed *Vartikas* on Panini *sutras* whereas Patanjali (circa 200 BC), wrote the *Mahabhaṣya*, the 'Great Commentary' on the Ashtadhyayi and Vartikas to suggest that language was created by Gods and was not subject to human intervention.

Bhartriharu (5th CE), in Vakyapadiya, equated the Absolute, or Brahman, with Language or *Shabda*. Thus, **language is the eternal truth** and Vedas are the essential expression of the language. Language is like a divine spirit *"descending and embodying itself in phenomena…"*. A derivative view was held by tantrists who ascribed incarnate divine powers to sacred syllables. Thus, metric hymns or **mantras are eternal** and metaphysical entities that can be read acoustically or astronomically through the same numerology. Mathematical accuracy of grammar ensured perfect accuracy in pronouncing every syllable in a prayer or sacrificial chant.

In *Surat Shabda Yoga*, initiation by an Outer Living Satguru (Sat = true, Guru = teacher) is required to reconnect the soul to the Shabda and stationing the Inner Shabda Master at the third eye chakra. In the Vedic age and later, linguistics, grammar, etymology and related sciences were so integrated and perfected that they have not been excelled even now anywhere in the world. Hymns and mantras were deified as Brihaspati whereas speech was similarly deified as *Vac* as the feminine principle of the universe sent by Prajapati to be transformed into various objects. In Rig Veda *vac* or speech is compared to a cow with abundant milk and *mantras* are considered more purifying than water. So, words must be chosen carefully because the power of words is not different from the power of thoughts.

In contrast with the rich and sophisticated vocabulary of the Sanskrit, **Latin and Greek had few words** in their most primitive stages. In the first dictionary of 1604 CE, **English** could boast of no more than **3000 words**. By avoiding verbs and compounding nouns, a great deal of information was condensed into mnemonic sutras or aphorisms for easy memorization with many plays on the sounds and meanings of words endowed with deep spiritual, philosophical and cosmological significance.

The poetry of the Rig Veda is of exceptional literary merit, produced by a refined sacerdotal class following a long period of cultural development. Each hymn may contain a **thousand layers of meaning**. For example, Panini's highly sophisticated Sanskrit grammar can be printed into thirty five octavo pages.

All Hindu gods have female consorts to form a complete whole as **Shakta** and **Shakti.** Without their consorts, the gods are powerless, in contrast to the all-male 'true' religions. The Phallus of Shiva or *Shiva lingam* is the most venerated object of worship since the Vedic age and has inspired art, architecture, literature etc. not only in India but around the globe (Chapter 5.I). Similarly, yoni (vagina) became an object of worship in Tantra. Torah implied that Sanskrit was confused on purpose: *"Let us then go down and **confound their speech** there, so they shall not understand one another's speech"* (Genesis 11:1-9) and replaced by belief. E. H. Johnston remarked:

"*The classical poets of India have sensitiveness to variations of sound to which literature of other countries affords few parallels, and their delicate combinations are a source of never ending joy"*.

Sir William Jones' was emphatic:

"*The Sanskrit language, whatever be its antiquity, is of a wonderful structure, more perfect than the Greek, more copious than the Latin, and more exquisitely refined than either, yet bearing to both of them a string affinity, both in the roots of verbs and in the form of grammar, than could possibly have been produced by accident; so strong indeed, that no philologer could examine them all three, without believing them to from some common source…both the Gothic and Celtic, though blended with a very different idiom, had the same origin with the Sanskrit; and the old Persian might be added to the same family…"*

Nehru, the first Prime Minister of modern India, was unequivocal:

"If I was asked what is the greatest treasure which India possesses, and what is her finest heritage, I would answer unhesitatingly, it is the Sanskrit language and literature and all that it contains".

St. James School in London eulogizes Sanskrit and explains its policy thus:

*"In St James School in London Sanskrit has been the basis of language teaching because it appears to be the **mother of all Indo-European languages**, is full of profound concepts, and alone among all tongues has not changed over the millennia......Sanskrit' Literally Means 'Well Formed' Or 'Refined.' It Is A Classical Language Predating Latin And Greek And Has The Ability To Act As A Model, Teaching Children The Fundamental Principles Of Language. Its Grammar Is Thought To Prevail As The Underlying Grammatical System Of Most Indo-European Languages. This Thorough Knowledge Of Grammar Ultimately Gives The Pupils A Greater Clarity And Accuracy In Thinking, Reading And Speaking, Thereby Preparing Them Well For Whatever They Will Undertake In Life."*

Two professors of Sanskrit, Wilson at Oxford and Lee at Cambridge, said that   Sanskrit was a language:

"Capable of giving a soul to the objects of sense and a body to the abstractions of metaphysics" (cited in Singhal).

3. Vedic Antiquity and Texts

Vedas form the epitome of spiritual ideation of the ancient Vedic-Hindu homeland and represent the raw energy of the spiritual experience, prior to any systematization, when the intellect had not yet taken toll on the intuitive human thought. Based on 53 astronomical references Rig Veda can be dated to 8th millennium BC. These are presented as 53 prayers to *Ashvinis* at dawn in the Aries constellation just before Heliacal sunrise after Winter Solstice that marks the new year *(Uttarayana).* The position of Ashvinis (Aries) matched that of the Winter Solstice about 9000 years ago (7000 BC).

Well horsed and celebrated, Ashvins come to our presence and drink madhuras! Your chariot, travelling along with the sun, marks with its track the farthest ends of heaven.

Worship the Asvins at early dawn; offer their oblations: the evening is not for the gods; it is unacceptable to them: and whether it be any other than ourselves who worships them or propitiates them, the worshipper who is foremost is the most approved of.

The town of Chemi Shanidar, later part of Iraq, shows that Vedas have been passed down through oral tradition and reached Florida Indians Aucilla river by 8000 BC.

In learning the Vedic mantras a correct pronunciation was of utmost importance, leading to **multiple recessions** through different schools (*shakha*) of oral transmission. Only Brahmins knew this speech to perform sacrifice, much as the gods had done to attain godhood. This mnemonic check and countercheck preserved the Vedas for posterity in an unadulterated form. Vedas became the essential personification of Sanskrit language where linguistics, grammar, etymology and related sciences were so integrated and perfected that they have not been excelled even now anywhere in the world. Philological and linguistic considerations suggest an age of well over 3000 years for the most recent strata but the descriptions of an extremely cold climate suggest that the Vedas are close to 20,000 years old. However, while Swami Dayananda Sarasvati concluded that the Vedas were revealed millions of years ago, the Communists have dated them to be as recent as 1200 BC.

Creation in Vedic hymns is described as the work of a divine craftsman via a fire sacrifice. Hymns and mantras were deified as Brihaspati whereas **speech** was similarly deified as *Vac* as the feminine principle of the universe sent by Prajapati to be transformed into various objects. Thought was considered internalized speech and compared to a cow with abundant milk; Vedic *mantras* were considered more purifying than the holy waters. So, words must be chosen carefully for their content of *sattva, rajas* and *tamas* qualities because the power of words is not different from the power of thoughts. Thus, the metric hymns or mantras are eternal and creative metaphysical entities that can be read acoustically or astronomically through the same numerology. Mathematical accuracy of grammar assured perfection in pronouncing every syllable in a prayer or sacrificial chant. Tilak was to declare:

"*Rig Veda is not a prayer book of Nature worshippers but inspired poetry that reveals the truths of existence. Thus, an ingrained and dominant spirituality, an inexhaustible vital creativity and gust of life and, mediating between them, a powerful, penetrating and scrupulous intelligence combined of the rational, ethical and aesthetic mind each at a high intensity of action, created the harmony of the ancient Indian culture*".

The Vedic age stemmed from pristine ideation by great rishis (seers) who had established their retreats on the banks of river Sarasvati or were associated with the great learning centers in Bharat. The **seven rishis** were identified with the stars of the Great Bear: Marici, Atri, Angoiras, Pulastya, Pilaha, Kratu and Vashishtha; other important rishis are Narada, Kashyapa, Daksha, Vishwamitra, Brahspati, Agastya, and Bharadwaja. The oldest University in recorded history could be Takshashila, circa 700 BC, followed by Telhara, Nalanda, and Vikramashila where the *lingua franca* was Meluhha, venerated as a divine manifestation in Rig Veda.Takshshila (Taxila) hosted Panini (grammar), Patanjali (Yoga), and Nagarjuna (alchemy).

Vedic age is reckoned by equinoxes and solstices. Vedanga Jyotish refers to a time when the vernal equinox was in the middle of the Nakshtra Aslesha (or about 23 degrees 20 minutes Cancer) around 1300 BC. Yajur Veda and Atharva Veda speak of the vernal equinox in the Krittikas (Pleiades of early Taurus) around 2400 BC but earlier eras are mentioned. Collectively, the Vedic period may be divided as follows: early Vedic 6000-4000 BC, composition of Rig Veda by Atri; late Vedic 4000-2000 BC, composition of Yajur Veda, Sama Veda and Atharva Veda; the age of Vashishtha, Vishvamitra; post-Vedic 3100 BC, beginning of Kaliyuga, the era of Krishna and Maha Bharat War, canonization of Vedas by Vyasa; late Brahminic, early Sutra 3000 BC, Vedic alters, composition of Brahmins, Sulbhashastra, Ashtadhyayi, by Baudhaya, Apstamba, Katyayana, Panini and Yaska; late Sutra 2000, decline of Harappa, drying up of Sarasvati. Vedas are *sanatan* (eternal) and *apaurusheya* not composed by human entity but uttered by Paramatma at the beginning of every cosmic cycle of Brahma and heard (*shruti*) by the Great Rishis during intense meditation thus unauthored (*apaurusheya*) and eternal.

Vedic literature is vast, containing some **4524 scriptures,** and far more abundant than the literature of the rest of the world put together. The four Vedas are followed by six auxiliary *Vedangas* viz: *Shiksha* (phonetics, phonology, morph phonology and sandhi), *Kalpa* (ritual), *Vyakarana* (grammar), *Niruktar* (etymology), *Chandas* (meter) and *Jyotish*, astronomy). *Dhanurveda* summarizes the Martial arts and self-defense, later picked up by the Chinese as acupuncture and related disciplines. *Stahapatyaveda* details architecture, sculpture and geomancy, used especially for Temple design and urban planning. Finally, *Gandharvaveda* concentrates on music, poetry and dance.

The major Upanishads are: *Brihadaranyaka, Chandogya, Taittiriya, Aitareya, Kaushitaki, Katha, Isa, Kena, Svetasvatara, Mundaka, Prasna, Maitri, and Mandukya.* Of the many texts designated as **Puranas** the most important are the *Mahapuranas* but 18-20 titles, totalling 429,000 verses, have been recorded. The eighteen Puranas, dated to the Gupta period, in decreasing order of antiquity are: *Brahma, Vayu, Matsya, Brahminda, Vishnu, Bhagvata, Garuda, Agni, Padma, Linga, Kurma, Markandeya, Bhavisya, Narada, Brahmavaivarta, Varaha, Vamana and Skanda.* Add to these *Manu Smriti, Artha Shastra, Agama Tantra Sutra, Dharmashastra, Divya Prabandha, Ramacharitmanas, Yoga Vashishtha, Swara Yoga, Shiva*

Samhita, Samarsar Narpatijacharya, the seven Yamalas, Goraksha Samhita, Panchadasi Vedantasara and more..

Attached to the four Vedas are *Brahminas* that interpret rituals in a prose form; *Aranyakas* (forest books) permit personal performance of sacrifice without the ritual paraphernalia of a priest. The **individual thus became a creator** in his own right as *purusha*. Some 108 **Upanishads**, literally meaning a session, follow Aranyakas and are written as dialogs in an attempt to break with the priestly rituals and magic, to inquire about truth behind external world for self-realization by perpetual questions and inference.

Vedas admit 1131 branches and each Vedic branch has a *Samhita, Brahmina, Aranayak and Upanishada*. Upanishads, literally meaning a session, follow Aranyakas and are written as dialogs to inquire about truth behind external world. Then there are 6 *Angas*,18 *Smritis*, and 2 Epics as well as *Yantras, Tantras, Mantras and Jantris*. The sutras and shastras together are known as *smriti* (remembered) as distinct from earlier Vedic *Shruti* (heard) revealed directly to the authors. Manu *smriti* and later *smritis* (200 BC-200 CE) developed from *Dharmashastras* and followed the *Puranas* of 700 BC or so. They are attributed to the primeval sage Manu, nominated by Brahma as the first king, who gave instructions in the sacred law.

The *Kalpasutras* are detailed instructions for performing rituals and are divided into *Srautasutras* (great sacrifices), *Grhyasutras* (ceremonies in the domestic life), *Dharmasutras* (religious and secular laws), and *Sulbhasutras* (measurements for altars etc.). Philosophical sutras, besides Samhitas and Brahamanas, consist of several *mimamsas* (investigation): *Purvamimamsa, Uttaramimamsa, Samkhya, Yogasutra, Nyaya* and *Vaisesika. Arthashastra, Nitishastra, Dandaniti, Rajaniti*, etc. deal with practical aspects of life such as administration, economics, politics, arts, techniques, mining etc. The most important *Arthashastra* of Kautilya (also known as Chanakya), is dated 300 BC and contains 6000 shlokas, 150 chapters and 180 subjects.

Although **over fifty thousand manuscripts** have been recorded, hitherto, mathematical historian David Pingree has estimated that there exist:

"…at present in India and outside of it some million manuscripts on various aspects of jyotishastra…neither cataloged nor translated and constitute a territory that remains remarkably unexplored".

In contrast this prodigious Vedic output, **Mycenaean writings** in Linear B are largely concerned with trade (lists, inventories, receipts, etc.),

Greek work is limited to *Iliad* and the *Odyssey,* attributed to Homer 700 BC, and Theogony by Hesiod dated 800 BC. Whereas Iliad and The Odyssey recount the victories of Achilles and Odysseus, Theogony systematically lists divinities in time periods and generations as well as unions between goddesses and mortals. Greek drama evolved only after 600 BC whereas History came of age in Greece with Herodotus (400 BC); philosophy was perfected by Plato but disappeared after the death of Aristotle. Roman literature is limited to epic poems about the deeds of brothers Vibenna and Mastarna, and of fighting between Etruscans and Celts. Homeric poems are prayers, vows and hymns to the gods and the dead. Elegies, Monodic lyrics, and love poetry by Sappho, predate tragedy which evolved slowly; other works deal with history and geography. Roman literature is limited to epic poems about the deeds of the brothers Vibenna and Mastarna, and of fighting between Etruscans and Celts.

The **Five Classics of China** go back to the first half of the 1st millennium BC and include I-ching, Shu-ching and Shih-ching (book of Odes) all of which have little literary merit. Although writing in ancient Egypt appeared in the late 4th millennium BC, the literature of the Old Kingdom (26-22 century BC) goes no farther than funerary texts, epistles and letters, hymns and poems, and autobiographical texts. A narrative **Egyptian** literature appears only 21-17 century BC to 17th century BC, concerned primarily with mythology. Assyrian literature under Ashurbanipal (669-626 BC) consists of mythological poem (Enuna Eliah) and Gilgamesh; other works record Hymns to Gods, incantations, ritual writings, genealogies of kings, victories and defeats. Persia produced the Avesta and Gatha, both religious and related to the Vedas. Gilgamesh ruled at Uruk and the epic got started by 2000 BC although the complete version goes back to only 700 BC.

The antiquity of the **Old Testament** is debatable and Pentateuch composed **800-600 BC** concerns the most obscure and the earliest periods of Hebrew life, probably conceived around time of Moses. Besides the 'Law', the 'Prophets' are divided into an earlier (Joshua, Judges, Samuel, Kings) and later (Isaiah, Jeremiah, Ezekiel) prophets and twelve Minor Prophets all of whom saw the **will of God** in all events to admonish their co-religionists. It is obvious from the foregoing that nothing in the ancient world can compare with the Vedic output in quality quantity, ideation and abstraction. Whereas the Sanskrit scriptures enumerated above were reserved for the priestly class, the Great Epics employed engaging frame tale episodes to weave moral codes and *dharma* for the masses. *Ramayana* was composed during the TretaYuga and predates MahaBharat which records events of

Dwapara Yuga. Ramayaṇa consists of 24,000 verses or 500 cantos (*kandas*), written in 32 syllable meters called *anustubh*. It is ascribed to a single author, Valmiki (circa 400 BC), who was the inventor of the Vedic poetic meter *shloka*, used in Sanskrit poetry of latter periods. In the Ramayana epic, Rama was to be enthroned as King of Ayodhya but was exiled by his father Dashrath for a period of fourteen years due to a promise given to Rama's step mother who wanted her son to mount the throne. Rama therefore left the kingdom with his wife Sita and faithful followers. Valmiki recorded the **birth of Rama** as Chaitra Shuddha Navami, in Punarvasu Nakshatra, when the five planets were positioned thus: Sun in Mesha up to 10 degrees, Mars in Capricorn at 28 degrees, Jupiter in Cancer at 5 degrees, Venus in Pisces at 27 degrees and Saturn in Libra at 20 degrees (Bala Kanda.18/Shloka 8, 9). Valmiki has beautifully described the sky (Ayodhya 41/10), when Rama left for the exile. He states, "*Crux (Trishankhu), Mars, Jupiter and Mercury have cornered the Moon. Vaishakha and Milky Way are shining in the sky*".

Dr. P. V. Vartak, in his book *Vastava Ramayan,* has shown the existence of Vedic culture as far back as 72,000 BC. Many astronomical references show that the Rig Veda was composed by 23,720 BC whereas Ramayana details events of 8th century BC. In *Punarvasu Nakshatra* (Bala Kanda.18/Shloka 8, 9), the description of the sky, 17 years after the birth of Rama, is perfect astronomically, thereby permitting the following tentative chronology:

Rama's Birth Date	**4 December 7323 BC**
Marriage of Rama and Sita	**7 April 7307 BC**
Rama Exiled	**29 November 7306 BC**
Rama Setu constructed	**26-30 October 7292 BC**
The War begins	**3 November 7292 BC**
Ravana killed by Rama	**15 November 7292 BC**
Rama returns to Ayodhya	**6 December 7272 BC**

On the other hand, aided by powerful planetarium software, Pushkar Bhatnagar calculated that the planetary positions for the date of Rama's birth were in place at 12.30 PM on 10 January 5114 BC. On the Amavasya of the 10th month of the 13th year of exile (7 October 5077 BC), a solar eclipse had indeed occurred and the particular arrangement of the planets in the sky was visible, followed by two subsequent solar eclipses. Rig Veda and Sanskrit scriptures mention several other dynasties of kings. Bharat dynasty includes Sudas, the patron of both Vishvamitra and Vashishtha and the hero of the Battle of Ten Kings (circa 3730 BC); Ikshvaku dynasty includes Rama, born 31 (or 32) generations before Brihadbala who was killed by Arjun's son Abhimanu at Kurukshetra. Taking 20 years per generation, one obtains 3800-3700 BC for Rama and Vashishtha who was Rama's contemporary senior.

The Ramayana, a compound of *Rama* and *ayana* 'going, advancing', translated as '*Rama's Journey*, was to **permeate around the globe** and exerted a profound impact on the lives of people for good. Rama was transformed into Ham, Ramallah, Ramasitoa, Ramadan, Ramsgate, Ramstein, Roma, and so forth, in most religious and secular traditions around the globe. Michelet wrote in 1864:

"*Everything is narrow in the West, Greece is small and I stifle, Judea is dry and I pant. Let me look towards lofty Sita and the profound East for a while. There lies my great poem, as vast as the Indian Ocean, blessed, gilded with the sun, the book of divine harmony where there is no dissonance. A serene peace reigns there and in the midst of conflict an infinite sweetness, a boundless fraternity, which spreads over all living things, an ocean (without bottom or bound) of love, of pity, of clemency*".

Consequently, Ramayana instills the Hindu social psyche with idealism to resolve crisis, in contrast to the Western society which thrives on conflict. Karan Singh remarked:

"*It is remarkable that the Ramayana story is by no means confined to India. Its fragrance has travelled across the whole of south and south-east Asia. The magnificent temple of Angkor Vat in Cambodia, the world's largest place of religious worship, displays on its walls magnificent sculptures telling the whole Ramayana and Mahabharat stories. In Indonesia, the Ramalila is performed with a grace and sensitivity far superior to our somewhat rowdy Ramalilas and, significantly, almost entirely by Muslim artists. The ruling dynasty in Thailand is known as the Rama Dynasty, and there is a shrine named Ayodhya in that country. Such examples can be multiplied. For the indentured laborers who were sent by the British to the ends of the earth and whose descendants now flourish in Fiji and Mauritius, Guyana and Surinam, their only source of cultural and spiritual sustenance was Tulsidas's classic Ramacharitamanas, perhaps the most popular retelling of the Ramayana epic in the world. Hindus in those and other countries around the globe look upon Rama as an incarnation of God, as the Maryada Purshotam, the ideal man. When Gandhiji envisaged his ideal society, he went back to invoking Rama Rajya*".

The Histiriocity of Ramayana is well documented. The Vayu Purana (70.48) says:

tretayuge chaturvinshe ravanastapasah kshayat I
Ramam dasharathim prapya saganah kshayamlyavan II

(Here, the misbehaving Ravana was killed with his kith and kin in a war with Rama in the 24th Treta-yuga).

The Ramayana is geographically very correct. **Every site on Rama's route is identifiable** and has continuing traditions or temples to commemorate Rama's visit. The route taken by Rama from Ayodhya to Ramaeshwaram is marked by as many as **195 ancient sites** testifying to his sojourn across Bharat during the 14 year exile. These are further corroborated in scriptures like Ayodhya Kand, Aranya Kand, Kishkindha Kand and Sunder Kand. Ravana is said to have brought Sita to Sri Lanka by a vehicle called *Pushpaka Vimanam* by the Hindus and *Dandu Monara Yanthraya* by the Sinhalese Buddhists. This vehicle is said to have landed at Werangatota, about 10 km from Mahiyangana, east of the hill station of Nuwara Eliya, in north-central Sri Lanka. Interestingly, a clear path runs through the densely forested areas there even today, marking Ravana's trail. A small pond in the shape of an eye always contains water and is believed to be the place where the tears of Sita fell.

Sita was taken to Goorulupota, now known as Sitakotuwa, the abode of Ravana's wife Mandodari, about 10 km from Mahiyangana on the road to Kandy. She was housed in a cave at Sita Eliya, on the Colombo-Nuwara Eliya road, where a temple for Sita exists. *Ashok Vatika*, where Sita was kept captive and which was later destroyed by Hanumana, is now in ruins. Hakgala, the exotic pleasure garden where Ravana insisted Sita should marry him still survives partially. In Colombo stands Kotte, one of the many places to which Ravana took Sita to confuse Rama. North of Nuwara Eliya, in Matale district, is Yudhaganapitiya, where the Rama-Ravana battle took place. According to another legend Sita was actually detained in the mountainous forest area of Rumassala near Galle. When she fell ill, Hanuman brought the whole mountain full of medicinal plants and dropped it at Unawatuna, which is near the present Galle harbor and which means 'here it fell'; the area is now known for its medicinal plants. Diwaurumpola is the place where Sita performed her Agni Pariksha (fire test) before returning to Rama. Continuing the practice, the villagers there still pledge their fidelity by walking over burning coals. According to a Sinhalese legend, Dunuwila is the place from where Rama shot the *Bramhashira* arrow that killed Ravana. Since Ravana was a Brahmin, it was considered a sin to kill him, even in battle. To wash off the sin, Rama performed *puja* at the Munneswaram temple at Chilaw, 80 km north of Colombo. Yahangala, meaning rock bed, is believed to be the site where Ravana's body was finally laid to rest.

Rama went to Sri Lanka via some sort of a bridge. **Rama Setu**, or Adam´s Bridge is made up of a chain of limestone shoals between the islands of Mannar, in northwestern Sri Lanka, and Rameshwaram, off the southeastern coast of Tamil Nadu in Bharata. The bridge is 30 miles (48 km) long and separates the Gulf of Mannar (southwest) from the Palk Strait (northeast). The bridge was first mentioned in the 9th century by Ibn Khordadbeh in his *Book of Roads and Kingdoms* and was called *Set Bandhai* or 'Bridge of the Sea'. The name *Adam's Bridge* probably came from an Islamic legend according to which Adam used the bridge to reach Adam's Peak in Sri Lanka, where he stood repentant on one foot for 1,000 years, leaving a large hollow mark resembling a footprint. The name *Rama's Bridge* or *Rama Setu* (Sanskrit *setu* = bridge) was given to it when Hindu legends identified it with the bridge built by the monkey army of Rama to reach Sri Lanka. The sea separating India and Sri Lanka, sometimes only 3 feet to 30 feet deep, is called *Sethusamudram* 'Sea of the Bridge'. According to Hindu legends, Rama Setu bridge was constructed under the supervision of the great *shilpkar* (architect) named Nal.

The earliest map that mentions Adam's bridge was prepared by a British cartographer in 1804 CE. Maps prepared by a Dutch cartographer in 1747 CE, available at the Tanjore Saraswati Mahal library, show this area as *Ramancoi*, a colloquial form of the Tamil *Raman Kovil* (Rama's Temple). A map of Mogul India prepared by J. Rennel in 1788 CE, retrieved from the same library, mentions a Rama Temple in this area. Many other maps in Schwartzberg's historical atlas and other sources call this area with various names like Koti, Sethubandha and Sethubandha Rameshwaram etc. while Valmiki Ramayana called the bridge *Setu Bandhanam* (verse 2-22-76). The bridge has been variously mentioned by Marco Polo, Thomas Horsfield, Sir William Jones, Sir Monier Williams, Arnold Herman, Charklotte Speir Manning, Geroge Scharf, Bowen maps of Netherlands, Lodovico de Varthema, Heorge Percy Badger, John Winter Jones, James Rennel, to mention a few.

NASA declared: *"The bridge's unique curvature and composition by age reveals that it is man-made. Legend as well as Archeological studies reveal that the first signs of human inhabitants in Sri Lanka date back to the primitive age, about 1,750,000 years ago and the bridge's age are also almost equivalent."*

Many studies quote Rama Setu as a land route between India and Sri Lanka. The Historical Atlas of South Asia by Joseph E Schwartzberg provides 20 maps as historical and geographical evidence about Rama Setu and its use as a land route between India and Sri Lanka during the last 2500 some years. In an Ajanta fresco, the landing of Ashoka's son King Vijay in Ceylon around 3rd century BC has been depicted along with elephants, horses and foot soldiers, possibly via a land route between Ramaeshwaram and Sri Lanka. During the Satavahan-Sak-Kushan Age (1–300 CE), Rama Setu was known as Ramaeshwarama Koti and used as a land route between India and Sri Lanka. During the reign of Gurjara Pratiharas, Palas and Rashtrakutas (700–975 CE), the region across the Rama Setu was under the rule of Rashtrakuta Kings. During the era of Khiljis and Tughlaks (1290–1390 CE), Rama Setu was shown as a land route between Ramaeshwaram and Sri Lanka, under the name Setubandha Ramaeshwaram. According to Hunter's Imperial Gazetteer, preserved in the Ramaeshwaram temple, a violent storm in 1480 CE breached the existing bridge. James Rennell (1742–1830 CE), the first Surveyor General of the East India Co (EIC), sometimes known as the Father of Indian Geography, refers to it as Rama's Bridge, later renamed as Adam's Bridge. The report by the Geological Survey of India says that this bridge could have been used as a land route between India and Sri Lanka about 7000 – 10,000 years ago. Post-16th century, some reports refer to two narrow channels, known as Pamban and Mannar, through which small ships could make their way (TOI 21 August 2013). The Nehru Dynasty wanted to eliminate the bridge altogether to obviate the historicity of Rama and placate their Muslim-Christian vote bank. Ambika Soni informed the Lok Sabha:

"There is no archeological or historical evidence regarding the existence or otherwise of the Rama Sethu Bridge or Adam's Bridge in Rameshwaram".

The actual BJP government has finally saved Rama Sethu by declaring it a national heritage.

From Ayodhya Rama travelled along the Gangetic belt to Tamsa Nadi Tal, 20 km from Ayodhya. After crossing the Gomti the party entered Shringverpur (Singraur) 20 km from Allahabad in the kingdom of Nishadraj Guh. This was the scene of 'Kewat Prasang' where a boatman refused to ferry them due to an old superstition whereby the dust of Rama's feet could turn a stone into a woman. After crossing Yamuna near Sangam, the party reached Chitrakoot (on the UP-MP border today), where memorials like Valmiki Ashram, Mandavya Ashram and Bharat Koop still exist. After Chitrakoot the advanced to Atri Ashram (Satana, MP) and crossed the dense forests (in Madhya Pradesh and Chhatisgarh today) to arrive in Dandak Aranya where they visited Sharbhang and Sutikshan Muni ashrams (in Satna). Several memorials in Panna, Raipur, Bastar and Jagdalpur retain relics of Mandavya ashram, Shringi ashram, Rama Laxman Mandir and so forth. Finally, the party landed at Agastya's ashram (Nasik) where weapons made in Agnishala were given by Agastya Muni. From Agastya ashram, the party went to Panchvati on the banks of Godavari (Nasik) where Shoorpanakha, Ravana's sister disguised as a deer, had lured Rama away from his consort Sita. Nasik region is full of memorials such as Mrigvyadheshwar, Baneshwar, Sita Sarovar and Rama Kund. Sarvatiratha memorial is still preserved in Taked Village, 56 km from Nasik.

Along Tungabhadra and Kaveri rivers, Rama and his younger brother Laxman met Jatayu and Kabandh, then moved south to Rishyamook Parbat. On the way, they visited Shabari ashram in Pampasarovar area (Sureban in Belgaon), still famous for its *ber* trees, and reached Rishyamook where they met Hanuman and Sugreev. Rama killed Bali in this area (Hampi in Karnataka) and, equipped with an army provided by Sugreev, reached the southernmost tip of Indian peninsula. Details of this phase, cited in Valmiki's Ramayana, can be corroborated with memorials which exist even now. After liberating Sita, Rama stopped at Dhanushkodi in Ramaeshwaram to perform a puja by building a Shiv lingum out of sand, to seek forgiveness for having killed the brahmin Ravana; the Ramaeshwaram temple stands testimony to that incident.

MahaBharat, the foremost of the Hindu epics, is the **longest and the oldest epic poem** in world literature, containing more than 74,000 verses, 110,000 couplets, plus long prose passages, or some 1.8 million words in total. Taken together with the *Harivamsa*, the *Mahabharat* has a total length of more than 90,000 verses, or fifteen Bibles, which stemmed from a shorter version simply called *Bharat* of 24,000 verses. The earliest known references to the MahaBharat, and its core *Bharat,* date back to the 6th-5th century BC, in the *Ashtadhyayi* (sutra 6.2.38) of Panini, the *Ashvalayana Grhyasutra* (3.4.4), and other Vedic literature. However, the earliest testimony of the existence of the full text of the MahaBharat comes from the Greek Sophist Dion Chrysostom, who exclaimed that **"the Indians possess an Iliad of 100,000 verses".** The copper plate inscriptions of Maharaja Sharvanatha (circa 533-534 BC) from Khoh (Satna District, Madhya Pradesha), also describe the MahaBharat as a 'collection of 100,000 verses' (*shatasahasri samhita*). This large body of text was finally committed to writing **emphasizing the numbers 18, and 12** and employing the frame tale structure of a story within a story. MahaBharat's scope and grandeur is best summarized by one quotation by the author himself from the beginning of its first sections:

"What is found here may be found elsewhere. What is not found here will not be found elsewhere".

The Bharat battle describes the dynastic struggle for the throne of Hastinapura between Kauravas and their cousin Pandavas in which kings from all over Bharat participated, along with the Greeks, Bactrians and Chinese. The war was fought for 18 days at Kurukshetra, now in Haryana, when only the Pandavas, Satyaki and Krishna survived. The survivors also included 18,000 warriors along with their wives and children, or a total of 144,000 **Yadus** and Yadavas who were to become the **forefathers of the Jewish** people. The MahaBharat itself ends with the death of Krishna which marks the beginning of the Kali Yuga. According to some accounts, **Krishna rose from the dead** and led his people to what is now Jerusalem where he ruled as Melchisedec. As All Vedic Kshatrayias had perished, Scythians were declared rajputs after a yajna around a fire sacrifice near Mt Abu around 7-8 CE to control fighting locals. Four lines of suryavanshis were thus created: Pratik Ara, Param Ara, ch Alukya and Ash Trak Uta.

The MahaBharat War has been dated variously from **5561 BC to 800 BC** and its history is also linked to the Battle of the Ten Kings in RigVeda. Dr. Manish Pandit, a nuclear medicine specialist, has declared: *'Lord Krishna existed. School texts are wrong'* (Rediff, 30 August 2009). Krishna was born in 3112 BC, so he must have been 54-55 years old at the time of the battle of Kurukshetra. More than **140 astronomical references** in the MahaBharat were used by Dr. B. N. Achar to extrapolate the first day of war to 22 November 3067 BC. However, Dr. P.V. Vartak comes up with the date of 16th October 5561 BC as the first day of MahaBharat War, based on 18 mathematical positions including the planetary positions, seasons, the two Amavasyas, two eclipses, the ancient tradition of *'Shravanadini Nakshatrani'*, *Kshaya Paksha*, and a Haley's Comet. Saturn was in Purva, as recited by Vyasa in MahaBharat, confirmed by: the positions of Rahu, Mars, Neptune, Uranus, Pluto and Jupiter; two eclipses; the ancient tradition of 'Shravanadini Nakshatrani' Kshaya Paksha, and a Haley's Comet. Aryabhata had posited the beginning of the war to 3100 BC, or just about 5000 years ago. Vedic Krishna is recorded by Megasthenes to have lived 138 generations before Alexander (325 BC); averaging 20 years per generation comes to 20 x 138 = 2760 + 325 = 3085 BC. The chronology of Professor Raghavan goes like this:

Lord Krishna departs from on the mission for peace 26 September 3067 BCE
Krishna reaches Hastinapura–September 28, 3067 BCE
Lunar eclipse–September 29, 3067 BCE
Krishna rides with Karna–October 8, 3067 BCE
Solar eclipse–October 14, 3067 BCE
The war begins–November 22, 3067 BCE
War ends in the wee hours of the morning 8 December 3067 BCE
Coronation of Maharaja Yudhisthir 36 years before the beginning of Kali-yuga, or about 3138 BCE
Balaram returns 12 December 3067 BCE
Winter solstice 13 January 3066 BCE
Bhishma passes away 17 January 3066 BCE
Lord Krishna departs 3031 BCE.
Vedavyasa composed the main Vedic texts 3000 BC
Sarasvati dries up or disappears 1900 BC

MahaBharat highlights all of the main teachings of the Vedic Aryans/Hindus, including the worship of Shiva, Vishnu and Devi, *Varnashram* (the Hindu stages of life), Samkhya, Vedanta and Yoga. Behind the symbolism of the narrative lies the essence of **dharma or righteous conduct** which is the ideal of the Hindu life and which is summarized thus:

Deal with others as thou wouldst thyself be dealt by. Do nothing to thy neighbor which thou wouldst not have him do to thee hereafter.

These were **picked up almost literally by Jesus**. The temporal nature of universe was summarized thus: *All this is rooted in Time, to be or not to be, to be happy or not to be happy*, later picked up by Shakespeare.

Bhagavada Gita is recited in the Bhishma Parva of the Maha Bharata consisting of 18 chapters from the 25th through 42nd, and 700 verses. One of its aims is to elucidate the four goals of life: *kama* (pleasure), *artha* (wealth), *dharma* (duty) and *moksha* (liberation), which explain the relationship of the individual to society and the world, and the workings of karma, leading to moksha.
Gita analyzes the conflict between an ethical problem along with the means required to achieve it and insists on the social duty or *dharma* for the man who has to participate in the common action. The essence of Gita is summed up in verses 65 and 66 of the concluding chapter where Krishna asks Arjuna to simply abandon all religious practices and pay homage to

Him, adore Him, worship Him and unconditionally surrender unto Him, after which Arjuna need have no fear. To achieve self-realization, Gita elucidates four different paths: Raja Yoga or meditation, Karma Yoga or work, Jnana Yoga or knowledge, and Bhakti Yoga or devotion. When Arjuna was reluctant to fight his kith and kin, Krishna reminds Arjuna of *svadharma* or ordained duty. Bhagavadagita explains the five basic concepts or 'truths: Ishvara (The Supreme Controller), Jiva (Living beings/the individual soul), Prakriti (Nature/Matter), Dharma (Duty in accordance with Divine law), and Kala (Time). Gita urges us to liberate ourselves from samsara, reunite with the Lord and thereby attain His nature of *sat-chit-ananda*, the state of being eternally existent, completely knowledgeable, and full of bliss. Consequently, the myopic personal salvation of M. K. Gandhi through ahimsa was **diametrically opposite** to the teachings of Gita where slaying of blood relatives was condoned to uphold a just cause for the fulfillment of dharma; Ramayana similarly espouses war for dharma. ***All paths lead to me*** is the universal message for peoples of all backgrounds. Krishna as God declares:

"Whenever virtue declines and vice predominates, I incarnate as an Avatar. In visible form I appear from age to age to protect the virtuous and to destroy evil doing in order to reestablish righteousness".

William van Humboldt admires Gita thus:

"*The most beautiful, perhaps the only true philosophical song existing in any known tongue*".

On the other hand, Gita has been belittled, berated, and insulted by the leftist writers in India and most recently by a writer from Harvard.

Krishna from MahaBharat was **transformed into Chrisn, Christ, Herakles, Melchidesec** and the like. Although written off as a myth by the ruling Dynasty in India, the historicity of MahaBharat is archeologically well documented. After the exile, the Pandavas had asked for three villages: Paniprastha, Sonaprastha and Indraprastha, generally identified with the modern Panipat, Sonepat and Delhi. These sites have yielded pottery, antiquities, building structures with drainage systems, iron arrow, and spearheads. The excavations in 1952, revealed the existence of Vidurka-tilla (Vidura's palace), Draupadi-ki-rasoi (Draupadi's Kitchen) and Draupadi Ghat, besides copper utensils, iron seals, gold and silver ornaments, terracotta discs and several oblong ivory dice used in the game of *chauper*. According to the Matsya and Vayu puranas, heavy flooding by the river Ganga destroyed Hastinapur and Nichakshu for which definite archaeological evidence exists. The submergence of Dwarka is described vividly in MahaBharat as Arjuna asked the residents of Dwarka to vacate the city immediately. Dwarka (Dvaravati) was submerged six times and the modern-day Dwarka is the 7th such city to be built on that site. Underwater exploration yielded two gateways, fort walls, bastions and a Jetty at a depth of 10 meters off **Dwarka** in the Sindhusagar (Arabian Sea); the pottery at Dwarka has been dated to **3520 BC** by Thermoluminence. Other finds at Dwarka include bronze and iron implements, a seal, a bull, unicorn and a goat all of which establish a **direct continuity with Harappa**. Ancient monuments, dated to the MahaBharat period, have also been found near Gwalior, Kotwar, Kumaon hills (Uttarkhanda), as detailed in my previous books. Kotwar has been identified with Kamantalpur, named after its founder, Kamant, father of Kunti, the mother of the five Pandava brothers.

In Kumaon hills (Uttarkhanda), **Bhimtal** is so named because, during the exile, Bhima prayed at the Bhimeshwara Mahadeva temple which still stands. Here, Bhima struck the ground with his mace to get water for the Pandavas while in Haridwar **Bhimagoda** yielded water when Bhima stuck the ground with his knee. **Naukuchiyatal** is believed to have been formed when the fourth Pandava brother Nakul shot an arrow into the ground and Pandavas are believed to have taken their last bath there before ascending to the other world. It is said that a dip in its waters with clean conscience will fulfill your wishes while good fortune will come your way if you can find a spot from where all nine corners of the lake are visible at once. **Sat Tal** is a series of interconnected lakes: Ram, Laxman, Sita, Hanuman, Nala Damyanati, Garuda and Sukha Tals. Legend has it that Raja Nala of Nishad fell in live with Damayanti but a demon created such a misunderstanding that Damayanti left Nala; once enlightened, he shared his wisdom with Arjuna who had married Ulipi, the daughter of the King of Nagas while Bhima married Hidimbu of Bachari tribe, both from Nagaland. Howey is of the opinion that Arjuna actually went to Patala (Americas) ruled by the Nagas. The city of Dimapur, known as Hidimbipur at the time of Pandavas, boasts of the ruins of Bhima's palace. Krishna married Rukmini in Arunchal Pradesh which is also linked to Krishna's grandson Anirudha, as detailed in *Bhagvata Purana* and other Vedic sources.

The current date for Gautam **Buddha**, some 500 BC, was derived by European historians from Ceylonese and Chinese records. Planetary alignments suggest that Buddha ruled during Krittika period (2621-1661 BC). Kshemajit (reigned 1892-1852 BC), the fourth in the Shishunag Dynasty, was a contemporary of Lord Buddha's father, Shuddhodana. It was during the reign of Bimbisara (reigned 1852-1814 BC), when Prince Siddhartha became the enlightened Buddha and departed from this world during the reign of King Ajatashatru (1814-1787 BC). Jain tradition holds that **Mahavira** left this world 15 years after Buddha (1807 BC), i.e., in 1792 BC, and since Mahavira lived for a span of 72 years, he must have been born in 1864 BC. Mahavira preached   during the reign of Ajatshatru 1814-1787 BC. Shankara, as per the current chronology, is dated 788-820 CE (derived from *Shankara Digvijaya Sara*). However, since the "sheet-anchor" is displaced backwards, it is apparent that the date of Shankara should be recalculated to around 600 BC.

The International Veda Conference held 20-22 February 2015 was to conclude that indigenous civilization has been developing on the Indian subcontinent for more than 10,000 years, that Aryans were native inhabitants of Bharat, that Vedas are the world's most ancient compilation of knowledge on all aspects of human endeavor (Chapter 5), that Vedas and Epics detail planetary alignments between 9000 BP & 7000 BP, although discrepancy exists regarding exact dates. By contrast, **few sites confirm the life and sojourn of Jesus**, whose very historical existence has been doubted, but Abrahamic faiths are nevertheless called 'true', as detailed in my previous books.

4. A Unique Marvel Called Arya

The brilliant discoverers who harnessed the fundamental principles underlying the fleeting reality were to call themselves **Arya** in their homeland **Aryavarta.** In his seminal book titled *The Arctic Home in the Vedas*, Bal Gangadhar Tilak advanced the theory that the North Pole was the original home of the Aryan people during pre-glacial period which they had to abandon 8000 BC or so due to climate change that produced great floods, and migrated to Northern Europe and Asia. This is supported by many Vedic hymns, passages in Avesta (Iran), Vedic chronology, and Vedic calendars. Mount Kailash and Mansarovar were the spiritual homes of the Vedic people, as described in a little known passage in MahaBharat known as *Uddyog Parva*. Similarly, *Valmiki Ramayan* describes Antarctica as a land of Yama situated to the south of Lanka, at the end of the earth, white in color because it is covered with snow.

The word 'Manasarovar' originates from Sanskrit *manas* (mind) and *sarovar* (lake) to personify purity such that drinking water from the lake would clean the devotee of all sins committed over even a hundred lifetimes, and attain the abode of Lord Shiva after death. Hindu scriptures state that the lake was first created in the mind of the Lord Brahma and then planted onto the Earth. It is also believed to be the summer abode of the Hamsa swan which represents wisdom and beauty. Buddhists associate it with the legendary lake known as Anavatapta in Sanskrit and Anotatta in Pali, where Queen Maya is believed to have conceived Buddha. Lord Buddha apparently stayed and meditated near this lake on several occasions. The lake now harbors several monasteries, most notably the ancient Chiu Gompa Monastery, carved straight out of the rock. Lake Manasarovar is also known as 'The Jewel of Tibet' in the meditative Tibetan tradition. In Jain scriptures, the Kailash-Manasarovar region is associated with the first Tirthankara Lord Shree Rishabhdev who attained nirvana (moksha) near Ashtapad Mountain adjoining the Kailash range. Lake Manasarovar is also mentioned in the Sri Guru Granth Sahib of Sikh faith and can be connected to the Ganga River basin through a fifteen km long tunnel.

Mount Kailash is a peak in the Kailash Range (Gangdise Mountains) of the Transhimalaya chain in Tibet. It lies near the source of some of the four longest rivers in Asia: Indus, Sutlej, Brahmaputra and Karnali. The word may be derived from *kēlāsa* in Sanskrit which means 'crystal'. According to Vishnu Purana, the four faces of the mountain are made of crystal, ruby, gold, and lapis lazuli. It forms a pillar of the world and is located at the heart of six mountain ranges symbolizing a lotus. In Hindu tradition, the Supreme Lord Shiva sits in a state of perpetual meditation atop Mount Kailash, along with his wife Pārvatī. In Jain tradition, Kailash is also known as *Meru Parvat* or *Sumeru*. Ashtapada, a peak next to Mount Kailash, is the site where the first Jain Tirthankara, Rishabhadeva, attained Nirvana or moksha. The ancient Koneshwaram temple at Trincomalee is heralded as 'Dakshina Kailasam' (Kailash of the South) as it lies on exactly the same longitude as Mount Kailash.

The Bön religion, which predates Buddhism in Tibet, maintains that the entire mystical region and the nine-story Swastika Mountains are the seat of all spiritual power, variously known as Water's Flower, Mountain of Sea Water, and Nine Stacked Swastika Mountain. Tibetan Buddhists call it *Kangri Rinpoche* or 'Precious Snow Mountain'. Numerous sites in the region are associated with Guru Rinpoche (Padmasambhava) whose tantric practices are credited with finally establishing Buddhism in Tibet in the 7th–8th century CE. Tantric Buddhists believe that Mount Kailash is the home of the Buddha Demchok (also known as Demchog or Chakrasamvara), who represents supreme bliss.

From this original habitat, during the pre-Orion period 8000 to 5000 BC, Vedic Aryans moved to what are now Afghanistan and Pakistan and founded the Indus Valley Civilization (ISC) whose origin could go as far back as 15000 BC. During the *Orion* period, 5000 to 3000 BC, when the vernal equinox was in Orion, Vedic bards still reminisced about the traditions of the original Arctic home. During the *Krittika* period, 3000 to 1400 BC, when the Vernal equinox was in Pleiades, the memory of the original Arctic home had grown dim and was often misunderstood, giving rise to the Sutras and philosophic schools that gained prominence around 1400 to 500 BC.

Although the Indus phase can be approximated with reasonable certainty by carbon dating, the original arctic homeland can only be gleaned by astronomic references in the vast Vedic literature as melting ice leaves no archeological residue. The early literature speaks of three constellations: *Mrighashira or the Orion* (4500-3500 BC, Rig Veda); *Rohini or Aldebaran* (3100 BC, MahaBharat), *Krittika or the Pleaides* (2900-1900 BC, Sutra and Brahamana). The seventh mandala of Rig Veda, which closed the Vedic age, records the vernal equinox in Mrighashira or the Orion era around 4500-3500 BC. The vernal equinox shifted from Mrighashira to Rohini around 3500 BC or a little earlier, as recorded in Aitareya Brahmina as well as in MahaBharat which speaks of Rohini-Krittika transition. MahaBharat records that the Rohini-Abhijit pair gave way to Krittika-Dhanishta pair around 3000 BC. Tilak was to observe:

"…we can now decipher these records inscribed on the specially cultivated memory of the Indian Aryans. Commencing with the Taittiriya Samhita and the Brahminas, which declare that the Phalguni moon was once the New Year's night, the Mrighashiras was designated by a name which, if rightly interpreted, showed that the vernal equinox coincided with that asterism (constellation) in old times".

The Vedas clearly state that there is only one God, other gods are only metaphor incarnations of the one God. **The almighty power of the Supreme Divinities is only One** (RV III.55.1). The Monotheism of Abrahamic religions completely turned this upside down in order to advance their only 'true' God. Metaphysical theories deal not with the ever-changing stuff of life but with some permanent reality behind it which is not affected by external changes. *Maya* is related to Brahman like the mirage to the desert. Whereas the religious and moral forces of the external cult could be understood or followed by the mass, the deeper truth was reserved for the initiate. For example, Surya, the sun god, personified the physical sun but he is also the giver of knowledge which illuminates the mind and spirit. All metaphors for Vedic gods have this **outer and this outer and inner functions**. This was the distinction between *shudra*, the undeveloped physical mind, and the twice born that could enter the world of Mysteries carefully disguised by symbols. However, many great teachers were men of inferior birth like Janashruti or Satyakama **Jabala**, son of a **servant girl** who knew not who his father was, **Vashishtha** was **born of a courtesan** and sage **Parthasartha's** mother was a **chandala.**

Vedic seers pioneered path breaking discoveries in all aspects of life to engender peace and prosperity around the globe, along the ideal of **krinvantum vishwam aryam** (we shall civilize the whole world). Great emphasis was placed on the right conduct (*karma*) throughout life to end the cycle of rebirths such that *Jivatman* would merge into *parmatman* and we would no longer be limited by our mind and body. Personal conduct was to be governed by one's thoughts and deeds, dharma and karma, and became established tenets by the sixth century BC. The **Transmigration** was first described in *Brhadaranyaka Upanishad* (circa 7th BC) as follows:

"*Those who have lived the lives of sacrifice, chastity and austerity pass to the World of Fathers, the paradise of Yama; thence to the moon; thence to empty space, air and finally rain on the earth where they become food… and are offered again in the altar fire which is man, to be born in the fire of woman. The unrighteous are reincarnated as worms, birds or insects*".

Yakkha prasna show Yakkha to be the arbiter of Dharma-Dhamma Yakkha, a Pali form of Vedic yakṣa, whose anthropomorphic representation as anray of light enlightened the viewer about the profundity and sacredness of dharma-dhamma. Neelkantha notes that Yaksha Prasna were intended to ascertain the truth about Atman, differentiating Atman from the Self. What is '*Dharma*'? Dharma is controlling the mind, synonym of yoga. These fundamental premises of being and becoming, dharma and karma regulated the life of *Bharatam janam* civilization from 5th millennium BC or earlier (Chapter 5.I) and all Bharatiya Hindu rites are now governed by them.

Mantras stem from divine inspiration and combine Samkhya, Vedanta and Yoga to reconcile the inner spiritual truth with outer actualities of man's life and action. The etymology of Yaksha called *Nirkuta*, dated some 500 BC, shows that Brahmins had forgotten the true meaning of many words at a very early period and less than 1000 scholars are so competent in contemporary India. Consequently, the household *havans* performed by the caste 'Brahmins' now have no ritual significance. Many racist writers, Western imperialists, and Communists, have condemned the Vedas altogether:

"*The hymns of Rig Veda are the sacrificial compositions of a primitive and still barbarous race written around a system of ceremonial and propitiatory rites addressed to Personified Powers of Nature and replete with a confused mass of half formed myth and crude astronomical allegories yet in the making. Only in the later hymns do we perceive the first appearance of deeper psychological and moral ideas – borrowed, some think, from the hostile Dravidians, the 'robbers' and 'Veda haters' freely cursed in the hymns themselves…This modern theory is in accord with the received idea of a rapid human evolution from the quite recent savage".*

Tilak was to set the record straight:

"Rig Veda is not a prayer book of Nature worshippers but inspired poetry that reveals the truths of existence". Thus, an ingrained and dominant spirituality, an inexhaustible vital creativity and gust of life and, mediating between them, a powerful, penetrating and scrupulous intelligence combined of the rational, ethical and aesthetic mind each at a high intensity of action, created the harmony of the ancient Indian culture".

The Upanishads emphasize fitness of the body and mind, knowledge, discipline, restraint, self-suffering, self-sacrifice. An answer was sought as to Brahmin, the Universe, self or *atman,* in *Brihadaranyaka* and *Chandogya* Upanishads. *Taittiriya* Upanishad asks: **What is Brahman**?

"The beginning and the source of all things, everything else is a consequence. The secret of everything else is explained by its secret; as it is the sum and end of all things, so everything else amounts to it and by throwing itself into it achieves the sense of its own experience. Matter is Brahma, from matter all existences are born, by Matter they increase and enter into Matter in their passing hence. Energy is Brahma."

"He whom the Shaivites worship as Shiva, whom the Vedantins call Brahma, whom the Buddhists call Buddha, whom the Nayakas call the creator, whom the Jains call the Arhat, whom the Mimamsakas call karma, may that Vishnu, the Lord of the three worlds, grant you the object of your desire.

*From non-being lead us to Being, from darkness lead us to Light, from death lead us to Immortality. (*Brihadaranyaka Upanishad I.3.28).

Jain tradition ascribed to Jinsena (500 BC) concluded:

"Time is without beginning and end, uncreated and indestructible, it endures under the compulsion of its own nature".

Chandogya Upanishad leaves gods out altogether:

"In the beginning this world was merely non-being. It was nonexistent…How from Non-being could Being be produced".

In *Chandogya*, the householder Uddalaka instructs his son Shvetaketu that the universe in the beginning was the Being or the Existent (*sat*) alone that became many by desire and thought:

"What is the Universe? From what does it rise? Into what does it go? In

Freedom it rises, in freedom it rests, and into freedom it melts away".

The use of the word **freedom** here is to be contrasted with the bias of those Europeans who attribute it to the Greeks only. Man was God *tat tvam asi* (Chandogya) while Gita prescribed that one should strive to **become like God**, or a perfect Arya. The soul can be defined both negatively:

It is no this, not this" (*neti, neti*), or positively *'That thou art'* (tat tvam asi):

Aham Brahmasmi (I am Brahma) Brihadaryanka Upanishad; *Yas tvam asi so ham asi* (You are indeed that I am) Isa Upanishad; *Idam sarvam asi* (thou art all this) Mundaka Upanishad; and finally as *Soham* (I am He, that am I) in the yogic practice. In later times, this was abbreviated to a simple Namaste. There is no attainment higher than Self-knowledge. A morning prayer affirms:

"O sun of refulgent glory, I am the same person as makes thee what thou art!"

The legend of Rudra (later called Shiva) affirms:

"God cannot destroy him who has conquered himself".

God looked in wonder and awe at the spirit of the man who had conquered his self and Rudra asked God:

*"Is he then a God like You?" And God said "No he is not a God like me, **He is Me**".*

This Vedic-Hindu **personification of God with man** is in contrast to the Abrahamic religions which disconnected them for good. In *Aitereya* Upanishad, the long endless journey is portrayed where every verse ends with *Charaiveti, charaiveti* , *"Hence, O traveler, March on, March along"*. In *Mimamsa*, devas are assigned a lower order of creation than man who can achieve self-realization and Buddhahood only through human birth which is the highest stage towards self-realization.

F. W. Thomas in 'The Legacy of India' concludes:

"What gives the Upanishads their unique quality and unfailing human appeal is an earnest sincerity of tone, as of friends, conferring upon matters of deep concern".

C. Rajagopalachari adds:

"The spacious imagination, the majestic sweep of thought, and the almost reckless spirit of exploration with which, urged by the compelling thirst for truth, the Upanishad teachers and pupils dwell into the 'open secret' of the

universe, make this most ancient of the world's holy books still the most modern and most satisfying".

Max Muller felt that:

"*The Upanishads are the …sources of …the Vedanta philosophy, a system in which every human speculation seems to me to have reached its very acme…I spend my happiest hours in reading Vedanta books. They are to me the light of the morning, like the pure air of the mountains, so simple, so true, if once understood*".

For Tagore, the message of Taittiriyaka Upanishad was final:

"*From bliss all these things are born; by bliss when born they live; into bliss they enter at their death*".

Havell affirms:

"*In India religion is hardly a dogma, but a working hypothesis of human conduct…the very raison d'etre …is its workableness, its conformity to life, to adapt itself to changing conditions…When it goes off at a tangent from the curve of life, loses contact with social needs, and the distance between it and life grows, it loses all its vitality and significance*".

The philosophical traditions of Bharat, transmitted to Europe as Islamic Arab achievements, were to assure European revival after Enlightenment. It is therefore obvious that the Vedic culture is:

"*More high-reaching, subtle, many sided, curious and profound than the Greek, more noble and humane than the Roman, more large and spiritual than the old Egyptian, more vast and original than any other Asiatic civilization, more intellectual than the European prior to the 18th century.*"

All this is in direct **contrast to the Divine Will** of the organized religions where man was not made of the same substance as God, again **contradicting Jesus himself**. For the Hindu, the Truth was a matter of investigation, not belief, and karma, not divine will, was to determine man's future. Theocracy does not permit deviation from the established principles and beliefs and is inimical to free thinking. It survives for religion and by religion where the word of God was revealed to the prophet, protected and propagated by priests. Pre-Christian kings were separate from the religious clergy but Christian **Church was fused with the state** by Constantine such that all wings of the state became wings of the church as well. The Church now institutionalized the **master-slave division** of society espoused by Aristotle and the clergy was to lead its flock in ritual obeisance to the Lord God. The secularism in Bharat of old contrasts with this and King was not the representative of God so religion had no place in governance.

Creation in Vedic hymns is described as the work of a divine craftsman via a **fire sacrifice.** The world was created by the prime self-sacrifice of Vishvakarman for creation. The gods themselves must perform sacrifice in order to ascend to the heaven. The sacrifice in the Vedas actually means sacrificing ones ego to the internal Agni, or Divine spark. The spirit of sacrifice inherent in Hindu psyche may be expressed as follows:

"I desire not the supreme state of bliss with its eight perfections, nor the cessation of rebirth. May I take up the sorrow of all creatures that suffer and enter into them so that they may be free from grief (Bhagvata)".

The *Purusha shukta,* or Hymn to the Primeval Man, underlines a careful correlation between sacrifice and causation (Rig Veda X.90). Consequently, sacrifice became the **center of Aryan social life** performed as *yajna* around a fire in *tapovans* that eventually gave way to temples in Hinduism.

"The individual should be sacrificed for the family, the family for the community, and the community for the country".

Vedic seers pioneered path breaking discoveries in all aspects of life to engender peace and prosperity around the globe (Chapter 5), along the ideal of **krinvantum vishwam aryam** (we shall civilize the whole world). To this end, the Vedic society was organized into *varnas* first mentioned in the **Purusha Shukta** verse of Rig Veda (X: 90), linked to professions. Here, the **four *varnas*** sprang forth from the body of the creative deity whose self-sacrifice lead to the genesis of the creative process: *Brahmins* from the head (knowledge), *Kshatriyas* from the arms (action), *Vaishyas* from the thighs (support) and *shudras* from the feet (servants) and a person could **change varnas** simply by adopting a different profession. Jatis were geographical or linguistic divisions within a Varna. Those who were outside these structures were known as *adhivasis*. All Brahmins are believed to have descended from seven great rishis: Kashyapa, Vashishtha, Bhrigu, Gautama, Bhardwaja, Atri and Vishvamitra; Agastya was added later on.

Unparalleled ideation by Vedic rishis finally perfected an ideal code of conduct that all humans were expected to follow. Just as the whole creation stemmed out of an original sacrifice by the omnipresent *Prajapati* so also all human beings were to **sacrifice their ego** by an exemplary conduct personified as a **noble Arya**. Great emphasis was laid on righteous deeds or *karma* to channel individual energy into socially prescribed goals. *Nitisara* of Shukracharya informs us that:

"Neither through color, nor through ancestors can the spirit worthy of a Brahmin be generated… No Brahmin is such by birth. No outcast is such by

birth. An outcast is such as by his deeds. A Brahmin is such by his deeds".

The origin of the word **shudra** is of doubtful etymology and occurs only once in Rig Veda. *Mleccha* meant barbarians of whatever color and race whose speech was unintelligible and whose nature could improve through adoption of Vedic principles. Untouchables were possibly derived from aboriginal tribes; *Chandalas* were to cremate corpses, execute criminals, and to dress in the garments of the corpses they had cremated, eat from broken vessels and wear only iron ornaments.

There is no mention of caste anywhere in Sanskrit literature.

The ancient Bharat was run as a **corporation** under the guidance of an elite Brahmin *varna* whose selfless ideation had assured peace and plenty around the globe. Most importantly, all of this was achieved **without slavery and no force** whatever was used to coerce peoples. Before the imperialists were to damage the system, education had turned the ancient Bharat into the **most creative and innovative civilization** in the world. There was a school in every village, and all groups enjoyed the benefits of gurukul-style education that created citizens, not drones. In his landmark work, The Beautiful Tree, Dharampal has quoted the imperialists themselves about the quality of indigenous education. Herder was to praise Brahmins who had ruled the world for thousands of years:

"The Brahmins have formed their people to such a degree of gentleness, courtesy, temperance and chastity…that Europeans frequently appear, in comparison with them, as beastly, drunken or mad".

In Rig Veda, the term Aryan occurs 36 times, always within the context of noble conduct in people as children of light, stemming from an illustrious family, characterized by gentle behavior, good nature and righteous conduct that worked for the equality of all and was dear to everyone defined thus: *mahakula kulinarya sabhya sajjana sadhavah.* Rig Veda employs Arya as an adjective *praja arya jyotiragrah* (RV, VII. 33.17) *Children of Arya seek and are led by jyoti.* In Ramayana, Valmiki defines Arya as one who cared for the equality of all and was dear to everyone, describing Rama as: **arya sarva samascaiva sadaiva priyadarsanah.**

In Amarkosha, the most authoritative dictionary of classical Sanskrit of 500 CE, Arya is defined as: **mahakula kulinarya sabhya sajjana sadhavah,** one from a noble family, of gentle behavior, good natured and righteous conduct; there is no mention of race or nationality. Dasyus are powers of darkness and are to be won over by the children of light. This is a cosmic struggle between good and evil, not a racial metaphor between light skinned invaders and dark skinned original inhabitants. The Aryan spirit of *Krinvanto Vishwam Aryam* and **Vasudhaiva Kutumbkum** (the whole world is one family) is perhaps most evident from the last prayer of an Arya who died in Gobi desert, 5003 BC:

"God, bring me not back, as I was, Let me come as a blade of grass
Or a droplet of dew and rain, so this waterless desert bloom again…"

Bhagvata was to epitomize the Aryan ideal as follows:

"I desire not the supreme state of bliss with its eight perfections, nor the cessation of rebirth. May I take up the sorrow of all creatures that suffer and enter into them so that they may be free from grief".

To be an **Aryan was not a matter of birth**. A beautiful tree is Aryan, the order of the cosmos is Aryan, Buddha called his teaching Aryan, and Jains also call themselves Aryans. According to *Manudharma Shastra,* or *Manusmriti* (X.43-45), the word Arya during the Vedic age denoted certain spiritual and humanistic values: An Arya became a **metaphor for God**, incessantly setting modes of behavior by his exemplary conduct, also true for Brahmin varna. Gita prescribed that one should strive to become like God, or a perfect Arya. Anyone regardless of birth, race or origin could become Arya by following this code of conduct.

.Manu was to insist that fall from the Aryan ideal resulted from the omission of scared rites, leading to the state of *Dasayus* (servants). By not heeding to sages, the following peoples have gradually sunk to the state of Dasayus: Paundrakas, Chodas, Dravidas (South India), Kambojas (North East Afghanistan), Yavanas (North West Afghanistan), Shakkhas, Paradas, Pahlavas (Parsis), Chinas, Kiratas and Daradas. Rig Veda also states:

"We pray to Indra to give glory by which the Dasyus will become Aryans."

Will Durant concluded:

"India was the mother of our race and Sanskrit the mother of Europe's languages. *She was the mother of our philosophy, mother through the Arabs, of much of our mathematics, mother through Buddha, of the ideals embodied in Christianity, mother through village communities of self-government and democracy. Mother India is in many ways the mother of us all"*

The British historian E. P.Thompson was prophetic enough:

"India is perhaps the most important country for the future of the world. *All the convergent influences of the world run through this society.... There is not a thought that is being thought in the West or East that is not active in some Indian mind".*

Senghor (1906-2001) had placed the 'cradle of mankind' in the Indian Ocean, just as H.G. Wells (1866-1946 CE) had done. Senghor then went on to suggest that the flood in the New Stone Age forced people to flee to Egypt and Mesopotamia (dubbed as cradles of civilization in the West) who derived their knowledge from the peoples fleeing this cataclysm. Buffon (1707- 1788) elaborated a coherent theory in which people emerged thirty thousand years ago east of the Caspian Sea and "*merited all respect as creators of arts, sciences and of all useful institutions…*" Diderot (1713-1784) likewise suggested that the "*sciences may be more ancient in India than in Egypt*". On the basis of his astronomical calculations, Jean Bailly situated earliest men in the valley of Ganges and Voltaire seconded this:

"*I am convinced that everything has come down to us from the banks of Ganges, astronomy, astrology, metempsychosis, etc…*".

Hugo (1802-188 CE) imitated an Upanishad in his poem *Suprematie* (1870 CE) while Voltaire (1885 CE) formulated the idea that Vedism comprised the oldest religion known to man. He discovered an old manuscript titled *Ezour Vedam* through which he placed the Hindus above the Jews:

"*We are a great people…The Egyptians, Persians, and Arabs came to our country in search of wisdom and spices, when Jews were unknown to the rest of mankind*".

Jews stole from the Aryans the idea of Adam as progenitor, the myths of Creation, and the Fall. As a polygenic, Voltaire could not place the origin of mankind in India, but strove to demonstrate that Adam had taken over everything including his name from the Vedic Hindu ancestry. Ampere (1800-18640), Le Charles (1798-1873), Jacolliot (1837-1890), Somerset Maughm's (1874-1965), Verlaine (1844-1896 CE), and Broussais(1772-1838) were all influenced by Vedic-Hindu thought. Alexander Hamilton (1757-1804) , a contemporary of Jones and Colebrook, introduced Sanskrit to Germany in 1802 CE and Schlegel brothers became the founder of Indian philology. Max Muller (1823-1900 CE) praised Indian thought and philosophy in almost lyrical terms:

"*If I were to look over the whole world to find out the country most richly endowed with all the wealth, power, and beauty that nature can bestow – in some parts a very paradise on earth – I should point out to India. If I were asked under what sky the human mind has most fully developed some of the choicest gifts, has most deeply pondered on the greatest problems of life, and has found solutions to some of them which well deserve the attention even of those who have studied Plato and Kant – I should point to India…"*

He pointed out that Alexander is not mentioned in the entire body of Sanskrit literature. Shakespeare and Bharat literature formed the main inspiration for the Romantic Movement, introduced to Germany by Friederich and Schlegel. Wilhelm von Humboldt (1767-1835 CE) was greatly moved by Bhagavad Gita which he described as "***the deepest and loftiest thing the world had to show***". Beethoven (1770-1827 CE) was attracted by Indian thought, as evident by numerous translated texts of Upanishads and Gita discovered in his manuscripts.

Herder (1744-1803 CE) described **India as the birthplace** of all languages, sciences, and arts and positioned the childhood of humanity in India. Both Herder and Goethe admired the graceful simplicity of Shakuntala by Kalidasa.

"Human mind got the first shapes of wisdom and virtue with a simplicity, strength and sublimity which have – frankly spoken – nothing, nothing at all equivalent in our philosophical, cold European world".

In Russia, Chadaiev declared in 1840 CE:

*"**We are the darling children of the East**….Everywhere we are in contact with the East, it is from there that we have drawn our belief, our laws, our virtue…"*

Sanskrit poetry provided the inspiration from which all poetry has descended.

"Asia impresses our imagination by virtue of her antiquity, her wonder, and her mystery. Hers is the land of buried story, the hidden records, of forgotten romance she fascinates, she baffles…Sphinx-like she propounds riddles which few can answer, luring us onward with illusive hopes of inspiring revelations, yet hiding ever in her splendid, tattered bosom the secrets of the oldest and least amply recorded of human histories".

Romantic poets Novalis (1772-1810 CE), Ruckert (1788-1866 CE) and Gutzkow, were also deeply influenced by Indian lyric poetry. Novalis observed:

"Poetry, pure and colorful like a beautiful India, stood opposed to the cold and deadening mountains of philistine reason".

Prussian minister of education described Gita as *"the deepest and loftiest thing the world has to show"*. Both Goethe (1749-1832 CE) and Schiller (1788-1805) found nothing in Greek literature compared to Kalidasa's Shakuntala. Schlegel (1804-1884) published his work On the Language and Wisdom of the Indians in 1808 CE and commented:

"If one considers the superior conception which is at the basis of the truly universal Indian culture and which, itself divine, knows how to embrace in its universality everything that is divine without distinction, then, what we in Europe call religion or what we used to call such, no longer seems to deserve that name. And one would like to advise everyone…to go to India for that purpose where he may be certain to find at least fragments for which he will surely look in vain in Europe".

Joseph Gores elevated Indian religion above Judaism. While Ritter characterized India as the vestibule of Western History since the oldest and the most important documents of history came from India. Schiller's Maria Stuart was inspired by Meghaduta 'The Cloud Messenger' of Kalidasa while Heine's finest poems *Die Lotusblume* and *Auf Flugen des Gesanges* breathe the very spirit of Hindu Lyrical poetry. Goethe's (1749-1832) Faust was inspired by Kalidasa. Immanuel Kant (1712-1804 CE) was very much influenced by Indian philosophy and some of his writings are very similar to the concept of Maya, transmigration and Buddhist philosophy. Kant placed the **origin of mankind in Tibet** and compared **Abraham with Brahma** while **Joseph** was compared **with Ganesha**. Kant declared that Indian religious thought was free of dogmatism and intolerance. Schopenhauer (1788-1860 CE) declared:

"I acknowledge that I owe the best part of my development, beside the impression of the outward world, to the works of Kant and to the holy scriptures of the Hindus and Plato…".

He regarded **Hindus as deeper thinkers than Europeans** because their interpretation of the world was internal and intuitive, not external and intellectual. Krause (1781-1832 CE) and Deussen (1845-1919 CE) were also influenced by Indian Philosophy.

Richard Wagner (1813-1883 CE) declared that he had become a Buddhist; Prakriti and Ananda were transformed into Kundry and Parsifal in his last opera Parsifal. In Gotterdammerung, *Wahnheim* (the abode of illusion) and *Wunschheim* (the abode of desire) are typically Indian concepts long with countless more. Nietzsche (1844-1900 CE) found in *Manusmriti* one of the sources of his own philosophy of the superhuman. Hermann Hesse, Nobel Prize for literature in 1946, felt that Indian thought offered the most radical possibility for undoing the curse of individuation. Other German writers who drew inspiration from Indian sources include: Dahlke, Munch, Winckler, Schaffer, Werfel, Zweig, Kasack, Keyserling, Meyrnik and Mann.

Sir William Jones (1746-1794), found **Aryans a superior people** who possessed a highly evolved moral wisdom and a fertile imaginative genius that had had discovered astronomy and metaphysics that the Greeks later appropriated. Colebrook (1805 CE) corroborated Jones and emphasized an **ideal Vedic age** that had degenerated. Indian philosophy influenced greatly English Romanticism as evident in the works of Blake (1757-1827), DeQuincy (1785-1859), Southey (1774-1843), Carlyle (1795-1881), and Coleridge (1772-1834). Shelley's (1792-1822) Adonais dedicated to Keats propounds the doctrine of Maya and Indian thought is recognizable in Wordsworth's poetry. Keats (1795-1821) was drawn to India, as a passage in Endymion reveals. Thomas Moore (1779-1852 CE) used Indian sources for his poem *Lalla Rookh* (1817) which was an instant best seller and went through several editions.

Whereas earlier British scholars had pointed out the depth of Sanskrit literature, the industrial revolution in England (fed by her colonies) produced a sense and power which was to manifest itself later in racial arrogance and imperialism. The 1857 CE mutiny in India left British with a taste of vulnerability in a world where they had become proud and arrogant so India was reduced to the 'White man's burden' by Kipling (1865-1936). Similarly, Ruskin (1819-1900 CE) dismissed Indians and their philosophy as 'childish' or restricted in intellect yet he became the idol of Gandhi.

Maxim Gorki (1868-1936) stated that Russia was more Oriental than China and Dostoyevsky declared that it would be beneficial for Russia to turn her soul towards the East. Eminescu (1850-1889 CE) borrowed heavily from Upanishads; his works even carried Sanskrit titles (*Tattwamasi, Kamadeva*). Yale University was founded in 1718 CE with the help of gifts raised in India by Elihu Yale, a governor of Madras. Johns Hopkins set up a chair in Sanskrit in 1878 CE, followed by Harvard. Emerson (1803-1882 CE) inspired the transcendentalist movement based on Vedanta:

"The Indian teaching, through its cloud of legends, has yet a simple and grand religion, like a queenly countenance seen through a rich veil. It teaches to **speak truth, love others as you, and to despise trifles***".*

Thoreau (1817-1862 CE) was deeply influenced by Vedas, Gita, and other Vedic texts. Walt Whitman (1819-1892 CE) stated that 'all religions are true' which forms the essence of Hindu thought. The Christian Science movement in the US, initiated by Mary Baker Eddy, was possibly influenced by Vedanta. T. S. Eliot (1888-1965) follows *niksha karma* of Gita in his '*The Dry Savages*' where he declared that all man's actions should be motivated by rightness and goodness, not by expectation of gain or merit.

Yeats (1865-1939 CE) discovered an **identity between Gaelic and Indian** civilizations, most evident in his poem *Meru* (1935 CE) based on Indian mythology. Carpenter, Havelock, Ellis and Lawrence found support in Kama Sutra for their revolt against the rigid sexual ethics of an earlier period. The mysticism of Eliot, Huxley and Auden clearly stems from Hindu roots which also influenced Maugham, Sitwell, Isherwood and Heard. Jung interpreted Hinduism and Buddhism in his psychological terms and stated:

"*We do not yet realize that while we are turning upside down the material world of the East with our technical proficiency, the East with its psychic proficiency is throwing our spiritual world into confusion. We have never yet hit upon the thought that while we are overpowering the Orient from without, it may be fastening its hold upon us from within*".

The Theosophical Society was founded in 1875 in New York to state that there is no religion higher than truth. The word itself is a translation of *Brahmavidya* and closely follows the concepts of Indian philosophies. Vivekananda, Ramakrishna, Coomarswamy, Radhakrishnan, and Gandhi have all found their way into Western culture, politics, and philosophy. Albert Einstein (1879-1955) was to remark:

'*The most beautiful and the most profound emotion we can experience is the sensation of the mystical...To know that what is impenetrable to us really exists, manifesting itself as the highest wisdom and the most radiant beauty which our dull faculties can comprehend only in their most primitive forms - this knowledge, this feeling is at the center of true religiousness.....The cosmic religious experience is the strongest and noblest mainspring of scientific research'.*

Niels Bohr (1885-1962) put it thus:

"*We are both spectators and actors in the great drama of existence. He himself is part of the world he seeks to explore. Man is thus his own greatest mystery*".

Vedic antiquity has not been dated accurately but Sanskrit scriptures, particularly the Epics, speak of a very advanced civilization some of whose accomplishments cannot be duplicated even in this day and age. MahaBharat describes weapons like *Brahamastra, Vajrastra, Narayanastra, Praswapastra, Divyastra* and so forth. Brahmastra was similar to the atom bomb whereas Vajrastra was able to powder even the mountains. Praswapa

Astra was known to only Bhishma who used it against Parashurama to induce a hypnotic sleep on the enemy. Sammohana Astra (Virata 61 / 11, 12) was used by Arjuna just by blowing his conch-shell to produce a hypnotic sleep on the Kauravas who threw down their weapons, sat down quietly, and soon became unconscious. The sound of Aum and that of blowing a conch-shell are similar and may produce such an effect if executed properly. Narayanastra was launched by Ashvatthama (Drona A.199) when thousands of fiery arrows appeared in the sky and the army was incinerated by fire, possibly a poisonous gas with a defined specific gravity. Many weapons like *Shataghni, Gada, Chakras* have been described whereas *Mayasabha* was a marvel of electronic technology. Using *Pashupatastra*, Arjuna could shoot 500 arrows in one 'Nimesha' (Udyog. 59/16, 19). Nimesh is equal to 0.2 seconds so **2500 arrows per second** could be launched whereas Modern machine-gun fires 600 bullets per minute. Arjuna killed the horses of Jayadratha from a distance of two miles (Arayanka 255/52-54) meaning a sophisticated weapon with telescope. Ground-to-air missiles and air-to-ground missiles have also been described in MahaBharat whereas antimissiles were named as 'Avapothika'.

'Kumbhakarna' was a war machine in the human form or a Robot, so described in Valmiki Ramayana. The Yoga Vashishtha has also described three robots or *Shambarasura* namely Dama, Vyala and Kata; Kata was like a modern tank protecting the army. Cannon balls (Huda) and explosive projectiles (Guda) have also been mentioned. Some devices could cause explosion of gases (Vayusphotah) and shockwaves. MahaBharat was an atomic war where four million soldiers died and one passage in MahaBharat actually describes the aftermath of an atomic explosion:

An iron thunderbolt contained 'the power of the universe...an incandescent column of smoke and flame, as bright as ten thousand suns, rose in all its splendor...clouds roared upward...blood colored clouds swept down onto the earth...fierce winds began to blow...elephants miles away were blocked off...the earth shook, scorched by the terrible violent heat of this weapon, corpses were so burnt that they were no longer recognizable...hair and nails fell out...birds were turned white...thousands of war vehicles fell down on all sides...never before have we seen such an awful weapon and never before have we heard of such a weapon".

Oppenheimer reacted similarly after the Hiroshima disaster. The survivors saw the disaster of *Astras* and decided to keep the new generation away from their devastating secrets; Arjuna did not reveal Brahmastra to his grand son Parikshit. Thus began the pacific phase of the Aryan miracle of old.

5.Civilization Originates in the Indus World

The Indus Valley Civilization (ISC) dating back to 8000 BC was to become the fount of discovery in all aspects of human endeavor. Bronze Age, Iron age, and pyro technology got started in Bharat whose centers of learning inspired immortal discoveries in Mathematical Sciences, Physics, Chemistry and Chemical Engineering, Mining and Metallurgy, weights and measures, coinage, and so forth. Phonetic linguistics and writing gave birth to Philology whereas secrets behind numbers, such as 7, 8, 33 and 108, led to divination by Numerology. Indus world invented writing as hieroglyphis, related to turner-lapidary-metalwork, read rebus in Meluhha language of Ancient *Bharatam Janam* sphere of influence. Consequently it is no longer necessary for historians to keep repeating that 'Indus script has not been deciphered so far.'

Advances in Architecture inspired the construction of centrally planned urban centers with geometrically designed streets, aligned in cardinal directions, endowed with sanitary drains and waste disposal, thousands of years before they were to appear in Europe. As far back as 3000 BC, Yoga and Ayurveda heralded discoveries in Biological and Medical Sciences that were to form the mother of healing in all medical traditions of the world. In fine arts, three dimensional painting, plastic representation of human figures, poetry, drama, fairy tales, fables, theater, musical octave, dance, martial arts, arena sports, dice and board games such as chess, ludo and backgammon, playing cards, and so forth, all originated in ancient Bharat of old.

All of these aspects have been detailed in my previous books but salient features are recalled here to contrast with European depravity, despair, disease, filth, hunger, superstitions and the like whose origin is to be found in Church despotism that kept Europe in Dark Ages. Besides the lack of archeology, Western society is also wanting in literature that got started only during the sixteenth century CE. Greece has become a fountain head of European traditions but has no written or archeological source to back it. Similarly, Egypt has no theoretical treatises to explain pyramids and constructors of Stone Henge remain unknown all of which were created by Vedic people who had migrated out of the ISC heartland. Enlightenment was promoted by philosophers and local to challenge the authority of monolithic institutions of the Catholic Church to emphasize reason, analysis and individualism rather than dogmatism.

I. Meluhha Linguistics and Industry

The Chalcolithic or the Copper age began at Mehragarh as of 7700 BC whereas the Bronze Age (tin plus copper alloy) on the Indian subcontinent began around 3300 BC, compared to 2900 BC in Mesopotamia. Copper-bronze metallurgy was used to produce household vessels, bolts, ornaments and weapons. The world's largest tin mines are to be found in the Tin Belt of the Malaysian Peninsula, extending northwards into Northeast Bharat (India) and eastwards into Vietnam. Tin deposits were exploited as early as 2000-1000 BC and there is evidence for bronze-working at Non Nok Tha in central Thailand, the Chota Nagpur plateau of the east-central subcontinent, Giridih in south Bihar as also in Afghanistan. Copper deposits were equally plentiful in mainland Southeast Asia at Phu Lon in the Phetchabun mountains along the Mekong river, West Bengal, Singhbhum plateau of Bihar, Tamkum in Bankura district, and Chhedapathar in Midnapur district. Tin extraction, alloying metals, *cire perdue* (lost wax) technique and metal casting were perfected by *Bharatam Janam* or 'metalcaster folk' (Meluhha), so mentioned in Rig Veda Chandas by Rishi Vishvamitra in the mantra: *visvāmitrasya rakṣati brahmedam bhāratam janam (*RV 3.053.12) translated as: This prayer, Brahma, of viśhvāmitra protects bhārata folk'. These artisans and traders of the Sarasvati-Sindhu civilization *sprachbund*, were Meluhha speakers, called Harappa culture in archeological parlance, and so identified in *Arya Sanghaṭa Sūtra*

The *lingua franca* of these metal casters developed as metalwork hieroglyphs read rebus in the Sarasvati-Sindhu doab along the 5000 km Tin Road from Hanoi to Haifa 5th millennium BC in Nahal Mishmar of Ancient Near East to circa 3rd century BC in Yunnan north of Vietnam. Khirsara (*Kshirsagar) in Gujrat* was a key transit point in the industrial complexes on the Tin Road. An abiding symbol of the Bronze Age was the oxhide shaped ingot, a signature of the metalworkers of Bharatam janam who developed a pictorial, sacred writing system. Meluhha language, recorded on seals, sculptural reliefs and so forth, also contains Munda and Khmer expressions, as evident on Candi Sukuh hieroglyphs in Java and identified as the language spoken by the Vedic people for trade transactions. The script used a rebus method, a form of picture writing referred to as hieroglyphs, such that words which signified the pictures were in fact mirrors of similar-sounding words which referred to metalwork. Thus, *bara Do* which meant metalcaster was denoted by *barad 'bos indus gaurus*, bull'.

The purpose of Indus Script corpora was to catalog, to engrave, to document in writing, metalwork practices and techniques of that era. Whereas the tablets denote consignments coming out of the smithy for shipment, the seals aggregate the information for bills of landing. The engraving of the 'lathe' on many Indus script inscriptions, mostly in front of the one-horned young bull , were organized as *ghā* 'lathe' *to* denote the tool central to the life-activity of the artisans, and as *anghāta or 'collection of word '*, listed as one of the 64 arts in *Vidyā amuddeśa* (purpose of education) in Vātsyāyana's *Kāmasutra*. The cognate word *an ṭa* refers to a metallic glue, or an alloy. The *Sanghaṭa Sūtra* refers to two profound glosses: dharma and karma which continue to be the founding gestalt of Hindu traditions. These mleccha words of metalwork were written down using 500 pictographs such as a bull (*barad*), zebu (*khunt*), elephant (*ibha*), tiger (*kol*), boar (*badhi*), rim of jar (*kand kanka*), rimless pot (*bata*), tree (*kuti*), crocodile (*kara*), fish (*aya*). These pictographs were chosen because the words which signified the bull, zebu etc. had similar sounding words which indicated metal alloys of zinc, tin, copper, unsmelted metal iron, as evident by the decipherment of over 3,200 pictographic scripts found in over 45 of the 2,600 ancient settlements.

Since Manu recognizes *Arya* and *mleccha* as a pair of dialects of Samskritam, Meluhha (mleccha) is reckoned as a speech form of Prakritam. Early Bharatam Janam did not reckon Meluhha (mleccha) to be a foreign tongue, but only a dialectical form with unacceptable mispronunciations. MahaBharat is replete with references to mleccha both as a language and as Bharatam Janam co-habiting with people who spoke Samskritam, adhering to grammatical rules and hence, referred to as speakers of *Arya Class.* Thus, mleccha or *Milakkha Bhasa* was a dialectical form of Samskritam, just like Prakritam.

Meluhha people had navigated the Persian Gulf during the Bronze Age to reach Sumer, Elam, Ur, Mesopotamia and even Haifa in Israel, suggesting a *sprachbund* (language union). The Gold disc in Kuwait National Museum is engraved with Meluhha metalwork hieroglyphs all of which also occur on Indus seals and tablets. The Dong Son bronze drums, found in an extensive area of Southeast Asia, from Salween river valley in Burma to the Island of New Guinea, highlights the renown achieved by Meluhha people. Dong Son was exemplified by both the *Cire perdue* (lost-wax) method of casting alloy metals and also production of tin-bronze alloys.

The hieroglyphs such as humped bull, Zebu, tiger, multi-pointed star (sun), rhinoceros are all related to Meluhha metalwork, practiced by *Dhokra kamar* of Sarasvati-Sindhu epicenter, so attested in Indus Script corpora.

That zebu, *bos indicus*, is an exclusive legacy of South Asia Neolithic has been conclusively established by genetic studies. The central role of Meluhha speakers is supported both by Pinnow's map of Austro-Asiatic language areas in Bharatam and Far East, and by Higham's map of Bronze age sites in ancient India and Far East, indicating the diffusion of Austro-Asiatic from Bharatam, recorded as Meluhha in ancient cuneiform texts of Sumer/Mesopotamia. *Ur-Nammu stela of* ziggurat builders of Ur is a Meluhha metalwork catalog denoting metal castings, weapons, and tools

The consecration is related to veneration of ancestors and is a metaphor for purification processes in metalwork, removing impurities from minerals to produce pure metals and alloys. The *gaṇá* are represented together with *makara* whereas akara is a combination of two glosses: *mahaa + kara*, 'great crocodile'. The *gaṇá* in art traditions of Bharatam are depicted as dwarves and associated with Kubera, the guardian of wealth and as assemblies of people working together to this end. Both *gaṇá* and *gaṇápati* are represented in sculptures of ancient Bharatam and many sites of Far East, dated 1st century CE. Comparable representations of gaṇápati in dance poses or dance steps also occur on sculptures from Bharatam. Consequently, the entire composition of the Candi Sukuh frieze could represent smelter working in forge with bellows.

Clay stela in fire altars suggest early Hindu temples of 3rd millennium BC and are likely to be hieroglyphic metaphors of *stambhas*, pillars of fire described in Atharva Veda, Skambha sukta, and the like. Metalwork Meluhha hieroglyphs, such as the ligatured eagle, duck, pine-cone, flowering creeper, pillar/post, bucket/wallet, further document hard alloys (*karaḍa*), metal casting (*dhokra*), and 'fire-altar' (*kaṇḍ*). Hieroglyphs on Gudimallam sculpture are all related to metalwork and reaffirm that a smithy was a temple. Here, Meluhha hieroglyphs occur as safflower, elephant, ram, tabor, drum, goblin, oxide ingot and more.

Rudra-Shiva was integral to Vedic Pantheon such that a lingam is a hieroglyph denoting metalwork in a smithy temple. In Ekamukhalinga of Mathura of 1st CE, the ligatured stake (lingam) is shown together with a tree which connotes a *kuṭi* 'tree' rebus: *kuṭhi* 'smelter'. An entire sukta in Rigveda is addressed jointly to Soma-Rudra whereas Vajasneyi rescension of Sukla Yajurveda addresses Rudra: *'Thou art gracious (Shiva) by name.'* Taittiriya Samhita of Krishna Yajurveda mentions Shiva several times while referring to Rudra. The lingam and Shiva are a Trans-Eurasian phenomenon from Haifa to Hanoi. One 1.82-metre lingam carries an inscription carved from top to bottom that translates "*Consecration of the Holy Ganges sudhi in ... the sign of masculinity is the essence of the world*". Sit Shamshi bronzes celebrate a gangga sudhi 'water purification' puja, much as on Candi Sukuh lingams in Java. *Gangga* is derived from glosses of both Thai and Lao origin: Mae Nam Khong.This is an elucidation of the meaning of *khong*, emphasized by the prefixes *mae*, 'mother' and *nam* 'water'.

The Indus Script was engraved on Harappa Seals (some 4200 to date) engraved in reverse (from right to left). Some 3000 ISC seals have been recovered to date from Mesopotamian sites, Umma, Lagash, Ur, Oman, Bahrain, and Failaka Islands, suggesting ongoing sea trade by 3rd-4th millennium BC from the ISC to the West. Some cylinder seals of Mesopotamia were made from bark of *Turbinella pyrum* which is a signature source material from Meluhha. The seals were engraved by a drill, also invented by Meluhha artisans and later used in Dentistry. Sculptures include the incomparable dancing girl and the Mohenjo-Daro Priest king in steatite. These clearly refute the fallacious notion of white imperialists that human figure was first depicted in Greek sculpture; in fact the other way around appears most likely. One Bronze statue shows a woman holding a small bowl for makeup including Lipstick 5000 Years old.

Neaqrchus, Alexander's General notes that the people of Punjab knew the art of preparing paper from cotton and tattered cloth for writing purposes. Curtius, another Greek writers, mentions the use of tender bark of certain trees, possibly, *bhurjipatra* (bark of bhuj, Himalayan birch tree), for writing. *Kharoṣṭī* is a compound of khara + *ū ṣṭ*/oṭha/hoṭ 'blacksmith + lip' (denoting the invention of writing by a metalsmith) leading to a 'smithy of nations' across many bronze-age settlements. The sculptures (pratimā) of Brahma at Khajuraho and Aihole show the divinity carrying a manuscript or a stylus. Sarasvati pratimā at Dhar is shown carrying a stylus, most are Now in British Museum. Gaṇapati is depicted in sculptures with broken tusk in his right hand, like a stylus.

In 1999, Richard Meadow of the Peabody museum, Harvard, announced the discovery of pottery inscribed with the '**world's oldest writing**'. Raja Rama deciphered the message as: ILA VARTATE VARA *'Ila (Sarasvati) surrounds the best and the most blessed land (vara)'*. This gives us a date of **3500 BC** for the third mandala of **Rig Veda** and its seer Vishvamitra. This is to be contrasted with the late arrival of other writing systems, enumerated below:

Indus script 5000 BC, Egyptian hieroglyphs 3400 BC; Sumerian tablets 3100 BC; Linear B 1450 BC; Archaic Chinese 1046 BC.

Both Hittie and Brahmi evolved from the Indus script. Subhash Kak concluded:

"My analysis of Indus and Brahmi based on computer-created concordances revealed obvious connections between the two scripts that could not be explained as arising out of chance…"

After comparing the geographical setting of ISC, Mesopotamia and Mid East, Wheeler conceded:

"In each of three lands so accessible to one another the immensely complex idea of an evolved civilization (or a writing system) should, within the narrow space of some five or six centuries, have emerged spontaneously and without cross-reference, is too absurd to merit argument".

Antiquity of Indus script is further validated by the discovery of a potsherd with hieroglyphs at Harappa, referred to as Meluhha in cuneiform texts of Mesopotamia and Elam, and by Samskṛtam word Mleccha. Hieroglyphs of Indus writing deployed on over 6000 inscriptions of Indus corpora, in a wide geographic contact area, from Meluhha to Mesopotamia, and incorporated words from Indo-Aryan, Dravidian, Munda, Tibeto-Burman and Khmer. The *vox populi*, popular speech, was referred to as Meluhha (later called Mleccha).

The syllabary (varṇamālā, 'garland of syllables') was also called siddham or siddhamātṛkā, derived, circa 600 – 1200 CE from late Brahmi and used all along the Silk Road. Siddhaṃ script was introduced to Japan by Kūkai when he returned from China in 806 CE, where he studied Samskṛtam with Nalanda-trained monks The best-known *bīja* syllable is OM written in varian orthography in Siddham or nāgar scripts. Kautilya's Arthaśhstra (ca. 4th BC) provides evidence for the wide use of writing. The system of varṇamālā or Samskṛta propounded phonetic sounds, uniquely structured and categorized sequentially: labial, dental, retroflex, palatal, velar, based on the locations of articulated sounds, produced by the movement of the tongue, and breath from thorax to lips/nose to throat.

Pre-Harappa Sarasvati site of Kunal, near Ambala, has yielded silver ornaments dated 3000 BC or earlier. Thus the Vedic people had mastered the **separation of silver from copper** ore which contains silver as a contaminant. The Vashishtha Head found near New Delhi in 1958 was carbon dated to 2800-3700 BC and predates Greeks by 2000 years. Recent archaeological research in the Ganges Valley in **India show early iron**

working by 1800 BC whereas the Iron Age in Europe is now seen to follow the Bronze Age collapse in ancient India, Iran, and Greece, and may be schematized as follows:

India 2800 BC; Hallstat C 800-600 BC; Hallstat D and 1/2 La Tene I 600-400 BC; La Tene I, II, part of III 400-100 BC; Remainder La Tene III 100-50 BC.

The Iron Age in China (600 BC), Japan (600 BC), and Korea (400 BC) appears obviously centrifugal from Bharat and is much more recent than in Africa (1200 BC).

Chakrabarti noted:

"*There is **no logical basis to connect the beginning of iron in India with any diffusion from the west**, from Iran and beyond… that India was a separate and possibly independent center of manufacture of early iron.*"

Here is one more blow to the Imperialist theory of Aryan Invasion from the West to the East.

II. Agriculture, Animal Husbandry

The most ancient archeological site in the Indus World is to be found at Mehragarh, carbon dated 8000 BC. At the end of the ice age, melting ice unleashed mighty rivers in the Asian heartland giving rise to sedentary agriculture at an unprecedented scale whereas ice age still persisted in Europe and northern hemisphere. The Indus-Mekong delta, united by a vast subcontinent known as the **Sunda Land**, was the **birthplace of agriculture**. R.E and E.H Huke of the International Rice Research Institute observed:

"*When viewed in conjunction with plant remains from 10,000 BC discovered in Spirit Cave on the Thailand-Myanmar border, it suggests that agriculture itself may be older than was previously thought.*"

Contrary to the colonial and racial models, the origin of agriculture can safely be schematized as follows:

Southeast Asia 12,000 BC; Indus Valley and Egypt 8,000 BC; Central; Europe (LKB Culture) 7,000 BC; Mesopotamia, Greece 6,000 BC; Africa 5000 BC; Northern Europe (Scandinavia, Britain) 4,000 BC; China 4,000 BC.

Along with floating rice cultivation, domesticated water-buffalo reached Mehragarh as the region was wet enough to support elephant, rhinoceros, swamp-deer and wild pig. Archaeological evidence for water buffalo in Harappa region comes in the form of buffalo horn motif of deities and depiction of this animal in the seals at Kot Diji, Kalibangan and Rojdi. Buffalo bones have been found from the Ahar-Banas site of Rajasthan. The buffalo, the cattle and rice then migrated to Sumer from northwest India between 5000 BC and 4000 BC, giving rise to a new economy which led the region into the earliest phase of urbanization and subsequently larger state formation.

Sumerian divinity is entirely Vedic where the gods and goddesses even conserve the Vedic Indo-European names. Kur is the 'serpent' but it could also mean the 'mountain', which has stolen all water, or just the 'land'. The serpent was killed by the warrior god to release waters, much as in the Rig Veda myth of the demon Vṛtra who had to be killed by Indra to release trapped waters. Conceivably, Sumerian script and astronomy too had been imported from India, very likely due to the considerations outlined in sections 5.I and 5.VIII

The cultivation of floating rice in warm climate of SE Asia revolutionized agriculture around 4000 BC. India was the native habitat for two sub-species of cultivated rice, and one wild semi-cultivated rice viz. *Oriza sativa indica* and and the *Oriza sativa nivara*, in the Ganga Valley from where it reached northwest India (Hakra-Ghagghar) by 5000 - 5500 BC. Genetic analysis has shown that Iraqi rice DNA matched Indian rice DNA, thereby proving the migration of the Indian domestic rice to South Iraq. Agrama found that 68% of the Iraqi rice consisted of Indian sub-species of Oryza sativa aus, the rest was mainly aromatic which too had originated in northwest Himalayas.

During floods, many Indian farmers and pastoralists from the Indus-Sarasvati region migrated westward to places like Sumer along with their caravans of buffaloes, cows, bulls, goats and rice. Consequently, about 8% of the male Marsh Arab population shows DNA of Indian origin. From the female mitochondrial DNA, a larger migration took place from India to Sumer. Marsh Arab population exhibits mitochondrial DNA U7, R2 and M33a2a markers, found in the Uttar Pradesh state of India. A 72.8% frequency of Hg J-Page08 in male Y chromosomal DNA expanded in the region around 2,800 BC, possibly through the Semitic speaking Akkadians who outnumbered the original Sumerians genetically and wiped them out linguistically.

Aryan people **domesticated** dogs, house, cats, sheep, goat, cattle, horse and camels; bred fowl, peacock, buffaloes, and other animals; cultivated wheat, barley, sugar cane and cotton for the very first time in the world; African millet, sorghum (*jowar*), peal millet (*bajra*) and finger millet (*ragi*), appeared somewhat later. Fruits (mango, plantain, coconut, date palm, tamarind, banana, melon, peach, apricot, and cucumber), vegetables (gourds, peas, cucumber, beans and lentils, onion), jute, and flowers were grown in abundance. Abundant agriculture was facilitated by the invention of artificial irrigation, hydraulic engineering, manure, crop rotation and the like, as detailed in the following section (5.III).

Raw agricultural produce was thereafter turned into sugar, bread, wine, beer and alcoholic drinks from honey and/or sugar cane juice by fermentation. Indeed, wheat was to become the staple diet of much of humanity such that the indigenous *nan* bread, well-known as *pita*, can now be found on supermarket shelves almost everywhere. Cotton cultivation led to the discovery of **thread, needle, pinning, weaving, tailoring** into kamiz (shirt), moza (socks), shoes, all of which went universal. Sesame seeds provided the edible oil whereas Viniculture gave birth to wine manufacture that was exported regularly.

Although Silk and silk yarn are generally said to have originated in China, a commercially-viable silkworm species (*Antheraea mylitta*) is present all along the western coastal mountain range of the peninsular Indian subcontinent. Randhawa comments that the Indian silk moth (*Bombyx huttoni*) of the north-western Himalayas is ancestral to the five silk-producing species of moth in India. The earliest silk in an archeological context comes from Nevasa (located on the western side of the subcontinent), dated as early as the 10-15th centuries BC. Early written materials also discuss silk use e.g. the donation of a temple by a group of silk-weavers in Mandasor in 437-38 CE. As **early as 2500 BC, silk** was used to produce brocades, embroidered fabric, carpets rugs, blankets, transparent muslins and so forth.

Archeological evidence from Mohenjo-Daro, establishes that the complex technology of mordant **dyeing** had been known in the subcontinent from at least the second millennium BC whereas **printing** by blocks is dated 3000 BC. Marco Polo recorded the export of Indian textiles to China and South East Asia from the Masulipattinam (Andhra) and Coromandel (Tamil) coasts in 'largest ships' of that period. Robyn Maxwell (in Textiles of Southeast Asia) notes:

"Prestige trade textiles such as Patola (double ikat silk in natural dyes) from Patan and Ahmedabad, and decorative cottons in brilliant color-fast dyes

from Gujarat and the Coromandel coast, were sought after by the Malaysian royalty and wealthy traders of the Phillipines".

By the late 1600s, there was such an overwhelming demand for Indian chintz that French banned them in 1686 and the English in 1701. While Kashmir was well known for its woolen weaves and embroidery, Benaras, Ujjain, Indore and Paithan were known for their fine silks and brocades; Rajasthan specialized in all manner of patterned prints and dyed cloths. Woolen carpets were known in Bharat of old as early as 500 BC; those from the Mughal period have been described by Daniel Walker as *"among the most beautiful works of art ever created".* Mother-of-pearl was one of the materials often used in the decoration of furniture, particularly small storage chests, produced principally at Ahmedabad, Cambay, and Surat.

Diet was rich, consisting of wild game including nilgai, sambhar, chital, and black buck, along with vegetables, rice, milk, curds, cheese, cereals and beef, as far back as 3000 BC, in contrast to the **extreme deprivation in Europe** and elsewhere. Greek historian Diodorus (50 BC) tells us that a visit to an Iberian Celtic chief may lead to the offer of a chunk of bread and some spit-roasted meat. The hospitality in ancient Cyprus at the time of Herodotus (450 BC) may have taken the form of cakes made out of minced, sun-dried fish (Herodotus 1957: Book 1, para. 200). Scythians (Herodotus Vol. 2 book 4: 61) stripped flesh from the bones of their victims and cooked it either in cauldrons or in their stomachs with some water. Outside of ISC, animals with hair, such as monkeys and peccaries, were first singed whole in fire, burned hair was scraped off with the fingernails or palms, and the animal was then gutted with a sharp piece of bamboo before being cooked. Birds were hastily plucked, singed in the fire and gutted. Small animal were usually cooked whole whereas shelled animals like the armadillo and tortoise were usually thrown on the fire and left there to roast in their shells.

III. Water Management, Hydraulic Engineering

Evidence for dams and barrages in Bharat of old goes back to as early as the second millennium BC. For example, the dam joining Sanchi and Nagauri Hills had a reservoir area of 1.7 square kilometers, along with sluice gates. Sudarshan Dam (located in Junagarh, Gujarat) was built during the reign of Chandragupta Maurya (4th-3rd century BC). The barrage near the Pitalkhora caves in Maharashtra, found at a site with seven Buddhist vihars (2nd century BC), is a showpiece landmark for ancient Indian hydraulic engineering, including a check barrage, a small bridge and catch pits extending over the actual flow of a seasonal river.

The first qualitative hydrological measurement of rainfall is noted in the *Arthashastra* (4th century BC). The *Brihatsamhita* (5th to 6th century CE) describes a round gauge that contained graduated units for rainfall measurement. The book also quantifies the variations in rainfall during different periods of the year, which is strikingly close to present estimates. Methods for locating underground water, and manufacture of mechanical water devices for producing artificial waterfalls, are also described.

The existence of government executives in charge of creation and maintenance of irrigation canals is noted in Arthashastra whereas technical details for canal construction and categorization of canals are available in the *Kashyapeey-Krishi-Sukti* to include the ratio of depth and width of the canal to regulate water flow, the terrain faults and their avoidance, extant of slopes etc. Canals excavated bear testimony to expert civil engineering knowledge and are lined with standard fire baked bricks. The book also devotes a chapter on wells and stepwells, and another one on water reservoirs. Both contain extensive surveys and different techniques for building reservoirs to ensure water supply in dry regions of North-West India. It has been recorded that the engineer Suyya during the reign of Avantivarman of Kashmir: '*Made the Indus and Jhelum flow according to his will*'. *Bhrigu Samhita* explains hydraulic engineering in a manner that astonished an irrigation expert like Sir William Wilcox:

"*Every canal…lined out and dug fairly parallel to each other…spaced apart and placed just above the distance apart that the canals should be placed…when I began to line out a system of canals for the irrigation of the country, I was astonished to find everywhere that so called 'Dead River' on the map was just where a canal should be placed*".

Babur, the founder of Mughal Empire, described a waterwheel, traditionally called Ghatiyantra or Arghat, in Punjab. :

"*In Lahore, Dipalpur and those parts, people lift water by means of a wheel. They make two circles of ropes long enough to suit the depth of the well, fix strips of wood between them and on these fasten pitchers. The ropes with the wood and the attached pitchers are put over the well-wheel. At one end of the wheel-axle, a second wheel is fixed and close to it another on upright-axle. This last wheel the bullock turns; its teeth catch in the teeth of the second and thus the wheel with the pitchers is turned. A trough is set where the water empties from the pitchers and from this the water is conveyed everywhere.*

However, Irfan Habib writes it all off as Persian wheel that imported into India from elsewhere.

Plenty of references to *arghat* are to be found in the Rig Veda (IV. 17.16l; VIII. 49.6l; X. 24.4), *Gathasaptasati, Mrichchhaktika, Kadambari, Upamitibav-Prapancha-Kathaand* so forth. Arghat is also depicted on a tiny relief at Jogeshvar temple, Sadri, Rajasthan and at Mandor, Rajasthan. No other literature describes such detailed techniques for water management at such an early stage of human history.

IV. Urban Centers and City Planning

Spread over some 2.5 million square kilometers, an area the size of Western Europe, the Indus cradle was the largest of the four ancient civilizations of Egypt, Mesopotamia, India and China. To date, some 650 sites have been excavated in the Indus basin constructed according to Vastu shastra that prescribes specific rules for site selection, soil testing, cardinal points, sculpture, architecture, household furniture, types of woods, landscape and garden and so forth. The knowledge of sacred architecture in India had existed in the oral tradition even before the Vedic Age under the title *Sthapatyaveda.* It was later recorded in the Sanskrit mantras and compiled under the title **Vastu Shastra,** the oldest known architectural treatise in the world, traceable to at least 3000 BC, possibly 6000 BC. In *Mayamata*, the general treatise on Vastu shastra from South India, Maya affirms that Vastu shastra cannot be divorced from Jyotish or astrology as it balances different forms of energy emanating from different planets. The chessboard system of city planning gave rise to rectangular or square patches, later picked up for the Mughal gardens. Andreas Volwahsen writes:

"Of all the possible sub-divisions, the Charbagh pattern predominated those two axes oriented towards four cardinal points and its basic square fitted exactly with Hindu cosmology".

The earliest known master of the *Vastu Shastra* was Maya Danava, recognized as the founder of Bharat's sacred architecture that **uplift the human consciousness.** Some 200,000 shlokas in various manuscripts deal with the Vastu science. References to Vastu are to be found in *Ayurveda, Dhanurveda, Gandharvaveda, Sthapatyaveda, Artha Shastra, Manu smriti, Kama sutra, Paak sutra, Mayamatam, Maya Vastu, Shilpa shastra, Shilpa ratana, Shilpa Prakash, Vasturatnakara, Visvakarma vastu shastra, Diparnava, Samaranganasutradhara, Mandana-sutradhara, Manasara*, and *Rajasimha-vastu.* Vastu is also mentioned in the Agamas: *Karnikagama, Suprabhedagama, Vaikhanasagama*, etc., in works on Tantra: *Hayasirsa-tantra, KiranastantraVedas*, and *Puranas: Agnipurana, Matsyaprana and Visnudharmottra-purana* etc. Jain and Buddhist Vastu texts include: *Gautamiyam, Bauddhamatam* and *Caitya, Vedanta, Brahmanas* and *Upansihads.* Lord of the ground is referred to as *Ksetrapati* in Rig Veda and described in hymn 57 of Mandala 4. This prodigious output has **no comparison anywhere else** in the world.

All **architecture grew out** of **altars** meant for Vedic sacrifice whose construction formed the subject of *Mahanava Sulbha-sutras* and *Maitrayaniya Sulbha-sutras*, again linked to Astrology. The temple was essentially a living **musical structure**, representing the Mount Meru, abode of the Cosmic *Purusha* balanced by female and male principles, right and wrong, the devas (gods) and asuras (demons), the body and mind, and so on. The pointed arch was the lotus petal or the eye of the Gods where the colors red (Brahma) white (Shiva) and blue (Vishnu) formed the Trimurti, whereas the bell shaped fruit was the Hiranyagarbha, to initiate a **spiritual rebirth,** perfectly coordinated time and space. The altar became the residence of the *Vastu-purusha* oriented via the *vastu-purusha mandala.* The construction followed a system of measurements where the smallest unit of scale was **1/8 the human hair**, called *paramount* or atom, followed by eightfold increments: 8 paramount = 1 hair end; 8 hair end = 1 nit; 8 nit = 1 louse; 8 louse = 1 barley corn; 8 barley corn = 1 angular = 3/4 inches; 12 angulas = 1 span; 2 span = 1 hasta; 4 hastas = 1 dhanush (bow) or danda (rod); detailed in Vastu shilpa, Deva shilpa, Manava shilpa, and Vastu kala.

Indus cities such as Mohenjo-Daro and Harappa are standing examples of the Vastu principles, much like Pataliputra and Taxila that came much later. Geometrically aligned streets were adorned with sidewalks, gardens, grain storage areas with sleeper cells and channels for movement of fresh air, citadels, residential houses complete with sewers, drainage, flush toilets, manholes, settling pools and taps, bathrooms, living room, bedroom, kitchen, and so forth. Administrative buildings, hospitals, sanatoriums, alms houses, rest houses, picture galleries, theaters etc were in the vicinity of the Royal palace in the center, surrounded by housing for officials, militia, police and spies. Several annexes were to be found in the garden: a cloister, a pavilion for games and exercise, storerooms, guest rooms, cellar and stables, aviary, and steam baths. Outside the main towns were to be found arenas for sports, cock and animal fights, a Royal park for the king which could be used by the public. Cities also had public baths and bathing Ghats, moats and step wells.

During 2700-1900 BC, some 40,000 to 80,000 people inhabited Harappa whereas Mohenjo-Daro occupied some 100 hectares and was the largest Bronze Age city in the world, housing 40,000 people in 2300-2200 BC; by contrast classical Athens counted no more than 10,000. Excavations carried out by a French team, headed by Jean-Francois Jarrige, at Mehragarh have pin-pointed the **beginnings of civilization** and shown that Indus-Sarasvati civilization had no moorings in Mesopotamia or any civilization outside India. It has been rightly observed:

"*The people in Mehragarh tradition are the people of India today*".

John Marshall compares the Indus phase IV with Egypt and Mesopotamia:

"*One thing that stands out clear and unmistakable both at Mohenjo-Daro and Harappa is that the civilization hitherto revealed at these two places is not an incipient civilization, but one already age old and stereotyped on Indian soil, with many millennia of human endeavor behind it….Thus, to mention only a few salient points, the use of cotton for textiles was exclusively restricted at this period to India and was not extended to the Western world until 2000 or 3000 years later. Again, there is nothing that we know of in prehistoric Egypt or Mesopotamia or anywhere else in Western Asia to compare with the well-built baths and commodious houses of the citizens of Mohenjo-Daro. In these countries much money and thought were lavished on the building of magnificent temples for the gods and on the palaces and tombs of kings, but the rest of the people seemingly had to content themselves with insignificant dwellings of mud. In the Indus Valley the picture is reversed and the finest structures are those erected for the convenience of the citizens.*

Gordon Childe continues:

"*…the craftsmen of the Indus cities were producing for the market…a strong and prosperous merchant community…A surprising wealth of ornaments of gold, silver, precious stones and faience, of vessels of beaten copper and of metal implements and weapons…Well planned streets and a magnificent system of drains, regularly cleared out, reflect the vigilance of some regular municipal government…to secure the observance of town-planning by laws and the maintenance of approved lines for streets and lanes…*".

Such planned cities in the ISC existed **thousands of years before the Romans** could come up with something similar albeit on a far more limited scale.

The ISC was a product of ideation by priest kings who were greatly concerned with bodily **cleanliness and ideology** which continues to this day in India. An elaborate water management in the mature Harappa phase removed the effluent away from the houses, below ground, safely out of the way and out of sight, in brick lined channels that prevented contamination of the earth and the city. The Great Bath, 39 feet long and 23 feet wide, sits upon an elevation, apart from the rest of Mohenjo-Daro, approached by a 7 meter wide staircase equipped with a hydrostatic filling and drains. Hands were washed regularly before and after meals as well as after passage through toilets. By contrast, Christianity throughout its history appears to have emphasized the **grace-giving quality of dirt and filth.** The Rule of Christ Church at Canterbury stipulated:

"The use of baths shall be offered to the sick as often as it is necessary; to the healthy and especially to the youths, it shall not be so readily conceded".

The Spanish Christians issued orders:

"...for the reformation of Moriscos neither themselves, nor their women, nor any other persons, should be permitted to wash or bathe themselves either at home or elsewhere; and that all their bathing houses should be pulled down and destroyed".

The **Church** favored a literal interpretation of aphorisms by Jesus ***"but to eat with unwashen hands defileth not the man"***, and **forbade hand washing** altogether. This practice has not entered in the contemporary western society even now such that the WHO spots on TV constantly remind audiences to wash their hands to stem Swine flu and other infections. Segregation was unknown in the West; the toilet 'potty' in England was kept inside the house until after WW II and hands or bottoms were never washed though rags were used.

Wealth generated by bounteous agriculture permitted the rise of skilled craftsmen for the manufacture of luxury items: faience, ceramics, lime plaster, baked brick, bitumen, vitreous paste, glazing and smelting to produce gold, copper and other metals. Indeed, the word copper is derived from *Kuvera* such that Afghan *Khyber*, Hebrew *Heber*, Egyptian *Khepri*, *Caberi*, Greek *Khyphera, Cabeiri*, *Babo-Quivari* (Kneevari) appear to be linked, as suggested by Pockocke and Matlock. Drilling technology, first mastered at Mehragarh 4000 BC, permitted the drilling of carnelian beads for local use export to Mesopotamia, Ur and Central Asia (Chapter 5.I). Europeans rarely succeeded in selling their own beads but successfully traded stone beads manufactured in Bharat that became the central giant in the Asian maritime trade.

V.   Maritime Technology and Trade Routes

The word *samudra* occurs frequently in Rig Veda, contrary to the idea of Muller that Vedic Aryans were barbaric nomads from the Steppes who did not know the ocean. Rig Veda observes:

"He who knows the path of the birds flying in the sky, he knows the course of the ocean going ships".

Shendje (cited in Matlock) described Harappans thus:

"*They participated in international trade, taking the caravans from place to place".*

A boatman's or navigators' song refrain: *ēlō ! ēlēlō* stands for Meluhhan journeys westward and eastward, southward and northward, moving with the waves of perennial streams of Himalaya and rhymes well with the tossings of the boat on the waves as also the 'splendor' of navigation.

The **Piri Reis World map** shows the coastline of Antarctica before it was covered by the mile thick ice cap. Air Force officer Lt Harold Z. Ohlmeyer made the following comment in a letter dated 6 July 1960 (cited in Matlock):

"We have no idea how the data on this map can be reconciled with the supposed state of geographical knowledge in 1513 CE".

Obviously, the map was the product of **maritime navigation around the globe**.

The antiquity of the Vedas leaves no doubt that Bharat began her maritime trade as early as 5000 to 3000 BC with Babylon (Baveru in Sanskrit) Iran, Bahrain, Central Asia, Oman, Phoenicia, Mid East, Assyria, Greece, Persia, Arabia, Mesopotamia, Egypt, Turkemania, Uzbekistan, China, Afghanistan, ancient Canaan (Israel) and Rome, thousands of years before Columbus.

"There is concrete evidence of a network of trade linking up the whole area

from Tigris to the Indus and the Oxus and its extension west of Euphrates as far as the Nile.

Khirsara, Gola Dhoro (Bagasra), Shikarpur, constituted the riverine hub of maritime trade by Meluhha seafaring merchants to link 2,600 sites of the Sarasvati-Sindhu Civilization mostly on river banks and along the coastline of Indian Ocean in Gujara.

A Sanskrit work of medieval times, *Yukti Kalpataru*, gives elaborate directions for colors, cabin dimensions, decorations, and mentions that Bharat built large vessels from 200 BC on to the close of the sixth century CE and continued shipbuilding until 1200 CE. Such ships were larger than those used by Columbus to negotiate the Atlantic a thousand years later; *Janaka Jataka* mentions a ship which could carry over **one thousand people** whereas *Sankha Jataka* details a ship 800 cubics in length, 600 cubics in width and 20 fathoms in depth, with three masts. A very detailed account of the seven ship fleet of Dhanapati sailing towards Ceylon is to be found in *Kavikankana Chandi.* The ships are said to have been equipped with the **Matsya Yantra** or magnetic needles that floated in oil for navigation, hundreds of years before the appearance of actual compass. Toussaint remarked:

"The Mauryan emperor Chandragupta, who ruled from 321 to 297 BC, had an actual Board of Admiralty, with a Superintendent of Ships at its head... Assam had its own fleets, while the Marathas had theirs on the West coast. Surat was then the most beautiful city of India, certain streets were paved with porcelain".

During the Mauryas (325 BC on) Alexander's fleet of two thousand vessels accommodated 8000 troops, several thousand horses, and vast quantities of supplies, according to Ptolemy. Nicolo Conti in the 15th century CE marveled:

"The natives of India build some ships larger than ours, capable of containing 200 butts, and with five sails and as many masts.

Sir John Malcolm observed:

"Indian vessels are so admirably adapted to the purpose for which they are required that, notwithstanding their superior science, Europeans were unable, during an intercourse with India for two centuries, to suggest or at least to bring into successful practice one improvement".

Many English merchants had their ships built at Madapollum while Parsi builders constructed ships for the Royal Navy even in the 19th century CE.

The revolution in maritime technology included ports, dockyards, harbors, *Yukti Kalpataru*, Matsya Yantra, triangular sail, monsoons and large ships. The world's first navy, mentioned in epics like MahaBharat and Ramayana, permitted the colonization of Java by immigrants from Bharat, as also the conquest of Sri Lanka.

As wealth poured into Rome from her colonies, demand for eastern luxury items reached an unprecedented scale. Because Europe was manufacturing nothing, Bharat became a depository of a large portion of the metallic wealth of the world. Pliny tells us that pepper and ginger from Bharat were worth their weight in gold in Roman markets and complained about the drain of gold to India:

"India, China and the Arabian peninsula take one hundred million sesterces from our empire per annum at a conservative estimate: that is what our luxuries and women cost us. For what percentage of these imports is intended for sacrifices to the gods or the spirits of the dead?" (Pliny, *Historia Naturae* 12.41.84.).

The maritime routes were fed by the Silk Road 1500-1300 BC that linked India to the Mediterranean; a long-distance trade route in the Steppes, and the Grand Trunk Road (Uttaraptha) that linked Calcutta to Peshawar 500 BC. The international trade had turned Bharat into by far the richest country in the world. Sir George Bidwood was to observe:

"The whole world has been ceaselessly pouring its bullion for 3000 years into India to buy products of her industries".

The *Silappathikaarum* (The Ankle Bracelet), a Tamil romance (circa second century CE), provides a glimpse of the maritime wealth and splendor of South Indian cities. Here, the markets offered a great variety of precious commodities such as coral, sandalwood, faultless pearls, gold, precious gems, silks, woven fabrics, and ivory carvings; Patliputra (now Patna) and Taxila were spectacular. Visitors like Ibn Batuta of Tunisia were to note bazars overflowing with precious metals, gems and stones:

"Gems dominate Mughal jewelry. India was a major source and trading center for precious stones."

VI. Discovery of Mathematical Sciences

Mathematical knowledge is to be found in Vedas, Sula Sutras, Jain texts, *Aryabhatia* of Aryabhat, *Brahmasiddhanta* of Brahmgupta, Panini, Pingala, Bkahsali manuscript, *Ganitasarasangraha* of Mahavira, Lilavati and *Bijaganita* of Bhaskara, *Ganita Kaumudi* of Narayana Pandita, Kerala School of Astronomy and Development of Calculus, Trigonometry and Spherical Trigonometry, Proofs, Combinatorics, and Place Value System. All modern science finds its roots in the Rig Veda. The poetry of the Vedas and other Sanskrit scriptures conceals coded mathematical secrets. Rig Veda (RV II.18.4-6) knows large numbers, a nascent decimal system, infinity (*aditi*), and zero (*kham*). Rig Veda gives names to simple fractions such as *ardha* (1/2), *trapada* (3/4) etc. Taittriya samhita mentions arithmetical series of odd (*ayugma*) 1.3.5 and even (*yugma*) 2,4,6, numbers. Terms like *dasa* (10), *sata* (100), *sahsra* (1000), *ayuta* (10,000) and others are mentioned in Yajurveda from 1 to 10^{12}. Buddhist literature mentions *tallaksna* for the number 10^{53}, obtained simply as multiples of 10. Taittriya samhita provides following denominations:

eka = 1; dasa = 10, sata = 10^2; sahasra = 10^3; ayuta = 10^4; niyuta = 10^5; prayuta = 10^6; arbuda = 10^7; nyarbuda = 10^8; samudra = 10^9; madhya = 10^{10}; anta = 10^{11} and parardha = 10^{12}.

Aryabhata (300-400 CE) in *Aryabhatiam* described the value of pi, heliocentrism, a round earth, elliptical orbits, zero, and much much more. *Lalita Vistara* gives five names for classes of numbers from 10^9 mounting by hundreds to 10^{53} above which there are other numerations. *This is to be contrasted with Greeks who had no names for numbers larger than 10^4 (myriad).* The abridged, specific place-value words (one, two, three, hundred, thousand, etc.) to designate numbers meant that mathematics was effectively **written in verse**.

Jain mathematical canons are: *Surya Prajnapati, Jamby Dwipa, Prajnapati, Sthananga Sutra, Uttaradhyayana sutra, Bhagwati sutra and Anuyoga Dwara sutra*; the first two are dated 300-400 BC and the last two came two centuries later; *Anugadvara-sutra* (ca. 100 BC) mentions places in powers of 10.

A. Seidenberg traced the **origin of mathematics** to Sulbhasutras traced back to **3000 BC** or more that preceded the mathematics of Old Babylonia (1700 BC), the Egyptian Middle Kingdom (2050-1800 BC), and Greece (600 BC). In fact, Greece acquired geometric algebra from Jain and Buddhist scholars via Thales of Miletus (ca 624 - 548 BC). Pythagoras of Samos (ca 580 - 500 BC) introduced concepts he learnt in Babylon, Egypt and India. In Egypt, true mathematics, on the base of 10, went no farther back than the 12th dynasty (ca 1990–1800 BC) as recorded in: The Moscow Mathematical Papyrus, the Egyptian Mathematical Leather Roll, the Lahun Mathematical Papyrus, Berlin papyrus (1300 BC), and the Rhind Mathematical Papyrus (ca 1650 BC). Babylonian mathematics, recorded on some 400 clay tablets in Cuneiform script dated 1800-1600 BC, is a sexagesimal (base 60) numeral system employing 10 and 6 in an alternative fashion: 60 = 10x6; 600 = 10x6x10; 3600 = 10x6x10x6. Traces of this circular system still remain in 60 minutes, 60 seconds, 360 degrees of the circle all of which were **passed on to Greece from Mesopotamia** and then to the present day Europe.

Zero is both a number and a numerical digit; its earliest use is dated 458 CE in the Jain text *Lokavibhaga*. Zero plays a central role in mathematics as the additive identity of the integers, real numbers, a placeholder and so forth, permitting **vast conceptions of time and space**. The zero symbol has been described in texts dated 200 BC and in 498 CE whereas Aryabhata (376-415 CE) described it as "*Sthanam sthanam dasa gunam*". The earliest depiction in English, is in *The Crafte of Nombrynge* (ca1350 CE), correctly identifies them as *teen figurys of Inde*. Fibonacci introduced these to Europe in 1202 CE but Zero was not accepted in Europe until 12th-13th century. The zero has been universally called the single most important development in the entire history of mathematics. The proof for nine digits and a zero, with place notation for tens of thousands, came finally from the **Bhaksali manuscript** of 4th CE According to Barrow:

"*The Indian system of accounting has been the **most successful intellectual innovation** ever made on our planet…adopted almost universally… far more extensively even than the letters of the Phoenician alphabet which we now employ… nearest thing we have to a universal language.*"

Like the crest of a peacock, like the gem on the head of a snake, so is mathematics at the head of all knowledge (Vedanga Jyotisha, 500 BC).

Halsted pays homage:

"*The importance of the creation of the zero mark can never be exaggerated..*

Dantzig asserts:

"*The discovery of zero will always stand out as one of the **greatest single achievements** of the human race*"; it marked a "*turning point*" in math, science and industry.

Charles Seif continues:

"Dividing by zero...allows you to prove, mathematically, anything in the universe...

Pierre Simon Laplace wrote this about the place value system:

*But its very simplicity and the great ease which it lent to all computations put our arithmetic in the **first rank of useful inventions**".*

Alfred North Whitehead adds:

*"The point about zero is that we do not need to use it in the operations of daily life. No one goes out to buy zero fish. It is in a way the **most civilized of all the cardinals**, and its use is only forced on us by the needs of cultivated modes of thought".* (All bold faces are mine).

Laplace in 1841 noted:

"Its simplicity lies in the way in which it facilitated calculation and placed arithmetic foremost amongst useful inventions. The importance of this invention is more readily appreciated when one considers that it was beyond the two greatest men of Antiquity, Archimedes and Apollonius".

In *Science in the Medieval World* Andalusi remarks:

*"**India is the first nation to have cultivated the sciences**, and although black, Allah ranked them above many white and brown peoples. It is a powerful, wealthy, and populous nation known for the wisdom of its people and their abilities in all branches of knowledge".*

French mathematician Pierre Simon Laplace (1749 – 1827 CE) affirms:

*"It is **India that gave us the ingenious method** of expressing all numbers by the means of ten symbols, each symbol receiving a value of position, as well as an absolute value.."*

Tobias Dantzig, the father of George Dantzig had this to say:

*"...the **achievements of the unknown Hindu,** who sometime in the first centuries of our era discovered the principle of position, assumes the importance of a **world event**".*

A.L. Basham concludes:

*"The **debt of the Western world to India** in this respect [the field of mathematics] **cannot be overestimated...**The unknown man who devised the new system was, from the world's point of view, after the Buddha, the most important son of India. His achievement, though easily taken for*

*granted, was the work of an **analytical mind of the first order**, and he deserves much more honor than he has so far received. Unfortunately, Euro centrism has effectively concealed from the common man the fact that we owe much in the way of mathematics to ancient India.*

Geometry Regulated the Life of Vedic Aryans in rites associated with birth, life and death. The planned cities of Harappa and Mohenjo-Daro, vast gardens planned for aesthetics, the brick making technology, the Indus seals, the Vedic altars for sacrifice, sacred architecture, marriage pavilions, and cremation altars, lead to the discovery of Geometry. The determination of auspicious dates for all foreseeable events stood behind the discovery of astronomy, astrology and various mathematical sciences. The spooked wheel, the docks for maritime trade, advanced civil engineering etc., all required the solution of complex mathematical problems such as squaring a circle and circling a square, i.e. getting a square and circle to be equal in area. **Geometrical drawing instruments**, dated 2500 BC, have been found in the Indus Valley ruins. The theorem of Pythagoras for Vedic Hindus is a theorem in geometry while for Babylonians it is so in arithmetic. Baudayana Sulbhasutra (800 BC, based on traditions dated 3000 BC), explains the so called Pythagoras's theorem as follows:

"The rope which is stretched across the diagonal of a square produces an area double the size of the original square".

The Katyayana Sulbhasutra gives a more general version:

"The rope which is stretched along the length of the diagonal of a rectangle produces an area which the vertical and horizontal sides make together".

The **Vedas** present five extremely simple proofs for this theorem, written simply as: $a^2+b^2 = c^2$.

The Vedic altars were based on astronomical reconciliation of the lunar and solar years, just like the female and male currents within the body and mind. The Sacrificial altars, whose size could be increased without change in shape, were constructed according to the instructions in *Sulbhasutras* that draw on the mathematical knowledge in *Kalpasutras* so ritual fire could be lit as per *Srautasutras*. Datta observed:

"Hence all Fire altars are either prisms or cylinders".

The spooked wheel is a common metaphor in Rig Veda, e.g. hymn I.164 (Rajarama translation):

"All worldly beings reside in the revolving five spooked wheel…The wheel with seven fellies, never decaying, rolls on forever…Wheel is one, fellies are twelve, and three are the axles".

Later Tantric traditions of *Shriyantra* required very precise calculation to achieve the intersections of more than two lines at single points in the perfect rendering. In all correctly constructed Shriyantras, the base angle of the largest triangle is 51.5 degrees, much as the Great Pyramid in Gaza (2600 BC). The **largest isosceles triangle** of the Shriyantra is one of the **face triangles of the Great Pyramid** in miniature, showing almost exactly the same relationship between π and Φ as in its largest counterpart. Seidenberg concludes:

"1) A common source for Pythagorean and Vedic Mathematics (Sulbhashastra) is to be sought either in the Vedic mathematics or in an older Mathematics very much like it. 2) The view that Vedic mathematics is a derivative of Old Babylonia having been rejected; a common source for this mathematics, different from Old Babylonia of 1700 BC, was indicated. 3) Thus, what we regard as the two main sources of Western mathematics, namely Pythagorean mathematics and Old Babylonian mathematics, both flow from a still older source…In geometry it (Sulbhashastra) knew the theorem of Pythagoras and how to convert a rectangle into a square. …Therefore I postulate a pre-Old-Babylonian source for the kind of geometric rituals we see preserved in the Sulbhashastras, or at least for the mathematics involved in these rituals…"The Sulbhashastras have geometric algebra…Greece and India have a common heritage that cannot have been derived from Old Babylonia, i.e., Old Babylonia of about 1700 BC".

Prof. R. D. Rawlinson adds:

*"Almost **all the theories**, religious, philosophical and mathematical, taught by the Pythagoreans **were known in India** in the sixth century BC".*

Thibaut also felt that:

*"**Greek Geometry was derived from the Sulbhas**"* and even Britannica notes: *"…the bulk of the intellectual tradition originating with Pythagoras himself belongs to mystical wisdom rather than scientific scholarship".*

Basham elaborates:

"While Greek mathematical science was largely based on mensuration and geometry, India transcended these conceptions quite early, and with the aid of a simple numerical notation…led to the study of number for its own sake".

Regarding reckoning Dantzig was puzzled by the fact that Greece did not stumble on this discovery and sums up:

"*An inflexible numeration so crude as to make progress well-nigh impossible, and a calculating device so limited in scope that even elementary calculation called for the services of an expert…Man used these devices for thousands of years without making a single worthwhile improvement in the instrument, without contributing a single important idea to the system…the achievements of the unknown Hindu, who sometime in the first centuries of our era discovered the principle of position, assumes the importance of a world event…Is it not strange that **algebra**, that corner stone of modern mathematics, also **originated in India**, and about the same time that positional numeration did*".

Hankel (1874) and Junge (1907) also deny Pythagoras credit for the discovery, as detailed by Datta.

The **westward movement** of Bharat science is also recorded in a book in Syriac written by Severus Sebokht, the Nestorian Bishop of Qinnesrin, in 662 CE:

"*I will omit all discussion of the science of Hindus…discoveries that are more ingenious than those of the Greeks and the Babylonians; and of their valuable methods of calculation which surpass description. I wish only to say that this computation is done by means of nine signs. If those who believe, because they speak Greek, that they have reached the limits of science, should know of these things, they would perhaps be convinced, even if a little late in the day, that there are also others who know something of value*".

Trigonometry, spherical geometry, and calculus are original inventions of Bharat. Bhaskaracharya (1114-1185 CE) was one the first to conceive **differential calculus** in *Siddhanta Shiromani* and the work was continued in Kerala. He **preceded Newton by over 500** years in the discovery of the principles of differential calculus. In *Lilavati* and *Bijaganita* he also established mathematically that: **infinity, however divided, remains infinity**, as represented by the equation: 00 /X = 00 in the Upanishads:

Poornamidah poornamidam poornat poornam-udachyate; poornasya poornamaadaaya poornamevavashishyate.

Other important discoveries include the **power series** of Madhava (1350-1425 CE) and **infinite series** of the Kerala School all now attributed to Europeans. Nilkantha (1444-1544 CE) wrote *Tantrasangraha* in 1501, an astronomical treatise, where he describes the use of epicycles and eccentrics to compute planetary positions which instituted a revolution in astronomical theory and preceded European Astronomy by two hundred years. Brhamagupta in his *Khanda Khadyaka*, advanced trigonometric computations by describing a method for obtaining the sines of intermediate angles from a given table of sines, Aryabhata introduced sine and versine functions for the first time which laid the foundation for modern Trigonometry. Jyesthadeva (1500-1575 CE) wrote *Yuktibhasa* where he used sine and cosine in capital letters e.g. Sin Θ = r sin Θ and Cos Θ = r cos Θ where r is the radius of the arc. The beginnings of algebra can be traced to the constructional geometry in the Shulbha Sutras. B.B. Dutta underlines:

*"The use of symbols-letters of the alphabet to denote unknowns, and equations are the foundations of the science of algebra. The **Hindus were the first to make systematic use of the letters of the alphabet to denote unknowns**. They were also the first to classify and make a detailed study of equations. Thus they may be said to have given birth to the modern science of algebra".*

Brahmagupta (598 CE) in his work *Brahmasphutasiddhanta* employed **Sanskrit letters and abbreviations** to represent several unknown quantities whereas Aryabhatiya unequivocally explained indeterminate analysis of the form: ***by* = *ax* ± *c*** where a,b,c are integral values and x, y are unknown. The Jayadeva-Bhaskaracharya method, known as *chakravala* or cyclic method is also a purely Bharat tradition. Selenius comments

*"The (chakravala) method represents the best approximation algorithm of minimal length that, owing to several minimization properties, with minimal effort and avoiding large numbers automatically produces the (best) solutions to the equation…**anticipated the European methods by more than a thousand years**.*

Jains may have developed the concept of logarithms to base 2, 3 and 4: the terms *ardhacheda, trakacheda* and *caturacheda* of a quantity may be defined as the number of times the quantity can be divided by 2, 3 and 4, respectively. *Anuyoga Dwara sutra* lists sequences of successive squares or square roots of numbers. The credit for the discovery of Algebra now goes to one Arab named **Algebre** who, in the first edition, was honest enough to note that he was only **translating** an Indian manuscript.

Planning urban centers (Chapter 5.IV) required the discovery of the **Indus inch, Plumb bobs, gnomon, saw with undulating teeth** and so forth are found frequently in Indus ruins 2500 BC and earlier, along with **place numerals, zero**, coins, weights and measures and the like, derived from the Gwalior inscription of 876 CE. These soon spread Persia and on to

Europe through the Arabs, Vasco de Gama and Portuguese.   Srinivas Ramanujan emphasized the relation between mathematics and religion:

An equation means nothing to me unless it expresses a thought of God.

VII. **Natural and Physical Sciences**

Vedas and other Sanskrit scriptures have been the source of natural and physical laws governing the universe. Atharva Veda (20.41.1-3) describes the principles of atomic energy:

"The atomic energy fissions the ninety nine elements, covering its path by bombardments of neutrons without let or hindrance…".

Teresi observed: "*Indians came **closest to modern ideas of atomism**, quantum physics and other current theories*".

The **theory of atom** was taught by Pakudha Katayana, a contemporary of Buddha, and thus centuries before Democritus and reached Greece via Persia. Jains described atoms, Chemical bonding, opposite electrical charges and advanced the idea of particle 'spin', whereas molecules were defined as:

'*aggregates of atoms capable of existing in gross form and undergoing the process of association and dissociation*".

Kanada (600) BC) in *Vaisheskik Darshan* surmised that atoms combine to form molecules, 2500 years before Dalton and that **light and heat are two forms of the same substance**:

"*Light is colored and illumines other substances; and to the feel is hot which is its indistinguishing quality. The heat of hot water is felt but not seen; moonshine is seen, but not felt*".

He also described the first three laws of motion attributed to Newton 16th CE.

Ist law: The change of motion is due to impressed force, 2nd law: The change of motion is proportional to the force applied and is made in the direction of the right line in which the force is impressed. 3rd law: To every action there is an equal and opposite reaction.

Varamihir (499-587 CE) in *Panchasiddhanta, Bruhad Jatak, Bruhad Samhita,* described fundamental principles in Astronomy, Astrology, Geography, Botany and Zoology.

The eminent historian T. N. Colebrooke was to remark:

*"Compared to Scientists of Europe, Kanada and other **Indian scientists were the global masters** in this field".*

Ancient Bharat knew both Newtonian and quantum physics. Capra observes:

"What we know today about universe was known to the Indians in very ancient days".

The first law of Thermodynamics, law of conservation of matter and energy, was known to the Vedic people as in Bhagavada Gita: *"That which did not exist cannot exist; that which exists can never be non-existent".* his was taken texto by Parmenides ca 575 BC:

"That which is, that which is not is not; how can that which is be about to be, for if it is about to be then it is not".

Sayana's commentary on Rig Veda calculated the speed of light to 2.5×10^8 which is quite near the accepted velocity of light.

Yajur Veda (6.21) mentions a number of sciences in one of the verses:

"O disciple, a student in the science of government, sail in oceans in streamers, fly in the air in airplanes, know God the Creator through the Vedas, control thy breath through Yoga, through astronomy know the functions of day and night…through astronomy, geography and geology, go thou to all the different countries of the world under the sun…".

In the *Brihad Vimana Shastrama* are to be found descriptions of 37 models of *vimana (*air ships). In fact, **airplanes** are mentioned time and over again in the Vedic literature e.g. Yajur Veda 10.19:

"O royal skilled engineer, construct sea boats, propelled on water by our experts, and airplanes, moving and flying upward, after the clouds that reside in the mid-region, that fly as the boats move on the sea, that fly high over and below the watery clouds. Be thou, thereby, prosperous in this world created by the Omnipresent God, and flier in both air and lightening".

The *Gayachintemani* mentions an aircraft shaped like a peacock.

"The privilege of operating a flying machine is great. The knowledge of flight is among the most ancient of our inheritances".

Bhardwaj (800 BC) also pioneered aviation technology in *Yantra Sarvasa.*

Aero plane, having three wheels which required no horses and which could fly in the sky, could move on waters and on ground. The 'Samarangana Sutradhara' gives a method of preparing an aero plane, using superheated Mercury. Valmiki describes Pushpaka aero plane which was just like a Jumbo jet. Supersonic fighter jet, Helicopter and gliders are also described vividly. The *Gayachintemani* mentions an aircraft shaped like a peacock. The descriptions in Ramayana, MahaBharat and different Vedas are replete with many astonishing feats based upon advances in chemistry and physics.

Shukra Neeti is an ancient text that describes the manufacture of **rifles, guns, rockets and machine guns** (shataghuni). Alexander wrote to Aristotle that **terrific flashes of flames** showered on his army in India (cited in Knapp). Higgins has provided evidence that the Vedic people knew **gun powder** from the remotest antiquity. *Agastya Samhita* describes the use of silk for balloons and another text describes the use of **hydrogen to soar** in the skies. *Shilpa Samhita* describes the manufacture of a **telescope**, by fixing glasses at either end of a hollow tube, to observe celestial bodies; it also describes the making of a **thermometer** with the help of mercury, thread, oil and water.

The ISC sites have revealed highly radioactive skeletons from Harappa and Mohenjo-Daro, melted remains, time capsules, spy ware, and other advanced products that have appeared in the modern world only in the last two centuries or so. One passage in Mahabharat actually describes the aftermath of an atomic explosion:

An iron thunderbolt contained 'the power of the universe…an incandescent column of smoke and flame, as bright as ten thousand suns, rose in all its splendor…clouds roared upward…blood colored clouds swept down onto the earth…fierce winds began to blow…elephants miles away were blocked off…the earth shook, scorched by the terrible violent heat of this weapon, corpses were so burnt that they were no longer recognizable…hair and nails fell out…birds were turned white…thousands of war vehicles fell down on all sides…never before have we seen such an awful weapon and never before have we heard of such a weapon".

VIII.Jyotish, Astronomy and Cosmology

Jyotish (Astrology) and Astronomy developed to determine auspicious time or *Muhurtas* to begin a job, start an enterprise, initiate a new relationship, births, marriages, business undertakings, festivals, agriculture, and indeed all else. Astrology or *Jyotishshastra* can be traced to the Atharva Veda. Jyotish considers the movement of the Sun and the Moon, the five major planets, (Mercury, Mars, Saturn, Venus and Jupiter) plus two additional nodal points known as ***Rahu and Ketu***. Furthermore, whereas the Western astrologers base their zodiac on the equinoxes and positions of the planets that continue to change with respect to the stars, Vedic Astrology bases its computations on the twelve zodiac signs plus 28 additional lunar constellations or *Nakshatras* in a complete Moon cycle. Kak (cited in Bryant) observed:

"Vedic sacrifice was meant to capture change in time, separation and unity, belonging and renunciation, permanence and death".

The size of planets, the motions of the sun and the moon, vernal equinoxes, etc. all speak of an **advanced Vedic astronomy** as far back as Harappa period people who oriented their streets and dwellings in cardinal directions. Rig Veda recognized the Sun as the source of life and foretold Heliocentrism. *Taittriya Brahmana* extolls *nakshtravidya* and *Surya Siddhanta* (13,902 BC – 490 CE) asserts that the universe was held together by **gravitation**, thousands of years before the apple opened Newton's head who probably got the lead **from Bharat through missionaries**. Bhaskaracharya remarked in Surya Siddhanta:

"Objects fall on earth due to a force of attraction by the earth, therefore the earth, the planets, constellations, the moon and the sun are held in orbit due to this attraction".

Around 425 CE, the *Paitamahasiddhanta* portrayed a **spherical earth** when everyone including Greeks thought it was flat. Hindus even knew that the **universe is an expanding sphere**: *brhamanda* means expanding sphere (*brah* = to expand or grow; *anda* = sphere), in contrast to the static universe of the Greek pseudo philosophers. Aryabhata explained that the glow of the **moon and planets** was the result of **reflected sunlight** with incredible astuteness, and proposed the elliptical orbit of planets a full thousand years before Keppler. Rigveda (1.84.15) informs us *"The moving moon always receives the light from sun to shine".*

Whereas the medieval British scientists believed that the earth was only 100 million years old, by the fifth century CE Bharat sages had calculated it to be **4.3 billion** years old, compared to 4.6 billion accepted now. Higg's field was known as *Maya* in ancient Bharat as an all pervasive, invisible principle that fills the universe like ether. Aryabhata was far ahead of his time but his editors changed his conclusions to conform to the accepted ideas of 500 CE. Duncan pays homage:

"In 476, far away in time and place from Charelamgne's dark, imposing castle in Aachen, beyond the eastern border of Frankland…a Hindu genius was born…A blend of Ptolemy the astronomer, Pythagoras the

mathematician and Bacon the rebel. Aryabhata was ...a pivotal figure on one of the stranger journeys ever taken by an assemblage of ideas across time and geography...to the west centuries later...landing the great centers of Islamic learning...to portals of Spain, Syria and Sicily...This was one of the dozens of critical documents that would contribute to the **knowledge base needed to propel Europe** into the modern age".

The early literature speaks of **three constellations**: *Mrighashira or the Orion (4500-3500 BC, Rig Veda); Rohini or Aldebaran (3100 BC, Mahabharata), Krittika or the Pleaides (2900-1900 BC, Sutra and Brahamana).* Tilak was to observe:

"...we can now decipher these records inscribed on the specially cultivated memory of the Indian Aryans. Commencing with the Taittiriya Samhita and the Brahmanas, which declare that the Phalguni moon was once the New Year's night, we found that the Mrighashiras was designated by a name which, if rightly interpreted, showed that the vernal equinox coincided with that asterism (constellation) in old times".

Spanish Arab astronomer Sai'id al-Andalusi (1029-1070 CE) had this to say:

"...Of the Indian astronomical systems, the three that are well known are the Sindhind...the Arjbadh...and the Arkand...we have received correct information only about the Sindhind which was adopted and further developed by a group of Muslim scientists".

As **no science was permitted** by the Church, medieval theologians of Europe argued about the number of angels that could fit on the head of a pin. Geocentrism and Aristotle were venerated until the era of Keppler (1671-1630). Burgess (quoted in Singhal) states:

"Very little astronomical borrowing between the Hindus and the Greeks...since in no case do the numerical data and results in the system of the two peoples exactly correspond'.

Arabs themselves tell us that India, and not a 'Semitic source', was used in their astronomy as no Semitic sources detail Nakshatras and the like. The notion of **proof in the Sulbhas** was also borrowed by the Greeks and perfected by Euclid.

Kapil (3000 BC) was the father of Cosmology that anticipated the Big Bang theory. Although Sagan calls it accidental, the similarities between Vedic and modern cosmologies are striking. Two Vedic concepts are remarkable: *Anantakoti Brahmanda,* or **billions of galaxies** or universe, and **eons of times** through which creation passes. A single day of Brahma of 4.32 million years closely approximates the age of the planet Earth. The drum in Shiva's left hand represents creation as the original Big Bang, or perhaps a continual series of Big Bangs, while the fire in his right hand represents their ultimate destruction. Sagan was to remark:

"The Hindu Religion is the only one of the world's great faiths dedicated to the idea that the cosmos itself undergoes an infinite number of deaths and rebirths…Its cycles run from our ordinary day and night to a day and night of Brahma, 8.64 x 10^9 years, longer than the age of the earth or the sun, and about half the time since the Big Bang".

Jain tradition ascribed to Jinsena (500 BC) concluded:

"*Time is without beginning and end, uncreated and indestructible, it endures under the compulsion of its own nature".*

Chandogya Upanishad leaves gods out altogether:

"In the beginning this world was merely non-being. It was nonexistent…How from Non-being could Being be produced".

IX.Excellence in Alchemy and Siderology

Jains had predicted Chemical bonding, electrical charge, and particle spin. In 600 BC, Kanada established a theory of atoms in his *Vaisesika sutra*, followed by the concept of elementary particles. *'The Jamakwala'* describes various metallurgical methods such as the chemical purification of silver alloyed with a large amount of copper and other metals; the extraction of gold; preparation of assimilable metals for internal administration in the form of oxides, sulphides and sometimes chlorides. Nagarjuna (300 BC) authored *Ras Ratnakar, Rashrudaya,* and *Rasendramangal* to describe chemistry, chemical engineering, and alchemy . By contrast, European chemists believed in **transmutation** e.g. water could be Trans mutated into earth because a solid residue was formed inside the pot in which water was boiled and evaporated completely. Patanjali in his *Lohashastra* gives elaborate directions for many metallurgic and chemical processes, preparation of metallic salts, alloys, amalgams, extraction, purification and assaying of metals. **Aqua regia**, a mixture of nitric acid and hydrochloric acid to dissolve gold and platinum, is ascribed to him. As of the sixth century, many acids, alkalis, and metallic salts were produced by calcination, distillation, sublimation, steaming, and fixing as described in *Rasaratna-*

Samuccaya. Harappa people made extensive use of copper, bronze and brass for household, utensils, weapons, and idols and knew basalt, granite, sandstone, alabaster, gold, silver and lead. They **alloyed tin and arsenic with copper** and extracted copper from sulphide ores and many Harappa objects have been found in Sumerian ruins. The *Rasvatnakar* 400 BC mentions the distillation of Zinc; in Europe, the metal could not be used on an industrial scale until William Campion patented it in 1732 CE, some 2000 years later. Lead oxide was used to purify pure metals or desired alloys of bronze or brass, described by a metaphor in Rasayana traditions as killing the *naga annaku*. American historian Will Durant concluded:

"*Something has been said about the chemical excellence of cast iron in ancient India, and about the high industrial development of the Gupta times, when India was looked to, even by Imperial Rome, as the **most skilled of the nations** in such chemical industries as dyeing, tanning, soap-making, glass and cement... By the sixth century the Hindus were far ahead of Europe in industrial chemistry; they were masters of calcinations, distillation, sublimation, steaming, fixation, the production of light without heat, the mixing of anesthetic and soporific powders, and the preparation of metallic salts, compounds and alloys. The **tempering of steel** was brought in ancient India to perfection unknown in Europe till our own times; King Porus is said to have selected, as especially valuable gift for Alexander, not gold or silver, but thirty pounds of steel The Moslems took much of this Hindu chemical science and industry to the Near East and Europe; the secret of manufacturing "Damascus" blades, for example, was taken by the Arabs from the Persians, and by the Persians.*

The **iron stele near Kutub Minar** of Delhi, The iron column, called the Kutub pillar at Delhi, weighs 6.5 tons, measures 23 feet 8 inches from the top to bottom, and the diameter diminishes from 16.4 inches below to 12.05 inches above, it carries an epitaph composed about 415 CE. The material is pure, rust less, malleable iron, weighs more than six tons, made by some sort of welding process. No one yet understands how so large a forging could have been produced at that time. V. Ball remarked in 1881:

"*It is not many years since the production of such a pillar would have been impossibility **in the largest foundries** of the world…*"

Basham adds "*…the column is of iron almost chemically pure. The process of oxidization demands a catalyst, and it is the great purity of the metal which has preserved it for so long…*".

"*The high quality of the native made iron, the early anticipation of the process now employed in Europe for the manufacture of high-class steels,* and the artistic products in copper and bronze gave India a prominent position in the metallurgical world…In India, steel was used for weapons, for decorative purposes and for tools, and remarkably high grade articles were produced. The old weapons are second to none, and it is said that the famous Damascus blades were forged from steel imported from Hyderabad in India.

The ***Wootz* steel** produced in Bharat was of the highest quality and formed the raw material for the **Damascus sword** made that reached Persia and Rome. Pliny refers to "*swords of good quality made of Indian steel*". Persians considered that swords from Bharat were the best and termed them *Jawabi Hind*. Gypsies were highly skilled craftsmen and the **art of forge spread to Europe** through them.

X.Numerology For Divination and Jyotish

Mathematics determined all aspects of life for the Vedic Aryans. Vedic seers saw numbers as symbols of certain types of cosmic powers, linked with spirituality. For example **0** is a number that encircles some part of the infinite universe whose inner part is separated from the vast outer space, similar to human body where the soul (*Jeevaatma*) resides. One (**1**) represents single-mindedness;
Two (**2**) represents flexibility and diplomacy;Three (**3**) represents ambition, self-expression and idealism; Four (**4**) represent unconventional behavior; Five (**5**) is dynamism and communication that makes a successful business man; Six (**6**) is love for family and enjoyment; Seven (**7**) is spiritualism and sensitivity;. Eight (**8**) is patience and discipline; Nine (**9**) is obsession with Maya. Each of the single digit numbers was attached to a particular planet in Astrology because certain planets reproduce vibrations of a particular number. Thus **1** = Sun, **2-** = Moon, **3** = Jupiter, **4** =Uranus or Rahu, **5** = Mercury, **6** = Venus, **7** = Neptune or Ketu, **8** = Saturn, and **9** = Mars. Number **0** was not attached to any planet,

The Sarasvati hymn in Rig Veda, venerates the number seven as **saptasindhu, saptarshi** etc that occurs constantly in Yoga, Ayurveda, and a range of Vedic-Hindu traditions e.g. the seven *Maruts*; the seven rays of Surya (Sun); the Seven Worlds; the seven rivers of heaven and earth; the seven creative Hosts, and the seven men, or primitive human groups; the Seven ancient Rishis enumerated in Jaiminiya Brahmana 2.218-221; the **Sapta Swaras** (*sa re ga ma pa dha ni*) in musical ocatve, seven Promises, seven rounds in Hindu Weddings, seven reincarnations; seven worlds in the universe, seven seas in the world, and the seven *Chakras* in the body; the seven Pleiades (*Kritikka*). The legend of seven was to eventually spread **around the globe** as: the seven Emperors of Rome the Seven Sages of Greece; the Seven Wonders of the ancient world, and so forth. The number seven appears very frequently in both the Old Testament and the, Islam, Judaism, and Zoroastrianism.

Eight is the symbol of **infinity** to the mathematician whereas in Vedic Astrology, Saturn (*Shani*) is linked to 8. Eight is **extremely lucky or unlucky** as it is a junction point in Vastu Shastra where 8 deities rule the 8 cardinal directions (N, S, E, W, NE, SE, SW and NW), 8 forms of *Mahalakshmi* (the Goddess of Wealth). Shri Krishna was the 8th child and was born on the 8th lunar day (*Ashtami*) and as the **8th Avatar** of Lord Vishnu. The **8th** shloka in Chapter 4 of Bhagavad Gita is cited the most:

PARITRANAYA SADHOONAAM VINASHAYACHA DUSHKRITAAM DHARMA SAMSTHAPANARTHAYA SAMBHAVAAMI YUGE YUGE

(For the protection of the righteous, for the destruction of wicked, and for the establishment of dharma, I am born in every age).

Buddha was enlightened at the age of 35 (=8) and attained Nirvana at 80. He preached the **Eight fold way** to salvation and his **dharma wheel** is endowed with Eight spokes. The legend around eight was eventually to enter European folklore e.g. Rotary International **R = 2, O = 7, T = 4, A = 1, R = 2, Y = 1** which totals up to **2+7+4+1+2+1 = 17, 1+7 = 8**. Polio eradication was the most significant ambition of Rotary. **P = 8, O = 7, L = 3, I = 1, O = 7** all of which add up to **8+7+3+1+7 = 26 = 2+6 = 8**.

The number **Thirty Three** (33) represents martyrdom and unconditional love, 33 major divinities, 330 million gods and goddesses in Hinduism. There are 33 bones in the spinal cord, 33 appearances of Kwan Yin, 33 measures in the construction of temples, solitary retreat of 3 years, 3 months and 3 days required to become a Tibetan lama, 33 temples of Taoism, 33 major religions in the world, and 33 rituals of Aura Mazda. Jesus died aged 33 and the number became a backbone of Judeo-Christian symbolism: *Elohim* appears 33 times in the story of creation in Genesis, 33) is a numerical representation of the Star of David and numerical equivalent of **AMEN:** 1+13+5+14=33. The number 33 is also venerated in Sufism, Sikhism and freemasonry.

One Hundred Eight (108) was the product of precise mathematical calculations by the Rishi philosophers and is central to Vedanta chants and Vedic constructions. The centrality of this number in Vedic ritual is stressed in the *Shatapatha Brahmana* where the numbers 108 and 360 appear as the axis and the perimeter dimensions of the temple to symbolize the **inner and the outer cosmos**; *Lankavatara Sutra* refers repeatedly to many temples with 108 steps. There are 10800 verses and 10800 stanzas in the Rig Veda. The total number of syllables in the Rig Veda is taken to be 432,000, closely related to 108, which equals the number of muhurtas in forty years such that the book was supposed to represent a symbolic altar.

In Hindu/Buddhist beliefs, there are 108 feelings, 108 earthly desires, 108 human delusions or forms of ignorance, 108 earthly temptations, humans tell 108 lies, 108 dance poses (*karanas*) in the *Natya Shastra*, 108 music talas and ragas, 108 Hindu deities, 108 gopis in Gaudiya Vaishnavism, 108 Upanishads, 108 qualities of praiseworthy souls, 108 Jain virtues, 108 paths to God. In Japan, a bell is chimed 108 times in Buddhist temples to finish the old year and welcome the new one. In astrology, there are 12 constellations and 9 planets, 12 x 9 = 108. The metal silver is said to represent the moon and the atomic weight of silver is 108. The sacred River Ganga spans a longitude of 12 degrees (79 to 91), and latitude of 9 degrees (22 to 31), 12 x 9 =108. Rama has been called by 108 different names. Pranayama and meditation are meant to reduce the number of breaths down to only 108 breaths per day. The prayer rosary (mala) contains 108 beads, plus a meru bead. There are said to be a total of 108 energy lines converging to form the heart chakra and 108 pressure points in the body, where consciousness and flesh intersect to impart life and form the basis of acupuncture, massage and martial arts. The mystery surrounding 108 was thereafter to enter all major religions and human enterprise as also the golden ratio, also named **divine proportion** that crops up in as plant growth, Mendelian genetics, Cosmology and so forth. The monument of Stonehenge is about 108 feet in diameter. There are 108 columns in the temple of Durga and 108 towers in Phnom Bakheng of Angkor.

Palmistry in India has a history going back thousands of years, generally known as *hasta rekha.* The most popular school in the north is known as *Samudrika Shastra*, based on the writings of Samudra whereas the school in the south is *sariraka shastra,* also known as *skanda* system, based on the writings of Kartikeya. From India, palmistry traveled around the globe through the gypsies and fortune tellers and has evolved into a lucrative industry.

XI.Yoga and Ayurveda Harness Life itself

Ayurveda evolved from Samkhya philosophy where the universal vibrations of **AUM (or OM)** had differentiated into In the Vedic concept of ***parasparopagrahajeevaanaam*** or all living beings were mutually interrelated so ecology and environment were to be respected, in contrast to Christian theology where nature was to be enslaved. Vedic Hindus were the first to recognize that **plants also have life** and kept man in the class of animals. Botany is treated in Vedic texts that also describe plant morphology, classification, physiology, diseases, pathology, reproduction, and so forth. Chandogya Upanishad attempts to classify animals according to their mode of reproduction, the number of senses they possess, physiology and embryology.

Important hymns dealing with medical knowledge are Rig Veda: 7.5, 10.97 and 10.162 whereas Atharva Veda hymns in this context are: are 1.3, 1.17, 1.22 – 1.25, 2.3, 2.4, 2.8, 2.31, 2.33, 3.7, 3.9, 4.12, 4.13, 5.4, 5.5, 5.22, 5.23, 6.14, 6.20, 6.21, 6.24, 6.25, 6.44, 6.57, 6.83, 6.85, 6.01, 6.95, 6.105, 6.109, 6.111, 6.127, 6.136, 6.137, 7.74, 7.76, 7.116, 8.7, 9.8, 19.34, 19.35, 19.36, 19.38, 19.39 and many Upanishads. *Shrimad Bhagwat Mahapurana*, composed 1650 BC, mentions homeopathy, embryology and cloning such that the three Ribhu brothers had cloned a whole animal from the skin of a cow and a horse from a horse, a feat not yet achieved by modern science. Vasistha and Agasti developed from a scientific utensil called *Vasatiwara*, without any mother, only from the semen of Mitra-Varuna. Gandhari could not conceive even after two years so aborted the embryo; Vyasa cut it into pieces to engender one hundred Kauravas in vitro.

MahaBharat, Shanti, 301, 320, 331, 356, and the Bhagawata 3/31 state that *Shukra* (sperm) conjugates with *Shonit* (ovum) during copulation to produce *Kalala* (Zygote) within 12 hours of coitus. Bhagawata described all of the microscopic changes taking place up to 15 days of the embryonic life in the womb, so confirmed by modern science. This is followed successively by the formation of head (30 days), lower and upper extremities (2 months), nails, hairs, bones, genitalia and skin (3 months), *dhatus* or tissues (4 months), appearance of hunger and thirst (5 months), fetus rotation (6 months), memory of past lives (7 months). *Bhagawata* (2/10/17-22, 3/6/12-15 and 3/26/54-60) details the formation of mouth, nostrils, eyes, ears and heart appears at the end of the second month.

Aitereya Upanishad elaborates further: first of all the mouth is formed that spews 'Vak' transformed into 'Agni'. Nostrils appear next and give rise to *prana* or 'Vayu' , followed by eyes, ears, skin, hair, heart, mind, umbilicus, Apana, penis, 'Reta' (the seminal fluid) and Apa. This description of fetal development is surprisingly accurate as compared to the modern embryology. Aitareya describes that directions come from ears. Apana energy pushes everything downwards: food, defecation, urination, seminal discharge, child birth and finally death. Yoga can reverse Apana, moving it upwards and thus leading to immortality. Chromosomes were numbered as 23; *Gunawidhi* and *Bhagwat* deal with the problems of infertility, birth, and so forth, not yet approached by modern science. Draupadi and Dhrushtadyumna were test tube babies developed from the sperms of king Drupada, without any ovum.

Taittiriya Upanishad postulates existence at five levels of consciousness, or **Pancha Koshas.** The physical body is called Annamaya Kosha, inhabited by inner Koshas and powered by prana. Manomaya Kosha contains mind, thoughts, emotions, passions, feelings etc. Vijnanamaya Kosha stores knowledge acquired in life. When Pranamaya Kosha and all other inner Koshas leave the body, they remain in *Bhuva Loka* for some time and then enter a new physical body whose brain in endowed with knowledge stored in the Vijnanamaya Kosha of previous life.

Vedic/Hindu anatomy lists **500 of the 513 muscles** in the human body, lymphatics, nerve plexus, vascular tissue, 360 bones, 800 ligaments, 300 veins, 500 muscles, 7 layers of skin, sutures, nerves plexus, adipose tissue, etc. **Marmas** (secret, hidden or vital) in the body are **junctions** where the flesh, bone, sinews, pipes, and ducts come together, and where the life **prana is most concentrated**. The 107 marmas have become the cornerstone for acupressure, acupuncture and martial arts. **Shrotas** are a network of 22 channel systems which permit undisturbed flow of life force and no comparable description is available in any other system of medicine. All this to be contrasted with absurd Greek theories where Aristotle, Plato and other philosophers, described human body like Geocentrism in place of Heliocentrism.

Yoga has been described as a **physiological treatise** where organs were used as metaphors for gods. It was recognized that the blood was made out of food and pumped by the heart in all four directions, a full **2500 years before** William Harvey was to establish it in Europe in 1628 CE. The constitution of the individual was decided by sperm, ovum, season, food, and *gunas*, at the time of fertilization, in contrast with the passive role assigned to the female in Greco-Roman and Christian traditions. Hereditary diseases have been described in Sushruta Samhita (24/6) as stemming from vitiation of sperm and ovum. Other branches included Geriatrics, Nosology, and Hypnotism which reached England in 1700 CE.

In view of this penetrating insight regarding human body, diagnosis and treatment were thorough and accurate, some far in advance of Europe even in this day and age. Health ensued from the right combination of *gunas* or humors that became the established medical theory around the globe until the 17th century CE as described in *Charak Samhita* , *Sushruta Samhita* and more, dated 1000 BC or earlier. Psychology was well developed whereas the Christian West believed that mind is controlled by evil and good; conversion from evil to good is possible only through Divine grace accessible only via the Church. In fact, psychology in the west is a direct borrowing from Hindu or Buddhist psychologists. Jung wrote:

"The Indian religions represented a higher level of development that reflected the maturity of the ancient civilizations of Asia; Europe and its indigenous faiths were younger and so less sophisticated. Just as a person must go through each development al stage to achieve full maturity, so also must each race".

Hall and Lindzey summarize:

"One of the richest sources of such well formulated psychologies is Eastern religions. Asian religions have at their core a psychology little known to the masses of adherents of the faith but quite familiar to the appropriate 'professionals'..."

The goal of psychology in Bharat was to alter a person's consciousness so as to transcend the limits imposed by habits. Medard Boss, the Swiss existentialist, felt that Western therapies lack the ability to bring an illuminating insight of power comparable to that of Indian methods:

"...the exalted figures of the sages and holy men...a living example of the possibility of human growth and maturity and of the attainment of an imperturbable inner peace, a joyous freedom from guilt, and a purified selfless goodness and calm..."

Vedic medicine was both **preventive and curative** and emphasized hygiene such as washing of hands and mouth. The diagnosis involved the **eight fold examination** (*Pariksha*): of Prakriti (face and general appearance), *Sara* (Tissue Vitality), *Nadi* (pulse), *Jivha* (tongue), *Shabda* (voice), *Sparsha* (skin), *Drka* (eye), *Mutra* (urine) and *Mala* (stool). In addition, the examination covered body constitution, pathological state, adaptability, psychological constitution, capacity for digestion, exercise, age, daily routine, dietary habits, the gravity of clinical conditions, as well as details of personal, social, economic and environmental situation. **Pulse** diagnosis was exceptional; **Pythagoras learnt these in Bharat** and imported them into Greece where no such prior knowledge existed. By contrast, in Europe, Physical diagnosis was introduced only at the end of the nineteenth century when Hospital medicine evolved in France 1789-1848 CE, in contrast to the age old traditions of Ayurveda 1000 BC or earlier. Dorothy Chaplin summarizes:

"Long before the year 460 BC, in which Hippocrates, the father of European Medicine was born, the Hindus had built an extensive pharmacopeia and had elaborate treatises on a variety of medical and surgical subjects."

The paramount importance of food was underlined by both Charaka as *Prakrititah Ahita Tama Ahara* which mentions 19 types of *Viruddha ahara,* and by Sushruta under the caption of *Ekanta Ahita Ahara* which mentions 10 types of *viruddha ahara*. The underlying maxim was: *You are what you eat.* Leech therapy was well known as were antibiotics from fungi and antiseptics from *neem* and other plants. Sushruta lists 760 medicinal plants many of which have now entered the western *materia medica*. Steroid hormones in urine and Ayurveda preparations were balanced by Ashwagandha which has also been patented in the US. Rasayana combines chemistry and alchemy whereas **Alchemy** was pioneered by Adinatha Siddha and Nagarjuna; the latter was compared to magic and therefore heavily censured by Christians. Metals used to heal, strengthen, and protect include gold, silver, iron, mercury etc. In the 16th century, Paracelsus was to emphasize the importance of gold, almost certainly borrowed from Ayurveda, and published *Prophecy for the Next twenty Four Years* in 1536 though he remained a fervent Catholic until his death in 1527. **Vaccination** was described in Dahnvantari's *Sacteya* before the Christian era and came to be known in Europe only in the 18th century. Finally, **Kayakalpa** was described in Siddha and Ayurveda medical literature as the ultimate fountain of youth, vitality, longevity, higher consciousness and *Jivan Mukti.* It goes back to thousands of years but was suppressed so severely by the British that few can perform it today.

Sushruta used some **125** different kinds of **surgical instruments** and described **300 surgical methods**. He remarked:

"Surgery is first and highest in the healing art, it is pure in itself, its use can never die, it is a product of the heavens and a sure source of renown on earth (to those who practice it)".

Asepsis was known in Bharat several thousand years before Leister along with Sterilization and bacteria were conceived as early as sixth century BC. Al Biruni found it strange that earthenware and banana leaves could be used only **once** and then discarded; two persons did not eat from the same plate. Narcotics from opium and cannabis were used to relieve pain.

Surgery excelled that of all other peoples and places in the world and surgeons accompanied the army in MahaBharat. Bharat surgeons were reputed for caesarian, plastic surgery, skin transplants, hernia, dentistry, amputation, catheterization, Rhinoplasty, craniotomy, prostate resection and cataract removal. Basham summarizes:

"*The caesarian section was known, bone setting reached a high degree of skill, and plastic surgery was developed far beyond anything known elsewhere. Ancient Indian surgeons were expert at the repair of nose, ear and lips…Indian surgery remained far ahead of European until the 18th century when the surgeons of the EIC were ashamed to learn the art of rhinoplasty from the Indians*".

By contrast, the **first caesarian in Europe** was recorded only in the **sixteenth century** albeit with 100 per cent maternal mortality; the first survivor of the procedure dates back to no earlier than the eighteenth century.

The man's **first known trip to the dentist** occurred as early as 9,000 years ago when at least nine people had drilled molars at the Mehragarh site (NYT 5 April 2006), as reported in *Nature*, push back dentistry to 7,000 BC. A Flint drill attached to a bow drill was used to treat molars, comparable to the one on an Egyptian mural, again confirming diffusion of Meluhha expertise.

Yoga Sutras were composed by Patanjali around 3000 years BC, based upon the theory that the main *nadis*, *Ida* and *Pingala,* run along the spinal column in a curved path and cross one another several times. At the points of intersections the two main nadis form strong energy centers known as **chakras**. In texts dating back to 1000 BC, breath or *prana* was the prime mover in physiology along with the bile and the pituitary gland. ***Pranayama*** (***pra*** = first unit, ***na*** = energy and ***ayama*** = expansion, extension or restraint) cleanses the lungs, heart and other organs. According to Swami Vishnu Devananda, meditation is "….*a continuous flow of perception or thought, just like the flow of water in a river*" that brings awareness, harmony and natural order into life. Herbert Benson at Harvard Medical School found that over **2,200 genes** were activated differently in the long-time Yoga practitioners relative to the controls, and **1,561 genes** in the short-timers compared to the long-time practitioners (TOI 4 July 2008; *Scientific American* February 1972, Lancet April 1970, *Am. J. Physiol.* September 1971, *Psychosomatic Medicine* 1971).

Oak has provided detailed comparison between some English and Sanskrit words: English fever, entrails, nasal, herpes, gland, drop, hiccups, muscle, malignant, osteomalacia, dyspepsia, surgeon, fertility, anesthesia, homeopathy, allopathy are derived from Sanskrit: *jwar, antral, naas, serpes, granthi, drups, hicca, mausal, malle, asthi-malashay, dush-pachanashay, salya-jan, falati-iti, anasthashayee, samaeo-pathy, alag-pathy*, respectively. P. N. Oak (quoted in Knapp) was to write:

"Thus, a close study of allopathic terminology, whether of ailments, physical organs, symptoms, remedies, or instruments will found to be based on Ayurveda because during the universal unitary Vedic administration it was only Ayurveda which was the sole medical system which was used throughout the world.

Yoga-Ayruveda practices have become the backbone of alternative systems of medicine and wellness such as Naturopathy, Pilate, Music therapy, Reiki and more. Although Britain closed thousands of Ayurveda institutions in India, all but decimated the Kayakalpa, and dubbed Tantra Yoga practice in temples as prostitution, it has now accepted Ayurveda as part of its National Health Service; Yoga is still denounced by the Anglican Church. Here is more proof that demonization followed by outright theft and elimination of the original source are the keys to success in the Abrahamic world.

XII.Plastic Arts Portray the Divine Ideal

Art permeated life in ancient Bharat and every person had knowledge of art, dance and music as essential elements of literary and aesthetic pursuit. Art galleries have been documented from the earliest times under the name *Chitrashalas*, so mentioned in Ramayana and Mahabharata, with specifications as to its location, dimension, surface area, illumination etc. Vast treatises such as *Natyashastra* and *Shilpasastra* portray the force of **spirit struggling to free itself** from the shackles of the medium that holds it captive. Consequently, the local artist all but eliminated the physical details to capture the spiritual beauty of the subtle soul of a Yogi. The power of thought was the highest Divine Ideal in Bharat such that Vedic/Hindu philosophy symbolized the Deity as pure form in the *yantra*, as sound in the Divine voice of the *mantras*, the *Ragas* of music, as pure contemplation in Divine Yogi, and as thought power in the Divine Mother.

Ajanta, Bagh, Sigiri and Pallava frescoes show **highest level of painted art**, as also the caves at Aurangabad, Ellora, Elephanta, Garapuri off Bombay, and Pallava cave temples at Mahabalipuram and Kanchipuram. Ajanta frescoes of the Gupta period (400-600 CE) depict three dimensional aspects of painting such that the side walls and the ceiling appear to have been created spontaneously. The spectator loses sense of time them as eyes pass effortlessly from one scene to the other. The world's **first ever oil paintings** were found in caves near two giant statues of Buddha at Bamiyan in Afghanistan but it was not until the 13th century that oil was added to paints in Europe and oil paint was not widely used in Europe till the early 15th century. Garratta observed:

"Ajanta is a world in itself, aloof and shut in…its beauty is surpassing…Ellora is more accessible and more human".

The influence of ancient Bharat is most evident in the paintings of Central Asia. Havell comments:

"Under this Indian inspiration Chinese painting by the seventh century had reached an extraordinary degree of eminence, far surpassing the contemporary art of Europe".

In contrast to the secular art in Bharat, European medieval painting was truly religious and could not go beyond the norms laid down by the theism of the Church. European painting before the fifth BC is often referred to as the childhood of art, a flat surface that was yet to be transformed into a tridimensional space. The outstanding quality of Bharat sculpture is its dynamism, attained through precise mathematical proportions for precise placement of gestures and body parts. The posture of Nataraja is plastic representation of a whole philosophy that embodies the primal energy of creation, destruction, and salvation through dance. Dr. Coomarswamy summarizes:

"No artist of today, however great, could more exactly or more wisely create an image of that Energy which science must postulate behind all phenomena".

Basham describes Nataraja as:

"*very essence of vital, ordered movement, eternal youth and ethereal light…depicting in plastic terms divine truth, beauty and joy*"

Similarly, the great image of seated Buddha represents:

"*…absolute immutability…an inexorable challenge to change and time…wholly absorbed in sublime meditation and that perfect peace which only dawns with the final annihilation of passion and desire…of complete and immense repose…liberation from the evil of existence; in a word Salvation*".

The Nataraja of Elephanta has been described thus by Havell:

"*Though the rock itself seems to vibrate with the rhythmic movement of the dance, the noble head bears the same look of serene calm and dispassion which illuminate the face of the Buddha*".

Epstein adds:

"*Our European allegories are banal and pointless by comparison with these profound works, devoid of the trappings of symbolism, concentrating on the essential, and the essentially plastic*".

The temple at Konark shows:

"*strength of treatment and of feeling for animal form rare in the world's art*" (Basham).

At the time when Ajanta, Ellora and Elephanta flourished in Bharat, artists poured into the other countries to inspire such wonders as Borobudur and Angkor. Havell concludes:

"*While there is no living artist within the boundaries of Europe who can produce anything, either in painting or sculpture, to be placed side by sides with these wonderful reliefs…we establish schools to teach Indians painting and sculpture as they are taught in Europe…Europe in the present day has in art far more to learn from India than to teach*".

Whereas the artist in Bharat was trying to reach the Divine Ideal by eliminating physical details, **European sculpture is purely static**, for esthetic pleasure by worshipping the human body only in a tradition that goes back to Greece and faithfully picked up by Romans.

XIII. Secular Folklore and Poetry

Sanskrit Literature began with the Vedas, continued with the Epics in the Iron Age Bharat, and finally culminated in the Golden Age of late Antiquity (3rd-8th centuries CE). *Maliki Ramayana*, the first poetry work in Sanskrit was followed by Ved Vyasa (3100 BC) who composed *Mahabharatham, Brahmasutras, and Bhagwat Purana.* Some 650 plays have been discovered so far, some as far away as the Gobi desert. Sylvain Levi declared:

"L'originalite de l'Inde s'est exprimée toute entière dans son art dramatique; elle y a combine et condense ses dogmes, ses doctrines, ses institutions…".

(The originality of India is expressed entirely in dramatic arts along with dogmas, doctrines

Abhijnanasakuntalam is considered to be greatest play in Sanskrit, eulogized by Goethe thus:

"Do you know by a single name heaven and earth, the flower of youth and the fruit of old age, something which is alluring and which is fascinating, which is both nourishing and palatable. I know it, it is Shakuntala, and so is said by all".

In Raghuvamsa by Kalidasa, the mastery of language is so remarkable that Kalidasa *"wedded sound to sense in a way rarely achieved in the literature of the world"* (Basham). Wilson pays tribute:

"It is impossible to compose language so beautifully musical, or so magnificently grand, as that of the verses of Bhavabhuti and Kalidasa".

In *Meghaduta* Kalidasa (375-455 CE) showed that he understood in the fifth century what Europe did not learn until the nineteenth. 'Mudraraksha' or the Signet Ring was performed in New York in 1924 when the following critic appeared in the Nation:

"…a genuine example of that pure art theatre of which theorists talk…to

meditate upon that real wisdom of the east which lies not in esoteric doctrine but in a tenderness far deeper and truer than that of the traditional Christianity which has been so thoroughly corrupted by the hard righteousness of Hebraism…Such a play can be produced only by a civilization which has reached stability…Macbeth and Othello…are barbarous heroes …produced by the conflict between a newly awakened sensibility and a series of ethical concepts inherited from the savage age.."

The *Katha-sarita-sagara* (An Ocean of Stories) by Somadeva was an 11th century poetic adaptation in Sanskrit of *Brihat-katha*, written in the 5th century BC in the *Paishachi* dialect. That was to **inspire mythological folklore around the globe**. Other masterpieces include: *Gita Govinda* (The song of Govinda) by Oriya composer Jayadeva, Dandin's (600-700 CE) *Dasa-kumara-charita* or the 'Tale of Ten Princes' portrays everyday life of ordinary people and confirms evidence from other sources that the means of subsistence were plentiful and cheap. A girl sends her nurse to sell a measure of rice husk and from the proceeds to buy "*some firewood, not too green, not too dry, a small cooking pot and two earthen dishes*". From the Gupta period flowers the genius of Subandhu who's only surviving work *Vasvadatta* uses puns, alliterations and assonances which was found in Europe only after the Renaissance. *Jatakamala* by Arya Sutra (3rd-4th CE) as also works by Banabhatta, the first Sanskrit novelist (6th-7th CE), the Kama Sutra by Vatsyayana, and the three *shataka*s of Bhartṛhari were to **inspire later poets in Europe**.

European colonialism proceeded by demonizing the colonized peoples despite such titles as: *The Triumph of Truth, Truth is dearer than life, The glory of sacrifice, Good for evil, Desire increases by fulfillment,* and so forth all of which confirm the importance of righteous conduct in daily life. Their ageless appeal was to later reappear as translations into the *Arabian Nights*, Grimm's *Fairy tales, Decameron* and *The Canterbury Tales*. The *Panchatantra* (Five Treatises) was translated into 200 versions in more than 50 languages. The Angles, Saxons and Jutes, imported legends and tales such the *Beowulf* (circa 1000 CE) adapted myths from Bharat that also reached Japan, Hawaii, Polynesia and Australia..

Mark Twain was to summarize it all succinctly by observing that India was:

"*The mother of history, the grandmother of legend, and the great grandmother   of tradition…Whatever sphere of the human mind you may select for your special study, whether it be language, or religion, or mythology, or philosophy, whether it be law or customs, primitive art or science, you have to go to India (Because) some of the **most valuable and*** *instructive material of the history* of man are treasured up *in* India and India only."

XIV. Gandharvaveda and Performing Arts

Drama or theater has been called a fifth Veda, drawn from Rig Veda (recitation), Sama Veda (music), Yajur Veda (acting) and Atharva Veda (sentiment) as an ideal combination of all the arts. Bhatta observed:

"The drama was among the first of the manifold achievements of the ancient Indians...in no field of creative activity did the artist or the author come nearer the people than in drama".

Bharat's *Natyashastra*, dated 2 BC-4 CE, is based on earlier books like *Nandikesvara*, and describes Kashmir as *shastrashilpin* or a maker of science. Sanskrit drama was fully established by **300-500 BC** and an ancient playhouse of the second century BC in Ramagarh Hills of Chota Nagpur fits in well with the general description of theater in *Natyashastra*. The text specifically describes stagecraft, auspicious occasions, theater design, selection of drama critics, development, action, sentiments, purpose, and specific instructions for actors, playwrights and producers. There is **nothing comparable to Natyashastra in the Western world**. The most outstanding feature of the dramatic theory and poetry was the *Rasa* which was akin to an experience of communion with some higher divine or spiritual object of universal appeal. Bharat emphasizes:

"No object can be comprehended without the aid of Rasa. Sentiment is produced from a combination of fundamental determinants, the excitant determinants, and the transitory states".

The spectator thereby relinquishes all other cognitive experience and, through the ennobling effect on human emotions, identifies himself with the absolute. Levi sums up:

"The Sanskrit drama still remains the happiest invention of the Bharat genius".

Keith remarked:

"The Sanskrit drama may legitimately be regarded as the highest product of Indian poetry...The Brahmin...was the source of the intellectual distinction of India. As he produced Indian philosophy, so by another effort of his

intellect he evolved the subtle and effective form of drama".

The stagecraft of Sanskrit drama is still ahead of the Greek drama that has been linked to the religious rites of Dionysus in Thrace, dated 1200 BC though it only took shape in Athens 600 - 200 BC and came to an end 200 BC. In contrast to the Greek tragedy which deals with the problem of evil and human suffering, violence or tragic end was not permitted in Sanskrit drama. British drama was initially performed in Churches and Inns and their first public theater appeared only in the 16th century.

Music arises when irregular sounds are made regular and indiscriminate sounds are rendered periodic. The emphasis on correct recitation of the Vedas led to studies in phonetics and sound manipulation giving rise to the Ragas (meter) and Swaras (rhymes), traced to the Indus valley civilization. Although he Vedic/Hindu scale existed 24 centuries ago, *Chandashastra* (500-400 BC), by Pingala, the earliest known treatise on prosody, notes were given seven initial syllables of Sanskrit: **sa ri ga ma pa dha ni**; Pingala is variously identified either as the younger brother of Panini (some 300 BC) or Patanjali. *Chandashastra* details the application of **binary numerals** for the enumeration of meters with fixed patterns of short and long syllables. It also contains the basic ideas of **Fibonacci number** (matrameru). Basham observed:

*"In the science of acoustics India made **real discoveries based on experiment, and the ear...**The octave was divided into seventy two shrutis or quarter tones and their proportions were measured with great accuracy.*

Nadi (Sanskrit 'tube, or pipe') are the channels through which the *pran shako* (vital force) and *manas shako* (mental force) are believed to flow, connected at the power centers, or the chakras. Some 72,000 or more of such channels or nadi permit the flow of auditive stimuli, as mentioned in the Chandogya Upanishad:

A hundred and one are the arteries of the heart; one of them leads to the crown of the head. Going upward through that, one becomes immortal (CU 8.6.6).

The seven chakras are related to the seven notes of the octave and form the basis of modern music therapy.

Naradiya Shisksha and *Sangitratnakara* by Sharangadeva are theoretical treatises replete with philosophical aesthetics, notes, swaras, intervals, scales and playing of veena, tala, drums, song types, and classes of instruments, movement of fingers, hands, head and so on. While *Bharatbhashya* by Nanyadeva treats **body as a source of musical sound,**

Parsvadeva (circa 1250 CE) mentions Kathak in *Sangistar, Sangitsud-hakara* (ca 1248 CE) by Raja Haripaldeva, *Sharangdharpaddhati* (ca 1350 CE) list some cures for vocal disorders, and *Sangitopanishad-saroddhara* (also1350 CE) mentions *tabla* drums. *Sangitsara* (1320-1380 CE) of Vidyaranya systematizes ragas into fifteen *melas*, and Sangitraja (circa 1456) divides music into Hindustani and Carnatic traditions.

Western orchestra has benefited from the gift of Indian **violin bow**. And European **flute and violin originated in Bharat;** Tambourin and the Tambour are adaptations of Tambora and Tanpura. F.W. Galpin (quoted in Garratt):

"From this great country, so rich in musical emotion, its little offspring was borne by Arab traders from the western coast to their own land and to Persia in the seventh or the eighth centuries...to adorn, as the legacy of India, the highest attainments of our European music".

The cross-blown concert flute, depicted in Amravati, Sanchi, and elsewhere, was adapted in China and reached Europe via Byzantium and North Africa. Besides the veena, cymbals, gongs, bells and drums, the singing **voice was often treated as a musical instrument**.

A *Raga,* first mentioned in *Brihaddeshi* by Matanga (6th-8th CE) was meant to define the nature of man and his place in the universe Ragas are timeless, follow a spiritual journey for human transformation and are supposed to have flowed out of the *Anhata Nada*. Whereas Western music is read as a particular mode in major and minor but a musician in Bharat invents as he goes along. **Raga** is **built on language** whereas **Western music** is **built on sound**. W. B. Yeats called Raga music *"not an art but life itself"*. The use of drum to accompany the voice goes back to antiquity. While a raga organizes melody, tala organizes the rhythm. Ancient texts speak of 108 *talas* that have no parallel in Western music. Pythagoras introduced Bharat notation in Greece but he has now become the discoverer of the octave. The seven notes of the **Vedic Hindu octave** travelled to Persia where they were transformed and introduced to Europe as **Do Re Mi Fa So La Si** by Guido d'Arezzo. Weber (cited in Knapp) concluded:

*"...even the 'gamma' of Guido (French gramma, English gamut) goes back to the Sanskrit grammar and Prakrit gamma and is thus a **direct testimony of the Indian origin of our European scale of seven notes**".*

Ethel Rosenthal confirms:

"...a regular system of notation had been worked out before the age of

Panini and the seven notes were designated by their initial letters. This notation passed from the Brahmans through the Persians to Arabia and then introduced into Europe…Hindu music after a period of excessive elaboration sank under the Muhammadans into a state of arrested development…"

In the 17th century, Aurangzeb banned music altogether as Allah's wish because Koran stood for total negation of all art forms except for calligraphy. Thus Muslim contribution to Indian music is zero. Yehudi Menuhin is convinced:

"…we would find all, or most, strands beginning in India; for only in India have all possible modes been investigated, tabulated, and each assigned a particular place and purpose. Of the many hundreds, some found their way to Greece; others were adopted by nomadic tribes such as the gypsies; others became the mainstay of Arabic music…Again its ability to paint the phenomena of existence, from terror to jubilation, from the waves of the sea to the steel and concrete canyons of a modern metropolis, has never been equaled".

Menuhin believes that the personal performance of the Western musician can benefit from:

"…the flexibility of the tone-row, melodic freedom and invention, including ornamentation, the peculiar technique of uniting melody and pulse of Indian music; the ability to improvise with requisite training and the release of creative energy in the performers…

Excavations at Mohenjo-Daro and Harappa have yielded conclusive proof for the existence of Bharat classical dance some 5000 years ago. Specific treatise dedicated to music and dance include *Natyashastra* by Abhinya, *Darpana* by Abhinavagupta and *Sangitaratnakara* by Sarangdeva. Princes were taught to dance and Krishna, Rama and Arjuna were all adept dancers. The approach to dance is holistic; Shiva performs *Lasya* for creation and *Tandava* destruction. Fritz Capra pays homage:

"The metaphor of the cosmic dance thus unifies ancient mythology, religious art and modern physics".

A ll classical dance styles of Bharat viz. Bharat Natyam, Kuchipudi, Kathak, Odissi, Mohiniattam, Kathakali, Manipuri, etc., are derived from the Natyashastra, incorporating stories from Epics, secular works, an elaborate pattern of facial expressions (*mudra*), movement of hands (Hasta), the simulation of various moods like anger (*krodha), envy (matsara)*, greed (*lobha*), lust (*kama*), ego (*mada*), etc. The importance of the gesticulation of the hand is described by Nandikesvara thus:

"Where the hand goes eyes follow: where the eye goes, there the mood (bhava) follows and where the mind goes there arises the sentiment (rasa)".

Each glance and movement of eyeballs and eyebrows is related to the *rasa* such that Natyashastra details **108 primary cadences**. The importance of music and dance in the spiritual life of Bharat are evident from the fact that Jagannath temple was constructed along the principles of a *Nat Mandir.* The sculptures arrest a dynamic moment rather than an ecstatic pose. Konark was conceived as a chariot on 24 wheels, dedicated to Surya, and reverberates with the movement of the dance.

In contrast to the spiritual orientation of dance in Bharat, Western dance is performed mostly for pleasure, and does not benefit from a theoretical treatise like the Natyashastra. The great leaps and gliding movements of the Western ballet try to cut space into chunks of intricate patterns, to arrest perfect dynamic movement free from gravity. Bharat dance strings together a number of highly stylized and symbolic poses to arrest spiritual timelessness. Western skirt, blouse and scarf are slight modifications of Indian *Choli, Laehnga and Dupatta* adapted from Indian slave girls and wandering gypsies.

XV. Games and Sports Celebrate Life

Classical history of Bharat is fraught with a haunting awareness of the perishability of material things and peoples. Life was therefore to be enjoyed and celebrated with vigor at all times. Mentioned in the Rig Veda (RV 6.75.2), Yajur Veda, Atharva Veda, Mahabharata and Ramayana are various styles of fighting and martial arts based on **107 vital points** on the human body of which 64 were classified as being lethal if properly struck with a fist or stick. The military accounts of the Gupta Empire (240-480 CE) identified over 130 different classes of weapons. The *Lotus Sutra* (circa 1st century CE) refers to a boxing art, addressed to Manjushri. *Dhanur Veda,* first mentioned in the *Agni Purana* (8th-11th century CE) states that it was revealed to the sages Vishvamitra, Bhrigu and Parashurama who trained 21 Kalaris to protect the land and maintain peace. Tony Nader-Rama summarizes:

"Dhanurveda represents the invincible quality of pure consciousness, which is able to always maintain itself undisturbed, unchanging, and self-referral

pure nature while upholding all transformations in the manifest creation. In the physiology, it is represented by all that maintains continuity within evolution and change. This is seen in the DNA, the biochemical and enzymatic reactions, the immune system, and the skeletal system".

All martial arts in the world are derived from Dhanurveda including Kung Fu and Karate in Japan: Karate = kar (hand) + hate (mouvement) from Sanskrit.

Polo, chariot racing, bullock racing, archery, martial arts, boxing, wrestling, gladiator contests, dueling, cock, quail, buffalo, bull, ox, peacocks, horse, elephant fights, have all been mentioned in literature as favorite pastimes while archery was the preeminent aristocratic sport. Bullfighting was a game of danger to test the manhood but was confined to the Dravidian south. Here the bull had the advantage in contrast to the Spanish where the beast is destined for death. The herdsman entered the arena and 'embraced the bull' that was neither irritated nor killed. Polo was the national sport of the Tibetans but modern polo is derived from Manipur where the Imphal Polo Ground is the oldest in the world. Cockfighting was a pastime in the Indus Valley Civilization by 2000 BC or earlier. The Encyclopedia Britannica (2008) holds:

"The game fowl is probably the nearest to the Indian red jungle fowl (Gallus gallus), from which all domestic chickens are believed to be descended."

The Aseel game fowl breed might well be 3500 years old as cockfighting has been mentioned in Manusmriti; thereafter it became universal.

Cubical dice and stick dice have been found at Indus sites and spread to Mesopotamia along with beads, jewelry, swastika designs, amulets, weights, copper implements, ivory objects, pottery, and writing on seals. Games like, chess, snakes and ladders, playing cards, all originated in Bharat and were later transmitted to foreign countries. The dice terminology of the *yugas* suggests that creation and cosmos were linked to the dice game between Shiva and his consort such that time itself progressed through the dice game. In the Ashvamedha tradition, the wandering of the horse was preceded by a gigantic dice game that:

"symbolically encompassed every possible permutation of family, social, political, and cosmic relationship of ties…every possible counterstroke to the royal horse, in the year of the wandering that is to follow, is played out and neutralized in advance".

MahaBharat itself is based on a dice game. The Upanishadic dice, a six-faced cube whose opposite sides sum up to seven, subsequently reached China and Japan. An ivory dice was found at Channu-Daro and later evolved into dominoes for fortune telling. The dice game played by Shiva was probably *chaupar*, variously mentioned in the puranas and MahaBharata, and also sculpted in Ellora and Elephanta caves. Other

variants of chaupar include *Pachisi* and *patolli*; English Ludo, a modified version of pachisi, was patented in 1896 during the Raj period. An early board game of *chaturanga* in Bharat during the Gupta Empire evolved from an earlier game called *ashtapada*; other variants include *Dashapada* and *Saturankam*. Chaturanga was taken to Persia during the reign of Anushirvan (531-579 CE) and came to be known as *chatrang* later modified to *shatrang* by the Arabs. The Encyclopedia Britannica maintains:

"About 1783-89 Sir William Jones, in an essay published in the 2nd Vol. of Asiatic Researches, mentions Bhawishya Purana in which is given a description of a four-handed game of chess played with dice"

The Chinese book *Hun tsun su*, written in the Sung period (960-1279 CE), suggests that the Chinese game *k'shu-pu* was invented in Western Bharat and reached China during the Wei dynasty (220-265 CE). Chinese *shwan-liu* and *wei-ki* originated and Japanese game of *sunoroku;* Chinese game *k'shu-pu* evolved from *chatush-pada* from Bharat.

The popular game of cards originated in ancient Bharat and was variously known as *Krida-patrama* and *Ganjifa*. Chatto has definitely traced the origin of playing cards to Bharat via linguistic affinities and skills required in chess. Some of the originals packs have survived e.g. the *Ramayana* pack and the *Dasavatara* pack. From South Bharat comes the game of *Chad* and its versions: *Nava Graha, Pancha Pandava, agad Mohan, Krishna Raj* , Persian *Ganjifa*, Chinese *che-pae* (pair sticks) or *yippee* (bone or ivory sticks). Playing cards travelled to Europe through Gypsies and fortune tellers, first documented as French *'jeux de cartes'* in 1393 CE. The 78 card Tarot is related to the 78 dim Lie algebra E6 and shows the Lie algebra structure of the D4-D5-E6 model; the South Part of the Temple of Luxor may represent a Tarot deck.

Gambling was so popular in ancient Bharat that a gambling hall was even attached to the King's palace in later Vedic times; the 'Gamester's Lament' in Rig Veda testifies to the popularity of gambling. Arthashastra advocates strict control of gambling via spies and a five per cent tax on the stakes. Modern mindset in India is unaware of its own past and relishes Abrahamic taboos.

XVI. Universal Symbols of the Vedic World

The word Calendar has no meaning in any European language and originated in Bharat from *kala* or time in Sanskrit. Pliny and Arrian have suggested that the *Saptarishi* calendar in Bharat started round 6676 BC, organized along a cycle of 2,700 years. Hindus ran two types of solar calendars simultaneously both of which are much more precise than the Gregorian (International calendar). In one solar calendar, the New Year's Day falls exactly on the 13th or the 14th of April and so practiced in Nepal, Bangladesh, Sri Lanka and Thailand. In the other, the year begins on 21 March as adopted by Iranians after Omar Khayyam. Bharat solar calendar is based on the zodiac sigs like *mesa* (sheep), *vrisha,* crocodile, scorpion etc. The claim that Indian solar calendar was imported from the West during the Gupta period is absurd as the West was in its darkest ages at that time and the so called European sources are nowhere to be found.

Hindu *mala* of 108 beads, plus the extra Meru bead, marks the 12 astrological houses and nine planets of the solar system. The three threads of mala represent the trinity: Brahma, Vishnu and Shiva, and it possibly **originated in 5125 BC**. The recitation of the primordial sound OM of creation, divided into the 50 basic sounds of Sanskrit, activates the seven chakras and the energy channels. Buddhists also use the same 108 bead mala and their lotus mantra could be '*Om Mani Padme Hum*'. The Hindu-Buddhist mala provided the model for the Christian rosary *of* 150 beads (= 150 psalms), as also for the Muslim rosary of 99 beads.

Sanskrit **swastika** is made of 'su' = good, 'asti' = to be, and 'ka' = to be good. In another translation, 'swa = higher self, 'asti' = being, and 'ka' = 'being with higher self'. The right-handed swastika **is** one the 108 symbols of Vishnu or Shakti that imitates the course taken daily by the sun. The earliest archeological evidence of swastika-shaped ornaments dates back to the Indus Valley Civilization and was to influence most cultures across the globe. Heinrich Schliemann discovered a Swastika artifact symbol in the ruins of ancient Troy and theorized that the swastika was a '*significant religious symbol of our remote ancestors'* that linked Germanic, Greek and Indo-Iranian cultures. The Nazi Party in Germany in 1920 adopted the swastika as a symbol of the Aryan race, fascism and white supremacy. Many contemporary political extremists and Neo-Nazi groups such as the Russian National Unity continue to use it in this context. In 2005, Tajikistan called for the widespread adoption of the swastika as a national symbol. President Emomali Rahmonov even declared that swastika is an Aryan symbol and that 2006 was to be 'the year of Aryan culture'.

In the Vedic-Hindu world, the three prongs of **Trishul** represent the Trinity: 1) brahma , Vishnu , Mahesh; 2) Sarasvati , Lakshmi and Kali; 3) creation, maintenance and destruction; 4) *kaals* past, present and future; 5) *gunas* sattva , rajas, and tamas; 6) *lokas*: swarg , bhu and patal; 7) forces: will, action and wisdom; 8) miseries: physical, mental and spiritual; 9) consciousness: cognition, conation and affection; 10) *Omkara*: A (akara), U (ukara) and M (makara). In the human body, the trishul may represent the junction where the three main nadis, or energy channels (ida, pingala and sushmna), meet at the brow. The ***Trishul-astra*** originated in the *Vishnu Purana* composed 1st- BC to 4th- CE and entered Buddhism and Taoism. In Egypt an inscription of Edfu relates how Horus was transformed into a winged globe in order to fight the armies of Set, using a three-pronged spear. In order to convert, the Church demonized the sacred symbols of all peoples around the globe and Trishul came to represent the Devil.

Reverence to Sun forms the very essence of the Vedic-Hindu way of life and hymns addressed to ***Surya*** (Sun) are found in all the four Vedas e.g. Saura Shukta of the Rig Veda, Surya Upanishad of Atharva Veda, Aruna Prashna of the Taittriya Aranyaka, the Puranas, Valmiki Ramayana, Mahabharata etc. These hymns describe the celestial body as the source of energy and sustainer of all life on earth. Surya is usually equated with Brahman as *Asaavaadityo Brahma* (the Sun is the icon of Brahma) and *Surya Atma Jagatastasthushashcha* (Sun God is the Soul of all beings). Although the Sun has been referred to under many appellations such as *Savitr* and *Adityas*, in later scriptures all of them merged into Surya. The charioteer of Surya is *Aruna,* personified as the redness in dawn and dusk, driven by seven horses depicting the seven days of the week. Surya is the most prominent of the *navagrahas* or nine celestial objects of the Hindus, to be placated with gold and Ruby.

Many temples dedicated to Sun have survived e.g. the Sun Temple at Konark, Dakshinaarka Temple in Gaya, Suryanar Kovil in Tamilnadu, Suryanarayana Temple at Arasavilli, and temples in Andhra Pradesh, Modhera in Gujarat, and in Rajasthan. The Most venerated Sun Temple in India, built by King Lalitaditya Muktapida (ruled c.724-c.760) of the Karkota dynasty, under whom both Buddhism and Hinduism flourished, is located at Anantnag (Kashmir) that came into existence as a market town around 5000 BC, possibly **visited by Jesus**. The temple was completely destroyed by Sikandar Butshikan in early 15th century who maintained a large establishment for one full year for the demolition of the grand Martand: *"But* *when the massive masonry resisted all efforts, fire was applied and the noble buildings cruelly defaced"*, cited in Tãrîkh-i-Firishta :History of the Rise of the Mahomedan Power in India, translated by John Briggs (1829–1981 CE).

As in almost all other contexts, Sun worship radiated out of ancient Bharat to reach, Asia, native Australia, China, Egypt, Greece, Roman Empire, Christianity, Islam, Central and South America.

The discovery and control of fire has been heralded as one the greatest discoveries. Vedic fire altars have been excavated at Kalibangan and Lothal in the Indus ruins and form the earliest archaeological evidence for **fire worship** in the world. Fire has been central to Vedic creation and sacrifice performed as *Yajna* in Tapovans where Fire, deified as god Agni, formed the mediator between the worshipper and the infinite. Most Hindu Samskaras and rituals (marriage, death, birth, religious festivals, etc) continue to be performed around a fire and Hymns to Agni are prominent in the Rig Veda. From the Vedic world, Fire worship was to influence Zoroastrianism, Greco-Roman Hestia and cults, Polynesian Pele, Celtic Belenus, Slavic Svarog, Hebrew Menorah and the New Testament 'tongues of flame'.

Vedic Hindus regarded creation as one the grandest miracles and have found divinity in the organs that facilitate it. Genitalia worship typically involves both the phallus (male organ) and the yoni (vagina). Evidence for **phallus worship** in India dates back to prehistoric times: Hohle phallus, a 28,000-year-old siltstone phallus discovered in the Hohle Fels cave in 2005, is among the oldest phallic representations. The famous 'man-size' lingam in the Parashurameshwar Temple in the Chitoor District of Andhra Pradesh, better known as the Gudimallam Lingam, is about 1.5 meters (5 ft.) in height, carved in polished black granite. Lingam-yonis have been excavated from Harappa and Mohenjo-Daro and entered modern Hindu practices. The *Yoni Mudra* in meditation is used to reduce distraction during the yoga session.

From ancient Bharat, Phallus Yoni worship spread to all of Asia, Japan, Egypt, Scandinavia, Greece and so forth to become universal during the Middle Ages but Christianity was to turn all this upside down and promoted an all-male God who created the universe with his own 'seed' such that women were not needed. In this world for men and by men, God grudgingly had to create women as a passive receptacle to rear the male seed. The Christian cross, the Jewish kippa, the obelisk, the Pyramid, the Vatican, are monuments for the male power only.

In Vedic-Hindu mythology, the **serpent deities** are semi-divine beings, who descended from the sage Kashyapa, and who play a paramount role in Hinduism. They inhabit the subterranean world of Nagaloka, ruled by Ananta at his capital of Bhogavathi. They act as guardians of subterranean gems, precious stones and minerals. The Snake primarily represents rebirth, death and immortality, as it casts its skin and is symbolically 'reborn'. Nagas are depicted in Hindu iconography with a lower snake body, covered by bejeweled garments, and a human-like head adorned by three to seven cobra hoods. Some of the prominent nagas are: Sheshnaga, or the 1,000 headed reptile, who supports the world on his many heads; Vasuki helped the churning of the Ocean; Kaliya subdued by Krishna; Manasa or the Universal mother. Padmanabha is the guardian snake of the south. The power of serpent is nowhere as important as in Yoga where *Kundalini* lies dormant as a snake at the base of the spinal cord, to be aroused by yogic discipline for eventual emancipation from reincarnation.

Vedic-Hindu snake symbolism found its way around the globe, particularly south East Asia and China. Egypt, Mid East and Greece; in Imperial Rome a sacred snake was kept within the city and was attended by the vestal virgins. In Australia, the Aboriginal people worship a huge python known as the *Rainbow Serpent*. Native American tribes revere snake variously as Fhahaha. Aztec deity *Quetzalcoatl* was a feathered serpent-god and Hopis do much the same. The tribes of Peru, The Mound Builders, Colombians and the Toltecs, all worship snake. In Christianity, the snake has been adored as a regenerative power, personifying Good, as Christ by the Gnostics, as a phallic deity, and as a solar deity. Contemporary Christian culture identifies the snake as a symbol of evil, thanks to the legend of the forbidden fruit eaten by Eve after she was tempted by Satan disguised as a snake. Snake handling is a religious ritual in some Christian churches in the U.S., probably dating back to antiquity, who quote the Bible to support the practice.

6. Vedic Patrimony Goes Global

Some Hindu traditions claim that from the remotest of times their *Naga* ancestors visited all parts of the earth, mapped it, and mined gold. The Nagas (Asuras) were expert navigators and had founded colonies around the globe, as postulated by Oldfield, Matlock and others. Mahabharata (VI.236 etc.) and Vishnu Purana (11.2 etc.) even describe the earth as seven circular islands, surrounded by seven seas. Based upon linguistics, shared deity and place names, mythology and customs. Matlock has surmised that Cassites or Kushites are the parent stock of all peoples around the globe. By 5000 BC or so, Hittie, Kassite, Cushite, Cuthite, Hurrian, Harri, and others, poured into what is now Afghanistan, Pakistan, Northern India and Tibet, from Chinese Turkestan; they stem from Kshatriya or Hattiya in ancient Bharat. China is also known as Cathy and was ruled by Cathatites (Hitties, Kassites etc).

Civilizing the whole world, *krinvantum vishvamaryam,* had been a declared mission of the Vedic Aryans who fared much danger and sacrifice to spread the Sanskrit language, idealism, spirituality, sciences, medicine, arts, and commercial technology of Bharat around the globe. The idea was to freely give the models developed in Bharat without expecting anything in return, in keeping with the spirit of sacrifice inherent in the Aryan ideation of the Vedas and indeed of the Creation itself (Chapter 4). This ideology transformed a vast area via a common philosophy whose unifying principle was the **well being of all humanity**. The peaceful penetration resulted in the flowering of a mixed ideal bubbling with vitality in all aspects of life. P. N. Oak summarizes the Vedic Society (cited in Matlock):

"Vedic society functioned as a silent, frictionless, noiseless machine with each component (individual) content with its role as a part of the entire social mechanism…there was no social strife or class struggle or economic competition. Everyone was trained to feel happy and contended in his social group…As long as Vedic civilization continued to be intact throughout the world, there used to be a worldwide network of Vedic priests…who used to ensure and regulate the hereditary social, professional guild system under which every individual, family group and organization adhered for the Varnashram Dharma regulation".

The following chapters briefly summarize that Vedic ideation indeed forms the core of human history. Detailed accounts have been published in my earlier books (amazon.com author central), substantiated by extensive references.

I. The Age of Myths and Legends

Based on the oral traditions, myths, and folk songs in the Near east, Far East, Central Asia, and Europe, Gidwani has concluded that the Aryans fanned out of ancient Bharat to find a land that was pure and free from evil. The legend has it that around 7000 BC a loosely held federation of **108 Hindu tribes** sealed an alliance with the *Rya* through a mala of 108 beads, **Sanatana dharma**, **Gayatri mantra** of the Rig Veda, *ahimsa* (nonviolence), *satya* (truth), *karma* (right action) and *dana* (charity). The Act of Union for the Merger of Lower and Upper Sindhu (5087 BC) stated:

> *"One land and One people of Sanatana Dharma and the Hindu.*
> *Aim High and Look Far, Traveler, Go On and On (5084 BC)".*

A memory song of 156 words has survived to speak of a **Hindu parliament** (5065 BC) that proclaimed:

"The first condition, then, for thinking minds to blossom, is a settled society which provides material needs, wealth, security and absence of external and internal enemies…"

The poetess Vidyapatni (3560 BC) speaks of the ***Ashvamedha*** tradition for the very first time while the song titled 'Brides of Sindhu Putra' (circa 5054 BC) states that **slavery was abolished** to join forces under a single name of Bharat Varsha, guided by *Sanatana Dharma*.

'Truth is the ultimate reality…Hindu must learn to refine everything by continuous testing and experience' (Song of the Hindu 5050 BC).

A seal maker produced seals with a **Swastika** sign of equal limbs in all directions, to symbolize the promise of Bharat Varsha in its timeless mission of spiritual unity, freedom from slavery, and equality for all.

Aryas fanned out of their Indus-Sarasvati home base to Hari Haran (Iran) that later got the name **Persia from Purus** while Sage Gandhara established an ashram in Avagna (Afghanistan). Sumer (Mesopotamia) may stem from ***Sumeru***, the great Meru of Hindu mythology, or from Sumaran who had led the first batch of Aryas to construct the tallest Ziggurat and they came to be known as '**Aryas of the Clay tablet**'. Aryas now advanced to Turkey, Egypt, Armenia, Palestine, Israel, the Gulf and the Russian republics. Kemi River was later called Ar, Ary or Aur and finally renamed as **Nile to honor Nilkantha**. In Egypt, the Aryan leader Lugal built a pyramid and became the undisputed leader of a united kingdom of Assyria and Sumeria.

Under Atul and Atal, the Aryas reached Stavropol and the area is now known as Aramvir. Arya Sakaru, whose mother came from Saketa (Ayodhya) and father from Sakkar (Sind, Pakistan), was eventually chosen as leaders and the tribe came to be called **Shaka tribe,** later named **Scythians**. Some Aryans reached Lithuania (5005 BC) where the Arya Bala married a local girl (Laima). Baltic folk tales and dances continued to be inspired by Devas, Saul (sun) like the Hindu Surya, and Rig Veda for long periods. The Aryas in Italy came to be called **Aryasenna** or Ryasenna; Herodotus confirms that people from the East arrived there through Lydia, or from the Aegean through Lemnos. Arya Gaipal **introduced the flute to Italy**. One source states (cited in Gidwani):

"…imprint they left would later blossom as the fountainhead of European civilization, culture, literature and philosophy…they found repulsive that men married men and women were regarded only as producers of offspring…and that land had neither real rivers nor forests nor tall trees".

West Germany was reached via the Dana River (Danube) sometime around 5000 BC. Writing in 98 CE, in *Germanica (De Origine et situ Germanorum)*, Cornelius relates ancient songs going back to Manu and the area that came to be known as Tungeri (Tungbhadra river). Black forest (Schwarzwald), black speech, and black arrows and the 'Black sea' were all named after the Aryans. In Greek mythology, Jason and the Argonauts set across the Black sea to look for the Golden Fleece to be found in the kingdom of the black people.

'Thus led by gold under the king of a sheep came the black from black deep. And the Black Forest, to which white river led with homage, bowed the golden head.'

Peace and unification ensued under Odin who combined the 12 tribes into one federation in the **Land of Tungeri (Germany)**. His wife Frigga, and son Bal Deva, were also honored as local deities Frigga came to be regarded as Terra Mater (Mother Earth) and even equated with Venus. Bal Deva was regarded as 'Spotless', innocent, suffering god. Friday is named after **Frigga** while **Thor,** the god of Odin, was honored by having Thursday named after him. Aryas did not go to England inhabited by a mongrel race, outside the periphery of any civilized knowledge or culture and practicing cannibalism (PTI 8 August 2009**)**. Even Germans ridiculed the English who practiced deviousness and deception and honored the god

Loki who was a 'changer of shape'. Contact with **Kosa Karas** (China) was also established as a weaver from Sindhu had installed himself there. The brown skinned weaver, distinct from Chinese features, was depicted in portraits and statues of Kosa Karas in gratitude for agriculture and chicken farming he had introduced.

Aryas from Bharat had colonized Italy around 5000 BC and Gaipal had introduced the flute. One source states (cited in Gidwani):

*"…imprint they left would later blossom as the **fountainhead of European civilization**, culture, literature and philosophy…they found repulsive that men married men and women were regarded only as producers of offspring…and that land had neither real rivers nor forests nor tall trees".*

II.   The Silk Road from Bharat to China

There are numerous references to China in various Sanskrit texts : Mahabharata, Arthashastra, and Manusmriti. French art historian Rene Grousset suggests that the name China comes from 'an ancient' **Sanskrit name *Cina*,** possibly derived from the small state of Chan-si in northwest China in the fourth century BC. The Chinese word for lion, *shih*, used long before the Chin dynasty, was derived from the Sanskrit word, *simha*, and the Greek word for China, Tzinista, appears to be a derivative of the Sanskrit *Chinasthana.* The arrival of **Buddhism** in China may be traced to **the 2nd century BC**; between 512 and 545 CE, there were thirteen thousand Buddhist shrines and monasteries, inhabited by three thousand foreign monks and two million Buddhist followers. By 845 CE, China counted 4600 monasteries, 40,000 Buddhist temples along with 260,000 monks and nuns. Chinese astronomy, statecraft, traditions of religious sacrifice, all suggest that **a readymade Vedic culture was simply planted in China** that was very much a part of the Vedic Empire. Professor G. Phillips, remarks in the Journal of the Royal Asiatic Society, 1965:

"The maritime intercourse of India and China dates from a much earlier period, from about 680 BC, when the sea traders of the Indian Ocean whose chiefs were Hindus founded a colony called Lang-ga, after the Indian named Lanka of Ceylon, about the present gulf of Kias-Tehoa, where they arrived in vessels having prows shaped like the heads of birds or animals after the pattern specified in the Yukti Kalpataru (an ancient Sanskrit technological text) and exemplified in the ships and boats of old Indian arts."

P.N. Oak (cited in Knapp) was to conclude:

*"Until the Mahabharata war, like the rest of the world, **China too spoke Sanskrit** and practiced Vedic culture".*

Hu Shih, (1891-1962), Chinese philosopher in Republican China, ambassador to the U.S. (1938-42) and chancellor of Peking University (1946-48) remarked:

"India conquered and dominated China culturally for two thousand years without ever having to send a single soldier across her border."

Lin Yutang, in his book *The Wisdom of China and India*, pays tribute:

*"The contact with poets, forest saints and the best wits of the land, the glimpse into the first awakening of Ancient India's mind as it searched, at times childishly and naively, at times with a deep intuition, but at all times earnestly and passionately, for the spiritual truths and the meaning of existence - this experience must be highly stimulating to anyone, particularly because the Hindu culture is so different and therefore so much to offer…Not until we see the richness of the Hindu mind and its essential spirituality can we understand India.. **India was China's teacher** in religion and imaginative literature, and the world's teacher in trigonometry, quadratic equations, grammar, phonetics, Arabian Nights, animal fables, chess, as well as in philosophy, and that she inspired Boccaccio, Goethe, Herder, Schopenhauer, Emerson, and probably also old Aesop."* (My emphasis).

Most recently, the State-run Chinese media acknowledged:

"The civilization of both China and India originated from the Himalayas and the Qinghai-Tibetan Plateau. And there was no conflict during their historical change that lasted thousands of years. Sages brought India's ancient culture to China. After the Han Dynasty (206 BC - 220 AD), China faced collapse. Buddhism contributed greatly to China's unification. Today, Indians have to come to China for documents if they want to know their cultural past." (Rediff 24 October 2012).

Yuag Xianji, member of the Chinese People's Political Consultative Conference, speaking at the C. P. Ramaswamy Aiyar Foundation, Madras, March 27 1984 said (cited in Knap):

*"Recent discoveries of ruins of Hindu temples in Southeast China provided further evidence of Hinduism in China. Both Buddhism and Hinduism were patronized by the rulers. In the 6th century CE the **royal family was Hindu for two generations**. The following Tang dynasty (7th to the 9th century CE) also patronized both Hinduism and Buddhism because the latter was but a*

branch of Hinduism…the Chinese worshipped Shivambu, the Chinese name for Durga". (My emphasis).

The Sanskrit language and literature influenced China enormously as evident by Shivalinga, Tamil inscriptions, the doctrine of karma, Yoga, an alphabetical system called **Hsi Yu Hu Shu** (Foreign writing) or *Po La Men Shu* (Brahmanical writing). In Chinese drama, the story, characters, and technique were all borrowed from Bharat initially; in the 12th CE the first known performance of a Buddhist play called *Mu-lien* is based on an episode in Mahabharata. Nehru commented:

"Sanskrit scholarship must have been fairly widespread in China. It is interesting to find that some Chinese scholars tried to introduce Sanskrit phonetics into the Chinese language. A well-known example of this is that of the monk Shon Wen, who lived at the time of the Tang dynasty. He tried to develop an alphabetical system along these lines in Chinese."

Bharat had invented **brown sugar** and Emperor Taizong immediately sent Wang Xuang to contact the Mahabodhi monastery in Magadha to transfer the **technology to China** where it came to be called 'stone honey' which transformed Chinese cuisine. Other imports included Sandalwood, cotton, Water clock, the Chinese pagoda (a modification of the stupa), mythology, painting and sculpture. Bharat music was eulogized by the Chinese poet, Po Chu-yi thus:

'It is a little wonder. An official publication of the Chinese Republic says: *"… when a Chinese audience today hears Indian music, they feel that while possessing a piquant Indian flavor it has a remarkable affinity with Chinese music".*

Even Joseph Needham, the well-known Hindu hater, admits:

"Indian music came through Kucha to China just before the Sui period and had a great vogue there in the hands of exponents such as Ts'ao Miao-ta of Brahmanical origin."

Professor Jin Kemu summarized China's indebtedness to Bharat in astronomy, mathematics, medicine, and calendar in a book published in 1957 in China:

"The Chinese were familiar with Indian mathematics, and, in fact, continued to study it long after the period of intellectual intercourse between India and China had ceased". (Cited in Sarkar: Hindu Achievements in Exact Science).

Hindu-Buddhist concepts such as the infinity of space and time, the plurality of worlds, time-cycles or Kalpas (***chieh***), **and *pralaya*,** calendar all reached China. During the T'ang dynasty, astronomers from Bharat were working at the Imperial Bureau of Astronomy such that a **zero symbol** and **table of sines** entered Chinese records. Regarding medical sciences, Terence Duke observed:

"Many Buddhists were familiar with the extensive knowledge of surgery common to Indian medicine and this aided them both in spreading the teachings and in their practice of diagnosis and therapy. Surgical technique was almost unknown within China prior to the arrival of Buddhism."

Acupuncture stems directly from Marmas in Ayurveda. **Black pepper** from India was known as '*hujiao*' and entered Chinese medicine. The Indian golden needle that could remove cataracts was introduced into China. Both Terence Duke and the history channel affirm that martial arts went from India to China. Bodhidharma introduced the **Shao-lin** style of boxing to China as did **Chuan Fa** (also **called Kung-Fu** or 'mastery'), racing games and chess. Terence Duke observes:

"In ancient Hinduism, nata was acknowledged as a spiritual study and conferred as a ruling deity, Nataraja, representing the awakening of wisdom through physical and mental concentration. However, after the Muslim invasion of India and its brutal destruction of Buddhist and Hindu culture and religion, the Kshatriya art of nata was dispersed and many of its teachers slain. This indigenous martial arts, under the name of Kalari or Kalaripayit, exists only in South India today. Originating at least 1,300 years ago, India's Kalaripayit is the oldest martial art taught today".

The name **Korea** is derived from the Sanskrit **Gauriya** where Gauri, the consort of Shiva, was the principal deity of the region. The wife of South Korean President Lee Myung-bak is a **descendant of Ayodhya princess** Heo Hwang-ok who married King Suro of Korea's Gaya Kingdom in 48 CE; former President **Kim** Dae Jung is one her descendants. According to *The Korea Times,* Korean archeologists have discovered a stone with two fish kissing each other, which was a uniquely linked to a royal family in Ayodhya. An analysis of DNA samples taken from the site of two royal Gaya tombs in 2004 in Gimhae, South Gyeongsang Province, confirms a genetic link between certain Korean and Indian ethnic groups (Rediff 26 Jan 2010). From China, Buddhism entered Korea, and then onto Japan by the end of the sixth century.

There was no Paleolithic culture in Japan and **Nippon stems from Sanskrit *nipun*** meaning dexterous. The ruins of a submerged city near

Okinawa suggest that it was probably developed by **Indo-Aryans some 8000 years ago**. Shinto (the way of spirits) stems from Brahman Okyo and adopted many Bharat gods: Varuna (*Sui-ten*), Sarasvati (*Benten*), Shiva (*Daikoku*), sun goddess Amaterasuc, Indra (*Taishakuten*), Naga (*Ryujin*), Hariti (*Kishimojin*) Kubera (*Bishamon*); Ganesha as Sho-ten or *Shoden* (literally holy god); Hariti and Dakini are also worshiped. The **Ainu** of Japan are said to be **Aryans** as are the Cust and the Galchas.

It is not uncommon to find **Devanagari inscriptions** in Japanese cemeteries and temples. In Japanese Katakana, the vowels were arranged as a, i, u, *e, o* and groups of consonants then followed e.g. *ka, ki, ku, ke, ko*, arranged into **fifty phonetic sounds, as in Sanskrit**. Other imports from India include cotton, graceful dance Bugaku, the Samurai tradition, and much more. Suzuki sumps up by suggesting that if one were to wipe out Buddhist traditions there would be nothing left in the rich culture for which Japan is known: gardens, tea ceremony, martial arts, landscapes, fencing, music, drama, painting, sculpture, industrial arts, philosophy, mythology, governance, education and social welfare.

Kashmir was a **seat of Sanskrit, sciences,** Buddhism and Brahmanical learning and an important place for the dissemination of the Divine Ideal. Kanishka of the Kushan Empire ruled during the lifetime of Jesus and convened the Fourth Buddhist Council in Kashmir, perhaps presided over by Jesus-Pravarasena. Prithvi Narayan Shah and his successors united and **Sanskritized Nepal 1743-1885** and Prithvi himself obtained the title of Bahadur Shamsher Jung from the Mughals in 1764 CE. Nepal is a replica of Vedic-Hindu state, modeled along Bharat, who's King was the only Hindu monarch in the world. **Tibet received Buddhism** in the 7th CE and became the national religion of Tibet in the 11th century whereas Brahmi of the Gupta period evolved into Tibetan.

III. East Asia-Bharat Connection

In the antiquity, South-East Asia was variously known as *suvarnabhumi* (the land of Gold) or *Suvarnadeep, Suwarndib (Susuvarnadvipa)*, the *Golden Chersonese*; or Chinese *kin-lin* (gold). Ancient texts such as *Brihatkatha, Kathakosa*, Jain *Jnatadharmakatha*, Buddhist *Milindapanka* and *Mahaniddesa,* and *Ramayana*, reveal knowledge of regions beyond the eastern seas; Kamboja became Cambodia, Java stems from Yavadvipa, and Malay from Malwa where intermarriages lead to complete fusion of population and culture without any torture or coercion or death or force. Prince Vijaya was sent by King Sinhala (Sinhavahu) of Bengal for the conquest of Ceylon around 550 BC and the Sinhalese language was thus born. Ashoka sent Mahendra and during the reign of king Devanampiya (247-207 BC) emissaries were sent **to ordain Queen Anula of Ceylon**. The Bodhi tree, Buddha's alms bowl, and his tooth also reached Ceylon and Buddhism was finally adopted with much enthusiasm. Early Sinhalese art was inspired by Amravati and Buddhist temples in Ceylon include Shiva, Vishnu, Ganesha, and others, along with Bharat dance and music

Fu-nan in the lower valley of Mekong, present day Cambodia and South Vietnam, was the oldest and the **most important of the Hinduized states**. By 357 CE, Fu-nan was ruled by a Hindu ruler identified as Chandan and later by Kaundinya. Fu-Nan inscriptions are in pure flawless Sanskrit and their content shows that religion, philosophy and mythology from Bharat were widely understood. **Champa** (Chiem-thanh) was a Hindu-Buddhist confederation of 4/5 principalities that included Indrapura (Dong Duang), Amravati (Quang-Nam), Vijaya (Cha Ban) Kauthara (Nha Trang) and Pandurang (Phan Rang). Sanskrit inscriptions in central Vietnam in 658 CE and in Cambodia in 668 CE, speak of a Hinduized Champa kingdom ruled by the Sri Mara dynasty (192-336 CE) where the cult of Shiva and Uma, along with cremation and immersion of remains, were widely practiced.

Hindu/Buddhist presence in **Vietnam** is most evident at Oc-Eo which was active as a port during the first millennium CE. **Cambodia** is a showcase example of the influence exerted by Bharat in Asia that led to the making of what is known as Greater India. The Kings of Kambuja claim descent from a mythical ancestor Kambu and a celestial nymph Mera, that represent the sun and the moon. Descriptions of Bharat influence could be multiplied indefinitely and Prince Nordom Sihanouk of Cambodia pays a befitting homage:

"In fact, it was about 2000 years ago that the first navigators, Indian merchants and Brahmans brought to our ancestors their gods, their techniques, and their organization. Briefly, India was for us what Greece was for the Latin Occident".

Materpieces of Khmer architecture, inspired by epics from Bharat, include *Phnom Bakheng* to celebrate the numbers of 33 and 108; *Preah Vihar* that stretched over 800 meters; *Preah Ko* and many more. Jayavarman VII planned *Angkor Thom* as city with cosmic significance around a central mountain *Bayon* to match the constellation Draco as it appeared in 10,500 BC, just the opposite of Orion connected with the ancient Egyptian pyramids. The city and suburbs of Angkor Thom and Angkor Wat **housed one million people** in the 13th century, the largest in the world at that time; the splendor and learning were so extensive that the public library, put on fire, burned for three days.

      Angkor Wat, dedicated to Vishnu, is the **largest religious monument in the world** depicting scenes from Ramayana and Mahabharat. The temple is actually a **coded religious text** where the **number 432** is related to 432000 syllables in Rig Veda as also to the four ages of Manu equal 432000 chords of Ptolemy. The total number of figures of men, animals and birds has been calculated to be nearly 20,000. The sacred 108 is 1/4 x 432, or the 10800 stanzas in Rig Veda as also the 10800 bricks in a Hindu fire altar. Henri Mouhot (1826 -1861 CE) exclaimed:

"It is grander than anything left us by Greece or Rome…At the sight of this temple, one feels one's spirit crushed, one's imagination surpassed. One looks, one admires and, seized with respect, one is silent. For where are the words to praise a work of art that may not have its equal anywhere on the globe? ... What genius this Michelangelo of the East had, that he was capable of conceiving such a work... This architectural work perhaps has not, and perhaps never has had, its equal on the face of the globe".

Lord Alfred Harmsworth Northcliffe (1865 – 1922 CE) marveled:

"No Sultan, no Mikado, no Viceroy of India could offer his guests a comparable spectacle."

      Sitwell observed:

"Let it be said immediately that Angkor, as it stands, ranks as chief wonder of the world today, one of the summits to which human genius has inspired in stone, infinitely more impressive, lovely and, as well romantic, than anything that can be seen in China…a civilization that flashed its wings of utmost brilliance…"

      The northern provinces of the Khmer empire reached Laos or *Lava,* the son Lord Rama. Laotian capital *Vian Chang* (Vientiane in English) is a corrupt form of Sanskrit *Vana chandan* meaning the forest of sandalwood. Burma is an abbreviation of the Sanskrit name ***Brahmadesh*** and its rivers bear Sanskrit names like Irrawati, Brahmaputra, and Chindwin, as do its cities The head of state of Burma is called Adipati, from Sanskrit Adhipati and the basis for her script, her literature, her art, her thought, her religion, Burma are all imported from Bharat.

The word **Siam or Sayam** is found in Vishnu Purana (6th CE) where most ancient cultural objects are all influenced by Bharat as is the mythology. Lopburi, 80 miles north of Bangkok, was a center of Mon-Hindu culture for many centuries whereas the kingdom of Sukhothai (1220-1350 CE) was founded by Rama Khamheng whose successors were crowned as Dharamarajas and founded the city of Shri Ayuthaya (from Ayodhya in Bharat) 1350-1767 CE. Thai Kings are considered to be descendants of Rama and the Royal Temple in Bangkok was once a Rama Temple. Hindu influence is all too obvious in festivals, dance, drama and music whereas the legal system descends directly from Manusmriti and Dharmashastra. Daniels and Bright conclude:

*"**Brahmi is the ultimate source** not only of all the indigenous scripts of South Asia but also of major SE Asian scripts (Burmese, Lao, Thai, Khmer etc.) of Tibetan, and other Central Asian scripts no longer in use. It thus constitutes one of the most important 'parent' scripts of the world, rivaling Aramaic and Arabic in the number and range of its varieties and derivatives".*

The word **Indonesia** is derived from Indo (India) and Nesia meaning Indian Islands, peopled by settlers from Bharat who reached Java circa 75 CE. Chinese accounts of the 4th century CE confirm Java to be entirely Hindu containing many Hindu temples and using Sanskrit dialect. Javanese people believe that Rishi Agastya came from Bharat and settled there whereas in 603 CE migrants from Gujarat and founded the Borobudur. Java is referred to as *Yavadvipa* in Sanskrit sources (Yawa means barley) or shaped like a barley corn. This attests to the skill of Vedic navigators in charting the world. Although almost all of the population in Java is now Muslim a monument in white marble, an 8 horse chariot driven by Krishna and Arjuna, right in the center of Jakarta, is known as *Arjun Vijay.* The Indonesian Kawi language borrows heavily from Sanskrit and Hindu numerals, and used the Pallava script of South India.

Around 775 CE, a Buddhist King carved out the **Shailendra Empire** of **Shri Vijaya** that covered Malaysia, Ceylon, Sumatra, Borneo, half of Java, Malay, Celebes, Philippines, parts of Formosa, and probably Champa and Kambuja; Malaysia was named Kalinga. Of Shailendra Quaritch eulogizes:

"This great conqueror, whose achievements can only be compared with those of the greatest soldiers known to Western history, and whose fame in his time sounded from Persia to China, in a decade or two built up a vast

*empire which endured for five centuries and made possible the marvelous flowering of **Indian art and culture in Java and Cambodia.** Yet in our encyclopedias and histories…one will search in vain for a reference to this far flung empire or to its noble founder…The very fact of such an empire even having existed is scarcely known, except by a handful of Oriental scholars".*

Bharat imprints on Javanese music, village organization, rural economy and property law, are all too evident. Borneo is called *Kalimanthan* and the Sultan of Brunei (in Borneo) bore the title of Seri Bhagwan. Borneo Sanskrit inscriptions at Maera Kaman in Kutei are dated to 4th century CE, dedicated probably to Shiva or Agastya. A Gupta style bronze Buddha has been found in Kutei at Kota Bangum and inscriptions in Sanskrit are also present; a gold tortoise and a gold Vishnu statuette were found at Kutei as well. **Bali is replica of Hinduism** but how it got there remains controversial. Singapore was simply **Singhpur** or Simhapurama of Mahabharat. It boasted of 500 temples consisting of the world's most artistic stone architecture. Both Shri Vijaya and Singapore were destroyed and on the ruins was built the Empire of **Madjapahit**.

Malaya was peopled by emigrations from Assam, Naga Hills and Yunnan 2500-2500 BC. Malaya is a Sanskrit word and the capital **Kuala Lumpur** stes from Sanskrit *Cholanampuram*, Seramban derives its name from Sanskrit *Shree Rama Van* or the bower of Lord Rama whereas Sungei Pattanai comes from Sanskrit *Shringa Pattan* or the mountain city. Chinese texts of the fifth century clearly state that in one of the Malay kingdoms:

"There are over a thousand Brahmins from India; the people practice their doctrine and give their daughters to them in marriage, so that many Brahmans stay there'.

Ramayana (Chapter 3) spread across South East Asia during the 8th century, and evolved into unique renditions incorporating local history, folktales, religion, literature, temple architecture, dance and theater. Some adaptations include: *Ramakien, Ravanavadham, Ramakavaca, Maradia Lawana, Kakawin Ramayana, Yogesvara Ramayana, Phra Lak Phra Lam, Hikayat Seri Rama* and *Reamker*; Buddha is even considered to be an incarnation of Rama and is known as *Preah Ream*. The *Rama Leela* is performed across South East Asia in numerous local languages and the story has been the subject of art, architecture, music, folk dance and sculpture.

Excavations conducted by Beyer in 1920s at Novaliches in **Philippines** revealed pottery, iron implements and weapons, beads and bangles, brought from Bharat over a long period of trade.The chiefs of many

Philippine Islands were called Rajas and their script was derived from Brahmi. Philippines literature, mythology and folklore are all traceable to Bharat as Philippines and Formosa were **part of the Shri Vijaya Empire**. *Maharadya Lawana* and *Darangen* of Mindanao (Philippines) were inspired by Ramayana but much of the history of Philippines was destroyed by the zealot Christians.

Archeology has revealed that the ancestors of **Polynesians left Bharat around 400 BC** and brought rice with them into Indonesia where they adapted bread fruit as their staple food; by 200 CE they migrated eastwards into the Pacific to reach Tonga or Samoa which was the final center of dispersion into Polynesia. It appears that the migration started from the mouth of the Indus and the Gulfs of Cutch and Cambay, to the south of the Punjab. J. Alden Mason (cited in Knapp) is emphatic:

"…the physical type of Polynesians, their language and the fundamentals of their culture connect them with South-eastern Asia rather than with America, and there is very little doubt that they originally came from the Malayan region…did not reach the Easter Island until the 14th century CE…the resemblances between certain cultural features in America and in Polynesia, Melanesia, Indonesia, or south-eastern Asia are too great and too close to be explained away as parallel developments".

Koi (Gonds of Bastar region) left Bharat about four thousand years ago and settled in New Zealand. They were later subjugated by a people called *Tutu-mai-ao* who also spoke a language with many Sanskrit words, suggesting even earlier emigration out of Bharat. Polynesian myths are adapted from Aryan folklore from the very earliest phase of Vedic religion in Southern Asia. A man named Kahukara, possibly from the valley of the Ganges 5th CE, introduced sweet potato (*kumara*) *Ipomoea batatas*, possibly 400-700 CE. A bell with Tamil inscription has been found in the coastal waters of Australia-New Zealand combine.

Maori migration successively followed the route Rarotonga - Tahiti – Hawaii but a stopover in South America is a distinct possibility. Tahitians had created a **society which came to near perfection**: enough food, warmth, beauty, leisure, fun, absence of disease, generous, happy, unselfish, all the time laughing, cheerful, everyone worked for the common good of everyone, no one was poor or rich, there was no theft because anyone could take whatever they wanted from houses left open. There was no envy, greed, avarice, cruelty because no one owned anything. Bougainville thought he had been transported into the Garden of Eden:

"Everywhere we found hospitality, ease, innocent joy and every appearance of happiness".

The London Missionary Society was Calvinistic and ready to destroy all world culture to save the wicked Tahitians from eternal hell fire by conversion. French took to burning, taking women and children hostage and starving them. Papeete provided organized brothels and illicit grog shops. The Missionaries introduced fleas, mosquitoes, syphilis measles, typhoid, mumps, whooping cough, tuberculosis and venereal diseases. Later epidemics included smallpox in 1853 and 1882, leprosy in the 1860s, cholera in 1895 and bubonic plague in 1899; one half of the women were infected with syphilis within three months of the arrival of Cook in 1769.

Cook had estimated in 1770s some 200,000 Tahitians as against 121,000 by Dr. Forester in 1791; by 1800 only 16,050 were left and the number went down to no more than six or seven thousand in the next fifteen years or so; 19/20 Tahitians had died without fathering a child. Cook was to write:

"We debauch their morals already too prone to vice and we interduce among them wants and perhaps diseases which they never before knew and which serve only to disturb that happy tranquility they and their forefathers had enjoyed. If anyone denies the truth of this assertion let him tell me what the Natives of whole extent of America have gained by the commerce they have had with Europeans".

On 30 November 1778 Cook discovered the island of Hawaii and described: *"a handsome people and a beautiful Land"* but Calvinist Hiram Bingham in 1820 saw:

"…destitution, degradation and barbarism among the chattering native savages…Can these be human beings! Can such beings be civilized? Can they be Christianized"?

Charles Stewart in 1823 CE further added:

"Can they be men-can they be women? Do they not form a link in creation, connecting man with the brute?"

According to Fraser and others, the Polynesian dialects come from Bharat and not from Malaya before the age of Buddha. There is no doubt that **Maori is related to Sanskrit, Prakrit, and Gonds** of Marian Hills in central Bharat. The most important Maori word *vari* and its numerous variants can be traced to the personification of the Sarasvati River; the union of Vari and Prajapati gave birth to waters and rivers, just as all things originated from the body of the Rarotongan goddess Vari. The all common

Maori root *fa* is related to Sanskrit *yava* meaning barley, wheat and grain in general. Polynesian numerals are related to Aryan languages and use the true decimal system with separate words for the numbers one to ten but words exist for powers as high as 10^9.

IV. Greater Bharat to West Asia and Arabia

Before the dawn of history, an extensive Chalcolithic culture connected lower Indus valley with the plains of Mesopotamia and Asia Minor (Turkey). Some authors such as Matlock believe that the Phoenicians and Aryans are the same people while Sumerians were Turk; Asuras (Phoenicians) flourished along the Indus valley. Turkish people call themselves Ari (Aryan). Southern Persia, Afghanistan and Pakistan were variously called **Shivapuri, Shivabhu, Shivapuni** and **Shivulba**. Meru resembles Sumer and Josephus was to state that Mount Meru was located in Eden. Sumerians seem to have arrived into an advanced Chalcolithic culture no earlier than 5000 BC; based on the decipherment of the Indo-Sumerian seals, L.A. Waddell (cited in Knapp) has concluded that an **Aryan society had existed in Mesopotamia** as far back as **3100 BC**. No western material has been found either in Indus sites or on Indus seals, and the rise of Gulf sites appears to coincide with the rise of the Indus cities.

Afghanistan (Sanskrit Upgan+Sthan meaning the land of compatriots) is mentioned in literature as **Aryana** whose borders are defined in Avesta and which stands for 'the land of Aryans'. **Buddhism reached Afghanistan** under Ashoka (ruled 273-232 BC) and became a great center for the spread of Shakiyamuni Buddha. Gondophanes took over the Kabul valley, Punjab and Sindh from the Indo-Scythian Kings and founded a capital at Taxila. Luv and Taksh (sons of Rama and Bharat in Ramayana) of Ayodhya dynasty are said to have founded the cities of Lahore (Luvpur) and Takshshila (Taxila), respectively. During his reign, Afghanistan was famous for Akhal-Teke horse farms, hanging gardens, complex irrigation systems, pools and ponds, huge palaces and temples, massive statues carved out of rocks and so forth, based upon Vedic-Hindu motifs, so confirmed by Arab chroniclers in Mohammad Kasim's, laid to waste by marauding Islamic hordes. The largest deposit of ancient coins was accidentally discovered in Afghanistan, about 55,000 specimens in gold silver and bronze.

Bamiyan, 240 kilometers northwest of Kabul, Afghanistan became one of the greatest Buddhist monastic communities in all Central Asia by the

4th century CE. The two standing Buddhas, 38 and 53 m high, were destroyed by the Taliban regime in March 2001. Bamiyan was described thus by Yakut in his geographical dictionary in 1218 CE:

"There one sees a structure of an elevation prodigious in height; it is supported by gigantic pillars and covered with paintings of all the birds created by God. In the interior are two immense idols carved in the rock and rising from the foot of the mountains to the summit....One cannot see anything comparable to these statues in the whole world."

Other important centers of Buddhist learning included **Balkh** housing in 7th CE some 100 Buddhist monasteries and about 3,000 monks in Balk̲, the capital of Tokharistan, Novasangharama (**Nava Vihara**) monastery, **Hadda** (ancient Nagarāhāra), near modern Jalālābād, **Kara Tepe** and **Fayaz Tepe** in Uzbekistan and Tajikistan, northern **Khotan** (Sanskrit Goshana), **Yarkand**, and **Penjikent** area of Sogdiana. By the 7th century all of the small kingdoms of the Tarim region had been entirely won over to Buddhism and Sanskrit but by the 11th CE all of that was destroyed by the peace loving sword of Islamicized Arabs. In the Steppes, Buddhism had penetrated Hun strongholds as early as the 2nd century BC. Kublai Khan clearly showed his preference for Buddhism even though most of the Mongol kingdoms had converted to Islam. Some of the Turkish emperors were foremost patrons of Buddhism who introduced a humane legislation and commissioned Buddhist Longmen caves, south of Loyang. However, in 515 CE Mihirakula suppressed Buddhism, destroyed monasteries and killed many monks throughout northwestern India, Gandhara, and especially Kashmir.

Khotan became the largest center of **Iranian Buddhism** and possessed a considerable number of Buddhist Sanskrit works from Bharat that were later on passed on to China. Persian poetry has preserved the word *bot* or Buddha, meaning 'idol, beauty, and the beloved'; other Buddhist traces can be found in the literature, art, and culture of the Islamicized Iranians. Balkh had been the birthplace of Zoroaster ca. 600 BC and venerated fire that had been central to Vedic creation and sacrifice. Ahura Mazda was totally avoided and substituted by Indra-Adbog, but Manichaeism was present.Mithraism of Vedic origin was also wide spread over Iran, Egypt and Europe. **Mithra** was a **Vedic Sun god** whose **birthday** was celebrated on **25 December** which later became the **birthday of Jesus**. Mithraism was definitely the principal religion in Europe when Christianity was absorbing the masses. Consequently, ethical monotheism of Judo-Christians originated in Hinduism.

MahaBharat mentions that **of the five descendants of Yayati two became Yavanas**, suggesting a westward emigration in the aftermath of the Battle of Ten Kings around 1900 BC. Linguistics has shown clear linkage between India and the Middle East, well tabulated by Matlock. The Mitanni, who worshiped Vedic gods and spoke a Vedic dialect, ruled an Indic kingdom in the region of Mesopotamia, Syria and Palestine around 1400 BC. **Mitanni were Vedic** and not Iranian because Indra, Mitra, Varuna, Vayu, Svar, Soma, Rta, Vasus and Nasatya are Vedic deities, not Iranian. A text by a Mitanni named Kikkuli uses words such as *aika (eka, one), tera (tri, three), panza (panca, five), satta (sapta, seven), na (nava, nine), vartana (vartana)*. Another text mentions *babru* (babhru, brown), parita (palita, grey), and *pinkara* (pingala, red). Over fifty years ago, R.T. O'Callaghan and W.F. Albright published in *Analecta Orientalia* of Rome a list of 81 names (13 from the Mitanni, 23 from the Nuzi, and 45 from the Syrian documents) with Indic etymologies. The initial *s* is maintained and the group *sv* is represented by the similar sounding *sw* and not the Avestan *aspo*; the initial *v* **is replaced by** *b*, while medial *v* **becomes** the semivowel *w*; *pt* transforms into *tt*, as in *sapta* becoming *satta*.

The word *sthan* or place stems from Sanskrit and a string of countries to the West of India carry this suffix. Jalalabad was earlier called *Nagarhara* or the town of Lord Shiva and **Karachi** was the Hindu city of *Debal* or *Devalaya*. Rai supports Biblical statement that Ophir and his progeny populated all of Mesopotamia and parts of India. Godfrey Higgins in *Anacalypsis* proved the **Indian origin of Jews** but it was suppressed by religious bigots in Europe and England. The Syrian writer, Zenob Glak, wrote of a Hindu community, complete with its own religious temples, on the upper Euphrates River in modern-day Turkey to the west of Lake Van in the second century BCE, and the Greek ex-patriot, Dion Chrysostemos (40–112 CE), wrote of a similar community in Alexandria. Archeological remains of Buddhist settlements have been found as far as the south of Baghdad, the lower Euphrates at Kufah, the eastern Iranian coast at Zir Rah, and at the mouth of the Gulf of Aden on the island of Socotra. So it is not the Muslims who introduced the **arch and dome** to India but **the Vedic Hindus who introduced them to Persia**.

The name **Persia** is derived from the **Sanskrit** *Parasu* who had overrun Persia and named it *Paarasika*. In fact, Iranians (Persians) are Zoroastrians who worshipped Ahura Mazda derived from Maha Rishi Shukracharya. Even the word Iran or Ariana means 'The Land of Aryans". The name Shah, taken up by the Pehlavi dynasty, is Vedic and also occurs in Nepal. **Bhrigus** were **Iranian priests** and their animosity with the Vedic seers is preserved in the **inversion of relationship** between Devas and

Asuras in Avesta. Talageri concludes that the Bhrigus were initially located in Punjab and Afghanistan but were driven out to Iran and Central Asia following the Battle of Ten Kings and later by hostilities in their new homeland of Afghanistan. The name **Rama appears in Avesta** as well.

Besides the Vedic-speaking Mitanni in West Asia, many of the early Mesopotamian rulers are mentioned in Indian mythology: Assurbanipal = Asura Bana; Semi Ramais = Sami Rama; Nimrod (the builder of the Tower of Babylon) = Nami Rud; Asshur = Asura; Na Rama-Sin = Nara Simha. Shri is derived from Suriya or Suri. The wandering monks and sea traders carried Buddhist and Vedic message to enlighten the whole area and a big Hindu community lived at Alexandria in Egypt while Iran has ruins of many Hindu temples. Monotheism of the Upanishadic literature reached Judaism, as well as Akhenaton of Egypt (1350 BC), and influenced Zarathustra.

Farther West, **Baghdad** is derived from Sanskrit *Bhagwad* or *Bhagwat nagar* until it was captured by the Muslim hordes. The **Kassaites** were a **Vedic people** who ruled for 500 years after the fall of the Hammurabi Empire and worshipped Vedic deities like Indra, Maruts and Surya in Western Iran as far back as 1800 BC. The name **Israel** is derived from **Sanskrit *Ishwaralaya*** which means the abode of Krishna whereas **Jerusalem** is derived from *Yerushaleim* or **Sanskrit *Yedu-Ishlayam*** which signifies a township of Lord Krishna. Gaza strip boasts of the city of Ramallah or the city of Lord Rama while the Jordan River derives its name from Sanskrit *Janardan*, another name for Krishna. **Palestine** gets its name from the **Vedic sage Pulestin** who lived there. Ramayana fragments have also been found in Uighur while an ancient Vishnu Idol has been excavated in Russia; recent archeological find in Kuwait unearthed a gold-plated statue of Ganesha. At the turn of the 19th century, sensational new finds from Central Asia (Eastern Turkemanistan) revealed Buddhist manuscripts now housed at the Institute of Oriental Studies at Leningrad as S. F. Oldenberg collection (27 items), N.N. Krotkov collection (some 100 items), and N.F. Petrovsky collection (582 items), and eight other smaller collections.

Arabia was known as *Arbasthan* from **Sanskrit *Arvasthan*** or the land of horses, inhabited by the Cushites and Semites. **Shem** is derived from *Shyam*, another name for Krishna, and Cusha or Kush was the son of Rama. A poem by Labi-bin-e Akhta-bin-e Turfa, who lived in Arabia around 1850 BC, pays devout tribute to the Vedas, (cited in Knapp):

"Oh, the divine land of Hindu, very blessed art thou! Because thou art the chosen of God blessed with knowledge. That celestial knowledge which like four lighthouses shown in such brilliance, through the (utterances of) Indian sages in four fold abundance. God enjoins on all humans, follow with hands

down the path of Vedas with His divine percept lay down. Bursting with divine knowledge are Sama and Yajur bestowed on creation, Hence brothers respect and follow the Vedas, guides to salvation. Two others, the Rig and Athar teach us fraternity, sheltering under their luster dispels darkness till eternity".

Another poem was written by Jirrham Bontoi, who lived 165 years before the prophet Muhammad, where he glorifies the reign of King Vikramaditya of Ujjain (Avantika), some 500 years before the prophet, translated into English as follows (cited in Knapp):

"Fortunate are those who were born (and lived) during King Vikram's reign. He was a noble, generous, dutiful ruler devoted to the welfare of his subjects. But at that time we Arabs, oblivious of divinity, were lost in sensual pleasures. Plotting and torture were Ramapant (amongst us). The darkness of ignorance had enveloped our country. Like the lamb struggling for its life in the cruel paws of a wolf, we Arabs were gripped by ignorance. The whole country was enveloped in a darkness as intense as on a New Moon night. But the present dawn and pleasant sunshine of education is the result of the favor of that noble king Vikram whose benevolence did not lose sight of us foreigners as we were. He spread his sacred culture amongst us and sent scholars from his own land whose brilliance shown like that of the sun in our country. These scholars and preceptors through whose benevolence we were once again made cognizant of the presence of God, introduced to his sacred knowledge, and put on the road to truth, had come to our country to initiate us in that culture and impart education".

These poems were inscribed on gold plate to be hung inside the Kaaba shrine and explain the almost identical tenets of Ayurveda and Yunani systems of medicine. The word **Mecca** is derived from **Sanskrit *Makha*** meaning fire worship or sacrificial fire but could also stand for Makka, a shortened version of Mahadeva or Shiva. The Black Stone (Sangay Aswad) in the Kaaba is really a **Shiva lingam**. Muslim pilgrims go around the Kaaba seven times, as in Vedic traditions such as marriages. Bakri-Id was initially a day set aside for revering the cows which are sacred to the Hindus, but now the Muslims have perverted the holiday and slaughter the cow for Id.

The city of **Petra** derives its name from the Sanskrit *Prastar* meaning stone and the name of its Temple El Dair is derived from the Sanskrit *Devalaya*. Oak has pointed out that the Arabs obliterated their own past history by destroying images and records, and by deliberate **falsifications of Sanskrit names**. The rediscovery of surviving Vedic accomplishments are then presented as Islamic. With the decimation of non-Muslims, only Muslims will be left to praise themselves in a mind controlled society.

British Lt. Col. Francis Wilford was certain that peoples from ancient Bharat colonized and settled in what is now Egypt. The name **Egypt** comes from **Sanskrit *Ajap* or *Ajapati***, the grandfather of Lord Rama, a name that was adapted by Egyptian ruling dynasties such as **Ramases** I and II. In another tradition, the history of Egypt dates back to Yayati whose descendant Puru founded the Purvas or Pharahos of Egypt. **Yayati was deified as Yahweh** by the descendants of his elder son **Yadu** whose progeny became **Yadus or Jews**. Of the other sons of Yayati, Druhya became French Druid, Anu went on to become the head of Anatolis, while Turvasu became the king of Turanians north of the Black Sea. Menes is Manasyu, the grandson of Puru, known as Manis or Manas in Mesopotamia and some Indus seals refer to Puru and Manis as rulers of the area Egypt-Mesopotamia whereas. Aryan **King Ikshvaku of Ayodhya**, who had started the solar dynasty, became **Osiris in Egypt**. This genealogy was later hijacked by the Aryan Invasionists to reflect nothing more than Biblical events. DNA from King Tut and other Pharaohs shows 99.6% identity with the Celts who were Vedic. Count Biornsttierna in his book *The Theogony of the Hindus* informs us about the Vedic culture in ancient Egypt:

"It is testified by Herodotus, Plato, Salon, Pythagorus and Philostratus that the religion of Egypt proceeded from India…The chronicles found in the temples of Abydos and Sais and which have been transmitted by Josephus, Julius, and Eusebius, all testify that the religious system of the Egyptian proceeded from India…We have Hindu chronologies (besides those of the Puranas concerning the Yugas) which go still farther back in time than the Table of Egyptian Kings according to Manteho".

Professor Brugsch agrees (Cited in Knapp):

"According to their own records the Egyptians came from a mysterious land (now known to lie on the shores of the Indian Ocean)".

These explain the **sudden rise** in **Egyptian civilization**, for which there are no historical or archeological records. Brugsch continues:

"We have a right to more than suspect that India, eight thousand years ago, sent a colony of emigrants who carried their arts and high civilization into what is now known to us as Egypt".

A report in Nava Bharat Times (18 April 1967) says that excavations of an Egyptian **Pyramid** 3000 BC revealed a famous **verse from Bhagavada Gita** (2.22): *vasamsi jirnani yatha vhiaya,* meaning:

"As a person puts on new garments, giving up the old ones, the soul similarly accepts new material bodies, giving up the old and useless ones".

In fact, most of the Biblical place names denote Indian exports to the Middle East e.g. Samaria, Judah, Bethpe or, Moab, Cush, Haran, Midian, Galilee, Ashkenaz, Terah etc. Jerusalem was founded by Indians, Hitties were a ruling clan in Bharat.

"Thus saith the Lord God unto Jerusalem, thy birth and thy nativity is the land of Canaan; thy father was an Amorite and thy mother an Hittie" (Ezekiel 16:1-3);.

Max Muller had observed that the mythology of Egyptians (and also that of Assyrians and Greeks) is wholly founded on Vedic traditions including the cult of Re whereas the Egyptian sun-god **Ra is derived from Sanskrit Ravi** while **Horus is derived from Hari** (Vishnu or Krishna). The creator-god Ptah rides a bull, just like Lord Shiva and is derived from Sanskrit Pitta, while Seb comes from Shib or Shiva. Shesh naga is believed to maintain the harmony of planets in Bharat and a cobra was to be found in the crown of the Pharaoh's. The river **Nile**, now called the Blue Nile, bears a **Sanskrit** name ***Neel*** or blue associated with the divinity like the hue of Krishna. Although the later Egyptian historians were to **remove all mention of Vedic sources** a centrifugal diffusion of Vedic culture from Bharat is obvious.

In Egypt, the Old Kingdom, the pyramids and the reign of Imhotep are dated 2900 BC, contemporary with the rise of Sumer and Akkad cultures in Mesopotamia, in between the early Harappa period around 3000 BC and the mature phase 2600 BC. The Egyptian Middle Kingdom (2050 BC) preceded by 100 years the rise of Babylonia 1950 BC while Zoroaster appeared 1900 BC, as Harappa declined and Sarasvati dried up. Greece enters history only with Pythagoras in 600 BC and Hellenistic Greece was founded 400 BC. Thus, only the Australian native culture is perhaps as old as the Vedic civilization.

Amenhotep III had a Mitanni mother Tiye, the daughter of the Mitanni king Artatama, who gave birth to Akhenaten or **Amenhotep IV**. The latter married Nefertiti, the daughter of Tiye's brother Ay **crowned as King Dashratta** (the name resembles the father of Rama). So the Egyptian 18th dynasty had obvious Vedic ancestry. The thought of an afterlife dominated the Egyptian psyche, much as it did in ancient Bharat and continues to the present day. The Pyramids were constructed in such a manner as to allow the rebirth of Pharaoh in the Orion where he would become immortal after union with Osiris. The **Great Pyramid of Giza** was built after much advanced mathematical calculations detailed only in the *Sulbashastras* in Bharat for the construction of Vedic altars. The step pyramid at Sakkara was designed like the pyramid-shaped *shamsana-cit* described in Baudhyana sulbha.

V. When Bharat Ruled the Americas

According to one legend, around 4000 BC, the **Vedic King Nahusha** is believed to have gone on a civilizing mission around the globe, possibly from the port of **Ramara in Gujarat**. The Nashua myth was to be found around the globe and became transformed to Dionysius in Greece. America, variously known as *amaraka or patala in Sanskrit*, is repeatedly mentioned in various Puranas, Ramayana and MahaBharat. When Nagas from Bharat arrived in Arizona, they found a huge stone peak that they named *Babu-Kheever,* resembling Kailasha, to honor their original and illustrious ancestor Kuvera. The Brazilian nuclear physicist Arysio Nunes dos Santos, at the Federal University of Minas Gerais, holds that the **Dravidians had colonized a vast region of South America** 11,000 years before the Europeans reached the New World, before the Ramayana period 7300 BC. Dr. P.V. Vartak mentions that Bali went to South America in 17,000 BC when the vernal equinox was at *Moola Nakshatra*.

"What is called the discovery of America is the meeting of two great currents of races of peoples, who, after a separation extending over many centuries, were again joined after going right around the earth...Those who first arrived on the continent later to be known as America were groups of men driven by that mighty current that set out from India towards the east."

Mazumdar concludes (cited in Matlock):

*"Hindu intercourse with America is still perhaps a startling point to many... bold **Hindu mariners had early circumnavigated the earth**, visiting foreign lands in every continent...Hindu knowledge of the roundness of earth, her vastness, her seven continents and seven oceans, 49 big islands, ocean currents, submarine volcanoes abounding in the Pacific etc., leave no doubt of the Hindu knowledge of, and intercourse with, America...The two*

prominent ports of North India were Broach in the west and Tamluk in the east…Vessels set sail from here to Ceylon, Eastern Archipelago, Islands of the Pacific, China, Japan etc."

Pococke opines that **Mexico** derived its name from **Makshika**, a mineral like gold. The parallels between the Brahma-Vishnu-Shiva trinity and the Mexican Ho-Huitzillopochtli-Tlaloc trinity are impressive where Shiva was worshipped as Chalma. Pococke believes that the city of Tjuana in Mexico got its name from Tehuana Cochimiri in Kashmir that was the seat of Hindu-Buddhist culture. The Mexican Eagle is actually a modified Garuda. The dishes Tamale and Corundas came from Tamil heartland. Matlock lists many similarities between Meso-Americans and Vedic Bharat whereas Sir William Jones observed that Peruvian **Rama Sitoa** festival recalls Hindu penetration of SE Asia by Rama. Chon remarks: *"The harvest festival of the Inca people is called Ramasitova (Rama is the plough and Sita the land)".* The first ruler of Mexico was a vassal of Angakaraka Sri Arya Manasa Tapa, the first ruler of Peru.

Cahitan and O'odham tribes in Northern Mexico worshipped two well know Hindu deities, Variseva and Vairubi, who were to beget all humanity. Variseva means Vira Shiva (Lord Shiva) in Sanskrit and Vairubi is simply Bhairavi or Durga, the consort of Shiva. The Spaniards also recorded that *Ahom*, cousins of O'odham, derived from the sacred AUM (OM), came from Assam. Ribas further explained that Northern Mexican natives worshipped *shiva lingum* as of the uniting mission of a **high priest called Shiva** who left Afghanistan for Arizona some 3000 BC, as per Matlock. The Huicholes in Central Mexico even remember the port in Gujarat from where they sailed for America whereas the Apaches worship Shiva as *Yusn* and natural forces like Diyi (Aditi). The Zunis worship **Shivani** and **Shiwanikoya** and could hail from Kerala; their King Azi Dahaka is shown wearing snakes around his neck.

The four Mexican icons known as The Vatican Codex correspond to the four Buddhist hells or purgatories whereas the Mexican doctrine of World Ages is reminiscent of Bharat *yugas;* the first age is exactly the same in both systems and totals up to 4800 divine years. Aztec pantheon of gods is very similar to the Vedic pantheon. The word OM, betel, coca and tobacco chewing, as well as the gourd container for lime, are common to people from Bharat and America. Tortilla (roti), vegetarianism, shell money, containers with curvilinear design, poisoned fish hooks, agricultural terraces, linguistics, the Aztec game *patolli* and Bharat *pachisi*, are also some of the common features. Evidence of sun and moon worship is plentiful in Mexico, thus linking them to the Asiatic branch of the Aryans.

Bhikshu Chamanlal (cited in Knapp) has shown that the **pre-Spanish rulers** of the Americas were of **Vedic origin**. The Inca ruler of Peru was Ayarmancotopa and his edicts in Mayan script carry Kannada-telugu titles at a place called Piedros Negros. The Inca ruler Atahuallpa carried a *kumkum* mark on his forehead (National Geographic December 1973) as in the Vedic-Hindu tradition. The words Aztec, Tezuco and Nahuatl are corrupted forms of *Astika, Talshaka,* and *Nahushadala* of the Naga tribes in India. They were forced out of Bharat as they practiced human sacrifice which was contrary to the Vedic tradition and which continued to be practiced in the Americas. **Surinam** derived from **Suri (Krishna)**. Apara Goyana has been described thus:

"When the sun rises in Jambudvipa, it is the middle watch of the night in Apara Goyana; sunset in Apara Goyana is midnight in Jambudvipa and sunrise is noon…" (cited in Matlock).

Guatemala is named after Buddha from Guatama-than or the land of Gautama but it could also stem from Sanskrit *Guadhaamala*. Mayas included Rama and Lenca tribes. Apaches call themselves Inde while the Incas use the words Inde and Inte. The Quecha tribe in Arizona carries names derived from Sanskrit e.g. Yuman (Yamuna) and Cushans (Kashi); Uto or Yuutaah derives from Sanskrit Yuti or Yutiya who were known as Yadus, Yadavas, and the like; Yaiowa the Creator God was later transformed into Jehovah, while Yadu was converted to Yahudi or Jews (Matlock). The Acoma natives of America have retained many Sanskrit names e.g. Akh (Sky), Koh (Mountain), Maha (great), Masewi (Shiva) and Ojuyewi (Jew-Yahweh). A number of Navajo deities, Cherokees customs and Yute natives of Utah exhibit similarities to Sanskrit names. **Belize** derives from Bal-Isha and Baleshwar (Shiva) with obvious links to Hebrew Baal (God), Assyrian and Mesopotamian Belusha or Belus.

The first **Maya** empire in Guatemala was evident as early as 700 BC but zenith of Maya civilization was reached at a time when Bharat also had attained an acme of culture during the Gupta period. They both calculated the length of one year as 365.2420 (Gregorian = 365.2425) which ran concurrently with a practical year of 18 months of 20 days and an additional month of only 5 days, all of which were given names. The astronomical symbols and methods for reckoning time in Mexico and Peru are identical with symbols and methods in Asia. The Mayas of Yucatan were the first besides Bharat people to use a zero sign but the expressions of the principle are dissimilar. The Mayan wise man called Maya, Mayasura or Maya Danava, was the leader in astronomy and navigation, as in Sanskrit

Suryasiddhanta that describes events as far back as 50,000 BC. An arch, called the Gateway to the Sun, at the Bolivian Site of Tiahuanaco, was used as an astronomical observatory. Mayan historical records were destroyed by the Spanish but their collective memory indicates *immigration from Greater Bharat some 20,000 years ago* and Vedic Mayasura reached Americas at that time. Mayan memory speaks of Shrilanka as their place of origin and their vocabulary is derived from Sanskrit. Pablo Jose de Arriaga, the head of Jesuit College in Peru, in almost unparalleled fanaticism, caused the destruction of all Inca state archives, codes of law, temples archives. Poindexter concludes:

"The unmistakable relationship of language, religion, architecture and art of prehistoric Aztec, Mayan and Inca peoples with various cultures of Asia, Europe and Africa can be reasonably explained by the hypothesis of the evolution of all from a common seed stock in Asia, spreading by various migrations in different epochs to the four quarters of the earth...A careful observation of the American Indian makes obvious his Asiatic origins. There is no doubt there were other infusions of blood, but the resemblance of the Indians of the northwest coast of America to the various tribes and nations of eastern Asia is so great that when they are placed under similar conditions as to dress, occupation, and exposure to the sun, it is difficult to distinguish one from the other. With due allowance for the vast range of conditions such as climate, mode of life, and means of subsistence, which have been constantly operating throughout untold ages to produce divergences and specialization of type, the same general similarity exists throughout the continent .

Shri V. Ganapati Sthapati underlines the similarity between stones used for Vedic constructions and Mayan sites built along the tenets of **Vastu Shastra**. The staircase leading to the *sancto sanctorum* at Angkor is almost identical to the pyramids of the Mayan city of Tikal where Temple 5 is also almost identical to the Ranchipuram temple in Tamil Nadu. Mayan sculptures in the pyramid temple of Pieadras Negras in Guatemala are like the Jataka bas-relief of Borobudur stupa in Central java. The lotus motif, interspersed with seated human figures, which has a deep symbolic meaning in Hindu and Buddhist mythologies, is found at Chichen Itza and resembles most closely with that of Amravati.

Hindu goddess Maya, the 'cosmic illusion', appears in the theology of Yucatan and Mexico under the same name performing the same functions. Poindexter underlines the joint family in Inca and Hindu societies and some other customs such as the dice games. **Swastika** is common in relics found in Arizona, Illinois, Ohio, Tennessee, Mississippi, Navajo and Hopi of New Mexico although race supremacists believe that it may have originated in

Greece. The Swastika also appears in Jewish and Celtic traditions. Poindexter concludes:

"*There is nothing strange in the fact that much of the religious mythology of the Mexicans and Peruvians was undoubtedly of Asiatic origin when it is considered that **all of our own religions come from Asia**...Both the Inca and Maya civilizations, even their languages, had much in common with our own, inherited from the same common, Far Eastern cradle-land of the race... **America** in race and culture was **but an extension of Asia,** and it is said that in pre-glacial times it was geographically so... The name Asia itself appears on the Peruvian coast south of Lim*".

Sorensen details plants, diseases, and animals from America that found their way around the globe before 1492 CE. Frank Joseph describes sustained contact between the Old and New Worlds leading to cultural splendor, political might, and incredibly advanced technology. North America's first civilization, the Adena, was founded by ancient Kelts with possible links between Hopewell Mound Builders and prehistoric Japanese seafarers. Gleaming stone pyramids stood amid smoking **iron foundries** from the Atlantic seaboard to the Mississippi River. Across from today's St. Louis, Missouri, Paul Schrag in his book mentions a walled city more populous than London one thousand years ago, with a pyramid larger, at its base, than the Great Pyramid of Egypt. During the 12th century, hydraulic engineers had laid out a massive irrigation network spanning the American Southwest and built a **five-mile-wide dam** from ten million cubic yards of rock, as in Bharat (Chapter 5.III). While Europe stumbled through the Dark Ages, a metropolis of weirdly shaped, multistory superstructures, precisely aligned to the sun and moon, sprawled across the New Mexico Desert. Other discoveries include archaeological proof of **giants**, the **fountain of youth**, and descriptions from Lewis's journals of a tribe of 'nearly white, blue-eyed' Indians. **Meriwether Lewis was murdered** to keep it all secret through a conspiracy hatched by the Smithsonian Institute in Washington, DC, and powerful vested interests run by US Secret Societies. A **vast network of tunnels** was believed to connect ancient Bharat to The Tunnel of the Incas in South America Geldern and Ekholm (quoted in Singhal) conclude:

"*The large number of highly specific correspondences in so many fields preclude any possibility of mere coincidental coincidence*".

Hopis came to America from Shipabu (Shiva-Bhu or Mt Meru) in North India, along with the Navajo, Supai, Paiute, Apache, Ute, Heheya and others sometime around 700-1000 CE to escape forced conversions under Islam, possibly through the port of Chetumal. Along the Hopi vertebral column were several vibratory centers which echoed the primordial sound of life throughout the universe, much like the eastern chakras. Zunis claim to have lived in a land called Itiwana in South India. Yaquis or Yeome could stem from Sanskrit Yah-am. New Mexico natives known as Taos trace their ancient ancestry to Indian Taos or Dyaus. Matlock concludes:

"All Native Americans, as well as the rest of us, must accept the truth that until we admit our 'India-Indian' ancestry, we are going nowhere".

The **Spaniards created an utterly distorted image** of the American past by stressing human sacrifice and homosexuality.

The Chimus of north Peru maintained the phallic cult of Shiva and the serpent is also sacred to them. Among the ruins of the Mayan city of Copan in Honduras are seen two elephant heads with mahouts wearing Hindu turbans, dated circa 900 BC. At the entrance to the ruins stands a large eagle, or Garuda in Sanskrit. In Mayan and Mexican codices and hieroglyphic reliefs, there are numerous representations of the elephant-headed god of rain, called *Chac* by the Mayas, and *Tlaloc* in Central Mexico, resembling *Indra*. Incas also had a 7.5 meter tall image of Ganesha. The name *Maya* itself is Sanskrit and their place of origin is Shivalva, later changed to Spanish Xibalba. The dwarf, hunch back god is frequently found among the burial *huacas* of Colombia and Peru. A falcon god is common to the Incas, the Garuda of Vishnu, and to the tribes of Peru. The *Makara*, a mythical sea monster with fish like bodies and elephant like trunks, was represented in various combinations in the Americas. Dr. E. Smith (quoted in Poindexter) observed:

"Nowhere is the derivation of American culture from Asia more obtrusively displayed than in the representation of men or gods emerging from the gaping mouth of some mythical monster analogous to the naga or makara of the Old World".

Diploid Bharat cotton has been found **in Peru** dated 2500 BC and in **Mexico** even earlier. Pre-Inca cotton goods include cotton garments along with instruments for weaving and spinning. Maize (*Zea mays*) is widely distributed in Asia and Africa, as also in pre-Columbian America; the sweet potato *Ipomoea batatas* was also cultivated both in Asia and Central America long before Columbus. Egyptian mummies have been found to contain traces of cocaine and nicotine although both are indigenous only to the Americas. Similarly, the parrot is genetically American but is also found in India and Polynesia. All these suggest **sea-borne commerce between Bharat and the Americas** via Polynesia, in keeping with the advanced ship building technology of the Vedic Aryans (Chapter 5.V)). Dr. Veny Goplacharya has shown that hundreds of words in various American languages are related to Tamil, Kannada and Sanskrit and tabulated in detail by Matlock. Denison observed:

*"The white man has always considered the (American) Indian as belonging to an inferior race, and has in consequence been somewhat indifferent to his language and his civilization. To a majority of the white race, the **Indian was once but little more than a wild beast to be robbed or killed at the pleasure** of his more elevated and civilized brother. His language was popularly supposed to consist of a series of grunts and exclamations, pieced out with gesticulations, a barbarous jargon without nicety of structure, or the power of expression and continuity of thought".*

Yet, the complexity of the barbaric language of the savages was used by white superiors for sending coded messages during WWII as it could not be decoded by the Germans.

Many languages spoken in the vast expanse of the Americas are all philologically related. Sanskrit is a highly inflective language yet capable of producing agglutinative combinations that form whole sentences. The North American languages are primarily agglutinative with little or no inflection and are thus related to the Siberian dialects. The Hopi language is especially rich in North Indian place names e.g. Homol'ovi (Himalaya), Hemis like the monastery in Tibet, and Neem-an (religious observance). The vocabulary of the **Mexican language Nauatl is pure Aryan**, Nauatl is closely related to Old Persian and Sanskrit. Similarly, Maya language and culture point to a common origin in Asia and possibly Peru. Denison concludes:

*"We must dismiss all notions that the Nahua developed an indigenous civilization on American soil despite assertions to that effect by prominent writers. They distinctly **inherited the old Aryan culture**...They may be classed with Vedic Hindus and the Greeks of the Homeric era".*

VI. Bharat Influence in Africa

Africa is mentioned as *Kushadvipa*, or the land of Kusha grass, that was part of the Empire of Rama and under the administration of **Rama's son Kush**. The Africans refer to themselves as Cushites where Rama is transformed into Ham. **Mauritius** derives its name from **Marichas** who was one of the generals in the army of Ravana defeated by **Rama (Ham).** Africa was also known as *Shankhadvipa* meaning the land like a conch shell, suggesting that the Vedic rulers were familiar with the shape of Africa as seen from miles above the earth. **Abyssinia** gets its name **from *App-Sindhu*** meaning waters of the Sindhu River where people from the Indus region had settled. **Somalia** is connected with **Soma** whose people worshipped the moon. **Tanganyika** (from **Sanskrit Tung Nayak** or the great leader) and Zanzibar later merged to become Tanzania. The port city Dar-es-Salaam is the Sanskrit Dwar-eeshalayam meaning 'Gateway to the Temple of God'. Philostratus had concluded that Ethiopians were an Indian race, forced to leave India for killing a monarch. Eusebius also concluded that the early **Ethiopians emigrated from the river Indus** and first settled in the vicinity of Egypt. **Lava**, the son of Rama, had a region named after him called **Laviya or Libya.** The African Swahili language and other local dialects retain remnants of Sanskrit; **Swahili *simba* is Sanskrit *simha* for lion**. African religions preserve many customs of their Vedic past such as divination, a Supreme Being or Supreme Creator, dancing, feasting, personification of natural forces as celestial spirits, and belief in a sort of karma for righteous life.

VII. Islamic Arabs Usurp Vedic Patrimony

By the time of the Christian era, ancient Bharat had become the only beacon of wisdom, knowledge, wealth, plenty, tolerance, personal freedom, and so forth. By contrast, Europe had remained mired in illiteracy, misery, hunger, disease, filth, superstition, magic, intolerance, privation and so forth where prayer to the divine was the only hope and escape. Armed with Qur'an in one hand and sword in the other, the nomadic tribes from Arabia desert were an illiterate lot and expropriated the clothing, dress, philosophy, science and arts of countries they invaded. Abbasid Caliphs initially **destroyed the lives, culture and books** of civilizations they had defeated but later (cited in Duncan):

"Seized on the clothing, dress, architecture, philosophy, literature – and science – of the Persian, Greeks and Indians they ruled…In 773, some two hundred years after Aryabhata's death, a delegation of diplomats from lower Indus River valley arrived in the new Arab capital of Baghdad…This particular delegation brought with them an astronomer…Kanaka. An expert on eclipse he carried with him a small library of Indian astronomical texts to

give to Caliph…the Caliph was amazed by the knowledge in Indian texts"

Stunned by the brilliance of Vedic Hindu ideation, the caliph ordered the translation of these astronomical texts, *Suryasiddhanta, Brhamasiddhanta* and *Khandakhadyaka,* into the *Great Sindhind* which was later translated into Latin in 1126 CE. The foundation of Arabic literature was laid only between 750-850 CE where everything is foreign. The Perso-Sassanian language was adopted officially as Arabic nomads did not have one of their own. Abbasid Caliphate under al-Mansur (745-775 CE) built a **House of Wisdom** to house manuscripts from around the world while Harun-al Rashid (786-809 CE) and his son al-Mamun (809-833 CE) invited scholars from India; Greek scholars also found refuge there after the closure of Plato's Academy in 529 CE. In part, this was necessitated by the practical needs of Islam to calculate the correct direction to Mecca, to solve the problems of inheritance under Islamic law, to calculate the beginning and the end of Ramadan, as well as for the floral Islamic art. The originals in Sanskrit and Prakrit were translated into Persian, then into Arabic, and finally into Latin.

Musa al-Khwarizmi (780-850) led three scientific expeditions to Bharat and translated Sanskrit texts on Logarithm, Algebra, Zero Trigonometry and positional notation all of which were translated into Latin as *Algoritmi de numero Indorum, Rasum al-Hind* (*Hindu Arithmetic*) and the like. The elimination of Bharat connection lead to 'Arabs using Arabic numerals'. Astronomy got started only in 771 CE after Siddhanta was translated whereas European science took off only in 1202 CE, thanks to Vedic-Hindu numerals and zero published by Leonardo Fibonacci of Pisa. Thus, Bharat played a determining role in the development of astronomical sciences around the world. Tang dynasty records show that as of 600 CE on Bharat astronomers were teaching astronomy in the Arab world.

Al-Biruni (973-1048 CE) went to India with the invading army of Mahmoud Ghaznawi and learned Sanskrit; his book *Kitab-il-Hind* was later translated into Latin as *Indica*. He recorded that the Hindus knew that the length of day varied according to the latitude and were aware of the existence of America which they variously called Siddhapura or Potala. Alexandrian scientists had earlier used the Babylonian sexagesimal system but Vedic-Hindu numerals had reached Alexandria by 500 BC. As Ibn Sina (987-1037 CE) was taught 'Indian calculation' by a vegetable vendor as Indian numeration was in popular use from Central Asia to Egypt and North Africa. The Arabs **altered the appearance** of Hindu symbols to be read from *right to left*, as described by Georges Ifrah. Sanskrit texts books on medicine, pharmacology, toxicology, philosophy, astrology, snakes (*sarpavidya*), poison (*vishavidya*), auguring and talisman, veterinary science, logic, ethics, politics, and the science of war etc. were all translated into Arabic by the Vedic-Hindu scholars at translation centers in Damascus, Spain, Palermo and Sicily.

To usurp non-Greek knowledge, Greek sounding names were invented by Latin translators of Arabic texts just as Sanskrit names were changed into Arabic by Arabs who had manipulated Sanskrit names, as the **Bible is culturally and scientifically barren**. Al-Biruni notes that the name *Aryabhata* was changed to *Arjbhad* and later to *Azjabhar* (Al-jabbar) so "*Hindus will not recognize it*". Copies of Latin translations were sent to universities in Bologna and Paris. Plotinus (204-270 CE) studied philosophy in Iran and Bharat in 242 CE:

"His ideas became the hallmark of Christian mystics for centuries after…Plotinus mapped out a world of experience beyond the bounds of sense reality, compared to which the normal world was illusory…Plotinus' version of ecstasy agrees with such classical Indian texts as Patanjali's Yoga Sutras which says that a person who can transcend the limits of their body, senses and mind will enter an altered state of ecstatic union with God".

His pupil Porphyry edited the works of Plotinus in fifty four volumes which, after the destruction of Alexandria University, were translated into Latin by Marsilio Ficino in 1492, and back again into Greek by Basel in 1580 CE. Plutarch, an Alexandrian scholar, was definitely influenced by Hindu reincarnation. In *Moralia* he consoles his grieving wife after the death of their two year old daughter:

"*The soul, being eternal, after death is like a caged bird that has been released…the soul will immediately take another body*".

Thanks to exposure to Sanskrit, the Arabic language was, for the very first time, systematized into noun, verb and particle. The simple mosque of Muhammad at Medina became the prototype for subsequent buildings and the mosque at Samarra shows clear Hindu influence. Priyadarshi has summarized it all succinctly:

"*The modern **Western Philosophy has borrowed heavily from India**, first through Pythagoras who influenced Socrates, Plato and Aristotle; Goethe, Schopenhauer and most German philosophers were influenced by Indian philosophy and influenced others in turn. Monism of Fichte and Hegel comes from the Upanishad translations of Anquetil-Duperron. Emerson, Thoreau and Walt Whitman, Carlyle, Richard Jeffries, Edward Carpenter,*

Stephen Zwig, Jung etc. all admitted Indian influence but the list is very long. Existential school as well as the Humanistic school from Nietzsche to Marlow revolves around existence which is not a Western concept at all. Upanishad Dialectics describes things in opposing couples: light and darkness, death and life, non-existence and existence. Human existence has been pictured in a dialectical manner in Hindu literature. Diwali is a festival of light over darkness whereas navratra celebrates good over bad. Rama and Ravana portray the same. Upanishads influenced Zoroaster which in turn influenced Judaism but Semites had non-believers to Satan whose elimination became a religious duty by good believers. Hegel's dialectical theory led Marx to propose dialectical materialism which sees all evolution as conflict between two opposite groups of interests in all ages. Ultimately this dialectics will be resolved in the social existence of communism hence **much of Marx philosophy owes to Indian philosophy**. *Yoga, Pranayama, Meditation, animals rights, religious tolerance, environmental concerns, anti-war movements etc. are entering the Western society more and more. The art of strategy of Nitishastra is now influencing defense services, diplomats and businessmen. Druids in Ireland may be related to Dravids as they share too many customs in common"*. (My emphasis).

VIII. Bharat Civilizes Europe

Europe traces its cultural roots to the Hallstatt and La Tène Celts who were possibly driven out of Bharat around 4000 BC and are known in the Vedic literature as Druhyus, as detailed in my previous books. The decipherment of Meluhha metalwork hieroglyphs (Chapter 5.I) along the Tin Road from Meluhha (Sarasvati-Sindhu doab) to Haifa, Israel, has confirmed contacts between the Indus world and Celts. Reverend Thomas Maurice has observed (cited in Knapp):

"The Asiatic origin of the Druids has long been an acknowledged point in the world of antiquities. Mr. Reuben Barrow, the great practical astronomer of India, was the first person who, after a strict examination and comparison of their mythological superstitions and their periods, directly affirmed them to be **race of Indian philosophers**…*These priests (Druids), Brahmins of India, spread themselves widely through the northern regions of Asia, even to Siberia itself, and gradually mingling with the great body of the Celtic tribes".*

In their native folklore, the supernaturally gifted people who instructed Celts are remembered as the children of Danu which in *Samskritam* means 'flowing water', the daughter of Daksha, wife of kasyapa Muni a goddess of rivers like Danube, Don, Dneiper, Dniestr. According to Irish Lebor Gabála,

Tuatha Dé Danann (or Tuath Dé) represent the main pagan gods who had resided in 'the northern islands of the world' where they were instructed in the magic arts, before finally landing somewhere near Connaught in Ireland. Tuatha De Danann brought with them four treasures viz. The Dagda's Cauldron, The Spear of Lugh, The Stone of Fal, and The Sword of Light of Nuada. The circular platform surrounding Lia Fáil is a Meluhhan artisan working platform, much as in Sarasvati-Sindhu civilization; it resembles Vedic Shiva Linga very closely. The stone pillars of Lia Fáil and Dholavira are comparable and denote early gestalt of Meluhhans for denoting a *stambha* (rebus: *tamba*, 'copper') as a fiery pillar, a hieroglyphic metaphor for Rudra-Shiva, inferred from a SkaSukta in Atharvaveda. The double ringforts of Forrad and Teach are comparable with the 8-shaped stone structures found in front of two polished stone pillars in Dholavira. Hindu Trimurti formed the model for Irish gods Eire, Banba and Forla, or the Celtic trinity, later adopted as Christian Trinity.

Gundestrup Cauldron Peat bog from Denmark, cast in silver in the 2nd century BC, is a religious vessel found at Himmerland in 1891 CE which shows Thracian in workmanship but carries decorative motifs of the Celtic pantheon consisting of Cernunnos, Taranis and others. Hieroglyphs on the cauldron are closely related to rebus in Meluhha metalwork. Art historian Timothy Taylor states:

"A shared pictorial and technical tradition stretched from India to Thrace, where the cauldron was made, and thence to Denmark. Yogic rituals, for example, can be inferred from the poses of an antler-bearing man on the cauldron and of an oxheaded figure on a seal impress from the Indian city of Mohenjo Daro…Three other idols are the goddesses with elephants (Indian goddess Lakshmi), wheel gods (Indian is Vishnu); the goddesses with braided hair and paired birds."

He further speculates that members of an Indian itinerant artisan class, not unlike the later Gypsies in Europe who also originated in India, must have been the creators of the cauldron. Renfrew opines that this civilization was:

"…erecting monuments in stone, setting up solar observatories (Stonehenge), smelting copper, and doing other ingenious things without any help from the Mediterranean".

The megalithic monuments of **Stonehenge** were constructed between 2000-3500 BC, contemporary with ISC. The stone alignment in the monument needed a profound knowledge of astronomy and mathematics, described in Vedic literature (Chapter 5.VI, VII, VIII).

Celtic language has much in common with Sanskrit; Celtic eventually gave birth to English and Irish languages. Irish sagas and epics grew out of verse dialogs in Sanskrit epics. Sylvain Levi maintains that Celtic poems were almost a chapter of the history of Bharat. The word Druid may stem from *drui-wid* or oak knowledge where *wid* means to know as in Sanskrit Vedas. Druids were considered the most just of men and Brehon Law is astonishingly similar to the *Manavadharmashastra* of Manu and meters of Rig Veda; same was true of the Welsh law. Celtic Druids were clean and fastidious and formed the Celtic intelligentsia as philosophers, judges, educators, historians, doctors, seers, astronomers, astrologers, much like the priest kings in the ISC. The Druids were skilled physicians and surgeons able to perform trepanning, caesarian, amputations, brain surgery, as in the tradition of Ayurveda (Chapter 5.XI), and founded the very first hospitals in Italy as well as in Ireland. English writers dismissed Scotts, Welsh and Cornish to be racially inferior. The Celts were now dubbed:

"...*savage and barbarous people, knowing no use at all of garments...destitute of the knowledge...to erect stately structures, or such remarkable works as Stonehenge...their chiefest glory to be wholly ignorant in whatever Arts*".

Besides Celts, Gypsies from Bharat epicenter fanned out as of the fifth century CE to reach Scandinavia by the early 16th century. Gypsies were perhaps the most persecuted people of all but continue to linger on their Bharat roots. The **affinity of Romani language to Sanskrit** was discovered by Jacob Bryant and confirmed by Pott 1844-45. According to Lal:

"*Researches based on their language, customs, rituals, and physiognomy, affirm that it is **Hindus from India who form the bulk of these people in Europe**".

Pre-Christian manuscripts in Europe were all Sanskrit scriptures of the Vedic Hindus but were fed to fire by the zealot Christian missionaries. Russia (from Sanskrit *rishis*) shares many Sanskrit based derivations: Moscow from *Moksha* (salvation), Soviet from **Svet** (white), Bolshevik from *Bal-Sevik* (learned sages), **grad** for towns from **graam** (village), Krasnoyarak, some 2000 miles east of Moscow, from Krishna, Lebedev from Sanskrit **Laba-dev**, Siberia from Sanskrit **shabir** and so forth. A Vedic temple dedicated to Jwalamai, inscribed with Gayatri mantra in Devanagari, was located in the port town of Baku on the Caspian Sea while another temple depicting a Vedic chariot was found in the region of Tajikistan (The Evening News of TOI 30 August 1982). In Soviet Central Asia, at Kara-tepe,

Fayaz-tepe (near Termez) and Dalverzin-tepe in Uzbekistan, are to be found entire Buddhist centers, wonderful monuments of art, Buddhist stupas, Buddha statues, inscribed pottery, inscriptions in Kharosthi and Brahmi, all from the Kushan period. A Sanskrit text of *Ashtanga Ayurveda* was also discovered in Russia while a Russian Veda speaks of Krishna who killed many demons and upheld spiritual truths as Christians could not penetrate the region easily to destroy pagan history.

In Eastern and Central Europe, Poland was closest to Bharat as evident from their saying: *"Kto poznal India, poznal coly swiant"* (he who has seen India has seen the whole world). Oak has pointed out that the terms Czech, Czechoslovakia and Czestochowa in Poland stem from the shaka clan; the Saxenas of India, Saxons of Europe and Anglo-Saxons of England originate from the same source. The town of Scope in Yugoslavia boasts of 50,000 families that carry the name Rama. Slav languages originated in Sanskrit, the Slav people worshipped many Vedic deities like Bog (*Bhag* or *Bhagwan*), Ogon (*Agni*) and Parun (*Varun*); Slav festivals also originated in Vedic rites. The Slavs were forced into Christianity around 980 CE and all Vedic relics were destroyed. Bulgaria, Ukraine, Lithuania continue to recreate Vedic Sanskrit traditions. Budapest (Hungary) is simply the Sanskrit *Buddhaprastha*.

The British Isles were designated as *Angulisthan* in Sanskrit, referring to the small size of the country as *anguli* compared to Europe. London was derived from *Londonium* from the original Sanskrit *Nandanium*, suffix *puri* was changed to 'bury' while 'shire' stems from Sanskrit *shwar*. Ramsgate in England is obviously related to Lord Rama whereas Italian Ravenna stems from Ravana. Eireland is derived from *Aryasthan*. Names like Kilkarny and Kilpatrick refer to the presence of fortifications from Sanskrit *kila* or *quila* while Dorothea Chaplin has suggested that Kent was founded by Jats who then migrated to the Isle of Wight. Scotland stems from *Kshatra-sthan*, and St. Paul's cathedral in London even has the word OM inscribed on the ceiling as it could have been a Krishna temple. The name France comes from the Sanskrit root *pra* while Paris, known during Roman times as Parisorium, stems from Parameshwari; Notre Dame was once Vedic temple to Parameshwari; Marseilles comes from *Marichalayas* and Versailles from *Vareshalayas* The cathedral at Sable in France appears to actually contain a Shiva lingum.

Scandinavia derives its name from Skanda, the son of Shiva by Vedic Daityas whose clans *Danu and Merk* gave rise to Denmark. Sweden and Norge (Norway) derive their names from *Swarga* (Heaven) and *Naraka* (Hell). Scandinavian names like Sorensen carry the suffix *sen* which is also used as a surname in India. The Vedas became known as the Eddas and remain the most ancient scripture of the region, now presented as fairy tales. For example, Norsk ballad Siegfried stems from the story of Karna in MahaBharat while Hildebrand Lied is an episode from Ramayana. Scandinavian Woden and German Odin are similar to the Vedic Varuna while the thunder god Donar/Thor resembles Indra. The concept of ages in Norsk is similar to the Vedic yugas. Count Biornstierna in The Theogony of the Hindus (cited in Knapp) states:

"It appears that the Hindu settlers migrated to Scandinavia before the Mahabharata war".

German stems from Sanskrit *Sharman* and Deutschland from *Daityasthan,* or the land of Daitya, born of mother Diti and Kashyapa muni; the Dutch also share the name Daitya and the biggest hotel in Amsterdam (from *Antardham*) is named Krisnapolsky derived from Krishna. Prussia comes from pra-Russia derived from Sanskrit *Rishiya*. Heidelberg is comes from Haya-dal-Barg meaning a fort garrisoned by a contingent of horses; Hindenburg is simply the fort of Hindus. The suffix *Mann* comes from Sanskrit Manav meaning man, as in Hahneman which is derived from Hanuman, while stein stems from *sthan.* Rama figures in many names such as Ramastein. German thank you or Danke is derived from Sanskrit *dhanya.* Germany also **worshipped the Shiva linga** which was found in the city of Schifferstadt. Simon Pelloutier (1740 CE) equated the religion of the Germanic Franks and the Celts as the one and the same thing. Regarding Spain, Marvin Mills (quoted in Knapp) summarizes:

*"...most important alleged **Moslem buildings in Spain are not Moslem at all**... Much like in India the Moslems came as looters and conquerors, preying on a superior culture where they found generous numbers of buildings to choose from. Thus I would guess that the (so called) Mosque of Cordoba, the Alhambra, and the palace city of Azhara outside of Cordoba as well as buildings in Seville and elsewhere will turn out to be non-Moslem. In short there is **need to rewrite** Spanish **history** as well as Indian history"*.

Both Greece and Rome were important trading partners of Bharat. The images of Shiva, Ganesha and other deities are found throughout Italy as are painted scenes from Ramayana. Some Etruscan Emperors have been portrayed with *tilak* marks on their forehead. Rome itself comes from Rama and is believed to have been founded on 21 April 753 BC on Rama's birthday. By adding *ha* to *Paap* (sin) Papa-ha signifies one who removes sin while Pontiff stems from *pundit* or *puntah.* Just as the Royal Vedic priest used to reside in a *Vatica* (hermitage) so also the Pope resides in *Vatican* whose Etruscan museum contains sculptures of Shiva linga, Shiva with a cobra, and so forth. Many of the contemporary papal rituals are rooted in the Vedic tradition e.g. baptism, purification with incense, chanting of hymns, washing of feet. However, when Constantine raised Christianity to the level of official religion of the empire, all connections with the Vedic past were suppressed.

Pre-Islamic Iran had been transmitting Vedic knowledge to Egypt for over two millennia and to Greece for over one millennium. Pliny refers to Herakles as Krishna who lived 138 generations before Alexander in 325 BC. Ravana of Ramayana appears to be Pluto and Rama is transformed into Mercury; Zeus can be compared to Indra: control weather, wield thunderbolts, live on mountains (Olympus and Meru, respectively), and both represent Thursday of the week. Greeks fused Durga, Sarasvati and Lakshmi into Athena. Vedic Rudra is described in Greek Odyssey:

*"With that he gathered the clouds and troubled the waters of the deep, grasping his **trident** in his hands; and he roused all storms of all manners of wind"*.

Here the trident is 100% Bharat. Pluto (Sanskrit Preta) was the guardian of Hades and could be no other than Yama. Pan, half man half goat, was like Prajapati Daksha, father of Parvati. Helios was Vedic Hari, following Greek practice of adding *os* to all nouns. The **Greek** language is largely derived **from Sanskrit** and the greeting *Hari Tutay* simply means May Hari (Krishna) bless you; this is equivalent to Hindu Rama Rama or Hare Krishna. Thanks to these interactions, the Greeks now learnt to domesticate pigs, sheep, and goat while agriculture also took shape along with sciences. McEvilley concluded:

"Indian ascetics followed an old overland route from Central Asia that ended at or near Sinope and came into actual contact with Diogenes personally before he left his native city and took the exotic craft he had learned to Athens to convert it, under the influence of Socrates/Antisthenes into philosophy…Diogenes lived in an entrepot on the ancient trade route between India and Greece, so did a Lakulisa whose reputed hometown of Broach…was the chief trading port in western India…from as early as Mauryan times".

Pococke confirms and feels that **India was far superior to Greece**:

"…the whole of Greece, from an era of the supposed god ship of Poseidon and Zeus, down to the close of the Trojan war (was) Indian in language, sentiment and religion, and in the arts of peace and war".

Deshpandey further adds (cited in Knapp):

"In respect of Philosophy, the Hindus were far in advance of the philosophy of Greece and Rome who considered the immortality of the soul as problematical... he Egyptians derived their religion, mythology and philosophy from the Hindus and the Greek philosophy too was indebted almost wholly to the Hindu philosophy...the resemblance between (them) is too close to be accidental. The Hindu being far more advanced must have been the teachers, and the Greeks, the disciples".

Pythagoras seems to have **visited Taxila** and in Himalayas he gave up his long Greek robes to adopt the local trousers worn by people in Nepal, Ladakh, Tibet, and Kashmir etc. Werthameir concludes that Pythagoras introduced trousers into Europe and thence on to the whole world. After twenty years he returned to Greece and settled in Croton (South Italy) where he founded a monastic order along the lines of an *ashram*. Neugebauer says Pythagorean Theorem *"was known more than a thousand years before Pythagoras..."* Junge has pointed out that Greek literature of the first five centuries after Pythagoras does not mention his theorem. Pythagoras also introduced Metempsychosis, Reincarnation H. G. Rawlinson affirms:

"Almost all the theories, religious, philosophical, and mathematical, taught by the Pythagoras were known in India in the sixth century BC".

In The Republic, the philosopher kings of Plato are the rishis and sages of Bharat, just like the priest king found in the Indus ruins. Urwick has shown that the Republic of Plato was based upon Vedic thought and finds that

"Conceptions, arguments and conclusions are in most cases identical with those of the Hindu scriptures".

Tarn sums up:

"Indian civilization was strong enough to hold its own against Greek civilization...in certain respect India was the dominant partner. Except for the Buddha statue the history of India would in all essentials have been precisely what it has been had the Greeks never existed".

The similarities between Vedic ideation and Platonic doctrine go on and on and McEvilley concludes:

"As the dialectical-logical dichotomy entered India from Greece, so the whole monism complex had entered Greece from India several centuries earlier, and has dominated the monistic and idealistic strands of western philosophy from Parmenides, Pythagoras, and Plato, to Spinoza, Hegel and

Heidegger…The comparative dating of the fifth century Pythagorean Philolaus and Tattriya Upanishad is uncertain – either might have come first. But at that time there is no Greek influence on India whereas Indian influence does seem to have arrived in Greece" (for other comparisons see McEvilley pp188-192 and 308-309).

The transfer of Bharat knowledge to Greece continued well into the early centuries of the Christian era and **Neoplatonism** of Plotinus (243 CE onwards in Rome) represents the last stage of **Hinduized Greek thought**. McEvilley (p.643-644) observes:

"*…every mystical element in Indian thought can be found in Greek thought too, and every rational element in Greek thought can be found in India…*"

Zeller adds:

"*…Greeks themselves were inclined from early times…to grant peoples of the Orient…that they had a share in the origin of their philosophy*" and, according to Halbfass, showed "*readiness to accept the possibility of a philosophical partnership, of debate and instruction, in what is foreign, specifically Indian*".

Yet, their successors in **modern Europe exclude Bharat from the history** of Philosophy, Mathematics, Natural Sciences and so forth such that Greece was propelled as the sole fount of knowledge. Chakrabarty ponders:

"*If Buddha's death date can be brought down from 544 to 371 BC then Buddha becomes younger than Pericles (492-420 BC), Socrates (461-399 BC), and Pythagoras. Vaishali, the ancient republic becomes younger than Athens…*"

Through such manipulations, the threat that the Vedic past presents to the 'Greek miracle' would be negated by chronology. Chaman Lal has concluded it all succinctly:

"*Humanity, which originated in Asia, was scattered by movements of expansion, on the one side towards the West (Asia Minor, Egypt etc.) to create western culture there, Greco, Latin or European, and on the other towards the east, to India, China, Japan, and the Islands of South Seas. And those who first arrived on the continent, later to be known as America, were groups of men driven by that might current that set out from India towards the East*".

The West also forgets that **Greek society was actually infested with oracles, witchcraft, ghosts, curse tablets, superstitions and the like.**

Fritz Graf observes:

"*The contemporaries of Plato and Socrates placed voodoo dolls on graves and thresholds (some found in modern museums)… The citizens of classical Teos cursed with spells whoever attacked the city and legislated against the magical transfer of crops from one field to another… the imperial Law books contained extensive sanctions against all sorts of magical procedures, with the sole exception of love spells and weather magic…. The accusation of having worked magic was wielded against many a prominent Greek and Roman, from Republican senators to philosopher Boethius in the sixth century…Greek spells from Egyptian papyrus books reappear in Latin guise in astrological manuscripts at the time of Christopher Columbus…Magical rites not only helped to harm enemies and rivals but also gave access to higher spirituality…Magicians had a direct link to the divine world, and magic was seen as a gift from the gods…Moses and Jesus were thought to have powers well beyond those of ordinary people*".

All Greek science was in fact the handmaiden of philosophers who had little respect for mathematical scrutiny. Some particularly absurd examples are recalled here as follows. Thales (594 BC) held that the Earth was a globular body in the center of the universe; Anaximanes agreed but Anaximander thought of it as cylindrical. Other Greek thinkers felt that the Earth was like a mountain around which revolved the stars. Erastothese 200 BC saw Earth surrounded by one great sea, an improvisation of the Homerian idea that the earth is an immense circular plain surrounded by a sea of darkness. Pliny asserted:

"*Europe appears to be greater than Asia by little less than half of Asia; and greater than Africa by the same quantity added to the sixth part of Africa*".

The late medieval science in Europe was dominated by **Aristotle** (died circa 323 BC) who was the **least enlightened pseudo-philosopher** of all and whose ridiculous theories have been thoroughly discredited by modern research. Aristotle's spherical universe rotated once a day moved by the unmoved mover, identified as God by Christian scholars. His world was formed by three continents (Asia, Libya or Africa and Europe) surrounded by three seas (Mediterranean, Caspian and Sea of India). Aristotle felt that western Spain was close to Eastern India, leading to the expedition of Columbus and the appellation of West Indies for the Americas. Aristotle rejected mathematics and heliocentrism altogether and saw Moon as a polished mirror. He also rejected Jain atomism to come up the idea of indefinite indivisibility of the matter and the absence of void. He divided the soul into rational (intellect) and irrational (desire) halves. To Aristotle

slavery was natural because slaves lacked a rational soul although his near contemporary Alcidamas was to assert that 'god has set all men free', as in the Vedic-Hindu world where slavery was nonexistent. Aristotle also reduced **women into second class citizens** because they lacked the rational soul.

Certainly the **most absurd** of all theories of Aristotle was his **medical ignorance** as dissection was not permitted in Greece. He placed heart as the nerve center and brain as the organ of sensations. Eyes were supposed to throw out a beam of light on objects to be perceived and sperm was believed to be synthesized in the brain from where it descended into testicles and got whitened in the process. Womb was supposed to be floating freely inside the body and female body was just a like a stove to cook the sperm into a full grown child. Aristotle finlly came with a model of The Great Chain of Being that was to become the backbone of Christian theology for mind control, enslavement of women, and colonization of the world.

The Arabs were to introduce Europe to the Vedic ideation (preceding section).The **Hindu numerals** appeared on a manuscript in 976 CE in Northern Spain, known as *Codex Vigilanus*:

"*So with computing symbols, we must realize that the **Indians had the most penetrating intellect**, and other nations were way behind them in the art of computing, in geometry, and in other free sciences. And this is evident from the nine symbols with which they represented every rank of number at every level*".

When Gerbert d'Aurillac became Pope Sylvester II in 999 CE, he embraced the abacus which incorporated zero and infinity and Hindu numerals adopted by the majority of merchants and nations in the West **under the name Arabic numbers**. Decimal fractions appear for the first time in *The Book of Chapters on Indian Arithmetic* written in 952 CE in Damascus by Abdul Hassan al-Uqlidisi. But Charles XII of Sweden (1682-1718) tried to ban the decimal system and replace it with a base 64 system. Hindu number names existed for denominations up to 10^{18}, in contrast to 10,000 for Persians, Greeks, Romans and Arabs. Laplace wrote:

"*It is India that gave us the ingenious method of expressing all numbers by means of ten symbols, each symbol receiving a value of position, as well as an absolute value; a profound and important idea which appears so simple to us now that we ignore its true merit but its very simplicity…it escaped the genius of Archimedes and Apollonius*".

Seidenberg concluded:

"*The elements of ancient geometry found in Egypt and Babylonia stem from a ritual system of the kind observed in Sulvashastra...Sanskrit scholars do not give me a date so far back as 1700 BC (for Sulbha). Therefore I postulate a pre-Old-Babylonian source for the kind of geometric rituals we see preserved in the Sulvashastras, or at least for the mathematics involved in these rituals*".

The Hebrew tradition was exposed to it by the traveling scholar Rabbi Ben Ezra in the twelfth century. Thibaut also felt that **Greek Geometry was derived from the Sulbhas** although he did not say so explicitly. Hankel (1874) and Junge (1907) also deny Pythagoras credit for the discovery, as detailed by Datta. Even Britannica notes:

"*...the bulk of the intellectual tradition originating with* **Pythagoras himself belongs to mystical wisdom** *rather than scientific scholarship*".

Lach (1965) mentions transfer of technology and products from Kerala to Europe that includes: the power series for the inverse tangent generally attributed to Gregory and Leibniz and the power series for the sine and cosine attributed to Taylor and the Newton. Later works on computing sine and cosine in Kerala produced expressions that predate the modern Taylor series by more than 300 years. Four books from Kerala are: Nilkantha's *Tantra Samgraha*, Jyesthadeva's *Yuktibhasa*, Somayaji's *Karana Paddhati* and Sankara's *Sadratnamala*, copied by the Jesuit missionaries. Ramanujan (1887-1920) has been called the greatest mathematician of the century thanks to his grasp of infinite series expansions.

Ptolemy compiled an encyclopedia of astronomy from Indo-Greek literature which was translated into Arabic in 827 CE and into Latin in the 12th century which is now called *Almagest* and which was the standard astronomical book for Arabs and Europeans up until the 17th century. The contents of the book are essentially the work of Vedic-Hindu astronomers and since the word *Almagest* has no meaning in Arabic so it could only have been a translation of **Sanskrit Mahishtha** which means 'around the earth'. Only one dot is needed in the Arabic script to change the word *'mahistha'* into *'magest'* and Al is usually added in Arabic to mean 'the', as explained by Priyadarshi. Diophantus (200-284 CE), called father of Algebra, wrote *Arithmetica* which is a meaningless word in Arabic and Greek but in Sanskrit it means calculation (*miti*) of money matters (*artha*). Europeans who translated from Arabic into Latin conveniently started calling them

Arabic although they predated Islam. By the time of Newton and Copernicus, all European universities possessed Latin translations of Vedic-Hindu astronomical and mathematical works such as the Great Sindhind and *Algoritmi de numero Indorum* that exposed Europeans to heliocentric universe, gravity etc, later passed off as 'European'. The translations of Panchatantra, *Hitopdesha* (Salutary Advice) MahaBharat, *Kathasaritasagara*, and others, permitted the genesis of Arabian Nights, Shakespeare's Merchant of Venice, Giovanni Boccaccio's (1313-1375 CE) Decameron, and Don Juan Manuel's Conde Lucanor. Singhal observed:

"*influence of Decameron on European literature has been incalculable, especially on Italian fiction*".

Hans Christian Andersen, Kipling, Aesop's fables and more were all inspired by Vedic sources. La Fontaine expressly stated in the Preface:

"*It is not necessary that I should say whence I have taken the subjects of these new fables. I shall only say that, from a sense of gratitude, that I owe the largest portion of them to Pilpay the Indian sage*".

Consequently, the **stolen Vedic patrimony** assured European resurgence. Louis Revel remarked that if Greek culture had influenced Western civilization, the ancient Greeks themselves were **"*the sons of Hindu thought*'**

"*…the germs of European arts and sciences. The mighty human tide that passed the barrier of Punjab, rolled on towards its destined channel in Europe and in Asia, to fulfill its beneficent office in the moral fertilization of the world…Still, the distance of the migratory movement was so vast, the disguise of names so complete, and Grecian information so calculated to mislead, that nothing short of a total disregard of theoretical principles, and the resolution of independent research, gave the slightest chance of a successful elucidation*".

7. Vedic Ideation in Dogmatic Religions

Preceding chapters have demonstrated that ancient Bharat was the mother of religion, myths and legends, sciences and indeed all human ideation, predating all other revelations, that was to influence the Egyptian Book of the Dead as well as The Old and the New Testaments. In his three volume seminal work Faber had remarked:

"*The various systems of Pagan Idolatry in different parts of the world correspond so closely…that they cannot have been struck out independently in the several countries where they had been established, but must have **originated from some common source**, and must thence as a common center, have carried it to all quarters of the globe*".

Matlock affirms:

"…**all our religions** *just appear to be fragmented. In reality they all descend from the same **Hindu source**"*.

Jewish Heritage

The antiquity of the Old Testament is debatable because the historiography was dominated by a religious missionary zeal as the writers saw the **will of God in all events** and they wanted to admonish their co-religionists. In fact, most of the 1500 years of Biblical history took place outside Israel. In his History of Jews, Josephus Flavius (32-100 CE) cites Aristotle (cited in Matlock):

"*These Jews are derived from the Indian philosophers; they are named by the Indians Caani…*".

Megasthenes also recorded that the Jews were an Indian tribe or sect called Kalani, derived from Kalyana or Kalienna, a port city, some forty six miles north of present Mumbai, whose archaeological ruins are traced back to 3000 BC. The port city of Sophir was situated about fifty miles north of Kalyan which formed the principal seat of trade with Mesopotamia, Persia, Arabia and Egypt. Sir Henry Rule (cited in Matlock) mentions a Chinese document where Adam is supposed to have come from India. Moses could well be Mahesh (Shiva), Moshe, Mushi, Mse as I Ramases, and so forth. Choudhury (cited in Matlock) was to note:

"*Much before the birth of Jesus, the whole of Bible land (not only Israel and Palestine) Jerusalem was colonized by the Indians Calani and became a major center of Krishna worship*".

The Epic of Gilgamesh mentions that Utnaphishtim, the Sumerian Noah, who survived a great flood that lasted forty days and landed at Mount

Ararat (Aryavarta) in Kashmir, much as Vedic Manu had done, is derived from Sanskrit Nu or Nau-a. The book of Genesis mentions that the **first home of Abraham** was in **Haran** which is a town a few north of Srinagar in Kashmir and where Christian era walls have been excavated. Well over 300 names of towns, regions, estates, geographical features, tribes, clans, families, and individuals in the Old Testament are phonetically similar to the names in Kashmir; the name Kashmir could stem from the Vedic seer Kashyap or from Kosher. The Identification Society of London in the 19th century proved that Kashmiri population is of Israelite descent. Moses climbed Mount Nebo to see 'the land of milk and honey' complete with place names such as Plains of Moab, Mount Nebo, Mount Pisgah, Beth-peor and Heshbon. Beth-poer could be Behat-poor, later Bandipur, 70 kms east of Srinagar. Some 20 km north east of Bandipur lies Hasba or Hasbal, the biblical Heshbon. A stone column at the foot of Mount Nebo is supposed to be the **tombstone of Moses** whereas a site on the riverbank in Bijbihara is referred to as the **birth place of Moses**. At the confluence of Jhelum and Sind is located Auth Wattu (eight paths) in the Hardwar district north of Sri Nagar where a Kohna-I-Musa, or the Cornerstone of Moses, forms the place where Moses used to recline. A 'Bathing Place of Moses' is marked by a stone lion, some 5000 years old. Kashmir is still known as the Garden of Solomon and a temple on one of the mountains is called Takht-I-Suleimna, Throne of Solomon.

Most religions had a King named David that stems from Da (Shiva) and veda/vida (knowledge). The word YHWH is derived from SHIVA. Both Abraham and Sarah were born in India but are believed to be buried in Hebron, Israel. Abraham really stands for A Brahman, but could also be Rama. The temple of Solomon and the tomb of Moses existed in Kashmir before the arrival of Muslims; Saul and David have also been traced to Kashmir. Fida Hassnain records that Emperor Claudius apparently found an ancient scroll of the Torah in Kashmir. Jeremiah could have been the first Jewish prophet to purge Judaism of Hindu elements. The Zion of the Jews was situated in Gujarat and Maharashtra in the region called *Seuna-Desa* or *Sion* that was also the original home of Yadavas. Bethlehem stems from Vatsaldham and Nazareth is simply Sanskrit Nandreth. Sion comes from Sanskrit Siyoni or The Source (Mt Meru). Many gates in Jerusalem are engraved with the Lotus symbol that is sacred in Bharat. After the Great Flood, the **Indo-Hebrew hordes moved to the Middle East** and renamed landmarks they had left behind in Bharata.

Thousands of years ago the **Jews worshipped Lord Chrisn playing** the flute and Oxford Dictionary admits that Easter corresponds with a pre-Christian Jewish festival and **Passover is a Hindu festival** around the

Spring equinox. The star of David, consisting of two interlocking triangles, is actually a Tantric symbol, a simplified Sri Yantra. Tell el-Amarna yielded 377 documents of 15th century BC in Acadian as correspondence between Prince Suwardata and Prince Indaruta of Vedic ancestry. Biryazawa of Damascus, Biridia of Megiddo, Widia of Askelon, Birasheshena of Scechem in Samaria, are all Aryan. The serpent of brass in the temple of Jerusalem is believed to be a Medianite who descended from Abraham's wife Keturah of Hindu mythology.

The Jews were among the first to rewrite history by reducing the legends of the neighboring countries into the Jerusalem Talmud (4th century BC) and the Babylonian Talmud (5th century BC). The earliest surviving written version of the first books of the Old Testament dates back to 200 BC, discovered among the Dead Sea Scrolls. The five books or the Pentateuch (*Genesis, Exodus, Leviticus, Numbers, Deuteronomy*) form the Jewish Torah whose authorship has been attributed to Moses but modern linguistic research has shown that they were composed by four authors during three different periods viz. 722 BC, 620 BC, and 444 BC (Dr. Knappert cited in Knapp); the sixth and the seventh books of Moses speak of spells, sorcery, magic, and esoteric doctrines of various backgrounds. French priest Alfred Loisy (1857– 1940 CE) observed:

*"The **Pentateuch, in its present form cannot be the work of Moses.** The first chapters of Genesis do not contain an exact and reliable account of the beginnings of mankind.... All the historical books of the Bible, including those of the New Testament, were composed in a looser manner than modern historical writing, and a certain freedom of interpretation follows.*

Jewish people approached Yahweh for land that they did not possess as Palestine was not large enough to satisfy the land greed of every tribe. Genesis mentions three waves of Hebrew settlements in Canaan (now Israel). In the first wave, Abraham left the family in Ur to enter Canaan where Abraham was told by Yahweh:

"I am with you; I will keep you safe wherever you go".

"To your descendants I will give this land" (Genesis 12:7)..."

"All the land you see I will give to you and your descendants forever" (Genesis 13:15).

"To your descendants I give this land, from the Wadi of Egypt to the Great River (Euphrates)" (Genesis 15:18).

"I will give to you and to your descendants after you the land in which you are now staying, the whole land of Canaan, as a permanent possession,

and I will be their God" (Genesis17:8).

Jewish people were ecstatic:

"Yahweh, you have seduced me and I am seduced, you have raped me and I am overcome..."

The land grab of the colonial era extrapolated these vague statements to mean the whole world as white man's property.

Successive waves of Jews went to India at different period of history. Around 500 CE or so, the Emperor of Kerala awarded his Jewish subjects their own small kingdom of around twenty square miles, as recorded in copper plate inscription displayed at the Synagogue of Cochin. This tiny Jewish kingdom lasted for but for 1000 years, destroyed in 1524 CE by the Arabs. In 1981, a researcher of north-east Indian tribes analyzed the oral traditions of several disjointed village communities who collectively called themselves Bnei Menashe (Hebrew for 'Children of God'), and concluded that they were descendants of one of the 10 lost tribes. In 2004, a DNA footprint at Kolkata's Central Forensic Science Laboratory reported that the tribe had indirect links to the Jews of Israel. In March 2005, a top clergyman from Israel formally recognized the Bnei Menashe as descendants of the lost tribes. Israel has now permitted the immigration of the remaining 7232 members of Bnei Menashe Jews from Kashmir and other parts of India (TOI 24 December 2012). Dr. S. Radhakrishnan asserted that the **Jews** were Indians whom the Syrians called Judea, the Sanskrit form of which is **Yadava**.

Hebrew Genesis really describes the history of Great Aryan Kings distorted by the rabbis such that the **Aryan King Adda or Addamu became Adam**. Hebrew genealogy of Adam, Cain, Enoch, Noah and Japhet are mere **distortions of the Babylonian Aryan Kings**. While Jesus had taught introspection, much like the Vedas, the Church preached blind faith in **predestination** where salvation was possible only through the clergy. Mark Twain (1835-1910) was quite vitriolic about missionaries who justified imperialism as an extension of religious duty.

"I bring you the stately matron named Christendom...returning bedraggled, besmirched, and dishonored from pirate raids in Kiao-chou [Tsingtao, China], Manchuria, South Africa, and the Philippines, with her soul full of meanness, her pocket full of boodle, and her mouth full of pious hypocrisies."

Christian Dogmatism

Vedic-Buddhist culture was the dominant force in pre-Christian Europe. Pope Gregory in 601 CE told the missionaries not to destroy the pre-Christian sites of worship but to bless and convert them "*from worship of devils to the worship of the true God*". In fact, Christian places of worship were implanted on to Vedic temples in Europe. Christian devotion is simply bhakti in Vedic worship. The Ashvin twins of Vedic lore were transformed into Castor and Pollux who descended from Kashmir/Afghanistan/Ladakh region. Rig Veda I.116, 3 and 5, mentions the first foreign invasion of Bharat. Carthage got its name from Sanskrit Kartikeya. When nascent Christianity met mature Buddhism, rosary was adopted along with other Paraphernalia of Buddhism.

As with Jewish faith above, the birth, life and death of **Jesus** are all closely linked to the history of ancient Bharat. Kashmir was ruled by Jayendra 4-17 BC and his minister was Sandimati who could be Jesus or Joseph; Sandimati could also have been James. Meghavana was to rule Kahmir (40-65 CE) after Sandimati and could have taken over as the guardian or husband of Mother Mary. Meghavana could have been Joseph of Arimathea and the real father of Jesus. The Houses of Wales and Brittany trace their ancestry to Joseph of Arimathea whose bloodline also produced Constantine as well as King Lucius related to the Merovigians through his sister and daughter. From 700 BC on, Celtic tribes from Central Europe had settled in Britain and various kingly branches emerged from Anna, the daughter of Joseph of Arimathea. The Stewarts arose from a marital union between the hereditary lines of Jesus and his brother James from the Merovigians and Celtic Britain, respectively.

Abhorred by the cruelty of Jewish butchers, Jesus travelled to Bharat by the Silk Road. Written accounts found in Lhasa and Leh speak of a lad of fourteen who arrived in the region of Sindh (Indus) in the company of merchants, traveled through Punjab, proceeded to Jagannath, went on to Nepal to study Buddhism, and finally returned to Palestine via Persia, Assyria, Greece and Egypt. Nicolai Notovitch, born in 1858, was told of a great prophet Isa (or Issa) at the Buddhist monastery of Hemis in Ladakh. Notovitch recorded his finds in *La Vie Inconnu de Jesus Christ*, followed by the Russian edition of *The Life of Saint Issa*; after 1916 CE Notovitch was heard of no more. Forty years before Notovitch, in 1853, a certain Mrs.

Harvey in her book *The Adventures of a Lady in Tartary, Tibet, China and Kashmir* mentions the same documents, as does Swami Abhedananda, born 1866 CE as Kaliprasad Chandra, in a book titled *Kashmir and Tibet*. Nicolas Roerich in 1925 CE confirmed that the people of Ladakh knew the legend of Issa. Lady Henrietta Maverick in 1931 in her book *In the World's Attic* mentions the existence of 1500 year old documents at the monastery of Hemis. In 1939 CE, a Swiss matron named Madame Elisabeth Caspari was shown manuscripts by the librarian at Hemis who said '*These books tell you of your Jesus*'. All the texts have since disappeared so Holger Kersten in 1979 could not access them. Nath Yogis, have preserved an ancient sutra known as *Nath Namavali* which speaks of the great saint Isa Nath who had come to Bharata at the age of fourteen, who later survived crucifixion as a result of the yogic powers he had attained under his teacher Chetab Nath, and who later returned to Bharat. Jesus married a Kshmiri girl named Marjan and sired a son Vima Kadphises who could have been the grandson of the founder of Kushan dynasty.

Jesus was crucified at about 12 noon on Friday and declared dead by three PM although his legs had not been broken and this hasty death surprised Pilate himself so much so that he asked the leading centurion if everything was all right. On Sunday the stone was found to be removed and when women came to anoint Jesus with oil on Monday, the tomb was empty; two men said "*Why seek ye the living among the dead*" (Luke 24:1-5) evidently meaning that Jesus was alive and had been saved. Mark was to record that when Mary Magdalene, Mary the mother of Jesus, and Salome, entered the tomb they saw a young man dressed in white who said to them:

"Don't be stunned. Are you looking for Jesus the crucified Nazarene? He was raised. He isn't here. Look, the place where they laid him. But go to the disciples and Peter. He is going ahead of you to Galilee. Then you will see him as he told you".

Later, Jesus assured the disciples that he has survived the crucifixion, felt hunger and had recovered:

"Behold my hands and my feet, that it is I myself: handle me, and see, for a spirit hath not flesh and bones, as you see me have. He said unto them, Have ye here any meat? And they gave him a piece of broiled fish, and of an honey-comb. And he took it, and did eat before them". (Luke 24:38-43).

To Peter he said: "*Take, handle me and see that I am not a bloodless phantom*".

The Treatise of the Great Seth at Nag Hammadi, composed around 200 CE, stipulates that Jesus was never crucified as there are no explicit references in the Bible itself to Christ's crucifixion. Qu'ran explicitly states: *'Yet they slew him not, neither crucified him, but he was represented by one in his likeness… They really did not kill him"* (Koran 4:156-157). Agapius in the 10th century mentions in *Kitab al'Unwan* that Jesus appeared to his disciples three days after crucifixion, and that *he* was alive. Kurdish people remember how Jesus after crucifixion was nursed back to health at Nisbis near Edessa, now called Nusaybin on the Turkish-Syrian border, and migrated east. Islam admits Immaculate Conception, as also the miracles, but clearly denies Crucifixion and supports Sanskrit sources. The second century historian Basilides of Alexandria wrote that crucifixion was stage managed. Jesus himself made a statement about his survival from crucifixion:

"For as Jonas was three days in the whale's belly, so shall the Son of man be three days and three nights in the heart of the earth" (Matthew 12:40).

Jesus had furthermore remarked:

"As for my death, which was real enough for them, it was real to them because of their own incomprehension and blindness".

Many passages in the gospels suggest that Jesus escaped crucifixion and he decided to go to Kashmir where the ten lost tribes had taken refuge more than 700 years before. Gospel of Philip (180-350 CE), from Nag Hammadi scrolls, mentions:

"Those who say that the Lord died first and (then) rose up are in error, for he rose up first and (then) died".

More than sixteen years elapsed before Jesus reached Kashmir via Persia with his three female companions, all named Mary, (mother, sister and wife). In Mari or Murree(70 km east of Taxila) a grave has been maintained as *Mai Marti da Asthan* 'The Final Resting Place of Mary' when she was 70 years old, aligned in an East-West orientation. Nicholas Roerich found a tomb near Ladakh believed to be that of one of the three Mary companions travelling with Jesus. Srinagar is 170 km away from Mari and between the villages of Naugma and Nilmag lays Yus-Marg, the *'Meadow of Jesus'* where Jews had settled as far back as 772 BC. Takht-I-Suleiman or 'The Throne of Solomon' bears the inscription:

'At this time, Yuz Asaf announced his prophetic mission, in the year fifty four. He is Jesus, prophet of the sons of Israel'.

Bhavishya Maha Purana, written in its final form around 115 CE states that Jesus came to India and met King Shalivahana (ruled 39-50 CE), the grandson of Vikramajit, some 10 miles north-east of Srinagar. The Jewish princess Maryan bore him eleven children whose genealogy is now in keeping of Sahabitzada Bashrat Saleem. No fewer than twenty one references relate the stay of Jesus in Kashmir, particularly in the Happy Valley. According to Olsson, *Rishi nama* is a document found in the sarcophage along with the rod which is now housed at the Aish Muquam mosque. The pillars at the Temple of Solomon carry an inscription in Persian Sulus script that reads: "*He is Yasu (Issa) prophet of the children of Israel*". Jesus was known under the name Yuz Asaf in Kashmir where he spent the last thirty to forty years and died at the age of 80 or so. His body lies in the Roza Bal tomb in the Khanyar quarter of Anzimar, in the heart of Srinagar, aligned east-west, whereas that of the Islamic saint Syed Nasir-ud-Din is aligned north-south. Not far from the tomb of Jesus are to be found the final resting places of Moses (died aged 120) and Aaron, as confirmed by Bible itself (Deuteronomy 31:2, 31:15 and 34:5).

There are many parallels between the lives of Hindu God Krishna and Jesus: evil kings tried to kill both of them so their parents took them to Mathura (India) and Maturai (Egypt), respectively. Finally, **Krishna and Jesus traditions fused together** to give rise to the modern Fundamentalist Christianity. The word Catholic derives from Ketu-Loka (Universal Leader). The Church simply turned all this upside down and tried to convert the Hindus to the teachings the latter had given to the world. Thus, Krishna could well be the real Messiah of the Jewish people as Israel and India share some 7000 years of history. Doane goes on state:

"*...the mythological portion of the history of Jesus of Nazareth, contained in the books forming the canon of the New Testament, is nothing more or less than a copy of the mythological histories of the Hindoo savior Krishna, and the Buddhist savior Buddha, with a mixture of mythologies borrowed from the Persians and other nations...*"

Godfrey Higgins (cited in Matlock) was to remark:

"*The Christians of the West probably descended directly from the Buddhists...The existence of the Christians both in Europe and India (existed) long anterior to the Christian era*".

Jesus was an avatar (incarnation) according to the Hindu scriptures and the essence of gospels can be summarized thus: "*I and my Father are One*" (John 10:30) and "*I am in the Father and the father in me*" (John

14:11), as in the Vedic tradition (Chapter 4). In the word AUM, A stands for *akara* (creative), U for *ukara* (preservative) and M for *makara* (dissolutive) vibrations and personifies the Holy Ghost that lies at the base of Creation. Christ Consciousness is obvious when St. John stipulates: "*As many as received him, to them gave he the power to become the Sons of God*" John 1:12-13). This is the divine union with God through Yoga and meditation using the vibrations of AUM. Baptism amounts to being permeated by God's presence in the cosmic vibration personified as AUM as extrapolated by Gerber and Walden. Jesus preached:

"*The light of the body is the eye: if therefore thine eye be single, thy whole body shall be of full of light*" (Matthew 6:22-23).

Yogananda has shown that all four gospels need to be understood in the Vedic-Yoga tradition. Jesus taught that '*Silence is the fount of* Wisdom' almost identical to Meditation in the Yoga tradition. The Second Coming may simply be summarized by one single parable of Jesus: "*Behold the Kingdom of God is within you*" (Luke 17:20-21). The Gospel of Mary says seek the Son of Man within You; look within yourself to find the divine source rather than to Jesus.

"*Ask and it shall be given you; seek and ye shall find; knock and it shall be opened unto you. For everyone that asketh reciveth; and he that seeketh findeth; and to him that knocketh it shall be opened*" (Matthew 7:7-8).

Astounding similarities exist between Buddhist and Roman Catholic monastic orders in priestly robes, hierarchical organization, chalice, staff and rosary, folding hands when praying, ringing bells, a circular halo around Jesus, incense, lamps (or candles), the red dress of Santa. Many of the parables in the New Testament are almost identical to those in the Upanishads e.g. '*the blind leading the blind, both fall in ditch*'(Mathew 15.14) stems from Katha Upanishad: "*Andhe andhi thelian, dono koop parent*". St Christopher carrying a baby Christ on his shoulder through a flooded river is clearly the story of Krishna and Vasudeva. Valentine's Day is nothing but the spring festival of youth or *Madanotsava* of Hindu tradition; the autumn festival of Diwali on 5 November is held roughly at the same time. Clement of Alexandria (150-218 CE) refers to the miraculous conception of Buddha, the star over his birth place, the twelve disciples, the miracles, much like the birth of Jesus. The similarities between Jataka tales and Christian parables are striking e.g. walking over water, feeding 500 disciples with a single piece of cake, and so forth. The cross was an auspicious symbol around the globe as Swastika. Miraculous birth was just as prevalent around the globe and Krishna was born of a virgin. Ammonius Sacccus observed (cited in Knapp):

"Christianity and Paganism, when rightly understood, differ in no essential points, but had a common origin, and are really one and the same thing".

T.W. Doane summarized in his book *Bible myths and their Parallels in other religions*:

"We have seen, then, that the only difference between Christianity and Paganism is that Brahma, Ormzud (Ahura Mazda), Zeus, Jupiter, etc., are called by another name: Krishna, Buddha, Bacchus, Adonis, Mithras etc. have been turned into Christ Jesus; Venus's pigeon into the Holy Ghost; Diana, Isis, Devaki, etc., into the Virgin Mary; and the demigods and heroes into saints. The exploits of the one were represented as the miracles of the other. **Pagan festivals became Christian holidays, and Pagan temples became Christian Churches"**.

More than one hundred passages in the New Testament may be traced back to Buddhism some coincide virtually word for word. Both seek the deliverance of mankind from suffering, both emphasize salvation through limitless Love and Compassion, both proclaim the necessity of a second death (death of the ego), both refer to man being asleep:

"Awake yourself and Christ shall give you light (Ephesians 5:14), *Earnest among the thoughtless, awake among the sleepers* (Dhamapada II:29)".

Origen firmly believed in **reincarnation** but the sixth Council of Constantinople condemned him. Elizabeth Prophet traces the history of reincarnation in Christianity, from Jesus and the early Christians through Church councils and the persecution of so called heretics. However, resurrection implies reincarnation as an immortal soul rather than physical reappearance. Even Christian creation is Vedic; the book of John says:

"In the beginning was the word, and the word was with God, and the word was God." (John 1:14).

This is a verbatim translation of Sanskrit:

Prajapatirvai idamagraasit, tasya vag dvitiyaa asit, vag vai paramam Brahma.

The Christian Trinity of Father, Son and the Holy Ghost is similar to Brahma, Vishnu and Mahesh. Holy Ghost is the invisible vibratory power of God that actively sustains the universe in the AUM. **Amen is** a corrupt form of **OM** (or Aum) and many Sanskrit words form the vocabulary of Christianity: bell from *bal*, Nazareth from Nandarath, Satan from **Sat-na**, vestry from **vastra**, and so forth.

The *Bhaviushyapurana* actually described the coming of Jesus. Both Buddha and Jesus were tempted by Satan and both commanded their first disciples thus: '*Come follow me*'. **Parables of Jesus come straight from Buddhism and Hinduism**. Both Buddha and Jesus performed similar miracles such as multiplication of food at a wedding, walking on water, visions, visual perception over extraordinary distances, healing, raising the dead to life, exorcism, simultaneous epiphany etc. all of which were accorded a special place in Christianity as miracles impress people more than spiritual truths. Both Buddha and Christ began teaching at thirty, both had twelve disciples initially, both found their first disciples sitting under a fig tree, both forbade theft, murder, bearing false witness and illicit sex. Buddha said: '*Believe in me Ananda! All those who believe in me will come to great joy*', Christ likewise. Much as in the Vedic tradition, Jesus had preached:

"I am not your master…He who will drink from my mouth will become as I am: I myself shall become he, and the things that are hidden will be revealed to him…Let the one who seeks not stop seeking until he finds…the kingdom (of God) is inside of you, and it is outside of you. When you come to know yourselves then you will become known and you will realize that it is you are the sons of the living father… If you bring forth what is within you, what you bring forth will save you. If you do not bring forth what is within you, what you do not bring forth will destroy you".

This echoed Taitttriya Upanishad (III.6.1.) **"*Out of bliss these beings are born, in bliss they are sustained, and to bliss they go and merge again*".**

On the archway of Fatehpur Sikri is engraved the inscription ascribed to Jesus:

"The world is bridge. Pass over it – but do not settle down on it"

A mosque shows the same saying in a modified form:

"*The world is an over-proud house. Take this as a warning, and do not build on it*'.

Jesus had argued that the whole of Law could be summed upon the maxim: "*do unto others as you would have them do unto you*". Mark's Gospel describes Jesus as perfectly normal man with brothers and sisters who said:

"Nothing that originates outside a man can make him unclean by going into

him since it doesn't go into his heart…What comes out of man's mouth is what makes him unclean. For it is from within – from the human heart- that evil intentions flow".

Plotinus (204-270 CE) studied philosophy in Iran and India and passed the wisdom to Christianity. Plotinus' version of ecstasy agrees with Patanjali's Yoga Sutras where a person who can transcend the limits of his body, senses, and mind, is expected to enter an ecstatic union with God (Britannica.com). Plotinus was the founder of **Neo-Platonism** which was Greek version of **ancient Hinduism and Buddhism**, as also of **Sufism.** Creuzer (1819) asserted that **'Brahmanism'** of Veda might well have formed the basis of the **Hebrew religion.**

So intimate was the link between ancient Bharat and Christianity that Paradise, mentioned in a dozen or so verses of Genesis, was believed to be a real place on earth (Genesis 2.8-14 and 2.10-14). According to the Bible, Paradise lay to the East near four rivers, close to five in Punjab, whereas Mesopotamia has only two. According to Rohl, the original Garden of Eden was perhaps an agriculturally rich plain, 60 miles wide x 200 miles long, near Tabriz in Iran. Rohl also plotted the four rivers that flowed out of Paradise: Tigris, Euphrates, Gihon and Pishon (Genesis 2.10-14); these ran underground and emerged at their respective sources known to Aristotle. Gihon and Pishon were equated with Araxes and Uizhun in Azerbaijan and Kurdistan by Rohl but Flavius equated them with the Nile and the Ganges, respectively; Gihon could also be Yamuna. Schopenhauer thought that both Christianity and the ancient Egyptian religion had originated in India:

"Sanskrit literature will be no less influential for our time than Greek literature was in the fifteenth century for the Renaissance…From every sentence of the Upanishads deep, original and sublime thoughts arise, and the whole is pervaded by a high and holy earnest spirit…In the whole world there is no study…so beneficial and so elevating as that of the Upanishads…(They) are products of the highest wisdom…It is destined sooner or later to become the faith of the people…The study of the Upanishads has been the solace of my life, it will be the solace of my death".

Contemporary Christianity is based on the two basic tenets of Death and Resurrection of Jesus. No Resurrection, no Christianity. Baptism, Sunday Sabbath, virgin birth, miracles, Eucharist, had all existed in the Middle Eastern and Asia communities; Paul simply ascribed them to Jesus. According to the Dead Sea Scrolls, the elder of the community as representative of God would stand over the bread and wine and say: *"This is my body, this is my blood".* This tradition of transubstantiation too was ascribed to Christianity. The fourth Lateral Council in 1215 CE decreed that the bread and wine of the Eucharistic sacrament were transformed into the body and blood of Christ by priestly action; the wafers thereafter possessed miraculous power, as per the Gospel of John, chapter 6 verses 51-57:

"Whoever eats my flesh and drinks my blood possesses eternal life and I shall raise him up on the last day".

Yet, just a few verses later Jesus says *"The Spirit alone gives life, the flesh is of no avail"* acknowledging that flesh and blood mentioned earlier were just spiritual transformation in men.

Nag Hammardi and Dead Sea Scrolls question the virgin birth and resurrection of Jesus as imagined by Paul. These scrolls describe Sodom and Gomorrah not as cities of debauchery and wickedness but as centers of wisdom and learning. The idea of the original sin of Adam did not emerge until the fourth century. John the Evangelist, at the end of the first century, started with a rewriting of Genesis. For the first time Jesus was called 'God' and the 'Only Son', in contrast to Mark, Matthew and Luke where Jesus is a modest, self-effacing 'Son of Man'.

The Pauline Church exploits human nature by putting the notion of guilt at the heart of its teachings which can be alleviated by confession and repentance through the medium of clergy whatever the enormity of prior sins. Pauline Church celebrates death and resurrection not the life and message of Jesus. The expulsion of Adam from the Garden of Eden, after Eve had tasted the forbidden fruit, was exploited to denigrate women as no better than second class citizens who were treated as property by her husband and had to submit to beatings at his will. Paul sets the tone:

"Let the woman learn in silence with all subjection. But I suffer not a woman to teach, nor to usurp authority over the man, but to be in silence".

Paul counseled wives to be **subordinate** to their husbands, comparing the latter's lordship to that of Christ over his church. Tertullian (born ca. 150-160 CE) in the third century continues:

"You are the Devil's gateway...the sealer of that forbidden tree...the first deserter of the divine law... You are she who persuaded him whom the devil did not attack...Do you know that you are each an Eve? The sentence of God on your sex lives on in this age; the guilt, necessarily, lives on too".

"It is not permitted for a woman to speak in Church...to Baptize...to offer the Eucharist, nor to claim for herself a share in any masculine function, least of all in priestly office".

Women were **dichotomized between a mother and a whore** and Chrysostom wrote in 386 CE:

"*What else is woman but a foe to friendship, an inescapable punishment, a natural temptation, a desirable calamity, a domestic danger? A delectable detriment, an evil of nature painted with fair colors*".

By 58 CE, Christianity had **severed virtually all connection with its roots** and was reduced to Paul's image of Jesus. Paine concluded (cited in Dershowitz):

"*Of all the systems of religion that were ever invented, there is none more derogatory to the Almighty, more unedifying to man, more repugnant to reason, and more contradictory in itself, than this thing called Christianity. Too absurd for belief, too impossible to convince, and too inconsistence for practice, it renders the heart torpid, or produces only atheists and fanatics. As an engine of power, it serves the purpose of despotism, and as a means of wealth, the avarice of priests, but so far as respects the good of man in general, it leads to nothing here or hereafter*".

Singhal points out:

"*Christianity is in essence a strict ecclesiastical hierarchy. It has inhibited the freedom of thought and individual liberty by relentlessly enforcing its presuppositions as eternal truths. No federation of states has been as comprehensive and universal in taking hold on people's minds, and no monarch or dictator has been given the complete and willing obedience of such a wide and vast body of peoples as has the church. Communism…is essentially a totalitarian doctrine, negating individual liberty, and is a typical, almost exclusive, Western concept*".

After the death of Charlemagne, the Treaty of Verdun in 843 CE established that **everything should have a lord** in a **Great chain of Being**, from the Emperor and the Pope on top to worms and flies at the bottom, along a model first proposed by evil Aristotle. By 1100 CE all rival Christian sects had been wiped out and the Catholic Church reached an acme of power and influence under Innocent III (1198-1216 CE) with **emphasis on wealth and politics** such that matters of spirit became less important than silk and gold. Europeans believed that **God controlled everything** and truth was revealed only as much as God permitted. The Bible was believed to be the sole reservoir of knowledge outside of which all else was the creation of Satan who had tempted Eve and precipitated the fall of man. Following the preambles of perverted Aristotle, Luther even reaffirmed that **Serfdom was the necessary foundation** of society. Christianity was based upon the **perpetuation of ignorance** where reasoning was not encouraged and people were asked to believe in what they were told. Worldwide **death toll** from the **Inquisitions** is put between **five and nine million**, nearly all victims being housewives, poets, or gypsies. **Witchcraft** trials claimed

another **nine million** lives whereas **Inquisitions** killed **five million** or more. However, the total number of casualties remains to be elucidated.

From the earliest period, the Christian Church had demonized **Pagan gods as devil**. Many of the Hindu Gods were demonized in this manner, along with Hindu sacred symbols like the Trident or Trishul and consigned to Žmuidzinavičius Museum, commonly known as the Devils' Museum, at Kaunas, in Lithuania. In 2009 the museum housed some about 3,000 exhibits including prominent Hindu deities like Ganesha, Mahakali and others. Potential converts were then asked to hate their ancient spirituality and their old relics were then identified with Christianity.

European missionary Roberto de Nobili published *L'Ezour Vedam* where he **intentionally faked Vedic works** to justify the conversion of Hindus. Abbe Dubois fled France and lived in India for thirty years in his mission to civilize the heathens and launched a **scathing attack** on Hindu belief and practice in his widely read *Hindu Manners, Customs and Ceremonies*. A Dutch preacher named Abraham Roger published a similar scathing account in his *Open Door to Hidden Heathendom*. Thomas Jefferson (1743-1826) noted:

*"**Millions of innocent men, women and children,** since the introduction of Christianity, have been **burnt, tortured, fined, imprisoned**: yet we have not advanced one inch towards humanity. What has been the effect of coercion? To make one half of the world fools, and the other half hypocrites. To support error and roguery all over the earth".*

Paul Brunton added:

"The survival of Western humanity depends on the reintroduction of the concept of karma to the minds of the populace at large".

Helen Ellerbe in her book, *The Dark Side of Christian History,* observed:

Christianity has distanced humanity from nature. Time, once thought to be cyclical like the seasons, was perceived to be linear. In their rejection of the cyclical nature of life, orthodox Christians came to focus more upon death than upon life.

Islamic Theocracy

The word Arabia is an abbreviation of Sanskrit 'Arvasthan' where the Sanskrit 'V' changes to Prakrit 'B'. Arva in Sanskrit means a horse so Arvasthan signifies a land of horses introduced there earlier by Vedic Hindus of old.

Arabia was essentially within the sphere of influence of Vikarmaditya (circa 376-415 CE). Professors Salibi and Mazumdar underlines the fact that Arabistan (was an extremely **rich and glorious center of Vedic civilization** worshipping many deities imported from Bharat: Vishnu, Brahma, Kuber and some 360 more. W.H. Siddiqui observed:

"The Arab civilization grew up intensively as well as extensively on the riches of Indian trade and commerce. Nomadic Arab tribes became partially settled communities and some of them lived within walled towns practiced agriculture and commerce, wrote on wood and stone, feared the gods and honored the kings."

The word **Kaaba** is derived **from *Garbha Graha***; it is also known as *Harama*, derived from Sanskrit *Hariyam* (the shrine of Hari or Vishnu). The word Rabi is derived from *Ravi* and many Islamic festivals like *Shabibarat, Ramadhan* and *Gyarahavi Shareef* stem from Vedic *Shivrata, Rama dhyan* and *Ekadashi*, respectively. The practice of taking seven steps (*Saptapadi*) is associated with Hindu marriage rites and fire worship. Since 'Makha' means fire, the seven circumambulations around the Kaaba also prove that Mecca was the seat of Vedic fire-worship in the West Asia. In fact, Mecca could well be makka from Makkeshvar or Shiva. The **Kaaba lingam is black with reddish tones and yellow particles** (15 inches high and 11 inches wide), much like the *lignum* in Bharat. It is covered by a silver foil so the pilgrim gets to view only small portion of the original fetish. The pinnacle of Kaaba even has a crescent moon, as on the head of Shiva, and the Zam Zam spring near it is equivalent to the Holy Ganga where G has been replaced by Z. Muslim pilgrims entering the Kaaba are required to shave their head, take a bath, wear white clothes, and refrain from eating meat, all of which are Vedic customs.

No one is allowed to enter the **Kaaba itself as its walls are believed to carry Sanskrit inscriptions**, including some from Bhagvata Gita.

However, Burckhardt and Leblich were able to gain entry to the Kaaba in the 19th century and concur with the accounts described here. All Arabic copies of the Qur'an have the mysterious figure 786 imprinted on them which is the Vedic 'OM' in Sanskrit; read backwards in Arabic, **OM becomes 786**. Islamic scholars simply translated the Vedic texts for their astronomy, folklore, sciences and medicine. The holy festival of **Ramazan** carries the name **Rama** that had permeated around the globe (Chapter 6). Many verses in the Qur'an are mere translations of Vedic scriptures. For example.

"Sight perceives Him not. But He perceives men's sights; for He is the knower of secrets, the Aware." in the Qur'an compares well with *"That which cannot be seen by the eye but through which the eye itself sees, know That to be Brahman (God) and not what people worship here (in the manifested world)"* in Kena Upanishad. Both of the above verses mean: *"God is one and that He is beyond man's sensory experience".*

The **temple of Mecca was founded by Brahmins** and Kaaba was a Vedic shrine that attracted Hindu pilgrims. Arab deities Lat, Manat and Uzza refer to planets whose worship is still practiced in India. An inscription on a gold dish, inside the Kaaba shrine in Mecca, was recorded on page 315 of a volume known as '*Sayar-ul-Okul*', at the Makhtab-e-Sultania library, Istanbul, Turkey (cited in Oak). In the Roman script it reads:

"ItrashaphaiSantu IbikRamatul Phahalameen Karimun Yartapheeha Wayosassaru Bihillahaya Samaini Ela Motakabberen Sihillaha Yuhee Quid min howaYapakhara phajjal asari nahone osirom bayjayhalem. Yundan blabin KajanbInaya khtoryaha sadunya kanateph netephi bejehalin Atadari bilamasa-rateen phakef tasabuhu kaunnieja majekaralhada walador. As hmimanburukankad toluho watastaru hihila Yakajibaymana balay kulk amarenaphaneya jaunabilamary BikRamatum."

An English translation would go something like this:

"Fortunate are those who were born (and lived) during king Vikrama's reign. He was a noble, generous dutiful ruler, devoted to the welfare of his subjects. But at that time we Arabs, oblivious of God, were lost in sensual pleasures. Plotting and torture were Rampant. The darkness of ignorance had enveloped our country. Like the lamb struggling for her life in the cruel paws of a wolf us Arabs were caught up in ignorance. The entire country was enveloped in darkness as intense as on a new moon night. But the present dawn and pleasant sunshine of education is the result of the favor of the noble king Vikramaditya whose benevolent supervision did not lose sight of us- foreigners as we were. He spread his sacred religion amongst us and

sent scholars whose brilliance shone like that of the sun from his country to ours. These scholars and preceptors through whose benevolence we were once again made cognizant of the presence of God, introduced to His sacred existence, and put on the road of Truth, had come to our country to teach their religion and impart education at king Vikramaditya's behest."

Kaaba was an extremely rich and ornate temple, containing innumerable gems and gold plaques inscribed with the names of the winners of an annual poetry competition known as the Okaj fair. No wonder Mohammad looted it first to finance his subsequent campaigns. It is significant that he **destroyed the 360 idols around it but permitted the fetish to remain** in place because it was the patron deity of the Kuru-ishi household or the **Shaivites**, now known as **Shias**. The Prophet also permitted a portrait of mother and child to remain on the wall; this could be Krishna in the arms of his Yashodhara and became the staple form of representation to depict Mary and Jesus.

Vedic influence shines through much of Islam, including the name **Allah which stems from *Allopanishad*.** Allah is the fusion of al and Ilah (goddess Durga). *Bhavishya Purana* even predicts (cited in Knapp**): "*An illiterate teacher will appear, Mahamada is his name,* and he will give religion to his class companions***"**. The word Islam is itself derived from *Isha-alayam* while Qur'an is related to *Karana*, both from Sanskrit. The grandfather and uncles of Mohammad were engaged in making temple deities and were hereditary priests of the Kaaba which housed the Shiva lingam whose worship was once prevalent amongst the Arabs. D.C. Sircar has this to say about the origin and traditions of the Kaaba (cited in Matlock):

*"According to a popular Bengali tradition, apparently influenced by the Tantras, in an underground room underneath the floor of the Kaaba at Mecca there lies **Shiva in deep sleep**; pious Hindus are never allowed to approach him; if, however, a devout Hindu could place on his head a bilva-patra (garland of cinnamon leaves) only once, the god would at once rise up and destroy all the Muhammadans of the world…the Temple of **Mecca was founded by a colony of Brahmins** from India…it was a sacred place before the time of Mohamed…Its great celebrity as a sacred place long before the time of the prophet cannot be doubted…the city of Mecca is said by the Brahmins, on the authority of their old books, to be built by a colony from India; its inhabitants from the earliest era have a tradition that it was built by Ishmael, the son of Agar. This town, in the Indus language, would be called Ishmaelistan…a large district on the Indus was called Arabia, and its inhabitants Arabi".*

P. N. Oak further adds (cited in Matlock):

*"The Kaaba temple in Mecca, which the Muslims have captured and misappropriated, was an international **Vedic shrine**. An ancient Vedic scripture is titled Harihareshwar Mahatmya… mentions that Vishnu's footprints are consecrated in Mecca…Arabia has been a prominent region of the Vedic civilization especially because of its huge temple complex of the Kaaba. The black stone which is the Shiva emblem still survives in the Kaaba as the central object of Islamic veneration. All other Vedic idols could be found buried in the precincts or trampled underfoot in labyrinthine subterranean corridors if archaeological excavations are undertaken".*

Oak has concluded that the **Kaaba** was actually one of the holy places that **carried Vishnu's footprint**: Gaya, Mecca and Shukla Teertha.

Aditi Chaturvedi is affirmative:

*"Many centuries before prophet Muhammad and the destructive advent of Islam, Arabia or Arabistan was an extremely rich and glorious center of Vedic civilization. Arabistan is derived from the original Sanskrit term Arvasthan which means The Land of Horses. Since time immemorial, proponents of the **Vedic culture used to breed exceptional horses** in this region. Thus eventually the land itself began to be called Arva (Horses) - Sthan (place). The people who lived in this land were called Semitic. **Semitic comes from the Sanskrit word Smriti.** Arabs followed the ancient Vedic Smritis such as Manu-Smriti as their revered religious guides and thus they were identified as Smritic which has been corrupted into Semitic. At that time the Uttarapath (Northern Highway) was the international highway to the North of India. It was via Uttarapath that Arabia and other Middle Eastern countries drew their spiritual, educational and material sustenance from India. Besides, this Sea-links were formed with India at least 800 years before the advent of Islam. Basra was the ancient gateway to India because it was at this port that the Arab lands received Indian goods and visitors. At that time the spoken language was **Sanskrit, which later dwindled into the local variation that we now call Arabic**. The proof of this is that thousands of words that were derived from Sanskrit still survive in Arabic today. Even various kinds of swords were referred to as Handuwani, Hindi, Saif-Ul-Hind, Muhannid and Hinduani. The Sanskrit Astronomical treatise Brahma-Sphuta-Siddhanta in Arabic translation is known as Sind-Hind, while another treatise Khanda-Khadyaka was called Arkand. Mathematics itself was called Hindisa. The Arabs derived technical guidance in every branch of study such as astronomy, mathematics and physics from India".*

"This particular practice of the Prophet, of taking down the sacred idol of a temple and using it as a doorstep to trample on, set a precedent that would be extensively followed by the pious adherents of Islam in the future…The most scared idols were to be turned into footstones or buried under entrances of mosques, so that every time a Muslim stepped into his place of

worship, the idols of the Hindus would be desecrated again and again…The place Mecca (Arabic Makkah) appears to be derived from Sanskrit word Maka meaning sacrifice or ritual".

Various Hindu customs still prevail in West Asia, despite Islamization over the last 1300 years. The Hindus have a pantheon of 33 gods and People in Asia Minor too worshipped 33 gods before Islam. Vedic descriptions about the moon, the different stellar constellations and the creation of the universe have been incorporated from the Vedas in Koran part 1 chapter 2, stanza 113, 114, 115, and 158, 189, chapter 9, stanza 37 and chapter 10, stanzas 4 to 7. Unani is just the Arabic term for the Ayurvedic system of health care when Arabia was part of the Bharat Empire of Vikramaditya. The Hindu lunar calendar was introduced in West Asia and the Muslim month of 'Safar' forms the extra month. The Islamic practice of observing the moon rise before deciding on celebrating the occasion derives from the Hindu custom of breaking fast on Sankranti and Vinayaki Chaturthi only after sighting the moon. The Muslim month Rabi is the corrupt form of Ravi meaning the sun where Sanskrit 'V' is changed to Prakrit 'B'. Muslim sanctity for *Gyrahwi Sharif* is nothing but the Hindu Ekadashi (Gyrah = elevan or Gyaarah). Id in Sanskrit means worship, and Griha means 'house', so the Islamic Islamic word Idgah signifies a 'House of worship' which is the exact Sanskrit connotation of the term. The Islamic practice of **Bakari Id** derives from the Go-Medh and Ashva-Medh Yagna of Vedic era. The Islamic term 'Eed-ul-Fitr' (worship of forefathers) is almost the exact equivalent of 'Id of Piters' or Pitr-Paksha of Hindu ancestor worship. The word Mesh in Hindu zodiac signifies a lamb, so in the Bakari Id festival Bakari simply stands for a goat. Similarly the word **Namaz** derives from two Sanskrit roots 'Nama' and 'Yajna' (Nama yajana) meaning bowing and worshipping. Recital of the Namaz five times stems from the daily Vedic Panchmahayagna (or five daily worships). according to A.F. Nizami, the daily **Namaz is simply yoga** as the devotees assume different postures. Muslims need to clean five parts of the body before prayers and this derives from the Vedic *'Shareer Shydhyartham Panchanga Nyasah'*. During four sacred months of the year the devout are enjoined to abstain from plunder and other evil deeds, possibly from the *Chaturmasa* in Hindu tradition. The Muslim festival for honoring the dead in battle, or by weapons, is called *Barah Vafat*, that compares well with Hindus *Chayal Chaturdashi* of similar significance.

Sayar-ul-Okul informs us that for thousands of years a pan-Arabic poetic symposium used to be held at Mecca during the annual Okaj fair in pre-Islamic times. The annual Okaj fair in Mecca was later translated into Haj. Arabic greeting *'Salam walekum'* is garbled form of *Ishalayam Balakam* which means obeisance to Krishna. Bintoi had lived 165 years before Prophet Mohammad and had received the highest award for the best poetic compositions for three years in a row. Bintoi informs us that Vedic-Hindu scholars, preachers and social workers spread the fire-worship ceremony, preached the Vedic way of life, manned schools, set up Ayurvedic health centers, trained the local people in irrigation and agriculture, and established a democratic, orderly, peaceful, enlightened and religious way of life. This is evident by the Sanskrit suffix **sthan** in Afghanisthan (now Afghanistan), Baluchisthan, Kurdisthan, Tajikiathan, Uzbekisthan, Iran, Sivisthan, Iraq, Arvasthan, Turkesthan and so forth. Obviously, the **Vedic Hindus ruled all of West Asia**, from Karachi to Hedjaz, gave Sanskrit names to these lands and the towns therein. Such ancient conquests permitted Vedic-Hindu Kshatriya families, like the Pahalvis and Barmaks, to hold sway over Iran and Iraq, turned Parsee Agnihotris into fire-worshippers, introduced a Sanskrit dialect to Kurds of Kurdisthan, and established centers of excellence in learning like the Nav Vihara all the way up to Soviet Russia. Recent excavations have yielded ancient **Hindu sculptures of Ganesha** in Central Asia, West Asia and Russia.

Ismailis turned to the Zoroastrian myths of Iran and developed the *tawil* (carrying back) method reading the Qur'an much like the **chanting of OM**. **Pranayama and yoga** were incorporated into all branches of **Sufism** where the sage says "*I cast off my own self as a serpent casts off its skin. Then I considered my own self and found that I was He* (God)". Jahangir identified the highest form of Sufism with Vedanta and Dara Shikoh proved that **Sufism and Vedanta were identical**.

Abrahamic tradition now stands for total destruction of pagan Hindu kafirs but repackages Vedic-Hindu patrimony to embellish its own depraved ancestry. Vedic spirituality has been replaced by blood thirst for symbolic, statistical, conversion such that Arabia and West are passed off as founts of World Religions and culture.

8. A Sick Old Orphan Called Europe

Europe is not an isolated land, continent, or entity but merely the westernmost extremity of the larger Eurasian landmass linked to Africa. The name Europe was concocted by Greek philosopher cum geographers in the sixth and fifth centuries BC when Herodotus argued for a tripartite division of the habitable world into Europe, Asia, and Libya (Africa). Europe displays a great diversity of geographical and climatic features. The great plains of the north and east, the steppes of the Ukraine, and the boulder clays of the Baltic, are to be contrasted with the mountain ranges of the Alps, the Pyrenees, and the Carpathians. The climate ranges from hot, dry, summers and cool, wet, winters of the Mediterranean region to the damper but more benign regions along the Atlantic coast endowed with dry summers and intensely cold winters of the East European interior. With an area of 3,998,000 square miles it ranks as the second-smallest of the continents, but in terms of population (727,000,000 in 2007) it is the third-largest.

Europe is ethnically diverse and Europeans have developed an awareness of being 'European' only since the colonial era. In fact, the term remains geographical rather than cultural, ethnic, or economic. Europe lacks both the great fertile valleys of Indus, Gangetic plains and fertile Nile delta, or great rivers required for bounteous agriculture. Due to cold climate, the Great Ice Age lingered on in Europe so agriculture was late to get started. Europe is also poor in natural resources and throughout pre-history had to import raw materials from lands outside its geographical confines. Coal is found extensively in Britain, Spain, France, Germany, Belgium, Poland, Slovakia, the Czech Republic, and Ukraine. Oil and natural gas deposits abound only in Russia and the North Sea. Nickel, tin, bauxite, copper, lead, gypsum, manganese, lead, and iron ore have been mined extensively.

The forests of Europe were destroyed by the seemingly inexorable 'advances' of civilization, industrialization and warfare. The earliest written accounts of forest destruction in Southern Europe date back to 1000 BC in the 'Histories' by Homer, Thucydides and Plato, and in Strabo's Geography. Countries in Europe with the largest percentage of arable land include the United Kingdom, France, Denmark, and the Netherlands; Norway, Sweden, Finland, and northern Russia have limited amounts of arable land due to a restricted growing season at high latitudes as well as extreme cold. Agricultural land covered 44% of the European Economic Union (EU) territory, down from 53% in 1975. . Agricultural land covers less than 10% of the territory in Finland and Sweden but accounts for 70% in Ireland and the United Kingdom.

Literacy came to the Mediterranean world from as early as the 8th century BC, while eastern and northeastern Europe remained in the prehistoric period until the Late Middle Ages, around 1400 CE. In contrast to the rich literary output in Sanskrit as far back as 2000 BC (Chapters 2,3), European literature took off only after the 17th century. The poetry of the year

1000 celebrated the hardened qualities of a hero in order to survive, as in *Fortunes of Men*:

> *Hunger will devour one, storm dismast another,*
> *One will be spear-slain, one hacked down in a battle.*

The writing of legendary histories to embellish depraved ancestry lead to the invention of the likes of King Arthur in the 12th century by a Welshman; an Irish Chronicler came up with the myth of High King Brian Boru who defended Christian Ireland against the Vikings.

Around the year 1000 CE European life was short, a boy of twelve was considered old and girls often got married to men significantly older than themselves. Most people died in their forties though England could boast a population of a million by 1000 CE who lived in small communities of a couple of dozen homes along a single, winding, street. Tall crosses in the middle indicated the place to worship as churches came up only later. Homes were built out of wood and covered in 'cob' – a mixture of clay, straw and cow dung – with roofs thatched of straw or reeds, while the windows consisted of gaps cut into walls covered with wattle shutters as glass was precious and probably imported. Wood was sometimes used to build houses, dishes, firewood, and the word carpenter is believed to have come from *'carpentum'*; the two wheeled chariot was developed by the Celts. There were no surnames; land was tilled by an oxen train of two men, invented in the first century CE, cultivation and pastures were organized on a community basis. Good and evil were living companions to people and the Church had its own army of spirits and saints. People wore simple tunics fastened with clasps and thongs, as the buttons had not yet been invented, colored with vegetable dyes of red, yellow and green.

Slavery was the common currency of the Arabs, Romans, Germanic tribes and Anglo-Saxon England. Everyone was beholden to someone in the hierarchy introduced by Normans in 1066 as feudal system consisting of serfs, villains and lords. People could not imagine themselves without a protector, there was a lord in heaven and one was needed on earth. The purpose of the war from the fifth to the tenth centuries was to **capture bodies for slavery**. Famine, disease and hardships were forever looming high and people dated their lives by them: great famines in 975, 976 and 1005, first great pestilence among cattle in 986, great sea flood in 1014, various diseases and bad weather in 1041. These compelled men to kneel and place their heads in the hands of a lord, sell their son under seven, and practice infanticide, all of which were permitted by the Anglo-Saxon law code. Although cannibalism had largely disappeared by 1000 CE people supplemented flour with weeds, bark, roots and nettles. Whereas drinking horns were known, fork was not invented until the seventeenth century and people took their own knives to the feast of the nobleman. Mead was a super sweet alcoholic beverage with quite a kick, brewed from crushed honeycombs. Wine was less popular as corked bottle was invented only in the 18th century. Ale was much safer to drink than water as boiling and brewing destroyed some contamination. Beer had to be consumed without delay as hops for brewing and longer shelf life were developed only as of the 14th century. Thirty or so monasteries in England provided solace in prayer from the impoverished life and Benedictine monks, who brought Christianity to England in 597 CE, administered the great cathedral churches.

Wheat and barley were consumed in England whereas rye was eaten in Central Europe. Watermills, some 5624 in England, about one for every village, were used to ground the grain. Animal excrement perfumed the air and latrines were built at the backdoor of most houses with no concern for either odor or flies that traveled from the latrine to the food; moss formed the toilet paper. The development of town life resulted in the adoption of surnames often based on trades and occupations: Carpenter, Tanner, Weaver, etc. People believed that venturing too far from Europe might entail the risk of ships falling off the edge of a flat world where stars etc. circled around the earth, as per Greek philosophers (Chapter 6.VIII). There was **no cotton** and only the wealthy could afford coarsely woven linen, everybody else wore hand woven wool undergarments, in contrast to Bharat (Chapter 5.II). Christianity throughout its history appears to have emphasized the grace-giving quality of dirt and filth in contrast to the ISC that was a model of cleanliness personified (Chapter 5.III,IV).

The flea hunter beat the insect to death with a cudgel, heavy cloth or the like. One monastery prescribed five baths per year for every monk and disease could be cured by faith as there was no notion of antiseptic at all. Bible listed thirty five miracles by which Jesus defeated illness by the power of faith. September heralded the culling of wild boars which was directly linked to survival through the winter as ailing and elderly livestock was turned into sausages and pies; sides made bacon, stomach lining provided tripe; intestines provided skin for sausage and blood was turned into black pudding. Sugar cane reached Venice only in 996 CE but sugar was not imported until the Middle Ages and Caribbean sugar plantations were developed only in the seventeenth century. Honey was so precious that people paid taxes with it while the bees wax commanded a higher price than honey as bees wax candle exuded a smell that was infinitely more pleasant than candle made from mutton fat.

Weather was interpreted as omens for people while the old magic lived in the country side or *pagus* that gave the word pagan. England was a **network of magical sites** and the altar of every English Church contained the physical relic of at least one Saint for miraculous cure. Heaven was visualized as a royal court where God sat in judgment and granted immediate access to saints without a wait in the purgatory. It was an age of belief and saints were a living community to whom one prayed and amongst whom one lived. There were no women in the Julius calendar and **Adam and Eve were represented as two men** but Mary came to wear a crown as a queen to separate her from worldly women.

The timing of Easter, the most important festival of the Church, was debated furiously as it was calculated by the lunar Jewish calendar of 29 and one half days that did not fit on with the solar calendar of 365 and one fourth days. Easter was sometimes celebrated twice in one year. Bede, the monk from Tyneside, popularized the Anno Domini (AD) system composed in 725 CE by Dionysius Exigus who dated the Christian era from the birth of Jesus as year 1 because zero was unknown. Worse still, the year 1 of Dionysius actually fell four years after the death of Herod which meant that **Jesus was probably born in 4 BC** (or earlier) and the second millennium of his birth should have been celebrated in 1996 or 1997, not 2000. Bede took it for granted that the year should begin with the birth of Christ on December 25; following that logic with the nine months of pregnancy one arrived at 25 March, the Feast of Annunciation or Lady Day. The Eucharist of Easter permitted ordinary members of the congregation to consume bread and wine, as on Christmas and Whitsun. The twelfth century could be summarized thus:

"Blessed are the rich for they shall be filled; blessed are they that have, for they shall not go away empty; blessed are the wealthy for theirs is the Court of Rome".

Archbishop Thomas Becket observed about the Roman Church

"......the Scribes and Pharisees... load themselves with fine clothes and their tables with precious plate...They oppress the churches, stir up law suits, bring clergy and people into strife, have no pity for the oppressed, and look on gain as the sole duty of man. Hey sell justice, and what has been paid for today must be bought again tomorrow...they imitate the demons...and the Pope himself they say is burdensome and oppressive to all: while the churches which our fathers built go to ruin, he builds palaces, and he goes about not only in purple but in gold".

It was possible to believe that:

The rich man in his castle, the poor man at his gate,
God made them high and low, and ordered their estate.

Cromwell maintained that the vote was rightly restricted to those who had a permanent interest in the kingdom i.e. who owned land for:

"If the master and servant shall be equal electors, then clearly those that have no interest in the kingdom will make it their interest to choose those that have no interest".

A doctrine of natural rights would lead to Communism. The House of Commons was elected by less than 10 per cent of English people as poor and women were not included. Win Stanley observed:

"The best laws that England hath are yokes and manacles, tying one sort of people to be slaves to another… all laws that are not grounded upon equity and reason, but respecting persons, ought not to be cut off with the king's head. He that hath no property was not free, nor were all Englishmen freeborn".

Judicial torture ceased after 1640 and a Habeas Corpus was enforced by the Whigs in 1641 CE. Universal male suffrage was introduced in England only in 1918 because voting rights had previously been granted to the privileged class. A major goal of the governments after 1660 CE was to protect the producer not the consumer or the subsistence farmer. Knowledge was denied to the lower classes by the Church as it would divert

"those whom nature or fortune had determined to the plough, the oar, or other handicrafts, from their proper design… (free schools) dangerous to the government".

Grammar schools were held responsible for educating people above their proper station and causing the Civil War of the 1640s. All but one of the Grammar Schools in Wales was dissolved as the propertied class and the Church hierarchy sought to suppress democratic ideas.

Old Testament mentions plagues and epidemic diseases as punishment by God e.g. the plague that Moses brought down upon Egypt, epidemic on the Philistines for their seizure of the Ark, the pestilence that punished David's sin by killing 70,000 out of 1,300,000 able bodied men in Israel and Judah, and the fatal visitation that *"slew in the camps of Assyrians one hundred and eight five thousand"* in just one night. The doctrine that **disease came from God** could mean that it was impious to interfere with God's purpose by trying to take precaution against it. People took it for granted that their bodies should provide hospitality to parasites including 30 cm long maw-worm that could emerge from any orifice including the corners of eyes; leprosy was a common European illness. The plague of Athens (430-425 BC) killed some 300,000 people. In Roman history, Livy describes at least eleven disasters; plague epidemics hit the Roman world 165-180 CE and again in 251-266 CE when 5000 died in the city of Rome, followed by outbreaks in 452, 565, and 590. Bede records pestilence in England in 664, 672, 678, and 683, no fewer than four in twenty years. Gibbon observed:

"Many cities of the east were left vacant, and in several districts of Italy the harvest and the vintage withered on the ground." He alleges...a visible decrease of the human species which has never been made good in some of the fairest countries of the globe".

Procopius reports that plague killed 10,000 persons daily in Constantinople 543 CE where it raged for four months. The bubonic plague of Justinian arrived in 542 CE and raged until 750 CE; it had appeared previously in Egypt and Libya in 300 BC. During 1346-50 CE, it came in waves every 21-25 years, killing one third of the total population in Europe and 45% of people in England. Six epidemics ravaged Europe between 540-600 CE when the power of prayer was the only cure in shelters attached to Churches; priests were doctors and nuns were nurses with no training in medicine or hygiene. In Spain one half million people died in 1596-1602 and subsequent outbreaks in1648-52 and 1677-85 more than doubled that number. In Venice, a third of the city's population died in 1575-77 and again in 1630-31. In London, plague in 1603, 1625, 1636, 1665 killed 33,500, 35,500, 10500 and 69,000 people, respectively. In 1771, plague killed 56672 people in a single season in Moscow. The last outbreak in Western Mediterranean occurred in Marseilles 1720-21. The Dance of Death became a common theme for art and the labor shortage had enormous impact on economy. The plague probably came via the Genoese settlers in Kafka (Crimea) to Sicily, then on to Pisa, Genoa, Marseilles, and Spain, finally claiming some 20 million lives.

. After 1900, plague continued in North America, Argentina and South Africa. Thus, plague appears to have reached **India from Europe,** not the other way around, along with tuberculosis, and typhoid. According to the British Gazetteer, **19 million people in India died of famine and 15 million more died of plague**, malaria and malnutrition during 1891-1900. Europeans introduced fawn (swine, cattle, horses) and flora (Kentucky blue grass, dandelions, daisies) into the Americas that killed 90% Amerindians. By contrast, there is no record any invader being ravaged by disease in

India such that all foreign observers lauded the cleanliness and the celebration of life prevalent in India, as described in appropriate chapters. **Yaws** appeared in Europe before 1346 and Syphilis broke out virulently in the 15th. Syphilis epidemic first appeared in Naples in 1493 but by 1498 **syphilis reached India** and by 1505 China. The populations of South Pacific island nations were wiped out to the extent of 95% by syphilis, smallpox, measles etc. all of which were used as a proof of the superiority of 'true' God.

Abject misery of life in Europe was balanced by sex, the only outlet available to the starving masses. To this end, sex and prostitution were organized by the state to generate revenue and to subdue the destitute masses. Sex was reduced to seminal ejaculation through street walkers as the society was not cultivated enough to enjoy fusing of all senses as in Kamasutra. Obscene works of art adorned the doors, arches, windows and niches of the finest Gothic cathedrals in France where some 800,000 flagellants, men and women, marched naked through the cities of France, using the whip freely on the bare back of the person ahead, and the aphrodisiac effect led thereafter to frantic debauchery. The number of prostitutes in Paris was recorded at 28,000 in a 1762 manuscript for a population of 600,000; assuming 200,000 men, there was a whore for every ten males. Other great centers of prostitution in France included Avignon, Carcassone, Toulouse and Strasbourg where churches and the Cathedral formed the recognized meeting ground for whores.

The Great Council of Venice declared prostitution to be "*absolutely indispensable to the world*" in 1358, and government-funded brothels were established in major Italian cities throughout the 14th and 15th centuries. In Russia, Peter I and Catherine the Great sponsored exclusive retreats for sex e.g. The Physical Club in Moscow, a worthy rival to Louis XV's *Parc aux Cerf*s at Versailles. The bishops of Winchester patronized the only officially recognized brothels in England, directly on church lands. Gladstone told the House of Commons in 1857:

"*As respects the gross evils of prostitution, that there is hardly any country in the world where they prevail to a greater extent than in our own*".

Howard Vincent of Scotland Yard admitted in the House of Lords in 1881:

"*I should think that prostitution in England is considerably in excess of the prostitution in other countries*".

Around 1700, the Dutch VOC established a large house of female **sex slaves** in Cape Town; Germans were particularly efficient in organizing prostitutes for their army. In the18th century, England permitted the grossest public display of sexual extravagance. During Victorian era, pornography became an industry and the 1869 number of prostitutes in London ranged anywhere between 60,000-80,000 (twice as many as in Paris). Even at midday, copulation was practiced at windows so all neighbors could see it. Many clubs such as the Cock and Hen club of Clerkenwell, combined sex with violence for aristocrats who indulged in rape, murder, perverse games, and other unbridled excesses. Strand was of course the place to pick up children as mania for virgins turned 8-9 year old girls into prostitutes. The servants themselves accepted sex with their masters to avoid the loss of their position. Some 921 brothels across the capital, offering full sex for between £15 and £250, employed 1,933 women aged between 18 and 55, an average of two per brothel (TOI 5 September 2008). One out of four men, and one out of 10 women, was prepared to sleep with someone to advance their careers, according to a poll for the Observer. Pornography became a big industry during the Victorian era. **Homosexuality** and **bestiality** were integral parts of European sexual practices and reached India through the British. Both Nehru and Gandhi, who had unbounded love for the British, apparently engaged in homosexuality.

The Bible prescribes **human sacrifice** to obtain favors from God. In the Old Testament, Abraham was instructed to sacrifice his son to God in exchange for the Promised Land because Canaan was too small to accommodate all of the tribes;

"Take your son, your only son – yes, Isaac, whom you love so much – and go to the land of Moriah. Sacrifice him there as a burnt offering on one of the mountains, which I will point out to you." (Genesis 22:1-18).

Consecrate to me every first-born that opens the womb among Israelites, both man and beast, for it belongs to me" (Exodus 13:2).

"And thou shalt offer thy burnt offerings, the flesh and the blood, upon the altar of the Lord thy God: and the blood of thy sacrifices shall be poured out upon the altar of the Lord thy God, and thou shalt eat the flesh". (Deuteronomy 12:27).

"Thou shalt not delay to offer the first of thy ripe fruits, and of thy liquors: the firstborn of thy sons shalt thou give unto me". (Exodus 22:29).

Samuel 21 prescribes blood sacrifice to appease Jehovah.

Archeological evidence from the British Isles seems to indicate that human sacrifice may have been practiced long pre-dating any contact with Rome. Child sacrifice, group sexual orgies, incest, castration, and cannibalism were practiced publicly, where the child covered in dough was put on a table, slaughtered by the neophyte and the onlookers would then dip bread in the victim's blood and eat. In 2nd century CE, children were still thrown from the top of the temple of Atargatis by parents who joked as they did so. Herodotus speaks of funerary **cannibalism** among the Iron Age Massagetae. Cannibalism was practiced as recently as 2000 years ago in Britain. Most recently, the Leeds Crown Court convicted a Mr. Morley for stabbing his own friend and consuming his flesh. The **Vedic-Hindu tradition does not sanction either human sacrifice, cannibalism or castration**. Some peripheral tribes that practiced human sacrifice were forced to move out of the Vedic heartland

Bible sanctified slavery along with rape and prostitution (www.evilbible.com).

Slaves, male and female, you may indeed possess, provided you buy them from among the neighboring nations. You may also buy them from among the aliens who reside with you and from their children who are born and reared in your land. Such slaves you may own as chattels and leave to your sons as their hereditary property, making them perpetually slaves. But you shall not lard it harshly over any of the Israelites, your kinsmen. (Leviticus 25: 44-46).

When you go out to war against your enemies, and the Lord, your God delivers them into your hand, so that you take captives. If you see a comely woman among the captives and become so enamored of her that you wish to have her as your wife, you may take her home to your house. (Deuteronomy 21:11-14).

Aristotle's thesis that certain peoples were slaves by nature was taken as an article of faith so Bible and Qur'an simply institutionalized the practice. Indeed, **slavery, rape, murder are all ingrained in Bible;** and these were institutionalized by successive hierarchies of various Church denominations. Slavery amounted to 25% of the population in Athens under Pericles. In the Roman Empire, probably over 25% of the empire's population, and 30 to 40% of the population of Italy was enslaved. The slave trade grew as a business subsidized by English, Spanish and Portuguese and Liverpool thrived as a great city based on slave trade. In 1452, Pope Nicholas V issued the papal bull *Dum Diversas*, granting Alfonzo V of Portugal the right to reduce any "*Saracens, pagans and any other unbelievers*" to hereditary slavery which legitimized slave trade. In 1619 the Dutch began the slave trade between Africa and America (Virginia), by becoming the pre-eminent slave trading country in Europe by 1650, but overtaken by Britain around 1700. Americas imported 275000 slaves in the sixteenth century, followed by another 340,000 in the seventeenth, six million in the eighteenth and two million in the nineteenth. By contrast, Greek historian Arian observed in his book *Indica*:

"*This also is remarkable in* India that *all Indians are free, and **no Indian at all is a slave**. In this the Indians agree with the Lacedaemonians. Yet the Lacedaemonians have Helots for slaves, who perform the duties of slaves; but the Indians have no slaves at all, much less is any Indian a slave*" (Book VIII, Chapter X).

Megasthenes had similarly declared that there was no slavery in Bharata and further confirmed by many Chinese scholars who visited Taxila and Nalanda.

The earliest accounts of **castration** by Herodotus (484-425 BC) refer to the lucrative practice of Panonius of Chios who: "*would procure beautiful boys and castrate and take them to Sardis and Ephesus, where he sold them for great price*". Herodotus further noted that Persians value castrates "*more than testicled men by reason of full trust they have in them*". Vedic record uses the term *vadhryasva* for castration of horses but makes no mention of human castration or eunuchs. The arrival of Islam in the 7th century lead to large scale castration of little boys for slave trade.

Europe was beset by religious wars, abject poverty, decadence, debauchery, superstition, disease and could boast of no scientific or medical tradition. Consequently, **superstition** was the only way out of frustration. Felix in the second century wrote that Christians worshipped the head of a donkey, the genitals of the presiding priest. The Initiation sometimes involved the stabbing to death of a child wrapped in dough with 'invisible blows' after which they drained his blood and fought for his limbs. Documentation for the ancient **magic** dates back to the sixth century BC to cure illness and to cast binding spells; curse tablets were found on tombstones but voodoo dolls were used as well. Ghosts were the chief motor of magic in curse tablets of Greece. Necromancy (ghost evocation technology) was fairly conservative and first described in Odyssey. **Divination** was so rampant that events were foretold by the flight of birds, entrails of slaughtered cattle, size, shape, color and markings on the liver and the gall bladder, croaking of ravens, chirping of wrens, flight of crows, and so forth; Roman armies carried sacred chicken whose appetite was directly proportional to the chance of victory. The Church counted on **miracles** to counter magic and to prove that the new religion was more powerful than the deities of the old. By contrast, Vedic ideation was based upon mathematics, jyotish, astronomy, reason, inquiry and spirituality (Chapter 5.VIII, IX).

Augustine of Hippo maintained that **everything was preordained** because Will belonged to God not man, in direct contrast to the law of *karma* by which each individual tried to emulate the Aryan ideal (Chapter 4). Pope Innocent VIII kept a mistress and fathered two children; for the last months of his life he was kept alive by suckling on women's breasts and blood transfusions resulting in the death of three boys. He authorized two Dominicans Springer and Kramer to stamp out the **heresy** of witchcraft and they authored the *Malleus Malefiacrum* which went into twenty eight editions 1486-1600 and entered the civil code known as the Carolina Code in 1532 which concluded that "*all witchcraft comes from carnal lust which is in women insatiable*". Gratian wrote the Church's Canon Laws around 1140 had said that God had given the devil power over the genitals.

Pope Innocent VIII issued a papal bull on 5 December 1484 which marked the official persecution of witches by being burnt alive. **Witchcraft** was made a civil as well as an ecclesiastical offence by the Paris Parliament in 1390 and in 1398 the University of Paris declared that the witch's pact with devil was an act of heresy. Inquisitors consisted of Dominican Friars reputed for their cruelty after torture had been sanctioned in 1252 CE and all trials were held in secret. Women were repeatedly raped before being tortured by instruments that were blessed by a priest. By the 17th century, as many as 200,000 or more were killed by Christian courts and witchcraft became a lucrative business as competing sects denounced each other.

Inquisition courts under the Dominicans turned torture into an art of organized cruelty using garrets, strapados, water, a German chair with spikes, bed with spiked rollers, the Nuremberg maiden, pendulum, the bone breaking wheel, melting lead poured into veins, skull crusher, iron mask, thumbscrews, cradle lined with spikes, boiling in oil or water, buried alive, burning slowly, poisons, mutilations, limb dislocation by horses for many hours, gouging out eyes, burning individual fingers, bilboes, the Spanish collar, the catchpole, the cage, bedsteads, ringing bell, mutilation, bastinado (beating with a bamboo), and many other devices. Many developed a mania for torture viewing, particularly in England where sometimes 30,000 or more gathered.

L'Abbe Guibourg was found to regularly conduct Black Masses in the presence of a naked woman made to lie in front of the altar with her legs open. Wafers were pressed against the breasts and vulva of the woman, a child would urinate in the chalice, the contents would be sprinkled over the worshippers, and the wafer would finally be inserted into the woman's vagina. An orgy of indiscriminate sex followed with incantations of Lord

Satan substituted for God and Christ including human sacrifice whose fat was used to make candles. Sometimes an infant's throat was split open such that the blood drained into the chalice on the belly of the naked woman. Guibourg would then smear the blood on his penis and have sex with the woman; fetuses were taken from unsuspecting women. Father Davot was supposed to have said a 'love mass' while a naked girl was kissing his private parts throughout the ceremony.

Europe was trapped in cycles of over population and under production. The years 1621-23, 1629-31,1646-51,1658-61, 1673-74, 1693, 1697-98 saw bad harvests, followed by catastrophic recession, famine and riots in 1686, 1696-97, 1701, 1706, 1708 and 1710. In 1300 Europe people were eating everything they could find: dogs, cats, grass and even their own children Between 1696 and 1697 CE famine killed a third of the population of Finland and close to a million starved to death in 1769. Anything that made a penny was tried. Adam Smith highlighted the absolute protection that English law gave to private property. There was no profits tax, no capital gains tax, no value-added tax on most manufactures. Most wars were waged in pursuit of trade by restricting imports and subsidized exports. Evangelicalism supported commercial capitalism – each man too paternalistic responsibility for himself and his family. Real National output, growing about 1% per annum between 1749 and 1780, was increasing by about 1-8% between 1780 and 1800. Export to Colonies and Latin America kept Britain afloat. Indeed, money was a passport up the social ladder. Porter paints a vivid picture:

"Crime was rife and often bloody…violence ran through public and political life…Force was used as matter of routine to achieve social and political goals…English political and legal institutions favored the propertied and privileged".

European rulers knew that there was only so much wealth to go around and one country could enrich itself only at the expense of others. In the late sixteenth century, 70% of Spanish state revenue was spent on weapons and two thirds of other European nations were doing likewise. Portuguese shipbuilders had already adapted the technology from Bharat to their own ships and armed them with canons under a crown-endorsed enterprise. Iron canons were invented in the early fourteenth century, bronze followed. Halifax in 1694 was to say:

"Trade… is the creature of liberty: the one destroyed, the other falleth to the ground".

A 1712 Act of Parliament was to establish free trade without any restrictions. Dryden accused: *"that kings were useless and a clog to trade"*.

Dean Swift observed:

"Law in a free country is, or ought to be, the determination of the majority of those who have property in land".

George Lockhart went even further:
"They don't so much value in England who shall be King, as those whose King he shall be".

Locke maintained that **security of property** was the reason for the existence of the state. Press freedom was all but assured after 1703 and the authors were granted copyright for the first time in 1711.

Such was the lewd and vulgar background of Europeans on the eve of their **civilizing mission** *around the globe.*

9. European Scramble for Bharat

Chaudhuri had rightly observed that Indian subcontinent and China possessed the most advanced and varied economies in Asia during the years1500 to 1800 CE. Pirenne was lucid:

"In the middle of the seventeenth century, Asia still had a far more important place in the world than Europe…The riches of Asia were incomparably greater than those of the European states. Her industrial techniques showed a subtlety and a tradition that the European handicrafts did not possess. And there was nothing in the more modern methods used by the traders of the Western countries that Asian trade had to envy. In matters of credit, transfer of funds, insurance, and cartels, neither India, Persia, nor China had anything to learn from Europe."

In the 13th Century India's share of world trade was 45%, after Moguls era it was 24%, when Brits left it was 4%, after 60 years of Congress rule it was 1.2%; India was the world economic leader for 1750 yrs.

Initially, British traders had come to India in the hope of selling British Broadcloth but found little demand for it. On the other hand, items manufactured in India could be sold quite profitably in their homeland. So, by the middle of the 17th century, the East India Com[any (EIA) was re-exporting Indian goods to Europe and North Africa and Turkey. The Indian Ocean trade was financed predominantly by metallic silver between 1220-1700 CE; gold was used only as a supplement of substitute. By 1650, Spanish America had exported some **181 tons of gold and 17,000 tons of silver** to Europe, most of this was used to purchase Asian manufacture. Dutch exported 25-30 thousand tons of silver from Japan each year to purchase raw silk from China. Spain looted **750,000 pounds of gold** from Americas between 1492-1600 that was to form the backbone for great banks in Italy, England and Amsterdam. Between 1600 and 1800, continental Asia absorbed at least 32 thousand tons of silver from the Americas via Europe, 3 thousand tons via Manila, and perhaps 10 thousand tons from Japan, or a total of at least 45 thousand tons, or nearly 40 percent of the world production of 116 thousand tons.

Nonmetallic currencies of the Indian Ocean included a nonedible, bitter almond (*badam*), imported into Gujarat from Persia in the seventeenth century for use as money; 36 of these badams equaled one paisa. The sea shell cowry was supplied by Maldives though Chinese had used cowry shells as currency as far back as 1200 BC. Their use in Bharata for small transactions can be traced to the fifth century but the EIC trade in **cowries** lasted at least until 1757 CE; even the rent was levied in cowries. Orissa used cowries as a legal tender even for big transactions and EIC received Orissa revenue in cowries. Cowries spread to Gujarat, Assam and adjoining areas but depreciated in the early 19th century. By the middle of the 18th century the Dutch had taken took full control of the cowry trade with the Maldives and the sea trade from Europe to Malacca.

In 1700, nearly all cotton goods sold in Europe came from Bharata whereas Manchester produced a poor imitation. Consequently, the new European bourgeoisie sought to ban the purchase Asian manufacture. Back in 1614, the Dutch Jan Pieterzoon Coen, had warned his directors:

"*Trade in India must be conducted and maintained under the protection and favor of your weapons, and the weapons must be supplied from the profits enjoyed by the trade, so that trade cannot be maintained without war or war without trade*".

Europeans were bemoaning the loss of 'European' silver to Asia as the silk and wool merchants of France and England could not compete with high quality textiles manufactured in Bharat. Eager to avoid the loss of bullion from England, after the battle of Plessey, the EIC was able to **force**

the cultivation of opium in India to purchase tea for British market whereas other European countries still had to suffer the loss of bullion mined in the Americas. Abbe de Pradt summarized the situation:

"The people who have enough control over India to reduce substantially the exportation of European metallic currency into Asia rule there as much for Europe's benefit as for their own; their empire is more common than particular, more European than British; as it expands, Europe benefits, and each of their conquests is also a real conquest for the latter."

By 1721 the East India Company had been prohibited from importing Indian textiles into Europe and this dealt a severe economic blow to the entire sub-continent; in particular, the Bengal *Nawabs*, who could no longer maintain navies powerful enough to resist the onslaught of the now richer and more powerful East India Company. The defeat at Plessey in 1757 was thus a monumental turning point in history. A nation that had long enjoyed a trade surplus from its manufactures was soon to be reduced to penury. The great merchants of India, who had earlier derived protection from the Mughals, and had benefited from Mughal naval patrols were by the end of the eighteenth century, practically extinguished in Bengal and elsewhere. Whereas earlier conquerors had taken full advantage of India's manufacturing, the British simply took away and never returned anything.

In the early 1800s, Indian cotton and silk goods imported into England were taxed to the tune of 70-80% whereas British imports into India faced only 2-4% customs duty. As a result, British imports of cotton, silk, wool, iron, pottery, glassware and paper into India increased by a factor of 50, whereas Indian exports dropped to one-fourth. Millions of ruined artisans and craftsmen, spinners, weavers, potters, smelters and smiths were consequently rendered jobless and had to become landless agricultural workers. The percentage of population dependent on agriculture and pastoral pursuits actually rose to 73% in 1921 from 61% in 1891. Mike Davis is lucid:

In the last half of 19th century, India's income fell by 50%. In the 190 years prior to independence, the Indian economy was literally stagnant - it experienced zero growth.

The EIC was helped by the fact that the British dominated the Atlantic slave trade transporting more slaves than all the other European powers combined. Carey was emphatic:

"Although the East India Company was not itself engaged in the transatlantic slave trade, the link was very close and highly profitable…It (the British System) is the most gigantic system of slavery the world has yet seen, and therefore it is that freedom gradually disappears from every country over which England is enabled to gain control."

Joshua Gee in 1729 had observed acutely:

"Slaves were the precious life-blood of the West Indian economy…All this great increase in our treasure proceeds chiefly from the labor of negroes in the plantations".

Political control also permitted Britain to tax Bengal, often by force. Sinha summarizes succinctly:

"For more than two centuries the Europeans had found that the trade with Bengal whether carried on by companies or by the individual free traders or by illicit means had always been so much in favor of Bengal that the balance had to be supplied in cash. Now after Plessey supplies were at last found in Bengal by means independent of commerce" (taxes).

The export, import, and manufacture of goods moved from the hands of independent Indian merchants to intermediaries hired by the EIC. Independent weavers who refused to work for the pitiful wages of the EIC had their **thumbs cut off**. After Plessey, the East India Company also moved to impose its monopoly on the internal over-land trade for virtual stranglehold on the economic and political life of Eastern India. Sinha continues:

The trade of the country merchant began to stagnate. Armenian, Mughal, Gujarati and Bengali merchants found their free trade daily fettered and loaded."

French, Dutch and Danish were also able to buy Indian goods at lower prices. Furber noted:

"The time had arrived when Europeans at home or overseas who had a stake in the maintenance of European power anywhere on the Indian continent were one and all forced to take part in the work of building a British empire in India".

The Portuguese trading monopoly on spice trade was complemented by the sale of Persian carpets to India, cloves from the Moluccas to China, copper and silver from Japan to China, Indian cloth to Siam, etc. Chroniclers such as Marco Polo, Ibn Batuta, Abdur Razzaq, Nicolo Conti, and Santo Stefano - all indicate that the Indian Ocean was the scene of peaceful and thriving trade in the 14th and 15th centuries. This last beacon of free trade became the prime envy of Portuguese imperialism and by the middle of the 16th century, a chain of fortified forces permitted them to enforce a semi-monopoly in the spice trade, by force, torture, mutilation, murder etc., if necessary. Local traders were coerced into buying safe passes and paying customs duties to the Portuguese. Further consolidation was achieved by the defeat of Hindu monarch of Calicut who capitulated following a two-day bombardment of that vital port city (largest spice market in the Indian Ocean); in 1510, Adil Shahi of Bijapur ceded the control of Goa to the Portuguese.

Armed ships provided such a technical superiority that Europeans could board Asian merchant ships, torture and slaughter the crew and passengers, loot the cargo, and burn the hulks. In 1505, the spice trade from Asia to Europe was declared a 'royal monopoly' by the Portuguese. In 1530, the Portuguese colonists looted and burned the ports of Cambay, Surat and Rander, and Diu; Daman was captured in 1559. Thus, the merchants of Gujarat were finally tamed and Gujarat, one of the richest provinces of India, saw constant decline. As trade from Goa to Bengal was even more lucrative than the Coromandel trade, Portuguese sought to control Chittagaon and Satgaon (near Kolkata), and later moved up-river to Hooghly. Smaller and less-established traders from the Southern and Eastern Indian coast were completely eliminated from the inter-Asian trade, and were never recovered. Unchallenged Portuguese monopoly now shipped highly-prized Indian textiles to Indonesia and picked up valuable spices in return for sale in Europe. Portuguese ordered that *cartaz* was applicable only to Christians: Hindus and Muslims had no claim to rite of passage in Asian waters. The Portuguese were so successful in opening up the routes to the East that their king took the title (confirmed by the Pope), 'Lord of the Conquest, navigation and commerce of India, Ethiopia, Arabia and Persia'.

The lucrative trade of the Indian Ocean soon spurred international rivalries between the Dutch, English and French. In 1656, Colombo fell to the Dutch, and in 1663, the Portuguese lost Cochin to the Dutch, Hormuz had been lost even earlier to the EIC. Control of Indian Ocean shipping thus passed successively from the Portuguese to the Dutch to the British. Indian ship-building industry continued to thrive, as ships built there matched, or even excelled, European ships in finish and craftsmanship. Dutch and British established factories not only on the coastal ports but also inland: so they could keep a much larger share of the profits that would have otherwise gone to local Indian middlemen.

As Mughal empire began to disintegrate, the British moved in India, followed up by that of Burma, Indo-China, Middle East, Africa, part of China, Caribbean and the Philippines. The conquest of India continued with conclusive defeats of the Marathas in 1818, the Sikhs in 1848 and the annexation of Awadh in 1856. The Indian colonies of the British East India Company became British Colonial India and thus began a new phase of colonial plunder for almost 200 years by a systematic transfer of wealth from India to Europe. British Banks used their Indian capital to fund industry in the US, Germany and elsewhere in Europe. The industrial revolution and the development of **modern capitalism** throughout Europe was based on the **colonization of India** and the rest of the world. It was the forced pauperization of the colonized world that allowed nations such as Britain, or the US to industrialize and 'modernize'.

Almost complete subjugation of much of the planet by the Western interests led to an enormous and unprecedented flow of wealth from the colonies to Europe and North America. Ernest Mandel has estimated that European colonial booty between 1500 and 1800 stood at 1,000 million gold pounds sterling, of which 100 to 150 million reached Britain from India alone between 1750 and 1800. While the plunder engendered numerous famines in colonies, Europe and North America witnessed astonishing developments. The wealth that funded the genesis of Western Civilization was stolen by force, torture, mutilation, and the like, from the South and the East. Armed intervention by Europeans, not free trade, destroyed Asia. Brooke Adams:

"The influx of Indian treasure, by adding considerably to the nations' cash capital, not only increased its stock of energy, but added much to its flexibility and the rapidity of its movement. Very soon after Plessey, the **Bengal plunder began to arrive in London** *and the effect appears to have been instantaneous, for all authorities agree that the* **'Industrial Revolution' began with the year 1770...***Before the influx of the Indian treasure, and the expansion of credit which followed, no force sufficient for this purpose existed...Possibly since the world began, no investment has yielded the profit reaped from the Indian plunder, because for nearly fifty years Great Britain stood without a competitor"*.

The words of Lord Curzon still ring loud and clear:

"India is the pivot of our Empire .... If the Empire loses any other part of its Dominion we can survive, but if we lose India the sun of our Empire will have set."

As early as 1812, an East India Company Report had remarked:

"The importance of that immense empire to this country is rather to be estimated by the great annual addition it makes to the wealth and capital of the Kingdom....."

Europeans transformed lying, cheating, swindling and stealing into acts of virtue. Before 1500 CE, there were hundreds of self-supporting and self-contained economies. But by 1800 CE, Africa, Asia and the Americas were integrated into a worldwide network of trade, slavery, murder, mutilation and outright theft.

Davis observed:

"Millions died, not outside the 'modern world system', but in the very process of being forcibly incorporated into its economic and political structures. They died in the golden age of Liberal Capitalism; indeed, many were murdered ... by the theological application of the sacred principles of Smith, Bentham and Mill"… Between 1875–1900—a period that included the worst famines in Indian history—annual grain exports increased from 3 to 10 million tons, equivalent to the annual nutrition of 25m people…Indeed, by the turn of the century, India was supplying nearly a fifth of Britain's wheat consumption at the cost of its own food security… India also had to finance British military supremacy in Asia. In addition to incessant proxy warfare with Russia on the Afghan frontier, the subcontinent's masses also subsidized such far-flung adventures of the Indian Army as the occupation of Egypt, the invasion of Ethiopia, and the conquest of the Sudan. As a result, military expenditures never comprised less than 25 percent (34 percent including police) of India's annual budget… During the famine of 1899–1900, when 143,000 Beraris died directly from starvation, the province exported not only thousands of bales of cotton but an incredible 747,000 bushels of grain".

An Englishman exclaimed:

Whatever happens, we have got the Maxim gun, and they have not.

10.Self Humanization by European Devils

Capitalism led to Imperialism and Nationalism with the idea **"my country right or wrong** under respective titles: "trusteeship", "good of the masses", "the training of backward peoples in self-government". The imperialist encounter between the English male aggressor and the colonized peoples appeared as a metaphor where the former was taming the latter, e.g. an imperial Tarzan taming wild animals. Hastings was to write in his diary on 2 October 1813 (cited in Knapp):

"The Hindoo appears a being nearly limited to mere animal functions…with no higher intellect than a dog or an elephant, or a monkey".

The trial of Warren Hastings in England revealed much **unscrupulousness and corruption of British regime** in India. Edmund Burke informed the Parliament:

"Those who could not raise money were most cruelly tortured; cords were drawn tight around their fingers, till the flesh of the four fingers on each hand was actually incorporated and became one solid mass; the fingers were then separated again by wedges of iron and wood driven in between them. Others were tied two and two by the feet and thrown across a wooden bar upon which they hung with their feet uppermost; they were then beaten on the soles of the feet till their toe-nails dropped off. They were afterwards beaten about the head till the blood gushed out at the mouth, nose and ears; they were flogged upon the naked body with bamboo canes and prickly bushes and above all with poisonous weeds which were of a most caustic nature and burnt at every touch. The cruelty of the monster who had ordered all this, had contrived how to tear the mind as well as the body; he frequently had a father and a son tied naked to one another by the feet and arms and then flogged till the skin was torn from the flesh and he had the devilish satisfaction to know that every blow must hurt, for if one escaped the son, his sensibilities were wounded by the knowledge that the blow had fallen upon the father…every blow that missed him had fallen upon the son…The treatment of the females could not be described. In the face of the sun, tender and modest virgins were brutally violated. Other females had the nipples of their breasts put in a cleft bamboo and torn off. Nay, some of the monsters had, horrid to tell, carried their unnatural brutality so far as to drink in the source of generation and life".

Theodore Greene summarized imperialism thus:

*"Imperialism is synonymous with the **appropriation by western nations** of the largest part of the rest of the world. The control of public mind connects propaganda to imperialism. Social Darwinism with the survival of the fittest, which he himself refused to apply to society, became an official thought on foreign affairs and justified ruthless treatment of the 'backward' races. **Christian missionaries were influential in the making of modern imperialism** that benefitted only the super-rich business people and manufacturers. Armed with modern weapons, as well as the Bible and the missal, the missionaries found that their unwilling "hosts" lacked the capacity to defend their beliefs or their lands. Ancient and flourishing cultures were shattered under the hammer of modern imperialism as people in the "white men's clubs' imposed crop-production quotas upon the conquered people.*

Adam Smith was the last major Western social scientist to appreciate that Europe was a Johnny come late in the development of world wealth. He had observed: *"China is a much richer country than any part of Europe"*. He also did not regard that the *"greatest events in the history"* had originated in European geopolitical space. Robertson observed:

"It is to the discovery of the passage to India by the Cape of Good Hope, and to the vigor and success with which the Portuguese prosecuted their conquests and established their dominion there, that Europe has been indebted for its preservation from the most liberal and humiliating servitude that ever oppressed polished nations".

Asia's rightful and historically authenticated place has been denied by the dominance of excessively Eurocentric perspectives of world economic and cultural history. Fernand Braudel astutely observed:

"Europe invented historians and then made good use of them."

Falsification had already permitted the Church to create an **anti-Christ** who adored wealth, in contrast to Jesus who glorified poverty as follows:

"It is easier for a camel to go through the eye of a needle than for a rich man to enter into the kingdom of God…Go thy way, sell whatever thou hast and give to the poor, and thou shall have the treasure in heaven".

Max weber was to turn Jesus upside down:

*"The **attainment of (wealth)** as a fruit of labor in a calling was a sign of **God's blessing**…an attitude toward life we have here called the spirit of capitalism"*.

The idea of equality was repulsive to Luther:

"This article would make all men equal and so change the spiritual kingdom of Christ into an external worldly one. Impossible! An earthly kingdom cannot exist without inequality of persons. Some must be free, other serfs, some rulers, other subjects. Therefore let all who are able hew them down, slaughter and stab them, openly or in secret, and remember that there is nothing more poisonous, noxious and utterly diabolical than a rebel. You must kill him as you would a mad dog; if you do not fall upon him, he will fall upon you and the whole land".

A sermon in 1609 asserted:

"The Lord hath given the earth to the children of men, yet ...is the greater part of it possessed and wrongfully usurped by wild beasts, and unreasonable creatures, or by brutish savages, which by reason of their godless ignorance, and blasphemous idolatry, are worse than those beasts which are of the most wile and savage nature".

The Puritans also appealed to the Bible:

"Ask of me, and I shall give thee, the heathen for thine inheritance, and the uttermost parts of the earth for thy possession". *(Psalms 2:8).*

World **history was now rewritten whole sale** and social science was advanced as a Eurocentric invention to highlight feigned White exceptionalism while the rest of the world was found to be deficient in some critical historical, economic, social, political, ideological, or cultural tenet. Eurocentric authors sought to create internal explanations for the presumed superiority of the West to explain its ascendance over the rest of the world. For all of them, the rise of Europe was a unique 'miracle' and not a product of European despotism. The Europeans did not in any sense 'create' either the world economic system nor 'capitalism'. China and India were the primary centers of the accumulation of capital in the world system. Asian production was much greater, and it was more productive and competitive than anything the Europeans were able to muster. Bairoch estimates that in 1750 Asia had a GNP of $ 120 billion (in 1960 US dollars) while all the 'West' meaning Europe and the Americas, also including Russia and Japan, had a GNP of only $ 35 billion. A century later in 1860, the respective amounts were $ 165 billion and $ 115 billion, respectively. According to Angus Maddison's estimates, per capita production or income were almost the same in China and Western Europe in 1400 CE.

Asians brought up in Europe-inspired anti-history believe that colonial powers were modernizing Asia. Nothing could be farther from truth. Although British built modern facilities for their administrative officers, 69% of Bombay's population in 1911 lived in one-room tenements, as against 6% in London in the same year and this increased to 74% in 1931 when one-third were living more than 5 to a room. After the Second World War, 13% of Bombay's destitute slept on the streets and 10-15 tenements typically shared one water tap. Yet, in 1757 (the year of the Plessey defeat), Clive had lauded Murshidabad in Bengal: *This city is as extensive, populous and rich as the city of London...*Dacca was even more famous as a manufacturing town and it's weavers had an international reputation unmatched in the medieval world. But in 1840 Dacca's population had fallen from 150,000 to 20,000, Surat and Murshidabad had suffered a similar fate. In 1854, Sir Arthur Cotton noted:

"Public works have been almost entirely neglected throughout India... the motto hitherto has been: 'do nothing, have nothing done, let nobody do anything.. ..."

John Bright was to observe in the House of Commons on June 24, 1858,

"The single city of Manchester, in the supply of its inhabitants with the single article of water, has spent a larger sum of money than the East India Company has spent in the fourteen years from 1834 to 1848 in public works of every kind throughout the whole of its vast dominions".

Another popular myth about British rule stipulates that the British modernized Indian agriculture by building canals although irrigation was invented by Vedic Aryans (Chapter 5.III). Thompson in 1838 noted:

" the roads and tanks and canals 'which Hindu or Mussulman governments constructed for the service of the nations and the good of the country have been suffered to fall into dilapidation; and now the want of the means of irrigation causes famines."

Montgomery Martin recalled that the old East India Company

"...omitted not only to initiate improvements, but even to keep in repair the old works upon which the revenue depended."

The Report of the Bengal Irrigation Department Committee in 1930 reads:

"In every district the Khals (canals) which carry the internal boat traffic become from time to time blocked up with silt. Its Khals and rivers are the roads end highways of Eastern Bengal, and it is impossible to overestimate the importance to the economic life of this part of the province of maintaining these in proper navigable order ...."As regards the revival or maintenance of minor routes, ... practically nothing has been done, with the result that, in some parts of the Province at least, channels have been silted up, navigation has become limited to a few months in the year, and crops can only be marketed when the Khals rise high enough in the monsoon to make transport possible".

Sir William Willcock wrote:

" Not only was nothing done to utilize and improve the original canal system, but railway embankments were subsequently thrown up, entirely destroying it. Some areas, cut off from the supply of loam-bearing Ganges water, have gradually become sterile and unproductive, others improperly drained, show an advanced degree of water-logging, with the inevitable accompaniment of

malaria. Nor has any attempt been made to construct proper embankments for the Gauges in its low course, to prevent the enormous erosion by which villages and groves and cultivated fields are swallowed up each year."

Life expectancy in India stood at barely 25 years in 1921 (compared to 55 for England) and actually fell to 23 in 1931. In 1934, there was one hospital bed for 3800 people in British India, including beds reserved for the British rulers. Infant mortality in Bombay was 255 per thousand in 1928. Between 1870 and 1910, India's population grew at an average rate of 19% but in England and Wales' population grew three times faster, by 58%; average population growth in Europe was 45%. Between 1921-40, the population in India grew by 21% but still less than the 24% growth in the US. In 1941, the density of population in India was roughly 250 per square mile, almost a third of 700 per square mile in England; Bengal was much more densely inhabited at almost 780 per square mile, only about 10% more than England. Yet, there was much more poverty in British India than in England and an unprecedented number of famines were recorded during the period of British rule.

In the first half of the 19th century, there were seven famines leading to a million and a half deaths. In the second half, there were 24 famines (18 between 1876 and 1900) causing over 20 million deaths (as per official records). W. Digby, noted:

"stated roughly, famines and scarcities have been four times as numerous, during the last thirty years of the 19th century as they were one hundred years ago, and four times as widespread."

In Late Victorian Holocausts, Mike Davis points out that there were 31(thirty one) serious famines in 120 years of British rule compared to 17(seventeen) in the 2000 years before British rule. This is not surprising, as the export of food grains had increased by a factor of four just prior to that period and export of other agricultural raw materials had also increased in similarly. Land that once produced grain for local consumption was now taken over by former slave-owners from N. America who were permitted to set up plantations for the cultivation of lucrative cash crops exclusively for export. Particularly galling is how the British colonial rulers continued to export food grains from India to Britain even during famine years. Annual British Government reports repeatedly published data that showed 70-80% of Indians were living on the margin of subsistence. That two-thirds were undernourished, and in Bengal, nearly four-fifths were undernourished.

Contrast this data with the following accounts by Tavernier, prior to colonization:-

"....even in the smallest villages rice, flour, butter, milk, beans and other vegetables, sugar and sweetmeats can be procured in abundance ...."

Manouchi, the chief physician to Aurangzeb, confirmed:

"Bengal is of all the kingdoms of the Moghul, best known in France..... We may venture to say it is not inferior in anything to Egypt - and that it even exceeds that kingdom in its products of silks, cottons, sugar, and indigo. All things are in great plenty here, fruits, pulse, grain, muslins, cloths of gold and silk..."

The French traveler, Bernier also described 17th century Bengal in a similar vein:

"The knowledge I have acquired of Bengal in two visits inclines me to believe that it is richer than Egypt. It exports in abundance cottons and silks, rice, sugar and butter. It produces amply for its own consumption of wheat, vegetables, grains, fowls, ducks and geese. It has immense herds of pigs and flocks of sheep and goats. Fish of every kind it has in profusion. From Rajmahal to the sea is an endless number of canals, cut in bygone ages from the Ganges by immense labour for navigation and irrigation."

Despite an 11 hour work day in 1922, a report in 1927-28 noted:

"all but the most highly skilled workmen in India receive wages which are barely sufficient to feed and clothe them. Everywhere will be seen overcrowding, dirt and squalid misery..."

In 1934, daily work was reduced to 10 hours but no restrictions were enforced on the use of child labor; Whitley Report found children as young as five working a 12 hour day.

Perhaps the least known aspect of the colonial legacy is the early British attitude towards India's historic monuments and the extent of vandalism that took place. Contrary to the pervasive myth, British not only did not protect India's historic legacy but actually vandalized it. Nath has underlined their fate:

"Relics of the glorious age of the Mughals were either destroyed or converted beyond recognition. Out of 270 beautiful monuments which existed at Agra alone, before its capture by Lake in 1803, hardly 40 have survived".

David Carroll confirms British greed for money:

" The forts in Agra and Delhi were commandeered at the beginning of the nineteenth century and turned into military garrisons. Marble reliefs were torn down, gardens were trampled, and lines of ugly barracks, still standing today,

were installed in their stead. In the Delhi fort, the Hall of Public Audience was made into an arsenal and the arches of the outer colonnades were bricked over or replaced with rectangular wooden windows."

The Mughal fort at Allahabad and Deccan fort at Ahmednagar were converted into barracks and nothing but their outer walls can hint at their former glory. Even the Taj Mahal was not spared. David Carroll reports:

"..By the nineteenth century, its grounds were a favorite trysting place for young Englishmen and their ladies. Open-air balls were held on the marble terrace in front of the main door, and there, beneath Shah Johan's lotus dome, brass bands um-pah-pahed and lords and ladies danced the quadrille. The minarets became a popular site for suicide leaps, and the mosques on either side of the Taj were rented out as bungalows to honeymooners. The gardens of the Taj were especially popular for open-air frolics....."

Vice Roy Curzon himself reports with glee:

"At an earlier date, when picnic parties were held in the garden of the Taj, it was not an uncommon thing for the revelers to arm themselves with hammer and chisel, with which they wiled away the afternoon by chipping out fragments of agate and carnelian from the cenotaphs of the Emperor and his lamented Queen.The Taj became a place where one could drink in private, and its parks were often strewn with the figures of inebriated British soldiers..."

Lord William Bentinck, first governor general of all India, went so far as to announce plans to demolish the best Mogul monuments in Agra and Delhi and remove their marble facades for sale in London. Plans to dismantle the Taj Mahal were actually put in place, and wrecking machinery was moved into Taj gardens, but news from London announced that first auction was disappointing, and all further sales were cancelled. Thus the Taj Mahal was spared along with the reputation of the British as *'Protectors of India's Historic Legacy'*.

Most of the important historical relics from barbaric Hindu India are now to be found in different British museums, thereby comforting the self respect of civilizing mission by the Aryan master race.

11.Racism and Eugenics Fuel Despotism

Racism is irreversibly linked to the search for self-identity in order to shape policies and societies. The **idolization of milky whiteness** debased the Greek heritage where color bias did not exist. In Homer, gods were pleased to dine with members of the Negro race. Both Jefferson and Charles White wrote in 1799 CE that only white women could blush. Buffon (1749-1804 CE) held that the white is the *"real and natural color of man"*. To Thomas Jefferson, Africans embodied animosity, lacked reason, imagination, self-restraint and the ability to make rational choices. Voltaire advanced the idea that **Indians, Negroes, and Europeans were separate species**. Cuvier's impact on social construction of race was horrific and the Africans were dubbed universally inferior to Europeans, further substantiated by Robert Knox's *The Races of Man* based upon the comparison of brain volume. The English physician Charles White in 1799 CE said that Negroes were closer to apes than to whites, based upon facial features, brains, bodies, hands, feet, penis and clitoris length (larger than in whites) and used Genesis to argue that negroes are a separate species. The prominent British polygenist Charles White asked in 1799 CE where but in Europe might be found:

"That nobly arched head, containing such a quantity of brain…? Where that variety of features, and fullness of expression; those long. flowing, graceful ring-lets; that majestic beard, those rosy cheeks and coral lips?… in what other quarter of the globe shall we find the blush that overspreads the soft features of the beautiful women of Europe, that emblem of modesty, of delicate feelings, and of sense? Where that nice expression of amiable and soft passions in the countenance; and that general elegance of features and complexion? Where, except on the bosom of the European woman, two such plump and snowy white hemispheres, tipt with vermillion".

The 1911 US presidential address states:

"We must see to it that our members no longer permit the sons of Shem, Ham and Japheth...to trample the mud of millions of alien feet into our spring. We must conserve the source of our race, the Anglo-Saxon race, mother of Liberty and self-government in the modern world...I dread the clouding of the purity of the cup with color and character acquired under tropical suns, in the jungle, or the paradisiacal islands of the seas..."

Hitler regularly read *Ostara* magazine whose editorial policy was "*the practical application of anthropological research for...**preserving the master race** from destruction by the maintenance of racial purity*". Blond, blue eyed Aryans must rule the earth by destroying their dark, racially mixed, enemies.

British writer Nancy Stephan asserted:

"On examination it is found that the European whites are at the top and the African blacks at the bottom, with others coming in between".

Racism took a new turn with the publication of *Survival of the Fittest* and *Struggle for Existence* (Herbert Spencer) along with the *Origin of Species* (Darwin) to give birth to the new science of Eugenics. The term Race Science was coined by Nancy Stephan in 1982 but Victorian British had already opposed dark skinned savages to light skinned civilized Europeans. The race scientists relieved the moral qualms of theologians and justified **colonial extermination of races** around the globe. Henry Treitschke (1834-1896) considered the white race the aristocracy of the world whose mission it was to divide and rule the planet. Eugenic societies sprang up in UK and Germany and Nietzsche came up with slogans such as "master race". Germany was seen to inherit the Roman tradition to rule the world for the spread of Christianity. The discovery of Amerindians challenged the Biblical Genesis since the 'Indians' there had been taken by papal decree into the human fold.

From the third century onwards, Greeks were credited not only with philosophy but also with the beginnings of the human race. British author Hugh Trevor-Roper agreed with the Hegelian view:

"It is European Technique, European examples, European ideas which have shaken the non-European world out of its past barbarism".

The German Edmund Husserl (1859-1938) argued that only in Greeks do we have a universal model and favored Europeanization of earth. Although he conceded that Indian thought was abstract he believed that India represented the 'childhood of humanity' with nothing to offer to the modern philosopher; India was otherwise "ahistorical". Shelley wrote in 1822 "We are all Greeks". John Locke was particularly vehement in his attack on Indian philosophy by deliberately confusing a myth with rational thinking because European technical, racial and cultural superiority was a forgone conclusion. Eurocentric isolationism underlined that other cultures had not separated philosophy from other intellectual activity. In contrast to scientific monogenism, polygenism saw **distinct parents for white and black races** by Voltaire and Hume. The latter declared in 1742:

"I am apt to suspect the Negros, and in general all other species of men (for there are four or five different kinds), to be naturally inferior to whites. There never was a civilized nation of any other complexion than white...the most rude and barbarous of the whites, such as the ancient Germans, the present Tartars, have still something eminent about them".

Cuvier: *"The people that composes this race (black) have always been savages...The Caucasian race has given rise to the most civilized nations, to those which have generally held the rest in subjugation".*

Saint Simon: *"Negro is organically incapable, in a situation where he can obtain the same teaching, of being educated to the same level of intelligence as the European..."*

Quatrfages: *"The Negro is an intellectual monstrosity. The Negro is a white whose body acquires the well-defined form of the species, but whose intelligence is halted along the way..."*

Hegel: *"The negro exhibits the natural man in his completely wild untamed state".*

Meiners: *"Only white peoples, especially the Celtic, possess true courage. The black and ugly differ from these by their deplorable lack of virtue..."*

Fabricius (1745-1808), a student of Linnaeus and a pious Lutheran, felt that Negroes issued from the union of white men and apes. He assured his pious readers that the skin of Adam was immaculately white. The mathematician Karl Peterson reasoned in 1893:

"we are struggling among ourselves for supremacy in the world which we thought as destined belong to the Aryan races and to the Christian faith..." Aryan rivalries were necessary because *"nations...cannot prosper and flourish except by intense competition like that of...Struggle for existence. That war should forever be banished from this world is not merely an absurd*

hope but something profoundly immoral".

Race hygiene became the order of the day as uncivilized races were procreating faster than the white Aryans. Dr. Muller-Lyer suggested that the right of procreation to 20% of the men and 75% of the women.

It was clear to Marx and Engels that the white race, as the bearer of progress, was more gifted than all other races. Engels wrote that "*the lowest of savages could return to an animal-like condition*" and blacks were genetically incapable of understanding mathematics. Marx was influenced by Germanomaniacs and believed that Russians were inferior to Europeans but all these differences were to disappear in the socialist city of the future. The emergence of molecular genetics has shown these race theories to be completely false. By creating this pseudo-science based on race, Europeans of the Age of Enlightenment sought to free themselves from their Jewish heritage. The creation of anti-history has become a hallmark of the Communists for their narrow political aims, particularly in India where vote bank politics is the road to political power.

Thomas Arnold saw in the Teutonic races a specifically designated **instrument of Providence**. Following Greeks and Romans, the Germans, including the Anglo-Saxons, were to dominate and civilize the world. Disraeli summarized the situation "*All is Race; there is no other truth*". In France Auguste Comte took it for granted that the leadership of humanity belonged to the white race of Western Europe, thereby supporting the British position. Gobineau stratified the racial pyramid into eight levels and felt that the white species will disappear henceforth from the face of the earth. Dunoyer, Charles Comte and others recognized the Germanic peoples as constituting the Master Race. Schelling (1775-1854) assumed that the white race was the noblest of all, the Africans the most savage, and Asians in between. The idea now gained currency where Catholicism = church of authority, Protestants = church of reason. The dolichocephalic Teutonic race is Protestant characterized by individualism, willfulness, self-reliance, independence. The brachycephalic Celto-Slavic race is Catholic, submissive and conservative in instinct. Richard Wagner identified **Jesus with Wotan** to promote a new world vision:

"*Long ago, in the golden age, men lived in a state of primitive innocence as vegetarians on the high plateau of Asia. But they were tainted by the original sin when they killed the first animal. Ever since a thirst for blood had taken possession of the human race...**Christ, who was either Indian or Aryan,** had tried to save mankind by showing the way back to the innocence of primitive vegetarianism...at the Last Supper changing bread into wine and flesh into bread...he gave up his life to expiate the blood shed by* *carnivorous man since the beginning of the world." The Jews being the "devil incarnate of human decadence", a new purification was called for. Rathenau (1867-1922) described the tragedy of the Aryan race: "A magnificent new nation is born in the North. Its overwhelming fertility spreads to the South. Each migration is a conquest, each conquest enriches the customs and civilization of the conquered".*

The German public was mesmerized by Heine:

"We Germans are the most powerful and intelligent of peoples. Our princely dynasties sit on all thrones of Europe, our Rothschild's control all stock markets of the world, our scientists dominate all the science, we have invented the gunpowder and the printing…".

The US Supreme court decision against Bhagat Singh Thind (1923) held that although Aryan he was not a "free white person" within the context of the 1917 naturalization act:

"…intermarriage did occur…destroying to a greater or less degree the purity of the 'Aryan blood'. Thus the effect of racialization of the Aryan theory is to deny the kinship of Indians and Europeans upon a new basis".

Race and skin color were used to justify colonization, slavery, and economic exploitation where black was evil and white was pure. Jesus himself was transformed from Jewish to European; his hair was no longer black but brown and the matching dark eyes became blue as everything black had to be removed as far as possible from the white redeemer. The Christian church was split cleanly and almost completely along racial lines. Long before the little signs "white only" and "colored" appeared in the public utilities, they had appeared in the church in the US. Jim Crowism had some of its first beginnings in the church. All this is in contrast to the idea of universal salvation in the New Testament where the entire human race was of one blood.

Intellectual justification for race now gathered momentum and Paracelsus in 1520 CE, the Swiss physician-alchemist-chemist, came up with the idea of **Polygenism** where whites descended form Adam-Eve to the Seth line and blacks from Adam-Eve to the Cain line. In 1591 CE, the Italian philosopher Giordano Bruno felt that God had either created separate Adams or Africans must have descended from pre-Adamite races. Lucilio Vanini in 1619 argued that because of their color, Africans must have descended from apes. French Protestant La Peyrere in 1655 CE challenged single creation and argued that pre-Adamite races had given rise to peoples in Asia, Africa and the New World; Africans were even more severely dehumanized through the Hamitic curse. Polygenesis justified the restoration of slavery by Napoleon. French ethnology was open to polygenesis and gained credibility between1800-1850 CE whereas the American School of Ethnology declared that whites, blacks and Indians were separately created and vastly unequal species.

Carolus Linnaeus (1707-1778) of Sweden described the European *Homo europaeus* (discoverer, active, acute) as the apex and *Homo afer* (crafty, lazy, careless) as the abyss of human varieties; *asiaticus* and *americanus* were in between. Dutch anatomist Petrus Camper (1722-1789) measured the facial angles and felt that the Negro was closer to monkey than humans. Comte de Gobineau (1816-1882) authored his Essay on the *Inequality of Human Race*, which stated that Aryan (white) race was superior to all other races. British writer Francis Galton used psychometry to classify dog intelligence into sixteen categories and postulated that the highest cognitive intelligence in the dog (X) was superior to that of the Australian native. Regarding Negros he observed:

"The mistakes the Negros made in their own matters were so childish, stupid, and simpleton-like, as frequently to make me ashamed of my own species".

All this was refuted by Molecular Genetics in 1982:

"The genetic distances for protein loci between Caucasian, Mongoloid and Negroid are of the same order of magnitude as those for local populations in other organisms and considerably smaller than those for subspecies…Therefore it is not appropriate to assign the rank of subspecies to the major races of man".

Colonization of indigenous peoples brought new questions to the long-assumed belief in a hierarchy held by Europeans. Hirschman raised pertinent questions and doubts:

*"Where do these new people fit in? Are they, in fact, people? Are they genetically human, placed in an animalistic environment, or are they animals themselves? **Are they now our property, just as their land is**? What is their relationship to us noble, conquering Europeans?"*

This sort of mentality led to the genesis of the Aryan Invasion model where white Christians came back to claim the lands of the colored peoples that had previously been civilized by the white ancestors.

Thus, Master Race was to hijack Hindu soul for his own salvation.

12. Europeans Hijack Aryan Ancestry

The colonial stranglehold of white Europeans on world peoples and resources led to the search for their own identity, ethnicity and cultural origins. In an Editorial Foreword, J. H, Plumb remarked

"In the 19th century all countries of Europe and America were preoccupied with the origins of national identity to forging a glorious past that would not only justify the present but also anticipate the future: Macaulay, Bancroft, Michelet…"

Another scholar had noted:

"How we see ourselves is shaped by the history we absorb, it fires our imagination and curiosity, rulers throughout history have recognized that the control of the past is to master the present and thereby consolidate their power".

During Renaissance, Europeans became aware of the naked contrast between their own cultural deprivation versus **richness of Indian history** and culture. It somehow did not seem right that while the 'civilized Christian' was toiling in superstition, illiteracy, poverty, hungry, misery and disease, before the colonial era, the pagans were scholars, teachers, poets, doctors and scientists, basking in luxury and plenty. Conscious of their own inferiority, the Europeans now sought to embellish their own ancestry after having demonized colored peoples around the globe (Chapters 10, 11).

Medieval monks, constrained by the Book of Genesis and political exigencies of their age, traced all human origins back to Noah and his three sons who had survived the flood after building the Tower of Babel against God's wishes in 2350 BC, or 1656 years after Biblical Creation. Genesis describes that the Semites (Asians, Arabs and Jews) and Hamites (Egyptians, Africans and Cushites) were the off springs of Shem and Ham, respectively. Noah's third son Japhet would then be responsible for fathering peoples in the rest of the world whereas Ashkenaz, a grandson of Japhet, would engender the Germans. During the Middle Ages, Ham became the ancestor of serfs, Shem as that of clerks, and Japheth that of nobles. Hamites or Africans were thus placed at the bottom rung of human hierarchy and Jews had the same fate. According to the Muslim theologians, Ham begat Hind (India), Sind (Sindhu or Indus), Habysh (Abyssinia), Zinge, Barber and Noah. Hind begat Purib, Bang, Decan and Nerwaal and their children gave rise to the great tribes. The children of Ham peopled the rest of the world, invented letters, calculated the Vedic astronomical period of 432,000 years, and named the stars. Shem begat Arabs and Persians;

Japheth was the most just with whom the lofty lineage of Mughal emperor Akbar is linked. Pere Coeurdoux derived Brahmins from Magot, son of Japhet. Muslim sources speak of India as the first of seven ancient nations to have cultivated sciences.

Jones proposed only three original stocks in Asia: Hindus, Arabs and Tartars, descending from Ham, Shem and Japhet, respectively. To Jones, the Biblical Cus or Cush is the same as Kush, the son of Rama who himself was the Biblical Raamah in the line of Ham. Rama started the Vedic civilization shortly after the flood of Noah and thus India (Bharat) became one of the oldest of civilizations. The story of the flood is also found in *Padma Purana* whereas *Narasimha* is remembered in the Tower of Babel. Incas and Mexicans are also classified with Hindus (hence Hamians) whereas nomadic Amerindians were tartars (hence Japhetites). Based upon Vedic and Puranic accounts, some scholars have compared Vedic and Mosaic traditions. Abraham is simply Brahma and the writing referred to could be the Vedas that appeared as the Talmud which is also derived from Sanskrit *tal mudra* or palm leaf manuscript. The British scholar John Marco Allegro showed (cited in Knapp):

"The names of the patriarchal heroes, as that of God Himself, are non-Semitic…and go back to the earliest known civilizations in the Near East, indeed of the world".

British Protestants had the matter settled by Archbishop Ussher in the 17th century such that The approximate age of events would be:

Adam	**Manu I**	**Karta Yuga**	**4004 BC**
Noah	**Manu II**		**2948 BC**
Flood	**fish, tortoise, boar**		**2349 BC**
Nimrod	**Narasimha**	**Treta Yuga**	**2217 BC**
Bel	**Bali**		**2105 BC**
Raamah	**Rama**	**Dvapara Yuga**	**2028 BC**
	Buddha	**Kali Yuga**	**1026 BC**

Here, the world was created 4004 BC (= Adam = Manu I Krta yuga), Noah was born 2948 BC (= Manu II), flood took place 2349 BC, Nimrod (= Narasimha) born 2217 BC (=Treta yuga), Bel (=Bali) born 2105 BC, Raamah (=Rama) born 2028 BC (=Dvapara yuga), Buddha 1026 BC = Kali yuga. Jones reconciled Sanskrit literature with the Biblical narrative of the flood by stating that the first three avatars of Vishnu (fish, tortoise and boar) were all related to water. The fish carried Manu II = Noah (the first human), his family, and seven sages (three sons, and four wives of Noah) in a ship (Ark of Noah) fastened to a horn on his head; Adam became Manu I. At the end of the flood, the rainbow is mentioned in Vedic-Hindu mythology as Kurma avatar of Vishnu. In *Skanda Purana*, the story of Noah and his three sons is retold when Sarma, Karma and Jyapati (Shem, Ham and Japheth) were born to Satyavarman (identified as Noah by Jones). *Shveta dvipa* could be England and Nila River Nile. By this manipulation, the **Sanskrit literature was reduced to confirming the account of Genesis.**

The Aryan Bible was published by Louis Jacolliot where Moses was derived from Manu, and the Bible from the laws of Manu. The origin of the Bible was traced to the highlands of Asia and the Old Testament was regarded as no more than a collection of superstitions. The Jews were now portrayed as a degraded and stupid people while Moses became a fanatical slave, charitably educated at the court of Pharaoh. Schopenhauer dissociated the Old from the New Testament such that the latter was windowed with Indian origins:

"Christian doctrine issuing from the wisdom of India has covered over the old trunk of Judaism…Indians of long time ago represented the most noble and the most ancient of peoples".

The chronological hegemony of the Bible was challenged by such Romantics as Voltaire, Schlegel, Herder, and Michelet. Bailly (1777) was to situate the earliest humans on the bank of the Ganges. The major races defined by the scientific community of 19th century were: Caucasian or the white race, Mongolian or the yellow race; Ethiopian or the black race of Africa; Red Indians of North and South America; Malayan of South-east Asia, Indonesia, Philippines and the like. Here, the original white race was believed to have civilize the whole world through ancient Bharat.

"Brahmins are the teachers of Pythagoras, the instructors of Greece and through her of the whole of Europe".

Romain Rolland continued in the same vein:

"If there is one place on the face of the earth where all the dreams of living men have found a home from the very earliest days when man began the dream of existence, it is India".

Cuvier (1817) was certain that **India was the birthplace of humanity**:

"Follow the migrations of mankind form East to West along the sun's course and along the track of the world's magnetic currents; observe its long voyage from Asia to Europe, from India to France…At its starting point, in

India, the birthplace of races and of religions, the womb of the world…"

Balzac was emphatic

:"It is impossible any longer to question the priority of the Asiatic writings over our Holy Scriptures…origin of man…on the mountains of Tibet between summits of Himalayas and Caucasus".

Gleason explicitly states: *"The **Vedas…are the oldest documents** in any Indo-European languages".*

Pavgee wrote in 1912 (cited in Bryant):

"We (Aryans) were autochthonous in India, that we born in Aryavarta on the banks or in the region of the reputed Sarasvati…our colony of young adventurers, having emigrated from and left Aryavarta, had colonized distant lands of Asia, Africa, Europe and America".

This view, also held by Michelet and Renan, contemplated *"mount Imaus"* **(Himalayas) as the birthplace of white humanity**. Jim Shaffer noted:

"Many scholars such as Kant and Herder began to draw analogies between the myths and philosophies of ancient India and the West. In their attempt to separate Western European culture from its Judaic heritage, many scholars were convinced that the origin of the Western culture was to be found in India rather than in the ancient Near East".

Stage was now thus for the white Master Race to usurp Hindu soul, even more precious than material wealth that the Europeans had already appropriated. How could anything good come out of slaves from children of Ham ???

Colonialism was to give way to Imperialism.

13. Demonization by Philology

Language was increasingly manipulated by European political elite as a road to social identity and power. Parsons concluded that all languages in Europe, Iran and India were derived from the common ancestor, the language of Japheth, who had migrated out of Armenia which was the final resting place of the Ark. The linguistic similarity between Sanskrit and European dialects led to the formulation of an Indo-European family of languages, at the top of the hierarchy of all languages hence the paradox: the supposed language of the slaves, turned out to be a language of masters as well. So India had a claim to priority because Western scholarship saw a close link between language, ethnicity and culture. India was thus catapulted into a hegemonic position and implicitly questioned the justification for British domination there. In the Indo-centric phase (1785-1820 CE), **India held the key** to West's quest for self-knowledge.

Thomas Young coined the term **Indo-European (IE)** in 1813 by comparing translated texts of Biblical prayers to denote kindred languages spoken in Europe and India. The term **Indo-Germans** was advanced by Klaproth in 1823 but it immediately became synonymous with a race or people who came from somewhere and implanted their blood and thought from the Indian Ocean to the Pacific Ocean. Being at the top of the philological pyramid, IE language and homeland now became the nucleus from which civilization took shape. The basic assumption required the hypothetical existence of a mother **Proto-Indo-European (PIE)** language which has **never been found** and which does not include Hebrew, Arabic, Aramic, Amharic and Hamitic. Thus, hypotheses engendered absurd hypotheses *ad infinitum*.

The word "veda" means "knowledge", more particularly "sacred book", and is derived from the root "vid-", Sanskrit for "know", reconstructed as being derived from the Proto-Indo-European root "weid-", meaning "see" or "know". "Weid-" is also the source of the English word "wit", as well as "vision" through Latin. The Czech and Slovak words for "science" are "věda" resp. "veda", derived from western Slavic "vědet" resp. "vediet'" for "know". Even the -uid in Celtic Dr*uid* seems to compliment "Weid-" (Druid meaning knowledge of the oak). To Schlegel (1808), Sanskrit itself was the Indo-European *Ursprache* rather than its descendant. The term Aryan was borrowed from Herodotus and found wide acceptance through the efforts of Schlegel in 1819 when he compared the root *Ari* with the German word *Ehre* (honor**).** Halhead (1776) had something similar to say:

"*The Sanskrit language is very copious and nervous but the style of the best Authors wonderfully concise. It far exceeds Greek and Arabic in the Regularity of its Etymology, and like them has a Prodigious Number of Derivatives from each primary Root. The grammatical Rules also are numerous and difficult, though there are not many Anomalies.*

The feigned racial superiority of the Europeans was based entirely on a linguistic extrapolation whose proof went no farther than the underlying hypothesis. Linguistics has thus enjoyed a veto power over all other sciences although few modern historians are linguists and few linguists are Vedic scholars.

Max Muller in 1853 CE introduced the word '*Arya*' into the English language as referring to a particular race and language although there is **no word for race in Sanskrit**. According to Muller's etymological explanation of '*Aryan*', the word is derived from '*ar*' (to plough, to cultivate). Therefore *Arya* means 'a cultivator, or farmer'. This is opposed to the idea that the Aryans were wandering nomads. V.S. Apte's *Sanskrit-English Dictionary* relates the word *Arya* to the root '*r-*' to which the prefix '*a*' has been added in order to give a negative meaning. Therefore the meaning of **Arya** in the Vedas is given as 'excellent, best, respectable, noble' and as a noun, 'master, lord, worthy, honorable, excellent, upholder of *Aryan* values, teacher, employer, father-in-law, friend' (Chapter 4). Leon Poliakov and others then perverted the notion of *Arya* to mean:

"*a white race which subsequently became Christian…which and descended from the mountains of Asia to colonize and populate the West*".

Anti-Semitism was the primary reason European scholars abandoned the idea of the Egyptian origins of Greek civilization in favor of the newly discovered Indo-European connection.

Latham minimized all connection between Sanskrit and Indian languages derived from Devanagari after Muslim conquests. Herbert Risley (1892) found a direct relation between the proportion of Aryan blood and the nasal index along a gradient from the highest caste to the lowest. Of the four races in Europe, the Iberians were Hamitic, Liguarians were Euskarian, German long heads were dolichocephalic, and Celts (Round Barrow people) were brachycephalic. Just as the intermarriage with the locals had sullied the purity of the original Aryan race in India, so also the Aryans in Europe had either disappeared or lost their purity. Herbert Hope Risley (1851-1911) used anthrometric methods to study noses and said that Vedic Aryans vaguely refer to aboriginal nose. Dugald Stewart felt that Sanskrit was a hoax, like a "kitchen Greek" produced by Brahmins after Alexander.

After having absorbed Vedic-Buddhist knowledge in the sciences and arts, the colonial powers did their best to belittle the past accomplishments of their subject peoples to justify colonialism. In a masterstroke, the achievements of the Vedic people were ascribed to a superior white skinned, blue eyed, **Aryan race, coming from somewhere or anywhere, to civilize the dark skinned native** who was deemed too inferior to have the capability to realize the marvels in the likes of the ISC. By this simple device, all ancient wisdom now ensued from the Europeans who had come to civilize the Asians in a remote past, though European contributions can be traced no earlier than the 17th-18th centuries of the Christian era.

The German people were weak, divided into 300 or so dukedoms, and treated with disdain by the great powers of Austria and France. The idea of the Aryan race was significant to German unification and nationalism. German intellectuals like Humboldt, Schlegel and Schopenhauer found solace in aligning themselves with the Vedic culture. Hegel (1770-1830) was fond of saying that **Germans were direct disciples of Indian tradition** while Humboldt declared in 1827: "*The Bhagvadgita is perhaps the loftiest and deepest thing that the world has to show*". German unification under the Prussian banner in 1871 gave birth to the most populous and powerful country in Western Europe, and the greatest threat to British expansion. Sir Henry Maine, Vice Chancellor of Calcutta University exclaimed "...***a nation has been born out of Sanskrit***". It was assumed that German physical traits, devoid of miscegenation, must be those of the original Aryans: blond, fair and blue eyed although the prehistoric graves in Germany contain mixed phenotypes. Nazis now usurped the Aryan myth and Swastika to endorse racism and genocide based on the myth of an Aryan master race of blond haired Teutons. **Thus comparative philology created twentieth century racism.** Wheeler emphatically described an Aryan race:

"*Sometimes during the second millennium BC...Aryan speaking peoples invaded the land of Seven Rivers...the Harappans of the Indus valley in their decadence, in or about the seventeenth century B, fell before the advancing Aryans in such fashion as the Vedic hymns proclaim*".

The 1920 edition of Oxford dictionary portrayed Aryans as tall, fair, blond, soma-belching, illiterate, Germanic superman nomads, riding chariots, hooting and tooting their trumpets as they trampled dark skinned, snub nosed, ugly, *dasas*.

German unification was a nightmare to the British, reeling from the uprising of 1857, and they now faced the dilemma of avoiding cultural equality, even indebtedness, to the Hindu subjects they intended to govern. The British wanted to ruin and demean the Vedic civilization to the point that Indians would hate everything about their own past. The Aryan Invasion Theory was therefore recreated and the Vedas postdated to a pre-Vedic stratum in which dissent could be sown. Deen Chandora has shown that the invasion theory was a conspiracy formulated on 10 April 1866 at a secret meeting of the Royal Asiatic Society to show that (cited in Knapp):

*"...no Indian can say that English are foreigners...**India was ruled all along by outsiders** and so the country must remain a slave under the benign Christian rule".*

William Archer (1856-1924) assailed the whole life and culture of India and lumped together all of her greatest achievements in philosophy, religion, poetry, painting, sculpture, Upanishads, Mahabharata, and Ramayana etc. in one wholesale condemnation, as a repulsive mass of unspeakable barbarism. Archer felt that **Asia must become culturally a province of Europe** otherwise Europe may become culturally a province of Asia. If India adhered to its spiritual ways, she will stand out as a living denial, a hideous blot upon this fair, luminous, rationalistic world. India must either Europeanize, rationalize, materialize her whole being and deserve liberty or else she must be kept in subjugation and administered by her cultural superiors. India is the quintessence of the Asiatic way of being, has never shared in the physical attacks of Asia upon Europe, and has freely infiltrated the world with her ideal. Just as the first wave of Aryans had brought a new language and superior civilization to India, the **British saw** themselves as the **second wave of Aryans** who were now bringing a new language and superior civilization. The great depravity in Hindu society was painted thus by Grant (1796 CE) and dominated British rule until 1947 CE.

"Between which and the European moral complexion there is a difference analogous to the differences of the natural color of the two races...They have had among themselves a complete despotism from the remotest antiquity; a despotism, the most remarkable for its power and duration that the world has ever seen...which has made them prey to every invader...void of public spirit, honor and attachment; and in society base, dishonest, and faithless...(Hindu law is) the work of a crafty and imperious priesthood...laws that promote oppression and injustice; and laws that show a spirit of cruelty...our light and knowledge to them would prove the best remedy for their disorders...to educate them in the elements of British arts, philosophy and religion...English is the key that will open to the Hindus a world of new ideas...". It would suit neither the British nor the Indian *"that the distinction between the two races should be lost"*.

Grant's policy was translated by Macaulay as of 1835, scion of an established Evangelical family, to form an elite class that was:

"Indian in blood and color but English in taste, in opinions, in morals, and in intellect".

Macaulay believed that 'knowledge and reflection' on the part of the Hindus, especially the Brahmins, would cause them to give up their age-old belief in favor of Christianity. In effect, his idea was to turn the strength of

Hindu intellectuals against them, by uprooting their own tradition. Macaulay wanted someone who would interpret Indian scriptures in such a way that the newly educated elite would prefer New Testament over their own cultural heritage, much as the German nationalism had been created. Max Muller was by now established in England and found himself in an extremely tight spot. With his background as a German nationalist, the last thing Max Muller could afford was to be seen as advocating German ideology in a Victorian England. He had no choice but to repudiate his former theories simply to survive in England. Just as he had been an upholder of this race theory for the first twenty years of his career, he was to remain a staunch opponent of it for the remaining thirty years of his life. Muller retracted:

"I have declared again and again that if I say Aryans, I mean neither blood nor bones, nor hair, nor skull; I mean simply those who speak an Aryan language...to me an ethnologist who speaks of Aryan race, Aryan blood, Aryan eyes and hair, is as great a sinner as a linguist who speaks of a dolichocephalic dictionary or a brachycephalic grammar."

William Jones too had suggested to Hastings, an avowed Hindu hater, that the Vedic heritage could be undermined by **manufacturing a Sanskrit scripture that would glorify Jesus**. Translations of Sanskrit literature were therefore produced to demean Vedic message and chronology. Max Muller was brought in contact with Macaulay and was promised 10,000 pounds if he could translate Rigveda in such a way as to destroy the belief of the Hindus in Vedas. This began his work "Sacred Books of the East" but he was given only 3000 pounds by the EIC. Julian Huxley, one of the leading biologists of the century, wrote as far back as 1939:

"In 1848 the young German scholar Friedrich Max Muller (1823-1900) settled in Oxford, where he remained for the rest of his life. ... About 1853 he introduced into the English language the unlucky term Aryan as applied to a large group of languages. ...He introduced a proposition which is demonstrably false. He spoke not only of a definite Aryan language and its descendants, but also of a corresponding Aryan race".

Colonel Bowden (d 1811) established a Sanskrit professorship at Oxford to:

"enable his countrymen to proceed in the conversion of the natives of India to Christian Religion" (p.22, Brawley).

Prizes were offered to literary works **undermining Indian traditions**. The first holder, Horace Wilson noted:

"these lectures were written…for the best refutation of the Hindu Religious systems" (cited in Brawley).

Max Muller declared:

"*There is more antiquity in Veda than in all the inscription of Egypt and Nineveh…old thoughts, old hopes, old faiths, and old errors, the old Man altogether*".

Rigveda was a monument without equal, its point of origin a pure utopia and its Aryan authors the best and the brightest. Muller was honest (cited in Frawley).

"*If I were to look over the whole world to find out the country most richly endowed with all the wealth, power and beauty that Nature can bestow – in some parts a very paradise on earth – I should point to India. If I were asked under what sky the human mind has most fully developed some of its choicest gifts, has most deeply pondered on the greatest problems of life, and has found solutions to some of them which well deserve the attention even of those who have studied Plato and Kant – I should point to India And if I were to ask myself from what literature we, here in Europe, who have been nurtured almost exclusively on the thoughts of Greeks and Romans, and one Semitic race, the Jewish, may draw that corrective which is most wanted in order to make our inner life more perfect, more comprehensive, more universal, in fact, more truly human, a life not for this life only, but a transfigured and eternal life – again I should point India…as it was a thousand, two thousand, it may be three thousand years ago – not of towns today but village communities*"

All translations of Vedas and so forth are the products of people like Max Muller to fill their political agenda. The reduction of Vedic culture as an offshoot of the hypothetical Proto-Indo-European (PIE) language, that has never been found, derives Asian civilization from the European. Muller placed the original Aryan ancestors in land-locked Sogdiana from where one branch migrated south to Europe (to counter Semitic origin in Bible) and the other east to Iran etc.

"*There was a time when the ancestors of the Celts. The Germans, the Slavs, Greeks and Italians, the Persians, and Hindus were living together beneath the same roof, separate from the ancestors of the Semitic and Turanian races (1855)…there was a small clan of Aryans settled probably on the highest elevation of Central Asia, speaking a language not yet Sanskrit or Greek or German, but containing the dialectic germs of all; a clan that had…invoked the Giver of Light and Life in heaven, by the same name which you may still hear in the temples of Benares, in the basilicas of Rome, and in our own churches and cathedrals (1861)*".

Max Muller had confided to Duke of Argyll, the Secretary of State for India:

"India has been conquered once, but India must be conquered again and that second conquest should be a conquest of education".

Two years later he was to write again:

"The ancient religion of India is doomed. And if Christianity does not take its place, whose fault will it be?"

There can be no doubt at all regarding Max Muller's commitment to the conversion of Indians to Christianity. Writing to his wife in 1866 he observed:

"This edition of mine and the translation of Veda will hereafter tell to a great extent on the fate of India and on the growth of millions of souls in that country. It is the root of their religion and to show them what that root is, I feel sure, is the only way of uprooting all that has sprung from it during the last three thousand years".

Max Muller came up with the **two race theory of India**: Aryan Brahmins (Japhetic or Caucasian) and black or Hamitic, by canceling his earlier statement regarding the brotherhood of Clive's soldiers and dark Bengalese. Now, only Brahmins, Kshatriyas and Vaishyas were Aryan, Shudras being un-arya based upon the word Anasas (noseless or bull nosed) in a single passage of Rigveda which does not mention skin color at all. **Caste now became a race** and the old theory was put into new package by Risley and Topinard, based upon the Nose index of the latter. *"Tall, fair, dolichocephalic, and lepto-rhine race" entered India from the north and collided with a black, snub-nosed race".* Muller declared:

"It is curious to see how the descendants of the same race (Aryan English) , to which the first conquerors of and masters of India belonged, returned, after having followed the northern development of the Japhetic race to their primordial soil, to accomplish the glorious work of civilization, which had been left unfinished by their Aryan brethren".

Max Muller further added in 1883 that many Europeans:

"would not believe that there could be any community of origin between the people of Athens and Rome, and the so-called Niggers of India".

India now became a land of two races where the lighter-skinned Aryans conquered the darker-skinned Dravidians. Although he had deliberately used the word Arya to mean race in his translation of Rigveda, Mueller abruptly changed and burst out in 1888: *"...if I say Aryan I mean neither blood nor bone nor skulls nor hair..."* and from then on he was a staunch opponent of the Aryan race theory. Muller even propounded a new 'linguistic theory' where the word race was changed to language: *"the same blood ran in the veins of the English soldiers as in the veins of the dark Bengalese"*. This did not go down well with the British pride that refused racial equality with the coloreds. Annoyed by the madness he had helped to create, Muller blasted those who spoke of an *'Aryan race. Aryan blood, Aryan eyes and hair'* as a lunacy comparable to a linguist who spoke of 'a dolichocephalic dictionary or a brachycephalic grammar'. But the superiority of the ancient Aryan Nordic race had caught popular imagination and had helped the Europeans to free themselves from the Jewish heritage. This theory was later transferred to India and Europeans, now calling themselves Indo-Europeans, became the invading Aryas and the natives became the Dravidians.

The Archeological Survey of India (ASI) was entrusted to a Major Cunningham who, in a letter to the Governor General Auckland, had suggested a scheme to **falsify Indian Archeology**. The Muslims had already razed most Hindu temples and palaces, burnt down libraries, and falsified records to glorify their own religion. The British simply took over these doctored Muslim records and danced to the Muslim tune to make the Hindus appear puny and insignificant compared to the invading cultures. The English common sense view held that the Indians were a separate, *inferior and unimprovable* race, often linked to the Irish whereas whiteness itself was narrowed down to a small, pure, original, Aryan stock, thanks the work of craniologists and archaeologists. Aryans thus became an exclusive group, much smaller than the people who spoke IE languages. The people of India were to get the message:

"Admire us, emulate us...but you can never be like us"

The colonial-missionary model turned Indian history and culture subservient to European rule and Christian expansion. Isaac Taylor made European history a double of the racial history of India. In both cases, light skinned Caucasian Aryans set out on their civilizing mission from anywhere, somewhere, anyhow and somehow. They also managed to efface all traces and memory of their invasion and came to regard themselves as original inhabitants of the lands from sea to sea. They were primitive enough to have no knowledge of the oceans but nevertheless imposed themselves from Bengal to Ireland. The invaders brought with them iron, chariot and horses to subdue and colonize the locals – much as the Europeans did during the colonial era. No one bothered to explain the transformation of the pleasure loving, soma drinking, dice playing, war mongering Aryans with Vedic asceticism and philosophy – all within 500 years of their arrival from 'somewhere'. As Shaffer has observed, religious conversion and colonialism were to go hand in hand; European Christian missions were an appendage of the colonial government, like an unofficial arm of the Imperial Administration. The same is true of many Catholic missions in Central American countries who were, and probably still are, in the pay of the American CIA, as admitted by the CIA director.

The missionaries portrayed Aryans as lusty marauding nomads, stealing cattle and defeating enemies in contrast to the traditional image of Vedas as being the product of enlightened people. While the invading Aryans were illiterate, their literature has survived whereas that of the literate Harappans has disappeared. They also held that Mathematics was introduced into India through Alexander although there is nothing comparable in Greece like the town planning of Harappa which required advanced mathematical knowledge. Seidenberg has demonstrated that all ancient mathematics is derived from Sulbhashastra that preceded Pythagoras by two thousand years. Here we have the paradox: instructions for construction of Harappa sites are found in the literature of the invading Aryans who destroyed them and who constructed nothing in their original land. The missionaries were propagating the idea that:

"Brahmins had entered India from across the Indus river, had brought Sanskrit language with them, and had foisted them on the aboriginal people of India" (Devendra Swarup quoted in Bryant)

"When the walls of the mighty fortress of Brahmanism are encircled, undermined, and finally stormed by the soldiers of the cross, the victory of Christianity must be signal and complete" (Monier Williams in Bryant).

Foreign Aryans were now supposed to have taught Indians their culture such that the racial justification for colonization did apply after all; modern British were now going to finish the job started earlier by the British Aryans. The contradiction inherent in these assumptions did not matter: Paradoxically, Aryans were portrayed at the same time as **illiterate marauders** and givers of an **advanced civilization**. British James Mills declared *"the Indian civilization never prospered except under foreign domination"* – a clear justification for imperialism as a civilizing mission. The Aryan connection was simply manipulated by self-serving dictates such the one by the evangelist Samuel Laing:

"Two races so long separated meet once more…the younger brother has become the stronger and takes his place as the head and protector of the family…we are here…on a sacred mission, to stretch out the right hand of aid to our weaker brother, who…has now fallen behind in race".

Depending upon their agenda and strategies, British glorified, minimized, shunned and stressed the Aryan connection to suit their intent. Whereas India had been viewed as the homeland of the Aryans and the cradle of Aryan civilization at the beginning of the 19th century, by the end of the same century it was considered its grave. Aryan Invasion model gave rise to a Vedic civilization after **Harappa which now became pre-Vedic**. The two race theory distinguished between an "aboriginal" population and Sanskrit speaking Aryans that arrived later. North Aryans were pitted against the Southern Dravidians, high-castes against low-castes, civilized orthodox Indians against barbaric heterodox tribals. The hypothesis of racial hatred between the Aryans and the dark-skinned Dasyus has no foundation in Sanskrit literature, yet some 'scholars' have misinterpreted texts to try to prove that there was racial hatred amongst the Aryans and Dravidians.

Philologists confused the linguistic age of texts with the historical age of contents. They tried to interpret Rigveda as a historical account of invading nomads called Aryans as an ancient replica of the 19th century European colonization. There is no reason to believe that there was an Aryan race that spoke Indo-European languages. In the Eurocentric approach, progress is a uniquely European phenomenon that becomes possible only by emulating European path. The British scholar James Mill even objected to the use of the word 'civilization' to describe ancient India. Developmental Studies, Anthropology and Oriental Studies served as the basis from which more elaborate Eurocentric theories were developed and tested. During the colonial stranglehold, the contributions of the colonized people were devalued or ignored as a rationale for subjugation and dominance. The colonization of Asia and Africa permitted the suppression of the knowledge of ancient peoples and Euro-centrism saw the **development of mathematics** in two stages: in **Greece** (600 BC to 400 CE) and **Renaissance** following the European dark Ages. European rebirth was possible only when the state was detached from religion so how could the Church institute reforms in India that it had failed to do in the parent country? In contrast to the iron cast organization of the military, religious and economic establishments in Europe, Indian tradition was based on complete freedom of individual thought, speech and belief.

Bankim was convinced that western scholars were deeply prejudiced against India and that racial arrogance was the mainspring of their judgment. India's literary heritage was either false or borrowed from other cultures. Ramayana was an imitation of Iliad, Gita an adaptation of Bible, Hindu astronomy was borrowed from Chinese and Greeks, the heroism of Pandava brothers was a poet's imagination and the legend of Draupadi proved that Indians were polyandrous and hence barbarous. The conjecture that a Sanskrit speaking Vedic Aryans invaded India in the second millennium BC hardened into an article of faith. Sri Aurobindo summarized thus:

"*To exaggerate the importance of their superficial discoveries…a conjecture supported only by other conjectures*".

Bloomfield was to criticize the very foundation of this sort of linguistics:

"*The earlier studies of Indo-European did not realize that the family tree (morphology) diagram was merely a statement of their method: they accepted the uniform parent languages and their sudden clear-cut splitting, as historical realities*".

When Tilak (1893) and Jacobi (1894) identified **astronomical statements in Rigveda** and other works that cast challenged the invasion, they were dubbed unreliable. Waradpande confirmed:

"*There is evidence in the published utterances of Western scholars themselves that Aryan invasion theory was not put forward as a serious scientific theory but as a politico-religious ploy…to sow dissentions among different sections of Hindu society…driving a wedge between the North and South Indians*".

Rathore (cited in Bryant) concluded:

"*The British wished to show that their invasion of India was the second great event, the first great event being its invasion by the Indo-Aryans*".

Anthropologist Edmund Leach observed (cited in Bryant 2005):

"*The origin myth of British colonial imperialism helped the elite administrators in the Indian civil service to see themselves as bringing "pure" civilization to a country in which civilization of the most sophisticated (but 'morally corrupt") kind was already nearly 6000 years old…the hold of this myth on the British middle-class imagination is so strong that even today…the Aryan invasions of the second millennium BC are treated as if they were an established fact of history*".

Crawford (1783-1868) was an Army medical Officer for whom:

"*the claim of a common descent between Hindu, Greek and Teuton would amount to allowing that there was no difference in the faculties of the people that produced Homer and Shakespeare and those that produced nothing better than the authors of Ramayana and Mahabharata; no difference between the home keeping Hindus, who never made a foreign conquest of any kind, and the nation who discovered, conquered, and peopled a new world*".

Based upon language reconstructs only, some **twenty regions** have been identified as possible places from where Aryans migrated none of which shows any evidence of philosophical, scientific, artistic, literary and spiritual heritage that flowered in the Indus culture unrelated to any other regions, and with no parallels and precedents elsewhere. Up until 1860's Aryan homeland was believed to lie in Asia but by 1870 Germany became the homeland (Lazarus Geiger cited in Mallory). By 1878 the homeland had been moved to the marshes of Eastern Europe where high incidence of albinism was linked to the blue eyed blond idea. But a swamp was hardly the place for the development of a Crocodile Dundee figure so in 1883 Penka placed this homeland in Scandinavia despite archaeological evidence for major intrusions into Northern Europe, not out of it. Another hypothesis suggested that Celts and Lithuanians formed the original Aryan tribe who are brachycephalic which is generally associated with high cultural development. American Charles Morris settled the earliest Aryans in Caucasus while Jyotiba Phule placed the Aryan homeland between Iran and Arctic and maintained that Aryans subjugated the existing peoples of the Indus valley. After much speculation, the Northern Andronovo course has been put forward as the base from where the Caucasian Aryans swarmed into Asia as the ISC was declining but the location keeps changing, based upon political exigencies.

While philology may be a study of a civilization, the orientation of the philologist is a necessary component for evaluation of the reliability and integrity of conclusions Cerquiliani was emphatic:

"Philology is a bourgeois, paternalist and hygienist system of thought about the family; it cherishes filiation, tracks down adulterers, and is afraid of contamination. It is though based on what is wrong (the variant being a form of deviant behavior), and it is the basis for a positive methodology."

Most of the works of European indologists suffused with Hinduphobia are works produced with racist overtones, a Eurocentric gestalt, assuming that nothing good could come out of a people who were merely fit only to be hewers of wood and drawers of water and hence, incapable of 'thought' and certainly not capable of producing 'knowledge systems'. Such prejudiced opinions do not constitute philology, meant to result in *abhyudayam* – a key determinant of dharma, but hate literature couched in Harvard Donkey Trial type of diction, evidenced during the California Text Books struggle to undo the bigoted depictions by some self-styled historians of Hindu civilization. Of late Witzel is holding the torch to lead Hinduphobia into a fathomless abyss of anti-history.

The term Mleccha was used by the Aryans much as the ancient Greeks used yhe term *barbaros* to indicate the incomprehensible speech and mannerism of foreigners. Akkadian as Mlakkha were the original mlecchas in northwestern India. Both Mleccha/Meluhha which had their cognates in Prakritam and Samskritam.Thus, Indian *sprachbund* is a sound framework to replace the Aryan-Dravidian-Munda divide splintering Bharatiya identity founded on Dharma-Dhamma gestalt. In a transition from the *cypro-lithic (copper-stone) phase* of civilizational progress to *Bronze-Iron phase*, the word mleccha refers to a people engaged in Bronze Age metalwork and trade. This is validated by the semantics of the two words: *mleccha* (cognate *meluhha*) and *bharat: Mleccha (Meluhha)* refers to copper work, *Bharat* refers to metal alloy work and metal casting.

According to Sâyana, 'He 'lavo' stands for 'He 'rayo (i.e. ho, the spiteful (enemies) which the Asuras were unable to pronounce correctly and he (who speaks thus) is a Mle*kkh*a (barbarian). Hence let no Brahmin speak barbarous language, since such is the speech of the Asuras. Thus alone he deprives his spiteful enemies of speech; and whosoever knows this, his enemies, being deprived of speech, are undone. The presumed distinctions were started with linguistic overtones suggesting 1) that mleccha speakers distorted the pronunciation of Chandas (grammatical Samskritam) words; 2) that some linguistic enquiries (like those of FBJ Kuiper) identified Munda words in Samskritam and 3) that Prakritam was a derivative from Samskritam, identifying *tatsamas* (cognates) and *tatbhavas* (etyma). The *Tamil Lexicon* of Madras University has conclusively documented that over 90% of the so-called ancient glosses of Tamil had, in fact, 'Indo-Aryan' or Samskritam cognates.

The absurdity of treating mleccha as a foreigner is negated unequivocally by the evidence of *Mahabharata* which contains thousands of references to mleccha kings and mleccha people. It is safe to conclude that mleccha was the *lingua franca* in *Bharatam Janam* mentioned in Rigveda by Rishi Viswamitra and dominated the Bharatiya polity. The Great War fully involved *mleccha Bharatam Janam* from both Kaurava and Pandava sides. Ramayana also mentions Mlecchas. Bharata Janam designation is a clear identity of artisans who had invented the new techniques of alloying metals and metal casting by control of fire. Mleccha-Chandas (speech and prosody) are two sides of the same *sprachbund* (language union) coin by Bharatam of the Early Bronze Age. Mleccha and Arya together formed Bharatam Janam metal casters but dichotomy was posited by reductionists to disintegrate and belittle India. Manusmriti (II. 17-23) is wrongly interpreted as setting apart mlecchas from Aryaavarta in terms of geography, culture and purity. In fact, Manusmriti simply distinguished between two dialectical versions of the one and the same language: while Chandas was the grammatical poetic diction for the mantras bequeathed to us by ancient texts such as the Rigveda, Mleccha was the parole, lingua franca of the seafaring artisans and merchants engaged in maritime trade.

14. Civilizing Mission by the Master Race

Racism is essentially a system of **negation and deformation** of the history of Third World peoples. Social Darwinism linked language to race; Sanskrit became the derivative of the lost language spoken by tall, blond and muscular people called Arya (noble or pure) who had vanquished the dark-skinned inhabitants of India and Persia. The fallacy of mixing race with language was based upon the premise that a language which is widely distributed throughout the world reveals the civilizing capacity of all those who speak. Hence the Aryan civilizing mission from the West to the rest of the world. New imperialism after 1870 lead to scramble for Africa, Asia, and near and Middle East based upon conjectures such as "a place in the sun", "manifest destiny", "lamp of life", and, particularly "the white man's burden". Hitler declared in 1930:

*"I know perfectly well that in the scientific sense there is **no such thing as race**. But a farmer cannot get his breeding right without the concept of race. And I as a politician, need a conception which enables the order that has hitherto existed on a historical basis to be abolished, and an entirely new and antihistoric order enforced and given an intellectual basis, and for this purpose the **conception of race serves me well**".*

Christian Identity has become synonymous with the "theology of hate" embraced by Aryan Nations at Hayden Lake, Idaho, where whites originated from one of the 10 lost tribes of Israel such that the Anglo-Saxon-Celtic peoples were true Israelites. The revised Biblical genealogy was published in Idaho by Aryan Nations and the Church of Jesus Christ. *Adam was "the first of the Caucasian race…a ruddy white man…literally and truly the son of God…the descendants of Adam… are the sons and daughters of God".* Victorian scholars conveniently joined forces with linguistics to place the Garden of Eden this in *"the high plateau of Asia",* in contrast to earlier theories that place it in India. By 1970's, Aryan Nations and Church of

Jesus Christ Christian were to state: *"Cain…was a result of Eve's original sin, her physical seduction by Satan…there is a battle being fought this day between the children of darkness (known as the Jews) and the children of light (God), the Aryans race, the true Israel of the Bible"*.

British Israelism stressed the two seeds doctrine whereby Bible was the exclusive history of the descendants of Adam whereas **Jews stemmed from the seduction of Eve by Satan** and the ensuing Cain. The Anglo-Saxon/Nordic Aryans civilized all barbarians like the puritan concept of the divine mandate which justified the conquest of North America as manifest destiny. The similarity between Dagestan (Persia) and Rigveda (Bharata) Sanskrit was taken as a proof for the west to east migration of PIE speaking peoples, after split from the Iranians, into India around 1300 BC when the Sanskrit language supposedly did not even exist; it mattered little that the PIE has never been found. Anthropological societies in France, UK and Germany used the term Aryan indiscriminately and in 1859 Pictet placed *primitive Aryas* in Iran, confused Christianity with Aryan race and excluded Semitic race from the fold of Aryans. Very soon, virility and superiority were endowed to tall, blond, dolichocephalic peoples (Germanics) who dominated short, dark, brachycephalic inferiors. Lapouge even fabricated that:

"The ancestors of the Aryans cultivated wheat when those of the brachycephalic were probably still living like monkeys".

By nineteenth century, a true Aryan appeared to be a **Westerner of male sex** of the upper or middle class. Following the line of Aristotle, Thomas Huxley remained convinced that women and Negros were congenitally inferior to the white male. Emile Burnouf maintained that the skull formation of Chinese and Semites made them incapable of metaphysics and Christianity. Renan concluded: *"The general laws governing the process of civilization are understood. The inequality of races is established"*. Buchner (1824-1899) attempted to demonstrate the congenital incapacity of primitives to raise their minds to the level of abstract ideas because of their impure blood. Karl Voigt applied the following law to women:

"The difference between sexes, so far as the cranial cavity is concerned, increases with the development of the race, so that the European male surpasses the female to a far greater extent than the Negro does the Negress".

Soon, the "prophylactic theory" of human origins affiliated each human race to one of the main branches of anthropoid apes, the whites related to some ape of a reputedly higher intelligence than others. Klaatsch derived the Negroes, the Mongols and Indo-Germans, to gorilla, chimpanzee and orang-outang, respectively. Even a plurality of separate Adams was postulated and the Jewish otherness was firmly established.

As no court of law would punish an author for providing false information in a book of history, the white race supremacists and Marxists grab the accomplishments of others and stick their own label to it. Indian history has been dictated by the West by bribing Indian historians, publishers and media to bark to their master's voice. One communist academic of India was paid professorship to UK simply because she had derogated the Indian civilization most efficiently. In Jan 2001, Michel Farrell of The Times, London made fun of Indians for thinking that they invented the chess, zero, Pythagoras' theorem etc. as in the soap opera "Goodness Gracious Me" in which a central character keeps claiming that whatever exists always originated in India. Such phantastic myths stem from the **European longing to secure for itself an illustrious ancestry,** "*fitted with exceptional mental endowments*" *and* "*promoters of true progress*" (Poliakov cited in Childe) when there is none.

The Indo-European crust forms a layer of civilization before the rise of Mesopotamia, Egypt and the Indus valley. In the reductionist view, this Aryan race, migrated out of its homeland and conquered advanced peoples, despite numerical inferiority. European intellectual and moral superiority was a foregone conclusion to the savants of the 19th and the 20th centuries. The Aryans, or Indo-Europeans, too must have been blessed with this superiority as conquerors. Race and language became intimately associated and Childe concluded in 1926: "…*the Nordic's superiority in physique fitted them to be vehicles of a superior language*". So an entire mythology was woven of an ancient, fair-skinned martial race of Aryans who invaded India and defeated the uncivilized natives. Dugald Stewart in 1826 CE went as far as to say that the Brahmins had learned Sanskrit from Alexander while the British claimed that the new invasion was a meeting of parted cousins. Indeed, what impelled them to leave their own advanced cradle to enter into inhospitable and unknown wilderness, across formidable mountains, in far recesses of Asia which was believed to be the home of decadence and darkness? How come they could not create the marvels of the likes of the ISC in their original homeland?

"This is paradoxical indeed for a people who had just arrived in this new and unknown land, far from their original and ancestral home, leaving behind all collective experience, memory, and associations that should form the most cherished part of their cultural universe".

People migrate to escape poor, depraved, and hostile environments to seek opportunity and plenty, not the other way around.

Based on excavations in 1922, and true to the racist colonial mentality of his age, Wheeler painted it as *'a dead end inflicted upon it by the invading Aryans'.* According to this theory, the 'Aryans' supposedly came riding down their horses, swinging their iron swords, and massacred the hapless 'Dravidian' inhabitants of Mohenjo-Daro. B.B. Lal (ex-Director General, Archaeological Survey of India) has this to say about the alleged massacre at Mohenjo-Daro which is the 'proof' given to us for the Aryan invasion:

"Had an invasion been the cause of these deaths, one expects that the skeletons would have been found in one level which also would have been the uppermost, after which the inhabitants are taken to have deserted the site and migrated to south India. Further, all the skeletal remains came from the Lower Town which was occupied by the commoners, but none from the Citadel area which was the seat of the government. Are we expected to believe that the 'invaders' killed the commoners and carefully spared the high-ups? The doubt about the deaths having been the result of an 'invasion' is also supported by that fact some of the skeletons bore cut-marks which had been healed – a process which must have taken quite some time. There would have been no healing had the deaths been due to a 'massacre'…

Dales observed in a paper titled *The Mythical Massacre at Mohenjo-Daro*:

"Despite the extensive excavations at the largest Harappa sites, there is not a single bit of evidence that can be brought forth as unconditional proof of an armed conquest and the destruction on the supposed scale of the Aryan Invasion".

Indeed, no site of the Harappa Civilization has yielded any evidence of 'invasion', much less of 'massacre'. Nor is there any evidence of an alien culture overtaking any of these sites. So the theory has now been recast into an Aryan Immigration scenario where an illiterate people from somewhere overpowered the mighty ISC strongholds and imposed their language. The Raj-era historians, and the modern communist historians of India, stick to the Aryan invasion theory to detach south India from rest of the country for conversion to Christianity, and to dismember India into a Dravidian Tamil Nadu, and a northern Aryan.

Barbarian Aryans from an Island nation invaded the far advanced Indus civilization of 1.5 million square kilometers and destroyed the Dravidian Indus townships, enslaved the dark Dravidians, pushed them to the south and imposed a caste system. The superior white Aryans then settled on the banks of river Sarasvati in 1500BC although the latter had to ceased to flow by 1900 BC. White Aryans brought the Proto Indo-European language with them which developed into Sanskrit, invented a written script and composed all of the vast Vedic literature as of 1000 BC of high philosophical and spiritual content (Chapter 3).but forgot to mention their original homeland. Later on, Hittite, Greek etc. also developed from the Proto Indo-European which has **never been found**.

Wheeler was furthermore of the view that not only the idea of a city came to India from Mesopotamia and that Mesopotamian masons actually built the first cities in India; the origins of the ISC would therefore lie in Mesopotamia: *'the stimuli are presumed to have arrived from the west'*. However, the two social philosophies and religious structures are at antipodes as are the two scripts. While the artisan guilds through seals appear during the early period of the ISC, the Egyptian and Mesopotamian systems are based upon absolute mundane and extramundane powers for the royalty, priests and noblemen who built monuments for themselves but devoid of towns or housing for people who lived in huts. Indus seals too depict no rulers and noblemen in contrast to those in Mesopotamia etc. Script, mythology, disposal of the dead etc. were also different in the ISC versus the west. In the New World, the religious institutions are self-aggrandizing, given to amassing great resources, and building permanent structures. In contrast to Mesopotamia and Egypt, the Indus age was not marked by kingships in the form of sculpture or palaces. Rather, the faceless socio-cultural system mastered food production and turned raw materials into luxury products for the benefit of all. There are **no planned townships for the common man in Mesopotamia of 2500 BC**?

Rigveda reflects a maritime culture along Sarasvati but Max Muller stated that Rigveda describes northwest India and Afghanistan and did not know the ocean. Interestingly, Mahabharata mentions Indraprastha, 1400 BC or earlier, somewhere between the Old Fort and Humayun's tomb. Many of the Indus sites have been found along the banks of the now dried up Sarasvati basin which is exalted throughout the Vedas as a very large and flowing river. If the dating of the Vedic literature is correct, then there is a discrepancy because the Sarasvati River **dried up around 1900 BC**, before the Vedas were supposed to have been written. Thus, either there was no influx of an invading people or that the Vedas were written by the people of the Indus Valley before 1900 BC. Dozens of Harappa seals and a horse training manual were found in West Asia and Anatolia, respectively. Other salient arguments against the West to East migration may be summarized as follows:

(i)   There is simply no archaeological evidence for the existence of Andronovo.

(ii)   Both BMAC and Andronovo are dubbed Indo-Iranian though their environment and archaeology are very different. Mallory wonders: "*How do we reconcile deriving the Indo-Iranians from two regions (Andronovo and BMAC).*

(iii)   The Mittany-Hittie treaty of the fifteenth century BC swears by a series Hindu gods Indra, Mitra, Varuna, and Ashvini twins. If the ISC people did not separate from the Iranians until 1300 BC, how could a record of 1400 BC in Anatolia, well west of Iran, possibly have Vedic-Hindu names still centuries into future? Some 100 such records exist. Glottochronology has revealed considerable divergence between Avesta and Vedic Sanskrit, contrary to earlier claims that both were almost identical.

(iv)   **The Hittie Empire compiled a horse training manual in** the 18th century BC **that** employs Sanskrit numerals such as: *aika* (1), *tera* (3), *panza* (5), *sapta* (7) and *nava* (9); the color of horses is similarly described in Sanskrit. **All of this is incompatible with the idea that Sanskrit and horse were brought to the ISC homeland by the Painted Grey Ware culture only in 1200 BC.**

(v)   Archeology records a continuous indigenous evolution of Vedic civilization going back to 8000 BC at sites like Mehragarh and Koldi.

(vi)   It was suggested that Aryans introduced the horse and chariot to Bharata. However, the remains of *Equus caballus* Linn have been excavated from both the Harappa as also from Karnataka to the Ganges region whereas there is no evidence for horse in Iran and in Mesopotamia until 2100 BC. A clay model of a horse was also found at Mohenjo-Daro.

(vii)   An Invasion of India from Central Asia would require crossing mountains and deserts, a chariot would be useless for such an exercise; one seal actually depicts a spoked wheel of the type used in chariots.

(viii) The word '*ayas*' in the *Vedas* was translated as iron but in other Indo-European languages, *ayas* refers to bronze, copper or ore. Vedas mention that the *dasyus* (enemies of the Aryans) also used *ayas* to build their cities. Thus there is no hard evidence to prove that the 'Aryans invaders' were an iron-based culture and their enemies were not.

(ix)   The *Vedas* are replete with references to fire-sacrifices (*yajnas*) and elaborate *vedhis* (fire altars) were uncovered in Harappa along a geometry explained in the Vedic texts such as the *Satpatha-*

brahmana. The University of California at Berkley has established that the geometry found in the Vedic scriptures should be dated before 1700 BC.

(x)   The Invasion theory argues that the inhabitants of Indus valley were *Shaivites* (Shiva worshippers) which is more prevalent among the South Indians so the inhabitants of the Indus valley region must have been Dravidians. However, some of the most important Shaivite sites are located in the North: Mount Kailasha, Varanasi, Pashupatinath. Many verses in the Rigveda mention Shiva along with Rudra, Indra himself is called Shiva several times in Rigveda (RV 2:20:3, 6:45:17, 8:93:3).

(xi) Whereas the Vedic-Hindus, Greeks, Romans and Hitties, cremated their dead, Kurgans went through elaborate burials that have not been found at the ISC sites.

(xii) The Rigveda itself contains nearly a hundred references to ocean (*samudra*), as well as dozens of references to ships, and to rivers flowing into the sea. The Vedic God of the sea, Varuna, is the father of many Vedic seers like Vashishta, and the Bhrigu seers. Indeed the basic Vedic myth is of the God Indra who wins the seven rivers to flow into the sea? How could such a myth arise in the desert of Central Asia?

Basham wondered:

"How did these primitive tribes conquer an area much larger than their homeland by overpowering peoples who were far advanced materially, culturally and technically and who were secured by the tallest mountain chains of the Hindu Kush and the Himalayas? No explanation is provided for the sudden transformation of these barbarian nomads into accomplished scholars after their perilous journey through the most inhospitable of all mountains in the world. Also, no mention is made of such barbarian conquests in the records of Mesopotamia that formed the Dilmun trade zone and the like".

Using Biblical chronology as their sole anchor, nineteenth century race supremacists had placed the creation of the world at 4000 BC and Noah's flood at 2500 BC. By assigning a period of 200 years to each of the several layers of the pre-Buddhist Vedic literature, the Aryan invasion was placed 1500 and 1000 BC. The great Sarasvati river that flowed "from the mountain to the sea" seems to belong to a date long anterior to 3000 BC. Thus the Rigveda, that describes the geography of Northern Bharat long before 3000 BC, must have been in existence no later than 3500 BC. More than 75% of some 2500 settlements, over a million and a half square kilometers, are concentrated not along the Sindhu, as was believed 70 years ago, but on the banks of the extinct river Sarasvati (now called the Ghaggar) in the Thar desert. Satellite imagery has shown that a great prehistoric river, sometimes over 7 kilometers wide, did indeed flow through the area at one time. Harappa settlements were east, not west of Indus. N. Rajaram analyzed:

"*The Aryan invasion theory is the fabrication of a version of ancient history and tradition that was highly advantageous to missionary and colonial interest…in the hands of politically driven historians of post-colonial India, these 19th century creations (Aryan invasion theory) have become handy tools to be used in support of their vested interest in Marxist ideology and the version of history that goes with it. Marxists maintain a defunct theory that the arrival of Aryans is analogous to the arrival of Muslims, Christians and others to the subcontinent. In such an amalgamation of immigrants, no one has more claim to indigenous pedigree or cultural hegemony than anyone else*".

Frawley and Rajaram remarked:

"*The prediction that an Aryan nation could emerge from the discovery that Aryans are native to India is irrelevant to the history of India; it is relevant, however, to modern politics*".

Talageri added:

"*The first principle of Leftist propaganda is that India is not a nation but a conglomerate of nations…if India breaks up in small 'nations' these would be easier for the Leftists to gobble up one by one*".

Rajaram concluded:

"*The chronology of ancient India found in history books-beginning with Rigveda is too late by several thousand years. Archaeology points to a continuum going back to 7000 BC. Astronomical references in Rigveda go back to 4500 BC…the Harappa civilization at the end of Vedic age was part of it*".

Renfrew believes that PIE may have extended to West Pakistan before 6000 BC such that Indus civilization could well become the original homeland.

Karl Marx did not believe India to be the home of any civilization as he was biased by the colonial-media accounts that had been distorted for political ends. So, Marxists supported the idea that Indo-Aryans brought with them the language that was to become Sanskrit later on. The metaphors in

Vedas were then reduced to a white-dark dualism by the Europeans and later picked up by the Marxists in India who came to support the colonial model which held that:

"Indigenism...is intellectually and historiographical barren with no nuances or subtleties of thought and interpretation...The next step to be moved from the indigenous origin of Aryans is to propagating the notion of an 'Aryan nation".

The Aryan invasion is now presented as a class conflict by the Marxists in India where **race is replaced by caste**. This is merely a continuation of the old colonial policy. "*The Indologists and Orientalists...introduced the till unheard of concept of Aryans and Dravidians which created mutual hatred* (Shankaracharya Chandrashekhar Saraswati quoted in Bryant). During the plenary session of the 1994 World Archaeological Congress in New Delhi, 'leftist' and 'rightist' historians physically wrestled each other in an attempt to snatch the microphone, and exchanged abuse in front of two hundred foreign delegates. Other periods of Indian history that are dubbed under 'revisionism' include the golden age of Chandragupta, Mogul period, and Babur. Frawley actually relates different shlokas of Veda to the major events.

Finally, there is no genetic or archeological discontinuity in the remains 4500 BC to 800 BC and **population genetics has formally ruled out** any large scale infusion of foreign genes into Bharata during the Vedic Age (chapter 5). Kenneth Kennedy of Cornell University has also recently proved that there was no significant influx of people 4500 to 800 BC. As the mitochondrial DNA extracted from Neanderthal bones people shows no relationship with modern Europeans or any other living humans the Aryan Invasion / Migration more likely happened not from West to East, but from East to West, from India to the Europe, not the way imperialist anti-historians would have us believe.

15. Civilization Followed the Westering Sun

How to reconcile the paradox: a concrete history and archaeology of a vast civilization of 'Dravidians', lasting thousands of years, left no literature whereas illiterate Vedic Aryans left no trace of history or archaeological records but a huge literature in Sanskrit ? Modern linguistics has not yet reached the level of sophistication attained by Panini 3000 years ago and his *Ashtadhyayi* and *Mahabhasya* are revealing rich dividends to computer scientists today. Vyaas Houston wonders about Sanskrit:

" …*a language infinitely more sophisticated than many of our modern tongues. How could language have been so much more refined in ancient times, especially among a people, the Vedic Aryans whom scholars tell us were nomadic barbarians from the north*".

How could the invading illiterates reach this level of linguistic sophistication? Aryan Indus shows city planning and sanitation that required knowledge of geometry and the world had to wait two thousand years to attain a comparable level in the Roman Empire. Seidenberg has demonstrated that. Egyptian pyramids were probably based on the Vedic funeral altar known as the *shamashana-cit*. all ancient mathematical knowledge is derived from mathematics in *Sulbhashastra* that made Indus possible. All this and more suggest a migration from Bharata into Iran, West Asia and Europe.

The Vedas, Puranas or other works do not mention an Aryan homeland at all and oral traditions are also silent in this context. On the other hand, the mythology of various countries indicates the arrival or Vedic Aryans. S. S. Mishra (cited in Bryant) concludes:

"*Therefore we are sure that India is the original home of Indo-Aryans and Iranians…as well as of Aryans, that is Indo Europeans…The Dravidians were also Aryans*".

According to Mishra, Indo-Aryans loan words in Uralic, Chinese and Korean indicate Indo-Aryans migrations out of Bharata in prehistoric times. Koenraad Elst adds (cited in Bryant):

"*On closer inspection, currently dominant theories turn out to be compatible with an out-of-India scenario for IE expansion. In particular, substratum data are not in conflict with an IE homeland in Haryana-Punjab…One after another, the classical proofs of a European origin have been discredited, usually by scholars who had no interest in an alternative Indian homeland theory…Invading Aryans could only initiate a process of language replacement by a scenario of elite dominance…at least some kind of military showdown must have taken place*".

Elst and Tilak suggest that from this ISC homeland Aryans went to south India and west to Central Asia. In 8000-5000 BC Aryans had to migrate out of their original Arctic home because of its destruction by the last Ice Age 10,000 to 8000 BC. Witzel (cited in Bryant) underlines the fact that even the earliest Vedic hymns are set in SE Asian realities; 40%

agricultural terms are Vedic. Varma observed:

"Further, little attention has been paid to the literary/astronomical evidence, available in the Vedic literature. The evidence which remains unchallenged is so decisive that the supporters of the low (i.e. late) dates for the Vedic literature and the Bharata war dare not even refer to it. ...The real fact is that unless the Vedic tradition is a gigantic forgery, the chronology propounded by Max Muller, and tacitly followed by the present day Indologists...can not be sustained".

Talageri, an accomplished linguist, compared mythologies and remarked:

"Among the speakers of the Indo-European languages, a great historical occurrence took place when a major part of the Indo-Europeans of south-eastern UP migrated to the west and settled down in the northwestern areas..the Purus (in Punjab), the Anus (in Kashmir) and the Dryhyus (in the northwest and Afghanistan)...Anus spread out all over Western Asia and developed into various Iranian cultures. The Druhyus spread out into Europe in two installments: the speakers of the proto-Germanic dialect first migrated northwards and then westwards, and then later the speakers of the proto-Hellenic and proto-Italic Celtic dialects moved into Europe by a different more southern route... it is all the more remarkable that the genealogical lists and traditional accounts given by the Puranas can be confirmed, in their geographical aspects, by comparing them with the relevant names attested by the Rigveda. The fact that the Rigveda seems to confirm the Puranic accounts in every case is positive proof of the geographical validity of the Puranic accounts...the Puranas provide incontrovertible evidence that there were dynasties...during and even before, the composition of the majority of the hymns of the Rigveda... and that the movement of these dynasties took place from east to west and not vice versa".

Puranas have actually **chronicled migrations out of Bharata** such that many of the ancient Europeans could be descendants of Aryans driven out of Bharata, first by Mandhatr before 4500 BC, from what is now UP, and later by Sudas in the Battle of Ten Kings. Druids of England were Druhyus, driven out of Bharata by Mandhatr, and Druids themselves trace their origin back to Bharata 4000 BC. Talageri identifies Druhyus with the Celtic Druids who trace their origins from Asia to 3900 BC. The Parthians (Prthu-Parthavas), Druids (Druhyu), the Ainas (Hellenes), the Simyus (Albanians), Balhanas (Bolans) the Pakthas (Pathans) were driven out in successive campaigns going back to 500 BC or more, and formed the seed of the Indo-European race. Shaivism is practiced in Nepal, Kashmir, UP, and Himachal, while the 150 BC Gundestrup Cauldron of Denmark carries Aryan symbols. Even the Iranian tradition firmly places Vivanhant (Vivasvan) outside Iran as their ancestor in their original homeland. The Avesta refers to '*Airayana Vajjo*' i.e. Aryavarta as their homeland and speaks of Rama whose guru Vashistha is mentioned in Avesta as Vashista and who figures in the Battle of Ten Kings as the chief priest and advisor to Sudas. Zoroaster is generally assigned to the sixth century BC but Xanthos of Lydia, writing in 470 BC, puts him six hundred years before the Trojan war or 1900-1800 BC just when Sarasvati was going dry. The fact that he was an uprooted heretic is evident from the lament in Avesta:

To what land shall I flee? Where bend my steps? I am thrust out from my family and tribe; I have no favor from the village to which I belong. Nor from the wicked rulers of the country.

The word Magi or Magus is mentioned in *Bhavishya Purana* and could well stand for the Median and Persian priests. According to Talageri, Anu people of Punjab and Kashmir became Persians, following the massive defeat of Prthu and Parsu people at the hands of Sudas in the Battle of Ten Kings 3730 BC. Talageri observed:

"*And then the Puranas make the most amazing and clear declaration of the emigration of major sections of these Druhyus from Afghanistan to strange and distant lands in the north. The evidence provided by this unique statement is so absolute that no honest scholar can deny that it constitutes evidence of migration of Into-Europeans…Five Puranas add that Pracetas' descendants spread out into the mleccha countries to the north beyond India and founded kingdoms there…*"

MahaBharata also tells us that the Aryans (and the Vedic seers) came from the east:

"*This quarter is called purva, O Brahmana for the reason that in far older times, it was first overspread by the Devas. Here first chanted the Vedas, the glorious God who promotes the welfare of the words. Here was recited to the chanters of the Vedas, the Savitri by Savirtar the Sun God. Here in the old days of yore, O best among twice born, took place the birth, the acquisition of renown and the death – of the ancient rishi Vashistha*".

Talageri concludes that the only way to reconcile the Aryan invasion theory with all this evidence is to assume:

"*…that the ancient composers of the Rigveda hymns and the editors of the Puranas hatched a deep, and extremely subtle conspiracy to doctor their texts in such a way as to give a false picture*".

The forgery theory implies fantastic back calculations more complex than the forward theory based on observations. Theosophists maintained that Aryans were indigenous to Bharata from where they migrated to Europe. The language structure of various mandalas suggested to Talageri that the Aryans were initially settled east of Sarasvati, present day Haryana and UP, and later expanded westwards towards Punjab and Afghanistan.

The east to west migration will be in accordance with the natural laws that stipulate a **centrifugal spread**, from the epicenter to the periphery, never the other way round. Centripetal theories, from the periphery to the epicenter, can only be formulated by linguists who do not know the languages but know about languages. The centripetal view would be tantamount to saying that the sun became the source of energy and life by absorbing light from the planets orbiting around it; the earth and other planets would then be the source of sun's radiance. As the Europeans trace their civilization to Greeks and Romans the latter were regarded as Aryan but it is now conceded that they are products of a stock composed of many consanguineous peoples who occupied the Mediterranean basin composed of Africa, Asia and Europe, following diffusion from Europe. Many East to West movements are well known: Buddhists, Gypsies, Dilmun trade, so a local South Asian homeland is obvious.

The destruction of Vedic-Hindu literature by Turko-Afghan invaders was so extensive that no record of pre-Islamic history remained in Bharata. Indian history was reconstructed from sources in Sri Lanka, China, Myanmar, Tibet etc. plus extrapolations from the Puranas and Vedas. In 1841 CE, M.S. Elphinstone, the first governor of the Bombay Presidency, wrote in his *History of India:*

'It is opposed to their (Hindus) foreign origin, that neither in the Code (of Manu) nor, I believe, in the Vedas, nor in any book that is certainly older than the code, is there any allusion to a prior residence or to a knowledge of more than the name of any country out of India. Even mythology goes no further than the Himalayan chain, in which is fixed the habitation of the gods...To say that it spread from a central point is an unwarranted assumption, and even to analogy; for, emigration and civilization have not spread in a circle, but from east to west. Where, also, could the central point be, from which a language could spread over India, Greece, and Italy and yet leave Chaldea, Syria and Arabia untouched? There is no reason whatever for thinking that the Hindus ever inhabited any country but their present one, and as little for denying that they may have done so before the earliest trace of their records or tradition.'

Western archaeologist Jim Shaffer is the most outspoken critic of the invasion theory:

"...invasion(s) as an academic concept in the 18th and 19th century Europe

reflected the cultural milieu of that period. Linguistic data were used to validate the concept that in turn was used to interpret archaeological and anthropological data…theory became unquestioned fact that was used to interpret and organize all subsequent data. It is time to end the 'linguistic tyranny' that has prescribed interpretative frameworks of pre- and proto-historical cultural development in South Asia".

Savarkar wrote in Hindutva in 1923:

"…The first important essential qualification of a Hindu is that…the system or set of religions which we call Hindu dharma-Vedic and non-Vedic is as truly the offspring of this soil as the men whose thoughts they are or who 'saw' the Truth revealed to them…it was in this land that the founders of our faith…from Vedic seers to Dayananda, from Jinnah to Mahavir, from Buddha to Nagasena, from Ramdas to Rammohan, our Gurus and Godemen were born and bred…in the case of some of our Mohamedan or Christian country men…Their holyland is far off in Arabia or Palestine…Their mythology and Godmen, ideas and heroes, are not the children of this soil …they do not look upon India as their holy land".

The above was adopted by Hindu Mahasabha as well as RSS as an authoritative definition of Hindutva. If the Vedic Aryans came from central Asia, the followers of the Vedic religion would have to be disqualified from being Hindus since the founders were not born and bred in Bharata. By extrapolation, the Aryan invasion theory would imply that followers of Vedic religion are no different from Muslims and Christians whose rootd are to be found outside the subcontinent. Golwalkar was more lucid abbot the pitfalls and political consequences of Aryan invasion paradigm:

"It was the wily foreigner, the British…carried on the insidious propaganda that we were never one nation, that we were never the children of the soil but mere upstarts having no better claims than the foreign hordes of Muslim of the British over this country".

Shrikant Talageri (1993) argued against Aryan immigration theory but nuanced it to suit Hindutva:

"Even if it is assumed that a group of people called Aryans invaded or immigrated into India…they have left no trace, if there was any, of any link, much less the consciousness of any link, much less any loyalties associated with such a link, to any place outside India…in any event Muslim country gives Indian Muslims the right to take to the streets and start vicious riots, all over the country, in an orgy of loot, arson and vandalism, especially vandalism of Hindu temples shops and houses situated near Muslim areas".

Talageri affirms that while Indian culture absorbs and assimilates new comers, Islam and Christianity do not: "Hinduism Indianizes foreigners,

Islam and Christianity foreignize or de-Indianize Indians. In these last two religions, all symbols owe allegiance to cultures outside India".

This position of Hindutva has been compared with Nazism by Leftists and other academicians in India who refuse to alter the paradigm of external origins of Vedic culture although this same has been all but discarded by Western scholars such as Renfrew, Gamkrelidze and Ivanov. Chakrabarty affirms:

"After independence, when the Indian ruling class modeled itself on its departed counterpart, any emphasis on the 'glories of ancient India' came to be viewed as an act of Hindu fundamentalism…It is the interplay of race, language and culture which has provided the most strong plank of the understanding of ancient India by the Westerns and the Indians alike. This plank was laid sown at the height of Western political hegemony over India, and the fact that it still has been left in its place speaks a volume for the post 1947 pattern of the retention of Western dominance in various forms…Rumblings against some of the premises of Western Indology have been heard from time to time, but such rumblings have generally emerged in uninfluential quarters, and in the context of Indian historical studies this would mean people without control of the major historical organizations, i.e. people who can easily be fobbed off as "fundamentalists" of some kind…of no intellectual consequence".

16. First they Stole Our Wealth then Our Soul

Cesare de Saussure had aptly noted:

"I do not think there is a people more prejudiced in its own favor than the British people…they look on foreigners in general with contempt, and think nothing is as well done elsewhere as in their own country"

Roy Porter painted the British thus:

"The English abroad saw the Continent with such prejudices: all was poverty and superstition, vain glory and tyranny".

Englishmen excused their vices as virtues and indulged them with brio. They liked being thought of as bloody-minded rough necks. *"Anything that looks like a fight, is delicious to an Englishman"* (Henri Misson). *"I love a mob, I headed one once myself"* (Duke of Newcastle). Duelling remained common among top people while the English ate to excess, drank like lords. The poet Southey observed: *"The English love to be at war but do not love to pat for their amusement".* Porter observed:

"They boast of the freedom of the press yet as surely and systematically punish the author who publishes anything obnoxious, and the book seller who sells it. They cry out against intolerance and burn down the houses of those they regard as heretics. They hate the French and ape all their fashions, ridicule their neologisms and then naturalize them, laugh at their inventions and then adopt them, cry out against their political measures then imitate them: the levy in mass, the telegraph, and the income tax are all from France".

The English thus fell in love with themselves in the 18th century. But did they really have anything to be proud about? In the 1700 theirs was still a second-rate rustic nation of hamlets and villages. Outside London it had no town. Nearly 80% of the population of five million lived in the country and 90% was employed either in agriculture or in processing rural produce. Millions of acres were waste heath, marsh or fen. The Roads were perhaps worse than the Romans had left them. In 1700 the harvest was still the heartbeat of the economy... ploughing, harvesting, fruit picking, chimney sweeping Would there be enough bread? And who could afford it? ...Weather alone held the answer...Industry still fed off the soil: timber, hides, hops, flax, madder, saffron, horn, glue, were the essential raw materials. And most industry was cottage industry: spinning, lace-making, stock-knitting, tanning, smithying.

Europe was trapped in cycles of over population and under production. Between 1696 and 1697 famine killed a third of the population of Finland and close to a million starved to death in 1769. Gregory King estimated that at the end of the seventeenth century about half the families in England were not commanding a subsistence. His figures are suggestive: landowners (1.2%), farmers and freeholders (24.3%), professionals including clergy (3.4%), laborers (26.8%), paupers (29.4%), armed forces (6.8%). Poor laborers, prosperous knights and peers made 10, 800 and over 10,000 pounds a year. The English social ladder was precisely graded and sealed attitudes even denied that rich and poor came from the same species so a merchant could never become a magistrate without buying an estate and a sailor could never rise to command a ship. Clive of India, an opium addict, took his own life and England became notorious as the world suicide capital. The resilience of its social hierarchy was cemented by profits from export. Money was a passport through social frontiers. British looted some **10 trillion dollas** from India and **decimated about 70 million people** in the process. After looting the wealth, British went after the rich patrimony of Bharat described thus by Max Muller:

"The bridge of thoughts that spans the whole history of Aryan world has its first arch in the Veda's and its last in Kant's critique of pure reason".

Demonization followed by conversion had been used by the Church to decimate peoples and cultures around the globe and British administration followed suite. Indians were written off as having no concept of nation, national feelings or a history. Worse still, Indians were fraught with casteism, religious bigotry, superstition and the like which had never existed in Vedic times and which had been implanted by Muslims, Portuguese and other invaders. The British, on the other hand, epitomized modernity, all that was rational and scientific. All conscious and subconscious means would be used by the British and Europeans to rape and conquer the Indian mind. The goal was entrusted in 1835 to the arch racist Thomas Babbington Macaulay (1800-1859) who had:

"never found one among them (Orientalists) who could deny that a single shelf of a good European library was worth the whole native literature of India and Arabia…It is, no exaggeration to say, that all the historical information which has been collected from all the books written in Sanskrit language is less valuable than what may be found in the most paltry abridgments used at preparatory schools in England".

Within a matter of years, J.N Farquhar (a contemporary of Macaulay) was to note:

"The new educational policy of the Government created during these years the modern educated class of India. These are men who think and speak in English habitually, who are proud of their citizenship in the British Empire, who are devoted to English literature, and whose intellectual life has been almost entirely formed by the thought of the West, large numbers of them enter government services, while the rest practice law, medicine or teaching, or take to journalism or business."

Charles E. Trevelyan, brother-in-law of Macaulay, stated:

"Familiarly acquainted with us by means of our literature, the Indian youth almost cease to regard us as foreigners. They speak of 'great' men with the same enthusiasm as we do. Educated in the same way, interested in the same objects, engaged in the same pursuits with ourselves, they become

more English than Hindoos, just as the Roman provincial became more Romans than Gauls or Italians.."

In his testimony before the Select Committee of the House of Lords on the Government of Indian Territories on 23rd June, 1853 Charles Trevelyan boasted

"..... the effect of training in European learning is to give an entirely new turn to the native mind. The young men educated in this way cease to strive after independence according to the original Native model, and aim at, improving the institutions of the country according to the English model, with the ultimate result of establishing constitutional self-government. They cease to regard us as enemies and usurpers, and they look upon us as friends and patrons, and powerful beneficent persons, under whose protection the regeneration of their country will gradually be worked out. ....."

In a speech before the Edinburgh Philosophical Society in 1846 Macaulay, offered a toast:

"To the literature of Britain . . . which has exercised an influence wider than that of our commerce and mightier than that of our arms . . .before the light of which impious and cruel superstitions are fast taking flight on the Banks of the Ganges!"

Realizing the danger of Indians discovering their real heritage through the medium of Sanskrit, Christian missionaries such as William Carey anticipated the need to transcribe and interpret Sanskrit texts in a manner compatible with colonial aims. Richard Fox Young hits the nail on the head

"To gain the ear of those who are thus deceived it is necessary for them to believe that the speaker has a superior knowledge of the subject. In these circumstances a knowledge of Sanskrit is valuable. As the person thus misled, perhaps a Brahman, deems this a most important part of knowledge, if the advocate of truth be deficient therein, he labors against the hill; presumption is altogether against him."

The Aryan invasion theory reduced Indian history to chronicle of invasions from the West viz: Aryans, Persians, Greeks, Scythians, Huns, Arabs, Turks, Portuguese, British, and so on, without any indegenoius input. Dravidians too were projected to immigrate into India from Central Asia, a few thousand years before the Aryans, pushing the native inhabitants into tribal areas thus further obviating India as an epicenter of civilization. Aryan Invasion scenario divided India into Northern Aryan and Southern Dravidian camps, hostile to each other. The Vedas, the genealogies of the Puranas, icons like Buddha and Rama, were reduced to myths, possibly derived from Mesopotamia and its Abrahamic patrimony. British could now claim to doing only what the Aryan ancestors of the Hindus had previously done millennia ago viz civilizing by superior Western culture and religion.

In this manner, India's awareness of her own history and culture was manipulated through colonial ideologues. British-educated Indians grew up learning about Pythagoras, Archimedes, Galileo and Newton without ever learning about Panini, Aryabhata, Bhaskar or Bhaskaracharya. The logic and epistemology in Nyaya Sutras, Buddhists and Jains were generally unknown to the them. Little did the Westernized Indian know that Western Science and Civilization stem directly from Vedic-Hindu discoveries. For instance, William Carey described Indian music as *"disgusting"*, bringing to mind *"practices dishonorable to God"*. Evangelist Charles Grant attacked almost every aspect of Indian society and religion, describing Indians as morally depraved: *"lacking in truth, honesty and good faith"*. British Governor General Cornwallis asserted *"Every native of Hindostan, I verily believe, is corrupt"*.

John Ruskin dismissed all Indian art with ill-concealed contempt:

"the Indian will not draw a form of nature but an amalgamation of monstrous objects…To all facts and forms of nature it willfully and resolutely opposes itself; it will not draw a man but an eight armed monster, it will not draw a flower but only a spiral or a zig zag".

Others such as George Birdwood opined: *"...painting and sculpture as fine art did not exist in India."*

James Mill, author of the three-volume History of British India (1818), William Jones, Henry Maine, all projected India as an essentially unchanging society devoid of intellectual debate, technological innovation or reform. Such stereotypes permitted influential philosophers such as Hegel to posit ethnocentric and self-serving justification for colonization and conversion. Arguing that Europe was *"absolutely the end of universal history"*, he saw Asia as only the beginning of history, where history soon came to a standstill.

"If we had formerly the satisfaction of believing in the antiquity of the Indian wisdom and holding it in respect, we now have ascertained through being acquainted with the great astronomical works of the Indians, the inaccuracy of all figures quoted. Nothing can be more confused, nothing more imperfect than the chronology of the Indians; no people which attained to culture in

astronomy, mathematics, etc., is as incapable for history; in it they have neither stability nor coherence."

Hegel was most vitriolic about Africans:

"It is characteristic of the blacks that their consciousness has not yet even arrived at the intuition of any objectivity, as for example, of God or the law, in which humanity relates to the world and intuits its essence. ...He [the black person] is a human being in the rough".

Max Weber focused exclusively on "material renunciation" and the "world denying character", insisting that: "Neither scientific, artistic, governmental, nor economic evolution has led to the modes of rationalization proper to the Occident."

With such distorted views of India, it was a small step to argue that:

"The British, or rather the East India Company, are the masters of India because it is the fatal destiny of Asian empires to subject themselves to the Europeans."

Gandhi came out to be the just the sycophant British had hoped for. In a conversation with General Smut, Gandhi appealed:

"General Smuts, sir we Indians would like to strengthen the hands of the government in the war. However, our efforts have been rebuffed. Could you inform us about our vices so we would reform and be better citizens of this land?"

Gen.Smuts replied: "Mr. Gandhi, we are not afraid of your vices, We are afraid of your virtues".

Dilip K. Chakrabarti summarized the situation:

"The model of the Indian past...was foisted on Indians by the hegemonic books written by Western Indologists concerned with language, literature and philosophy who were and perhaps have always been paternalistic at their best and **racists** at their worst."

17. Native Despots Hoist the Beacon

India was particularly unfortunate in having Gandhi and Nehru at the helm of affairs in the post independent era both of whom have been described most recently as British agents by high ranking polity in India. The following quotes betray their perverted mind set. The so called 'Mahatama' Gandhi was to prescribe at a prayer meeting New Delhi 6 April 1947 (CWOMG, vol 87 pp 217-219, Govt India ND,1958-1982).

Hindus should not harbor anger in their hearts against Muslims even if the latter wanted to destroy them. Even if the Muslims want to kill us we should face death bravely. If they establish their rule after killing Hindus we would be ushering in a new world by sacrificing our lives.

Gandhi even condoned rape of Hindu women by Muslims. J.N. Nehru despised Hindus as well and his political leaning was spelled out in a letter, dated 17 November 1953, to President Dr. Rajendra Prasad:

"I am proud to be reared up as an Islamist, an English man by education, and Hindu by accident....The Hindu is certainly not tolerant and is certainly more narrow minded than almost any person in any other country except the Jews".

The cultural colonization by British continues to be most successfully echoed by Western educated native despots of India who hate everything associated with the glorious Vedic past. Education in India has estranged Hindus from their marvelous patrimony in order to create cultural slaves for the West. Priya Joshi writes:

"Often, the implementation of a new education system leaves those who are colonized with a lack of identity and a limited sense of their past. The indigenous history and customs once practiced and observed slowly slip away. The colonized become hybrids of two vastly different cultural systems. Colonial education creates a blurring that makes it difficult to differentiate between the new, enforced ideas of the colonizers and the formerly accepted native practices."

Ngugi Wa Thiong'o asserted that the process:

"...annihilates a peoples belief in their names, in their languages, in their environment, in their heritage of struggle, in their unity, in their capacities and ultimately in themselves. It makes them see their past as one wasteland of non-achievement and it makes them want to distance themselves from that wasteland. It makes them want to identify with that which is furthest removed from themselves".

Consequently, there is **no pro-Hindu school** of history, newspaper, news channel, or the like, in a Hindu majority India as all political parties have taken the easy road to garner the minority votes. Christians, Muslims, anarchists and Marxists espouse the dismamtling of Indian as a nation on the feigned anti-history that India had nothing to boast about its past and to prepare Hindus for conversion into 'true' faiths. Indian Council for Historical Research (ICHR) is the dominant voice regarding the information and account of Aryans origins to be presented in school textbooks. Arun Shourie has placed the Marxist control of ICHR as follows:

"They have made India out to have been an empty land, filled by successive invaders…No such thing as 'India', just a geographical expression, just a construct of the British; no such thing as Hinduism, just a word used by the Arabs to describe the assortment they encountered, just an invention of the Communists to impose uniformity-that has been their stance. For this they have blackened the Hindu period of our history and…strained to whitewash the Islamic period…These intellectuals and their patrons have worked a diabolic inversion: the inclusive religion, the pluralist spiritual search of our people and land, they have projected as intolerant, narrow-minded, obscurantist; and the exclusivist, totalitarian, revelatory religions and ideologies-Islam, Christianity, Marxism-Leninism-they have been made out to be the epitomes of tolerance, open-mindedness, democracy and secularism".

Worse still the Bharatiya Janata Party (BJP), dubbed communal for Hindu revival, is doing its best to go down the minority appeasement abyss to secure a secular label for itself. Yet, the stoic Hindu sits aloof in his own corner, totally oblivious to the decimation of his kind and his shining past. One thousand years of slavery appears to have permamnently damaged Hindu dignity, self respect and instinct for survival. Heidegger and others have equated modernism with westernization but the trend is to steal and copy from Vedic Mythology and Sanskrit concepts to impart respectability to their own products. This scramble for **Aryan ancestry** is the best proof yet of its **eternal timelessness**. However, History has yet saved a ray of hope for Hindu revival:

"Fierce and warlike tribes again and again invaded its (India's) northern plains, overthrew its princes, captured and laid waste its cities, set up new states and built new capitals of their own and then vanished into the great tide of humanity, leaving to their descendants nothing but a swiftly diluted strain of alien blood and a few shreds of alien custom that were soon transformed into something cognate with their own surroundings".

18. Bibliography

Achar, B. N., Origin of Indian Civilization, Bal Ram Singh (Ed), Center for Indic Studies, Dartmought, USA, 2010.

Agarwal, M. K. The Vedic Core of Human History, iUniverse, 2013.

Agarwal, M. K., From Bharata to India, Vol. 1 Chrysee the Golden, iUniverse, 2012.

Agarwal, M. K., From Bharata to India, Vol. 2 The Rape of Chrysee iUniverse,2012.

Agarwal, M.K. and Sharma, A.K., The Yoga-Ayurveda Miracle, Dog Ear, 2011.

Agrawal, V. S., India in the Days of Panini, 1953.

Agarwal, D.P., Ancient Metal Technology and Archeology of South Asia, Aryan BooksInternational, ND, 2000.

Agarwala, Vasudeva Sharana (Ed) Vedic Mathematics, Motilal Banarsidass, ND, 1992.

Agrawala, Dinesha, Demise of the Aryan Invasion Theory, Oxford U Press, Delhi, 1998.

Ahmad, Mirza Ghulam, Jesus in India, Islam International Publications, 2003.

Albinia, Alice, Empires of the Indus: The Story of a River. First American Edition W. W. Norton & Company, NY, 2010.

Al-Biruni, *Kitab-il-Hind* (later translated into Latin as *Indica,* Aldred, Cyril, Akhenaten, Thames and Hudson, 1988.

Allchin, F.R., The Archaeology of Early Historic South Asia: The Emergence of Cities and States, Cambridge, 1995.

Allen, Charles, A Mountain in Tibet: The Search for Mount Kailash and the Sources of the Great Rivers of Asia, André Deutsch, London, 1982.

Allen, Charles, The Search for Shangri-La: A Journey into Tibetan History. Little, Brown & Co,1999, Abacus, London, 2000.

Allen, W. S., Phonetics in Ancient India, London, 1953.

Alpers, Edward, A., Ray, Himanshu P., (eds) The History of the Indian Ocean World, Oxford, 2007.

Amma, Saraswati, Geometry in Ancient and Medieval India, Motilal Banarsidas, ND, 1979.

Anant, Sadashiv Altekar, Education in Ancient India, Nand Kishore Brothers, Varanasi, 1965.

Ankaroo, Bengt and Stuart, Clark, Witchcraft and magic in Europe, Ancient Greece and Rome, U. Pennsylavia Press, Philadelphia, 1999.

Armstrong, Karen, Islam: A Short History, Random House, NY, 2002.

Arnold, D., Science, Technology and Medicine in Colonial India, Cambridge U Press, 2000.

Auboyer, Jeannine, Daily Life in Ancient India: from 200 BC to 700 AD, Phoenix Press, London, 2002.

Bag, A. K., Mathematics in Ancient and Medieval India, Chaukhambha Orientalia, Varanasi,1979.

Bala, Saroj and Mishra, Kulbhushan, Historicity of Vedic and Ramayan Eras: Scientific Evidences from the Depths of Oceans to the Heights of Skies, Vision India Publications, ND, 2012.

Balachandran, Premalatha, Govindarajan, Rajgopal, Ayurvedic Drug Discovery, Information Healthcare, 2: 1631-1652, 2007..

Bapudeva, Surya Siddhanta: Translation of an Ancient Indian Astronomical Text, Varanasi, 1860.

Barriedale, Keith, A., Sanskrit Drama, Oxford, 1924.

Barrow, J. D., Pi in the Sky, Oxford University Press, 1992.

Basham, A. L. The Wonder That Was India, Rupa & Co., Calcutta,1967; ND, 2002.

Basham, A.L. (ed), A Cultural History of India, Clarendon Press, London, 1974.

Beal, George, Playing Cards and their Story, Arco Publishing Co., NY, 1975.

Begley, Vimala, De Puma, Richard Daniel, Rome and India: The Ancient Sea Trade, U. Wisconsin, 1991.

Bell, Robert Charles, Board and Table Games from Many Civilizations, Courier Dover, 1979.

Bellwood, Peter (ed), In Search of Suvarnabhumi: Early Sailing Networks in the Bay of Bengal, Indo-Pacific Prehistory vol. 1, Indo-Pacific Prehistory Association, Canberra, pp. 357-365, 1990.

Belvalker, S. K., Systems of Sanskrit Gramamar, Poona, 1915.

Benner Larsen, E., The Gundestrup Cauldron, Identification of Tool Traces, Iskos, 5: 561-74, 1985.

Berggren, Lennart, J. and Jones, Alexander, Prolemy's Geography, Princeton U Press, 2000.

Bergquist, A. K., and T. F. Taylor, The Origin of the Gundestrup Cauldron, Antiquity, 61: 10-24, 1987.

Berkowitz, Stephen C. (ed) Buddhism in World Cultures, Abc-Clio, Santa Barbara, 2006.

Berriman, A. E., The Babylonian Quadratic Equation, 1956.

Beye, C. R., Ancient Greek Literature and Society, Oxford, 1987.

Bhaskaracharya. Lilavati, H. T., Colebrooke (trans) Kitab Mahal, Allahabad, 1967.

Bhatt, S. C., Drama in Ancient India, Amrit Book Co., ND, 1961.

Bidyaranya, Swami, History of Hindu Mathematics: a Source Book, Asia Pubilishing House, Bombay, 1962.

Billard, R., L'astronomie Indienne, Paris: Publications de l'ecole francaise d'extreme-orient., 1971.

Bird, Henry Edward, Chess History and Reminiscences, Forgotten Books, London, 1893.

Biswas:, S.K., Autochthon of India and the Aryan Invasion, Genuine Publications, ND, 1995.

Bloom, Jonathan, Blair, Sheila, Islam: A Thousand Years of Faith and Power, Yale U Press, 2002.

Bodin, H., Migrations of Mankind, J. Polynesian Soc., 44: 124-129, 1934.

Bokonyi, S., Horse Remains from the Prehistoric Site of Surkotada, Kutch, Late 3rd Millennium BC, South Asian Studies 13: 297-307, 1977.

Bose, D. M., Sen, S. N. and Sunnarayappa, B. V. (eds), A Concise History of Science in India, Indian National Science Academy, ND, 1971.

Bostom, A. G., The Legacy of Jihad: Islamic Holy War and the Fate of the Non-Muslims, Prometheus Books, NY, 2005.

Bowra, C. S., Ancient Greek Literature, Oxford, 1960.

Boyer, Carl B., A History of Mathematics, Princeton, 1985.

Braudel, Fernand, A History of Civilizations, Penguin, 1988.

Brockington, John, The Sanskrit Epics, Blackwell, 2003.

Bronson, Bennet, The Late Prehistory and Early History of Central Thailand with Special Reference to Chansen. In R.B. Smith and W. Watson (eds), Early South East Asia, Oxford, NY, 1979

Bryant, Edwin, The Quest for the Origins of Vedic Culture, Oxford, NY, 2002

Buhlerg, Geroge, The Laws of Manu, Motilal Banarsidas, ND, 1970.

Burgess, Collin, The Age of Stonehenge, castle Books, 2001.

Burton, David M., The History of Mathematics: An Introduction, McGraw-Hill, 1997.

Bynum, William, F.,The Great Chain of Being after Forty Years: An Appraisal, History of Science 13: 1-28, 1975.

Cajori, F., A History of Mathematics, The Macmillan Company, NY, 1894.

Capra, Fritjof, The Dance of Shiva: The Hindu View of Matter in the Light of Modern Physics, Flamingo, 1972.

Casson, L., Libraries in the Ancient World, Yale U Press, 2002.

Catherine, Perry, A History of Playing Crads and a Bibliography of Cards and gaming, Houghton Mifflin , NY, 1930.

Cavalli-Sforza L. L., and Feldman M. W., The Application of Molecular Genetic Approaches to the study of Human Evolution. Nat Genet 33 Suppl: 266-275, 2003.

Cerquiliani, B. In Praise of the Variant: a Critical History of Philology, Baltimore, 1999, .

Chakrabarti, Dilip K., Colonial Indology, Munshoram Manoharlal, ND, 1997.

Chakrabarty, D.K., The Early Use of Iron in India, Oxford, ND, 1992.

Chakrabarty, P. C., Naval Warfare in ancient India, The Indian Historical Quarterly, 4: 645-664, 1930.

Chakrabarty, B. B., Indus Script - the Artistic Version of Brahmi, Calcutta, 1991.

Chandler, David. A History of Cambodia, Silkworm Books, Thailand, 2003.

Chaplin, Dorothy, Matter, Myth and Spirit, or Keltic and Hindu Links, Scot Rider & Co., London, UK, 1935.

Chapman, Malcolm, The Celts, St. Martins, NY, 1992.

Charles John Erasmus, Patolli, Pachisi, and the Limitation of Possibilities, South-Western Journal of Anthropology Vol. 6, 369, 1950.

Chatterji, B.R., Indian Cultural Influence in Cambodia, Calcutta, 1928.

Chatto, William Andrews, Facts and Speculations on the origin and History of Playing Cards, John Russell Smith, London, 1849..

Chaturvedi, Aditi, Vedic Past of Pre-Islamic Arabia, Google.com.

Chaubey G, Metspalu M, Kivisild T, Villems R, Peopling of South Asia: investigating the caste-tribe continuum in India. Bioessays 29: 91-100, 2007.

Chaubey G The Demographic History of India: A perspective based on genetic evidence Evolutionary Biology, 2010.

Chaudhuri, K. N.,Trade and Civilization in the Indian Ocean, Cambridge, 1985.

Chhabra, B. C., Findings in Indian Archaeology, ND, 1991.

Childe, Gordan V., The Aryans: A Study of Indo-European Origins, A. A. Knopf, NY, 1926.

Choudhury, Nishipada Deva 1985 Historical Archaeology of Central Assam, B.R. Publishing, ND, 1985.

Chowdhury, Abdul Momin 1977 Geography of Ancient Bengal-An Approach to its Study, Bangladesh Historical Studies (Dacca) 11: 31-53.

Chon, Kuttikhat Purushottam, Remedy the Frauds in Hindusim, Bombay, 1991, Digitized U. California, 2007.

Choudhury, Parmaesh, Indian origin of the Chinese nation: A challenging, Unconventional Theory of the Origin of the Chinese, Amazon.com., 1990.

Choudhury, Parmaesh, North East India: Cradle of the Chinese Nation, Amazon.com., 1996.

Choudhury, Parmaesh, Aryan Invasion Myth, Amazon.com., 2003

Choudhury, Paramaesh, Did India Civilize Europe: Europe Learnt Science, Mathematics, Technology, Medicine from India, Amazon.com., 2007.

Christianidis, Jean (ed), Classics in the History of Greek Mathematics, Kluwer Academic Publishers, 2004.

Clagett, Marshall, Ancient Egyptian Science: A Source Book, Memoirs of the American Philosophical Society 232. Philadelphia: American Philosophical Society, 1999.

Coedes, George, *Histoire ancienne des etats hindouises d'Extreme-Orient. The Indianized states of Southeast Asia* Ed. Walter F.Vella, translated by Susan Brown Cowing. Hawaii: East-West Center Press, 1968.

Cooke, Roger, The History of Mathematics: A Brief Course, Wiley, 1997.

Coppa, A., Bondioli, L., Cucina, A., Frayer, D.W., Jarrige, C., Jarrige, J.F., Quivron, G., Rossi, M., Vidale, M., Macchiarelli, R., Palaeontology: Early Neolithic tradition of dentistry, Nature 440: 755–756, 2006.

Corn, Charles and Glasserman, Debbie, The Scents of Eden: A History of the Spice Trade, Kodansha, 1999.

Cox, Jeffrey, Imperial Fault Lines, Stanford University Press, 2002.

Craig, Steve, Sports and Games of the Ancients, Greenwood, 2002.

Crego, Robert, Sports and Games of the 18th and 19th Centuries, Greenwood Press, 2003.

Cunliffe, Barry, The Ancient Celts, Oxford, NY, 1997.

Dales, George F., The Mythical Massacre at Mohenjo-Daro, in G. L. Possehl (ed)   The Ancient Cities of the Indus, pp 293-29, Vikas, ND, 1979.
Daniels, Peter, D., Bright, William, The World's Writing Systems, Oxford, NY, 1996.
Dasgupta, S. N., Dey, S. K., A History of Sanskrit Literature, Calcutta, 1962.
Datta, B., The science of the Sulba, Calcutta, 1932.
Datta, B. B., Singh, A. N., History of Hindu Mathematics, Asia Publishing House, NY, 1938.
Davey, Christopher J., The Early History of Lost-Wax Casting, Archetype Publications, London, 2009.
Davis, Mike, Late Victorian Holocausts, Verso, 2000.
DeBlois, Francois, Burzoy's Voyage to India and the Origin of the Book of Kalilah wa Dimnah, Royal Asiatic Society, London, 1990.
Denison, T. S., Mexican Linguistics, T.S. Denison & Co. 1913.
Denison, T. S., Primitive Aryans of America, T. S. Denison & Co.1908.
Deo, Ashwini S., The Metrical Organization of Classical Sanskrit Verse, J. Linguistics 43: 63–114, 2007.
Deo, S.B., New Discoveries of Iron Age in India, in C. Margbandhu, K.S. Ramachandran, A.P. Sagar and D.K. Sinha (eds.), Indian Archaeological Heritage I: 189-97, Agam Kala Prakashan, ND, 1991.
Derbyshire, John, Unknown Quantity: A Real And Imaginary History of Algebra,   Joseph Henry Press, 2006.
DeSalle, Rob and Tattersall, Ian, Human Origins, Texas A&M Press, 2008.
Dickinson, G. L., The Greek View of Life, Methuen & Co Ltd, London, 1938.
Diehl, Richard A., The Olmecs: America's First Civilization, Thames & Hudson, London, 2004.
Diffloth, Gerard, The Contribution of Linguistic Paleontology to the Homeland of Austro-Asiatics. In: Sagart, Laurent, Roger Blench and Alicia Sanchez-Mazas (eds). The Peopling of East Asia: Putting Together Archaeology, Linguistics and Genetics, Routledge Curzon, 2005.
Dikshit, S.B., Bharatiya Jyotish Shastra, Gov India Press, Calcutta, 1969.
Dillon, Matthew and Garland, Lynda, Ancient Greece, Routledge, NV 1994.
Dowling, Levi, H., The Aquarian Gospel of Jesus the Christ, De Vorss & Co., 1972.
Duncan, David Ewing, The Calendar, Avon Books, New York, 1998.
Durant, William, Our Oriental Heritage, Simon and Schuster, NY, 1925.
Dutt, Romesh C., Ramayana, Kessinger Publishing, 2004.
Dutt, Romesh, C., The Civilization of India, Rupa, ND, 2002.

Earl of Ronaldshay, The Heart of Aryavarta, Houghton Miffin, NY, 1925.
Ebenezer, Burgess, Surya Siddhanta, A Textbook of Hindu Astronomy, Motilal Banarsidas, ND 1989.
Elisseeff, Vadime (ed), The Silk Roads: Highways of Culture and Commerce,

UNESCO, Paris, and Berghahn Books, NY, 2000.

Ellis, Peter B., The Ancient World of the Celts, Constable, London, 1998.
Ellis, Peter B., The Druids, Carroll and Graf, NY, 2002.
Elphinstone, M.S., History of India, Atlantic , 2002.
Eves, Howard, An Introduction to the History of Mathematics, Rhinehart, NY, 1953.
Ewald, William B. (ed.) From Immanuel Kant to David Hilbert: A Source Book in the Foundations of Mathematics, Oxford, 1996

Fairservis, Walter, The script of the Indus Valley Civilization, Scientific American, 1985
Feurstein, George, Kak, Subash, Frawley, David, In Search of the Cradle of Civilization, Motilal Banarsidas, ND, 1999.
Flacelière, Robert , A Literary History of Greece, Aldine Publishing , 1964.
Forbes, Duncan, The History of Chess: From the Time of the Early Invention of the Game in India Till the Period of Its Establishment in Western and Central Europe, W. H. Allen & Co, London, 1860.
Francis, Peter, Asia's Maritime Bead Trade, U. Hawaii, Honolulu, HI, 2002.
Francis, Peter Jr., Beads, the Bead Trade and State Development in Southeast Asia, In Ancient Trades and Cultural Contacts in Southeast Asia, Office of
the National Culture Commission, Bangkok, pp. 139-152, 1996.
Frank, John Ninivaggi, An Elementary Textbook of Ayurveda: A Six Thousand Year Old Healing Tradition, International Universities Press, 2002.
Frank, Andre Gunder, Asian-based world economy 1400-1800: A horizontally integrative macrohistory, U Amsterdam, 1995.
Fraser, John, The Malayo-Polynesian theory, J. Polynesian Soc., 4: 241-255; 5: 92-107, 1895.
Fraser, John, The Polynesian numerals, J. Polynesian Soc., 11: 1-120, 1904.
Frawley, David, The Rig Veda and the History of India, Aditya Prakashan, ND, 2001.
Frawley, David, Ayurvedic Healing: A comprehensive guide, Motilal Banarsidas, ND, 1997.
Frawley, David, Gods, Sages and Kings: Vedic Secrets of Ancient Civilization, Motilal Banarsidass, ND, 1999.
Frawley, O'Dea, Mary Gail, Perversion of Power, sexual abuse in the Catholic Church, Vanderbilt U., TN, 2007.
Freke, Timothy and Gandy, Peter, The Jesus Mysteries. Was the Original Jesus a Pagan God. Harmony Books, Random House, NY 1999.
Friedman, Richard, E., Who Wrote the Bible, Summit, NY, 1987

Gabriel, Brigitte, Radical Islam: The Plan to Destroy America from Within: Infiltration, 2011.

Gajjar, Irina, On Hinduism, Axios Press, 2013.

Gamer, Helena M, The Earliest Evidence of Chess in Western Literature: The Einsiedeln Verses, Speculum 29: 734–750, 1954.

Ganeri, Anita, The Story of Numbers and Counting, Oxford, NY, 1996.

Garg, Ganga Ram, Encyclopedia of the Hindu world, South Asia Books, 1992.

Gershevitch, Ilya, The Avestan Hymn to Mithra, Cambridge, 1959.

Ghurye, G.S., Caste and Race in India, Popular Prakashan, Mumbai 1969.

Gidwani, Bhagwan S., Return of the Aryans, Penguin, 1994.

Gillings, Richard J., Mathematics in the Time of the Pharaohs. MIT Press, 1972.

Goel, R. G., Goel, Veena, Encyclopaedia of Sports and Games, Vikas , ND 1988.

Goel, Sita Ram, The Story of Islamic Imperialism in India, Voice of India, ND, 1994; South Asia Books, 1996.

Goel, Sita Ram, Arun Shourie, Harsh Narain, Jay Dubashi and Ram Swarup. Hindu Temples – What Happened to Them, Voice of India, 1990, 1991.

Goldenberg, D. M., The Curse of Ham, Princeton U Press, NJ, 2003.

Goody, Jack, The Theft of History, Cambridge, 2007.

Gordon, D.H., The Early Use of Metals in India and Pakistan, J. Royal Anthropological Institute, 55-78, 1950.

Govinda, Lama Anagarika. (1966). The Way of the White Clouds: A Buddhist Pilgrim in Tibet. Shambhala Publications, Inc. Boulder, Colorado. Reprint with foreword by Peter Matthiessen: Shambhala Publications, Inc. Boston, Massachusetts. 1988.

Green, Thomas M., Hamberg, Charles L., Pascal's Triangle, Dale Seymour Publications, 1986.

Grover, Sudarshan, History of Development of Mathematics in India, Atma Rama & Sons, ND, 1994.

Guicharnaud, June, History of the Indian Ocean, U. Chicago Press, 1966.

Gulati, A.N., A Note on the Early History of Silk in India, In J. Clutton-Brock, Vishnu-Mittre and A.N. Gulati (eds) Technical Reports on Archaeological Remains, Deccan College Post-Graduate and Research Institute, Poona, 1961.

Gupta, R.C., New Indian Values of π from the Manava Sulbha Sutra, Centaurus 31, 114-125, 1988.

Gupta, R.C., Baudhayana's Value of √2, Math. Education, 6:B77-B79,1972.

Gupta, S.P., The Indus-Sarasvati Civilization, Pratibha Prakashan, ND, 1996.

Gupta, S.P., Ramachandran, K.S. (ed.), MahaBharat: Myth and Reality, Agam Prakashan, ND, 1976.

Gurjar, L. V., Ancient Indian Mathematics and Veda, Pune, 1947.

Gutzwiller, Kathryn, A guide to Hellenistic literature, Blackwell, 2007.

Hadas, Moses, A History of Greek Literature, Columbia University Press, 1950.

Hall, D.G.E. A history of South-east Asia. London: Macmillan Limited, 1955.

Halsted, G. B., On the Foundation and Technique of Arithmetic, Chicago, 1912.

Handelman, Don and Shulman, David, God Inside Out, Shiva's game of dice, Oxford, NY, 1997.

Hasnnain, Fida, The Fifth Gospel: New Evidence from the Tibetan, Sanskrit, Arabic, Persian and Urdu Sources, Blue Dolphin, 2008.

Hasnnain, Fida, A Search for the Historical Jesus, Down to Earth Books, 2004.

Havell, E.B., Indian Architecture, John Murray, London, 1913.

Havell, E.B., Indian Sculpture and Painting, John Murray, London, 1908.

Havell, E.B., Ideals of Indian Art, John Murray, London, 1920.

Havell,E. B., The Art Heritage of India, John Murray, London, 1964.

Hearn, William E., The Aryan Household, Longman, London, 1879.

Heath, Thomas Little, A Manual of Greek Mathematics, Dover, 2003.

Heidtmann, Horst. "Swastika." In Encyclopedia of the Third Reich, Macmillan, NY, 1991.

Heller, Steven. The Swastika: Symbol Beyond Redemption? Allworth Press, NY 2000.

Herodotus, The Histories, Penguin, NY, 1983.

Higgins, Godfrey, The Celtic Druids, Radgway & Sons, Picadilly, UK, 1929.

Higham, Charles, The Bronze Age of Southeast Asia, Cambridge, 1996.

Hoffman, Detlef, The Playing Card, An illustrated History, New York Graphical Society, NY, 1973; Leipzig, 1972.

Hopkins, E. W., The Great Epics of India, New York, 1901. ..

Hunter, G.R., The Script of Harappa and Mohenjodaro and its Connection with other Scripts, Kegan, Paul Trench, Trubner & Co., London, 1934.

Huson, Paul, Mystical Origins of the Tarot: From Ancient Roots to Modern Usage, Destiny Books, Vermont, 2004.

Ifrah, Georges, The Universal History of Numbers: From Prehistory to the Invention of the Computer, Wiley, 2000.

Ifrah, G., From One to Zero, Viking, London, 1985.

Ingalls, Daniel, H. H., Sanskrit Poetry, Harvard U Press, 1967.

Jacobs, Alan, When Jesus Lived in India, Watkins Publishing, 2009.

Jaggi, O. P., Science and Technology in Medieval India, Atma Rama & Sons, ND, 1977.

Jain, Jyoti Prasad, The Jaina Sources of the History of Ancient India (100 B.C. to A.D. 900, Munshi Ram Manohar Lal, ND,1964.

James, Simon, The Atlantic Celts, Ancient People of Modern Invention, U. Wisconsin Press, Madison, 1999.

Jarrige, J. F., Meadow, R.H., The Antecedents of Civilization in the Indus Valley, Scientific Americam, August, 1980.

Jenkyns, Richard, The Victorian and Ancient Greece, Cambridge, 1980.

Johnson, G., SriRaman,B., Saltztstein, Where are the plans? A socio-critical and architectural survey of early Egyptian mathematics, in Bharath SriRaman, (ed) Crossroads in the History of Mathematics and Mathematics Education. The Montana Mathematics Enthusiast Monographs in Mathematics Education, Information Age Publishing, Charlotte, NC, 2012.

Johnson, Russell and Moran,Kerry, The Sacred Mountain of Tibet: On Pilgrimage to Kailash, Park Street Press, Rochester, Vermont,1989.

Jones, E. L., The European Miracle, Cambridge, 1981.

Joseph, G. G., The Crest of the Peacock, Penguin, 1991.

Kak, S., Āyurveda, in Encylopedia of India, Stanley Wolpert (ed), Scribner's/Gale, NY, 2005.

Kak, Subhash, The Astronomical Code of the RigVeda, Aditya Prakashan, ND, 1994. MunshiRam Manoharlal, ND, 2000.

Kak, Subhash, The Architecture of Knowledge, CRC-Motilal Banarsidass, ND, 2004.

Kak, Subhash, Early Indian Art and Architecture, Migration and Diffusion, 6: 6-27, 2005.

Kak, Subhash, The Ashvamedha: The Rite and its Logic, Motilal Banarsidass, ND, 2002.

Kak, Subhash, The Axis and the Perimeter of the Hindu Temple, Mankind Quarterly, 2006.

Kak, Subhash, The Vedic Religion in Ancient Iran and Zarathustra, Indian Historical Review, 2003.

Kak, Subhash, Three old Indian values of π, Indian J. Hist. Sci., 32: 307-314, 1977.

Kak, S., Logic in Indian Thought, in Logic in Religious Discourse, ed. A. Schumann (ed), Ontos Verlag, Frankfurt and Paris, 2009.

Kak, S., Archaeoastronomy in India, in Heritage Sights of Astronomy and Archaeoastronomy, C. Ruggles and M. Cotte (eds.), ICMS, Paris, 2011.

Kalyanaraman S., 1999, Sarasvati River, Godess and Civilization, in: Memoir 42, Vedic Sarasvati, Geological Survey of India, Bangalore, India, 1999.

Kalyanaraman, S., 2000, River Sarasvati: Legend, Myth and Reality, All India Sarasvati Association, Mumbai, 2000.

Kalyanaraman S., Indian Alchemy: Soma in the Veda, Munshiram Manoharlal, Delhi, 2004.

Kalyanaraman, S., Indus Sript Encodes Mleccha Speech (Language, Writing, Epigraphica Sarasvati, Dictionary, Indian Lexicon), Chennai, 2008.

Kalyanaraman, S., Indus Script Cipher: Hieroglyphs of Indian Linguistic Area, Amazon, 2010.

Kalyanaraman, S., Rastram – Hindu history in United Indian Ocean States, Amazon, 2011.

Kalyanaraman, S., Indian Hieroglyphs – Invention of Writing, Amazon, 2012.

Kaplan, Robert, The Nothing That Is: A Natural History of Zero, Oxford University Press, 2000.

Kapoor, S. K., Vedic Mathematics, Arya Book Depot, ND, 1998.

Kazanas, Nicolas, Vedic and Indo-European studies, Aditya Prakashan, ND, 2015

Keith, Arthur Berriedale, The Sanskrit Drama in its Origin, Development, Theory and Practice, Motilal Banarsidas, ND, 1992.

Kendrick, T. D., The Druids, Metheune & co., London, 1927.

Kenoyer, Jonathan M., Uncovering the Keys to Lost Indus Cities, Scientific American, July 2003.

Kenoyer, Jonathan. M., Kimberley, Heuston, The Ancient South Asian World, Oxford University Press., 2005.

Kenoyer, J.M. and Vidale, M., A New Look at Stone Drills of the Indus Tradition. In Material Issues in Art and Archaeology, III,eds., PB Vandiver, JR Durzik, GS Wheeler, and KC Freestone (Eds), Pittsburgh, 1992.

Kersten, Holger, Jesus Lived in India, Element Books Ltd., 1994.

Kivisild, Toomas et al, An Indian Ancestry: a key for Understanding Human Diversity in Europe and Beyond, pp267-275. In Renfrew, Colin and Boyle, Katie (eds), Archaeogenetics: DNA and the Population Prehistory of Europe, McDonald Institute for Archaeological Research, Cambridge, MA, 2000.

Klindt-Jensen, O., The Gundestrup Bowl-a Reassessment, Antiquity, 33: 161-9, 1979.

Knapp, Stephen, Proof of Vedic Culture's Global Existence, Booksurge, Charleston, SC, 2000.

Knighton, William, The History of Ceylon, Colombo, 1845.

Knox, Robert The Races of Man – a Fragment Kessinger Publishing, 2010

Koch, John (ed), Celtic Culture: a Historical Encyclopedia, ABCCLIO, 2006.

Koenraad, Else, The Aryan Non-Invasionist Model, Aditya Prakashan, ND, 1999.

Koven, Seth Slumming, Social and Social Politics in Victorian London, Princeton, NJ, 2004.

Kuiper, F.B.J., 1948, Proto-Munda words in Sanskrit, ord-Hollandsche Uitg. Mij., Amsterdam, 1948.

Kulaichev, A. P., Sriyantra and its Mathematical Properties, Indian J. His. Sci., 19: 279-292, 1984.

Kulakarni, Raghunatha Purushottama, Geometry According to Sulba sutra, Tilak Maharastra Vidyapitha, Vaidika Samsodhana Mandala, Pune,1983.

Kulkarni, R. P., The value of π Known to Sulbasutrakaras, Indian J. Hist. Sci. 13:32-41., 1978.

Kumari, G., Some Significant Results of Algebra of Pre-Aryabhata era, Math. Ed. (Siwan) 14: B5-B13, 1980.

Kuzmina, Elena Efimovna, (Victor H. Mair ed), The Prehistory of the Silk Road, U. Penn., 2008.

Lacey, Robert, and Danziger, Danny, The Year 1000, Little Brown, 1999.

Lach, Donald Frederick, Asia in the Making of Europe: The Century of Discovery, University of Chicago Press, 1994.

Lal, B.B., Frontiers of the Indus Civilization, Aryan Books, ND, 1984.

Lal, B.B., The Saraswati Flows on: the Continuity of Indian Culture, Aryan Books, ND, 2002.

Lal, B.B., The Earliest Civilization of South Asia, Aryan Books, ND, 1997.

Lal, B. B., The Homeland of the Aryans, Aryan Books Internl, ND, 2005

Lal, B. B., Rama, His Historicity, Mandir and Setu: Evidence of Literature, Archaeology and Other Stories, Aryan Books International, ND, 2008.

Lal, B. B., How Deep Are the Roots of Indian Civilzation?: Archaeology Answers Aryan Books International, ND, 2012.

Lal, B. B., The Rigvedic People: 'Invaders'?/'Immigrants? Aryan Books International, ND 2015.

Lal, Chaman, India: Cradle of Cultures, Aryan Books International, ND, 1976.

Lal, P., Great Sanskrit Plays, New Directions, NY, 1957.

Leshnik, Lawrence S., The Harappan "Port" at Lothal: Another View, American Anthropologist, New Series, 70: 911–922, 1968.

Lesky, Albin, A History of Greek literature, Hackett Publishing, 1966.

Lichtheim, Miriam, Ancient Egyptian Literature, London, 1975.

Lindsay, W.S., History of Merchant Shipping and Ancient Commerce, Adamant Media Corporation, 2006.

Litvinskiĭ, B. A., Outline History of Buddhism in Central Asia, Dushanbe, 1968.

Lomperis, Timothy, Hindu Influence on Greek Philosophy, Minerva, Calcutta, 1984.

Londhe, Sushama, A Tribute to Hinduism, Penguin, ND, 2007.

Lovejoy, Arthur, O., The Great Chain of Being: A Study of the History of an Idea, Harvard U Press, Cambridge, MA1936, 1964.

Luijendijk, D.H., Kalarippayat: The Essence and Structure of an Indian Martial Art. LuLu.com, 2008.

Lynch, John, Pacific Languages, U Hawaii Press,1998.

Mabbet I.W., The 'Indianization' of Southeast Asia: Reflections on the historical sources, J. Southeast Asian Studies, vol.8, No.2, 1977.

Mabett, I.W., Buddhism and the Rise of the Written Vernacular in East Asia: The Making of National Languages, J. Asian Studies, 53: 707-75, 1994.

MacDonell, Arthur A., A History of Sanskrit Literature, Kessinger Publishing, 2004.

MacFie, J. M., Myths and Legends of India, Rupa, ND, 1993.

Majumder, Partha, P., The Human Genetic History of South Asia, Current Biology, 20: R184-R187, 2010.

Majumdar, R.C., Ancient India, Motilal Banarsidass, ND, 1987.

Majumdar, R.C., History of the Hindu colonization and Hindu culture in South-East Asia, Classical Pub. Co, 1996.

Malhotra, Rajiv, Breaking India, Amaryllis, 2011.

Manich Jumsai, M. L., History of Thailand and Cambodia, Cahlermnit Press, Bangkok, 1979.

MarkaL jean E., King of the Celts, Inner Traditions, Vermont, 1994.

Martin, Thomas, R., Ancient Greece, Yale University Press, 2000.

Mason, Colin A., Short History of Asia, St. Martins, NY, 2000.

Maspero, Georges, M., Le Royaume de Champa, Paris, 1928.

Ocean   Arena, 1860-1920, U. California Press, LA, 2007.

Matilal, B.K., Epistemology, Logic and Grammar in Indian Philosophical Analysis, Oxford U Press, 2005.

Matlock, Gene, What Strange Mystery Unites the Turkish Nations, India, Catholicism, and Mexico?, iUniverse, 2006.

Matlock, Gene, India Once Ruled the Americas, iUniverse, 2000.

Matlock, Gene, Jesus and Moses Are Buried in India, Birthplace of Abraham and the Hebrews, iUniverse, Author's choice, 2000.

Matlock, Gene, The Open Secret of India, Israel and Mexico from Genesis to Revelations, iUniverse 2008.

Mazoyer, Maradl and Roudart, Laurenad, A History of World Agriculture: from the Neolithic Age to the Current Crisis, Earthscan, 2006.

Mazumdar, Ashok, K., Hindu History, Rupa, 2008.

McEvilley, Thomas,The Shape of Ancient Thought, Allworth Press, New York, 2002.

McLeish, John, The Story of Numbers, Fawcett Columbine, NY, 1991.

McPherson, Kenneth, The Indian Ocean. A History of People and the sea, Oxford, Delhi, 1993.

Metcalf, Thomas, R., Imperial Connections: India in the Indian

Meyer. J.J., Sexual Life in Ancient India: A Study in the Comparative History of   India and Culture. Barnes & Noble, NY, 1930.

Mitchiner, J. E., Studies in the Indus Valley Inscription, Oxford, ND, 1978.

Mitra, Parimala and Santhali, S., The Base of World Languages, Firma KLM, 1988.

Monica, I. smith and Miksic, John N.,Evolving Archaeological Perspectives on Southeast Asia, 1970-1995, J. Southeast Asian Studies 26, 46-62, 1995.

Mookerji, Radhakumud, History of Indian Shipping, Longmans, London, 1912.

Mookerji, Radha Kumud, The Gupta Empire, Motilal Banarsidas, ND, 2007.

Moro, Javier, The Red Sari, Planet Publishing, 2008.

Morrison, Kathleen D., Trade, Urbanism, and Agricultural Expansion: Buddhist Monastic Institutions and the State in the Early Historic Western Deccan, World Archaeology 27, 203-221, 1995.

Morse, Michael, A., How the Celts came to Britain, Tempus, UK, 2005.

Mukhopadhyay, A., Adhikari, M.R., The Concept of Cyclic Quadrilaterals: its Origin and Development in India (from the age of

Sulba Sutras to Bhaskara I), Indian J. Hist. Sci., 32: 53-68, 1997.

Mukhopadhyaya, Girindranath, The Surgical Instrument of the Hindus, with a Comparative Study of the Surgical Instruments of the Greek, Roman, Arab and the Modern European Surgeons, Calcutta, 1913.

Muller, F. M., History of Ancient Sanskrit literature, Varanasi Chowkhamba Sanskrit Series, 1968.

Muller, F. M., The Sacred Books of the East vols. I to 40, Clarendon, Oxford, 1879-1897.

Nagarajarao, M.S., Iron Age in South India: Fresh Evidence on Chronology, in A.K.

Nguyen, Thi Dieu,The Mekong River and the Struggle for Indochina: Water, War, and Peace, Praeger, Cambridge, MA, 1999.

Nicol, Manicol, Hindu Scriptures: Hymns from the RigVeda, five Upanishads, the Bhagavadgita, E. P. Dutton & Co., NY, 1938.

Nizami, Ashraf, F., Namaz, the Yoga of Islam, Bombay: D.B. Taraporevala, Bombay, 1977.

Nomachi, Kazuyoshi, Tibet, Boston Shambhala, 1997.

North, John, The Norton History of Astronomy and Cosmology, W.W. Norton, NY,1995.

Notovitch, Nicolas, The Unknown Life of Jesus Christ, Wilder Publications, 2008.

Oak, Purushottam, Nagesh, World Vedic heritage, Hindi Sahitya Sadan, 2003; digitized 2008.

Oak, P. N., Some Blunders of Indian Historical Research, Hindi Sahitya Sadan, India, 2003.

Oak, P. N., Some Missing Chapters of World History, Hindi Sahitya Sadan, India, 2003.

Oldfield, M. O., The Encircled Serpent, Amazon.com, 2005, Kessinger Publishing, 2005.

Olivelle, Patrick (ed), Between the Empires, Society in India 300 BC to 400 CE, Oxford, 2006.

Olsson, Suzanne, Jesus in Kashmir: The Lost Tomb, Kindle, 2011.

Opie, Iona, Taem, Moira, A Dictionary of Superstitions, Oxford, NY, 1992.

Ogden, Daniel, Magic, Witchcraft and Ghosts in the Greek and Roman Worlds,   Oxford, NY, 2002.

Paliwal, K.V., Atrocities on Hindus by Christian Missionaries in Goa, Hindu Writers Forum, ND, 2005.

Paliwal, K.V., Max Muller; A Secular Christian Missionary & Distorter of the   Vedas Hindu Writers Forum, ND, 2006.

Pande, G. C., Foundations of Indian Culture, Motilal Banarsidas, ND, 1995.

Pande, Shyam Narain, Geographical Horizons of the Maha Bharata,

Bharata-Bharati, 1980.

Panikkar, K. M., India and the Indian Ocean, Allan and Unwin, 1945.

Pappas, Theoni, The Magic of Mathematics, Wide World Publishing, San Carlos, CA, 1994.

Parashuram, T. V., India's Jewish Heritage, Sagar Publications, 1982.

Parker, Grant, The Making of Roman India, Cambridge, UK, 2008.

Parlett, David: The Oxford history of Board Games, Oxford University Press, 1999.

Parpola, A., The Indus Script: a Challenging Puzzle, World Archaeology 17: 399-419, 1988.

Parrinder, Geoffrey, World Religions: From Ancient History to the Present, Himalayan Publishing Group, USA, 1971.

Pearson, M. N., The World of the Indian Ocean 1500-1800, Ashgate, VT, 2005.

Peck, Foreman, James, (ed), new Perspectives on the Late Victorian Economy, Cambridge, NY, 1991.

Peterson, Ivars, The Formula Man; the Legacy of India's Greatest Mathematician Continues to Influence Modern Mathematics, (Srinivasa Ramanujan), Science News, 131: 266-268, 1987.

Piggott, Stuart, The Druids, Thames and Hudson, London, 1968.

Piggott, Vincent C., The Study of Ancient Metallurgical Technology: A Review, Asian Perspectives 35, 89-97, 1996

Place, Robert M., The Tarot: History,Symbolism,and Divination, Tarcher/Penguin, NY, 2005.

Plumb, J., H., England in the 18th century, Pelican, 1950.

Pococke, Edward, India in Greece, Google, 2010.

Poindexter, Miles, The Ayar-Incas, Quinn & Boden Co., Rahway, NJ, 1930.

Poliakov, Leon, The Aryan Man, Basic Books Inc., NY, 1971.

Porter, Roy, English Society in the Eighteenth Century, Penguin, 1982.

Porter, Roy, English Society in the Eighteenth Century, Penguin, 1982.

Possehl, Gregory L., The Indus Civilization, Brown and Littlefield, Latham, MD, 2002.

Possehl, Gregory L., The Indus Writing System, U. Pennsylvania Press, PA, 1996.

Possehl, Gregory L., The Ancient Cities of the Indus, Vikas, ND, 1979.

Powell, Arthur, B. and Frankenstein, Marilyn, (eds) Ethnomathematics: challenging Eurocentrism in Mathematics Education, SUNY Press, 1997.

Prakash, B., Tripathi, V., Iron Technology in Ancient India, Historical Metallurgy: 568-579, 1986.

Priyadarshi, P., India's Contribution to the West, Standard Publishers, ND, 2004.

Priyadarshi, P., First Civilization of the World, Siddharth Publications, ND, 2010.

Priyavrat Sharma, KaRamabekar, V.W., The Atharvaveda and the Ayurveda, Nagpur 1961.

Prophet, Elizabeth Clare, The Lost Years of Jesus: Documentary Evidence of Jesus' 17-Year Journey to the East, Summit University Press, 1988.
Puri, H.S., Rasayan: Ayurvedic Herbs of Rejuvenation and Longevity, Taylor and Francis, London, 2003.
Puri, B. B., Vastu Science, New Age Books, ND, 2002.
Puri, B.B., Applied Vastu Shastra in Modern Architecture, Vastu Gyan, ND, 1997.

Quaritch, H. G., Towards Angkor, Harrap, 1937.
Quinn, Malcolm. The Swastika: Constructing the Symbol. Routledge, London 1994.
Qureshi, Samina, Legacy of the Indus, Weatherhill, NY, 1974.

Radhakrishnan, S., History of Philosophy, Eastern and Western, 2 vols. London 1952-1953.
Radha, Kumud Mookerji, Ancient Indian Education: Brahmanical and Buddhist, Motilal Banarsidass, New Delhi, 1989.
Raftery, Barry, Pagan Celtic Ireland, Thames and Hudson, London, 1994.
Rajaram, N. C., Search for the Historical Krishna, Prism Publications, 2005.
Rajaram, N.S., Christianity's Scramble for India and the Failure of the Eecularist Elite, Hindu Writers Forum, ND, 1999.
RajaRama, Navaratna, S. and Frawley, David, Vedic Aryans and the Origins of Civilization, Voice of India, ND, 2001.
RajaRama, Navaratna, S., The Politics of History: Aryan Invasion Theory and the Subversion of Scholarship, Voice of India, ND, 1995.
Ramasubramanian, K., and M.D. Srinivas, Development of Calculus in India, in Studies in the History of Indian Mathematics, C.S. Seshadri (ed) Hindustan Book Agency, Gugaon, ND, 2010.
Ramachandran, K.S., Archaeology of South India Tamil Nadu, Sundeep Prakashan, ND, 1980.
Randhawa, M.S., A History of Agriculture in India, Indian Council of Agricultural Research, ND, 1980.
Rao, S. R, The Lost City of Dwarka, Vedam, ND, 1999.
Rao, S. B., Indian Mathematics and Astronomy, Jnana Deep Publications, Bangalore, 1994.
Rao, S. R., Dawn and Devolution of the Indus Civilisation, Aditya Prakashan, Delhi,1992.
Rao, S. R., Lothal, Archaeological Survey of India, 1985.
Rasmussen, Ann, Kinney, Marijke J. Klokke. J. Kieven, Lydia Worshiping Siva and Buddha: The Temple Art of East Java. University of Hawaii Press, 2003.
Ray, Himanshu, P., and Salles, J. F. (eds), Tradition and Archaeology: Early Maritime Contacts in the Indian Ocean, Munshiram Manoharlal, ND, 1996.

Ray, Praphulla Chandra, History of Hindu Chemistry from the Earlies Times to the Middle of the Sixteenth Century AD, Calcutta, 1903.

Ray, Himanshu Prabha, Alpers, Edward A. (eds), Cross Currents and Community Networks, The History of the Indian Ocean World, Oxford, ND, 2007.

Ray, Priyadaranjan, The Cultural Heritage of India, The Ramakrishna Mission, ND, 2000.

Reat, Noble Ross, Buddhism: A History, Asian Humanities Press, Berkeley, 1994.

Rele, V. G., The Vedic Gods as Figures of Biology, Taraporevala and Sons, Bombay, 1931.

Rhyner, Hans, H., Ayurveda, The Gentle Health System. Motilal Banarsidas, Delhi, 1998.

Rizvi, S.A.A., The Wonder that was India Volume II, Rupa, ND, 1993.

Roberts, B.W. and Christopher Thornton (eds), Archaeometallurgy in Global Perspective: methods and syntheses, Springer.

Roberts, B.W., Thornton, C.P. and Pigott, V.C., Development of Metallurgy in Eurasia. Antiquity 83, 112-122, 2009.

Robins, R. Gay, Mathematics, Astronomy, and Calendars in Pharaonic Egypt in Civilizations of the Ancient Near East, Jack M. Sasson, John R. Baines, Gary Beckman, and Karen S (eds), Harcourt, Inc., New York, 2003.

Rossen, Milev, Scriptura Mundi, Writings of the world, Vol. 1, Balkan Media, Sofia, 2014.

Sachau, E.C., Al Beruni's India, Kegan Paul, FrenchTrubner & Co, London, 1910.

Sahoo, Sanghamitra, A prehistory of Indian Y chromosomes: Evaluating demic diffusion scenarios, Proc. Nat. Acad. Sci. (USA), 103: 843–848, 2006.

Said, Edward, W., Culture and Imperialism, Alfred A. Knopf, NY, 1994.

Saraswati, Amma, Geometry in Ancient and Medieval India, Motilal Banarsidas, ND, 1979.

Sarton, George, A Guide to the History of Science, Chronica Botanica, MA, 1952.

Savarkar, V.D., Hindutva, Hindi Sahitya Sadan, 2003.

Scafi, Alessandro, Mapping Paradise. A History of Heaven on Earth, U. Chicago,Il., 2006.

Schrag, Paul, Haze, Xaviant and Tsarion, Michael, The Suppressed History of America: The Murder of Meriwether Lewis and the Mysterious Discoveries of the Lewis and Clark Expedition, Bear & Co., 2011.

Seidenberg, A., The Ritual Origin of Geometry, Arch. Hist. Exact Sciences 1: 488-527, 1962.

Seidenberg, A., The Origin of Mathematics. Arch. Hist. Exact Sci., 18: 301-342, 1978.

Sen,Parasher Aloka, Mlecchas in Early India, Munshiram Manoharlal

Publishers, 1991.

Sengupta, S., Polarity and Temporality of High-Resolution Y Chromosome Distributions in India Identify Both Indigenous and Exogenous Expansions and Reveal Minor Genetic Influence of Central Asian Pastoralists. Am. J. Hum. Genet., 78: 201–221, 2006.

Sethna, K.D., The Problem of Aryan Origins, Aditya Prakashan, ND, 1992.

Shaffer, Jim G., The Indo-Aryan Invasions: Cultural Myth and Archaeological Reality', Ninth Annual Wisconsin Conference on South Asia, November, 1980.

Shah, Khushal, T., The Splendor that was India, Taraporevala, Bombay, 1930.

Shaikh, Anwar, Why Muslims destroy Hindu temples? Hindu Writers Forum, ND, 2001.

Sharma, Madhulika, Fire Worship in Ancient India, Jaipur Publication Scheme. 2002.

Sharma, S., Saha, A., Rai, E., Bhat, A., Bamezai, R., J. Hum. Genet. 50: 497–506, 2005.

Sharma, Tej Ram, A Political History of the Imperial Guptas, Concept Publishing, ND, 1989.

Shastri, Subbaraya, Discovery of Ayurveda, Nagarjun, 1976.

Shekhar, I., Sanskrit Drama: Its Origin and Decline, Eur. J. Brill, Leiden, Holland, 1960.

Shendge, Malati J., The Civilized Demons: Harappans in Rgveda, Abhinav Publications, ND, 1977.

Shukla, D.N., Vastu-Sastra: Hindu Science of Architecture, MunshiRama Manoharlal, ND, 1993.

Shukla, S.P., A review of Water Management and Hydraulic Engineering in India (c. 600 BCE – CE 1200), (O. C. Handa ed), Pentagon Press, 2001.

Siculus, Diodorus, Library of History, Cambridge, 1935.

Singh, Bal Rama, (ed) Origin of Indian Civilization, Center for Indic Studies, Dartmought, USA, 2010.

Singh, Natwar, One Life is Not Enough, Rupa, 2014.

Singh, P., The So-called Fibonacci numbers in Ancient and Medieval India, Historia Mathamatica, 12: 229-244,1985.

Singhal, D.P., India and World Civilization, Michigan State University Press, 1969.

Singhal, G.D., Patterson, T.J.S., Synopsis of Ayurveda, based on a translation of Susuruta Samhita. Oxford, ND, 1993.

Smith, Adam, The Wealth of Nations, London, 1776.

Smith, D. E., History of Mathematics, Dover, NY, 1951.

Smith, Monica L, The Dynamic Realm of the Indian Ocean, Asian Perspectives,36: 245-259, 1997.

Smith, Percy, S., The Fatherland of the Polynesians, Aryan and Polynesian points of contact., J. Polynesian Soc., 19: 84-88, 1912; 20: 37-38, 1913; 20: 170-171, 1913; 28: 18-30, 1919.

Snelling, John, The Sacred Mountain: The Complete Guide to Tibet's Mount

Kailash. East-West Publications, London and The Hague, 1990.

Somadeva, Tales from the Kathasaritasagara, Penguin, ND, 1994.

Srinivas, M.D., Sriram, M. S. and Ramasubramanian, K., History of Mathematics in India from Vedic Period to Modern Times. IIT Bombay

Srinivasiengar, C. N., The History of Ancient Indian Mathematics, World Press, Calcutta, 1967.

Staal, F., Universals: Studies in Indian Logic and Linguistics, U Chicago Press, 1988.

Stannard, David E., Before the Horror : the Population of Hawai'i on the Eve of Hawaii, 1989.

Stannard, David E., American Holocaust: Columbus and the Conquest of the New World, Oxford, NY, 1992.

Stannard, David E., The Puritan Way of Death: a Study in Religion, Culture, and Social Change, Oxford, NY,1977.

Stewart, D. S., Mexican Linguistics, T.S. Denison & Co., Chicago, 1913.

Stillwell, John, Mathematics and its History, Springer Science, 2004.

SubRamanyam, B.R., Appearance and Spread of Iron in India – An Appraisal of Archeological Data, J. Oriental institute, Baroda, 13: 349-59, 1964.

Susan Whitfield, Ursula Sims-Williams (eds) The Silk Road : trade, travel, war and faith, British Library, 2004.

Swami Jagadguru, Shri Bharati Krishna Tirthaji Maharaja, Vedic Mathematics, Motilal Banarsidass, ND, 1988.

Swamy, Subramanian, Virat Hindu Identity, Concept and its Power, Pragun Publication, ND, 2012

Swamy, Subramanian, Hindutva And National Renaissance, Har-anand Publications, ND, 2010.

Swamy, Subramanian, Hindus Under Siege: The Way Out, Har-anand Publications, ND, 2010.

Szabo, Arpad, The Beginnings of Greek Mathematics, Reidel & Akademiai Kiado, 1978.

Tadgell, Christopher, The History of Architecture in India, Longman, London, 1990.

Talageri, Shrikant, G. The Aryan Invasion Theory: A Reappraisal. Aditya Prakashan, ND, 1993.

Talageri, S.G., The RigVeda: A Historical Analysis. Aditya Prakashan, New Delhi,   2000.

Tanner, Marcus, The Last of the Celts, Yale, New Haven, 2004.

Taylor, I., The origins of Aryans, Scribner, New York, 1890.

Taylor, Keith Weller The Birth of Vietnam, U. California Press, Berkeley, 1983.

Taylor, T., The Gundestrup cauldron, Sci. American 266; 84-89, 1992.

Thapliyal, K. K., Studies in Ancient Indian Seals, Lucknow, 1972.

Thibaut, George, Mathematics in the making in Ancient India, K.P.Bagchi, Calcutta, 1984.

Thiong'o, Ngugi Wa, Decolonizing the Mind, Heineman, 1986.

Thompson, G., India and the Colonies, London, 1838

Thompson, Jason, A History of Egypt, American U Cairo, 2008.

Thubron, Colin, To a Mountain in Tibet, Harper Collins, 2011.

Thurman, Robert and Tad Wise, Circling the Sacred Mountain: A Spiritual Adventure through the Himalayas. New York: Bantam, 1999.

Tilak, Bal Gangadhar, The Arctic Home of the Vedas, Tilak Bros., 1903.

Tilak, Bal Gangadhar, Orion: Researches into the Antiquity of the Vedas, Tilak Brothers, Poona, 1893 and 1955.

Tougher, Shaun, Eunuchs in History and Beyond, Duckworth, 2002.

Toussaint, Auguste, History of the Indian Ocean, U. Chicago, 1996.

Trachtenberg, Joshua, The Devil and the Jews, meridian Books, NY, 1943.

Trautman, Thomas, R., Aryans and British India, Vistaar Publications, ND, 1997.

Trevor Fisher, Prostitution and the Victorians, St. Martins Press, NY, 1997.

Tripathi, Amish, The Immortals of Melhua, India Research Press, 2010.

Trypanis, C. A., Greek Poetry from Homer to Seferis, U. Chicago Press, 1981.

Tudge, Colin, The Time Before History, Scribner, NY, 1996.

Underhill et al., Separating the Post-Glacial co-ancestry of European and Asian Y chromosomes within haplogroup R1a, Eur. J. Human Genet., 18: 479-484, 2009.

Vartak, P. V., Vastav Ramayana, Vedvidnyana Mandal, Pune, 2000.

Vasu, Srisa Chandra, The Ashtadhyayi of Panini, Motilal Banarsidas, ND, 1962.

Vasudev, Gayatri Devi, Vastu Astrology and Architecture, Motilal Banarsidas, ND, 1998 and 2001.

Vatsyayan, Kapila, Bharat: The Natyasastra, Sahitya Akademi, ND, 1996.

Verghese Joseph George, The Crest of the Peacock, Penguin, UK, 1991.

Verma, Vinod, Patanjali and Ayurvedic Yoga, Motilala Banarsidas, ND, 2001.

Vermes, G., The Dead Sea Scrolls in English, Penguin Books, 1962.

Vibhuti Chakrabarti, Indian Architectural Theory: Contemporary Uses of Vastu Vidya, Routledge, NY, 1998.

Vivek, Lies, Lies and More Lies: The Campaign to Defame Hindu/Indian Nationalism, iUniverse 2007.

Von Ihering, Rudolph, The Evolution of the Aryan, Henry Holt & Co., NY, 1897.

Warmington, E. H., Commerce between the Roman Empire and India, Cambridge, 1928.

Warpande, N. R., Aryan Invasion: A Myth. Baba Saheb Smarak Samiti, Nagpur, 1989.

Waters, Frank, Book of the Hopi, Penguin, NY, 1977.

Weeks, Lloyd R., Early Metallurgy of the Persian Gulf, Brill, Boston, Leiden, 2003.

Weiss, H. M., Courty, M. A., Wetterstrom, W., Guichard, L., Meadow, R. and Curnow, A. The Genesis and Collapse of Third Millenium North Mesopotamian Civilization, Science 261: 995-1004, 1993.

Wertheim, Margaret, Pythagoras' Trousers, W.W. Norton & Co., NY, 1997.

Wheeler, Mortimer, Civilizations of the Indus Valley and Beyond, McGraw Hill, NY, 1965.

Wheeler, R.E.M., Arikamedu: An Indo-Roman Trading-Station on the East Coast of India, Ancient India 2: 17-124, 1946.

Wheelright, Phillip, Aristotle, The Odyssey Press, 1935.

Whelpton, John, A History of Nepal, Cambridge, UK, 2005.

Whitmarsh, Tim, Ancient Greek Literature, Cambridge Polity Press, 2004.

Winters, Clyde, African Millets carried to India by Dravidian Speakers, Annals of Botany, March 19, 2008.

Wolters O.W. Early Indonesian Commerce: A study of the Origins of Srivijaya, Cornell U Press, 1967.

Wolters, O.W. History, Culture and Region in Southeast Asian Perspectives. Institute of Southeast Asian Studies, Singapore, 1999.

Wood, Jacqui, Food and Drink in Prehistoric Europe. European J. Archaeology, 3: 89-111, 2000.

Wujastyk, Dominik, The Roots of Ayurveda, Penguin India, ND, 1998.

Yogananda, Paramahansa, The Sacred Coming of Christ: The Resurrection of the Christ within You, Self-Realization Fellowship, 2011.

Zysk, Kenneth, G., Medicine in the Vedas, Motilal Banarsidas, ND, 1996.

19. Web Resources

www.come let us create a mahan bharat
www.dr.pvvartak
www.indicethos.org
www.indicstudies.us
www.mera bharat mahan
www.the religion of peace.com

www.hindudatabase.blogspot.com
www.rarebooks onweb.com@hinduidf
www. he korean brahmins, Kim Heo Clan (ajit vadakayil)
www.babri masjid demolition, mughal emperor babur (ajit vadakayil)
www.jewish russian mafia (ajit vadakayil)
www.the unquantified holocaust and genocide (ajit vadakayil)
www.sikh24.com/2012/10/the-immoral-life-of-maimuna-begum-aka-indira-gandhi/via @sikh24
www.History of Hindu- Christian encounters AD 304 to 1996. Voice of dharma.com/books/hhce
www.The Story of Islamic Imperialism in India (w singh)
Indian Mathematics: Redressing the Balance, www-history.mcs.st-andrews.ac.uk/history/Projects/Pearce/index.html. (IG pearce)
ajitvadakayil.blogspot.in/2011/10/tipu-sultan-unmasked-capt-

ajit.html ...www.mythicalireland.com/ancientsites/tara/
www.docstoc.com/docs/4430971/Gundestrup-cauldron-and-Sarasvati-hieroglyphs
www.jblstatue.com/gundstrup/home.html
www.abaxion.com/jbgcaul.htm
www.traditionalwitchcraft.org/celtic/gundestrup.html
www.aboutulverston.co.uk/celts/gundestrupbuddha.htm
aolsearch.aol.com/aol/search?query=Gundestrup%20cauldron
www.themystica.com/mystica/articles/g/gundestrup_cauldron.html
www.cyberwitch.com/wychwood/Temple/kernunnos.htm
www.sniffout.net/home/simontodd/herne.htm
www.realtime.com/~gunnora/vik_pets.htm
www.swampfox.demon.co.uk/utlah/shift/wolfbane.htmlwww.csp.org/chrestomathy/hallucinations2.htm
www.indigogroup.co.uk/edge/bdogs.htm
www.collect.com.au/_numismatics/00000016.htm
sacredsource.com/gundestrup/
www.djames.demon.co.uk/celtic/cr01.htm
www.celtic-cauldron.com/images/gcauld.jpg
www.realtime.net/~gunnora/graphics/gundstrp.gif
www.celtica.wales.com/arddangosfa/gof/index.english.html
www47.pair.com/lindo/Classical.htm
www.britannica.com/bcom/eb/article/4/0,5716,119804+5,00
.html en2.wikipedia.org/wiki/Celtic_mythology
www.celtic-cauldron.com/
www.jamesmdeem.com/bogphotos.htm
www.angelfire.com/me/ik/pics.html
www.en.wikipedia.org/wiki/Dravida_Kingdom
www.sites.google.com/site/kalyan97 Saraswati Website with 40,000 files
www.hindunet.org/hindu_history/sarasvati/ (including Indian Lexicon for 25 ancient Indian Languages; R.gveda text and trans. based on Sayana bhashya www.hindu-tva.com http://kalyan97.wordpress.com

www.tinyurl.com/c5ovj5q (Saraswati Research Center)
www.indiadivine.org/news/history-andculture/
ancient-shiva-linga-in-ireland-r831
www.en.wikipedia.org/wiki/Four_Treasures_of_the_Tuatha_De_Da
nann
www.en.wikipedia.org/wiki/Celts).
www. bharatkalyan97.blogspot.in/2013/11/two-lingaskambhas-
of-dholavira-ca-2500.html
www.bharatkalyan97.blogspot.in/2011/12/indus-valleymystery-
and-use-of-tablets.html
www.en.wikipedia.org/wiki/The_Dagda
www.en.wikipedia.org/wiki/Gundestrup_cauldron
www.hindunet.org/saraswati/gundestrup1.pdf
www.en.wikipedia.org/wiki/Tuatha_D%C3%A9_Danann#cite_refkoch1693_
1-1
www.en.wikipedia.org/wiki/Lia_F%C3%A1il
www.megalithic.co.uk/modules.phpop=modload&name=a312&file=in
dex&do=showpic&pid=23878
www.megalithic.co.uk/modules.php?op=modload&name=a312&file=i
ndex&do=showpic&pid=19084
www.megalithic.co.uk/article.php?sid=11511
http://www.bham.ac.uk/TAG98/pages/abs
www.sarasvatihieroglyphs.wordpress.com/2005/04/20/meluhhan-smiths--
gundestrup-cauldron/
www.bharatkalyan97.blogspot.in/2015/02/ancient-history-of-
www.bharatkalyan97.blogspot.in/2015/02/vedic-indians-in-iraq-in-5000-bce
www.bharatkalyan97.blogspot.in/2015/02/vedic-indians-in-iraq-in-5000-bce
http://bharatkalyan97.blogspot.in/2015/02/unmasking-motives-of-aryan.html
http://bharatkalyan97.blogspot.in/2015/02/the-rigvedic-people-
invadersimmigrants
www.bharatkalyan97.blogspot.in/2015/02/archaeometallurgy-of-cire-perdue-
lost.html
www.bharatkalyan97.blogspot.in/2015/02/maritime-meluhha-tin-road-links-
far.html
www.bharatkalyan97.blogspot.in/2015/01/sekkizhar-periya-puranam-
candisukuh.html
www.archive.org/stream/historyofhinduch01rayprich/historyofhinduch01rayp
rich_djvu.txt
www.aakkl.helsinki.fi/melammu/pdf/vidale2004.pdf
www.bharatkalyan97.blogspot.in/2013/08/bronze-age-kanmer-bagasra.html
www.bharatkalyan97.blogspot.in/2013/05/indus-writing-on-gold-disc-
kuwait.html
www.facebook.com/BenoyKBehlArtCulture/photos/pb.369573056429568.-
2207520000.1423199373./505466802840192/?
www.academia.edu/8795289/Ligatured_eagle_pinecone_
www.bharatkalyan97.blogspot.in/2015/01/stepped-socles-of-assur-
meluhha.html

Stepped socles of Assur.

www.bharatkalyan97.blogspot.in/2015/02/vajra-sanghata-binding-together.html

www.bharatkalyan97.blogspot.in/2015/02/the-indus-inscriptions-are-collections.html

www.bharatkalyan97.blogspot.in/2015/02/proof-for-cipher-key-of-indus-writing.html

www.http://bharatkalyan97.blogspot.in/2014/01/course-on-mathematics-in-indiafrom.html

www.bharatkalyan97.blogspot.in/2015/02/ancient-history-of-bharatam-janamalong.html

www.bharatkalyan97.blogspot.in/2015/01/meluhha-hieroglyphs-and-candi-sukuh.html

www.en.wikipedia.org/wiki/Substratum_in_Vedic_Sanskrit

www.bharatkalyan97.blogspot.in/2015/02/chandas-and-meluhha-mleccha-are-prosody.html

www.visual-arts-cork.com/site/about.htm

www.academia.edu/9643316/A_review_of_Dr_S._Kalyanaraman_s_trilogy_by_Dr_Shrinivas_Tilak).

www.islamicity.com/Mosque/IHAME/Ref6.htm

www.tumblr.com/search/bow%20drilling

www.youtube.com/watch?v=iH0Ep2XHstY

www.youtube.com/watch?v=DmjpdiSZjaM

www.youtube.com/watch?v=Jp31J9qAWJE

www.youtube.com/watch?v=OFnADN8c_Es&sns=tw … @RSS_ORG

www.ejvs.laurasianacademy.com/witzel-philology.

www.hdl.handle.net/10062/15240

The End

CPSIA information can be obtained
at www.ICGtesting.com
Printed in the USA
BVHW061520150822
644636BV00003B/210

9 781508 714774